Narendra Modi
THE GAMECHANGER

Narendra Modi
THE GAMECHANGER

Sudesh Verma

Vitasta
Let Knowledge Spread

Published by
Renu Kaul Verma
Vitasta Publishing Pvt. Ltd.
2/15, Ansari Road, Daryaganj,
New Delhi - 110 002
info@vitastapublishing.com

ISBN 978-93-82711-18-6
© Sudesh Verma, 2014

Cover Design by Sandeep Singh
Layout Design by Vitasta Publishing Pvt. Ltd.
Printed by Vikas Computer and Printers, New Delhi

To
"the poorest and the weakest"
who looks at
Narendra Modi
with hope

Contents

Acknowledgement		ix
Preface		xiii
Abbreviations		xix
Introduction		xxiii

1. Rebellion and Direction
   A Peek into Modi's Growing Years   1
2. Political Baptism by Emergency Fire   31
3. Delhi Calling   45
4. Destiny Takes a Turn
   Modi Sent Back as Gujarat CM   60
5. Expediting Relief and Rehabilitation   86
6. History of Riots in Gujarat
   Godhra Contextualised   94
7. The Dark Days
   Godhra and Post-Godhra Riots   102
8. Dispelling Myths
   'Hang Me If I Am Guilty'—Modi   125
9. Modi's Resignation had no Takers   140
10. Three Victories in a Row   150
11. Development Challenges   176
12. Surmounting Challenges
    Infrastructural Development   188
13. Governance   215
14. Profitable Agriculture & Prosperous Villages   227
15. Unleashing Entrepreneurial Energy
    Favoured Destination for Industries   241
16. Showcasing Gujarat to Investors   252

17. Urbanisation: Changing Gujarat's Landscape
'Aatma Gaanv Ki, Suvidha Sheher Ki'   262
18. Raising Green Consciousness   271
19. Khushboo Gujarat Ki
India's New Tourism Destination   281
20. Healthcare to Every Citizen   288
21. Making Women Count   296
22. Harnessing Human Resource:
Education and Skill Development   304
23. Statue of Unity   314
24. BJP's Trump Card: PM Candidate Modi   317
25. Modi and the Muslim Community   336
26. The Fuss Over Visa   357
27. The GameChanger   363

Bibliography   386
Endnotes   392
Index   420

Acknowledgement

Without mincing words, I wish to thank my friend from JNU days, Amitabh Sinha, for being the inspiration and the guide for this book. When I got stuck in my daily journalistic existence, he egged me on to take leave and finish writing the book. But for him I would not have been able to meet the important contacts that proved useful during collection of the material and research. He took time off from his busy schedule, accompanied me to some of the interviews and then joined me on a fortnight tour of Gujarat to get a real perspective on the impact of development. The Team had decided I would write what we saw.

The dream about this book would not have translated into reality without the young lawyer Nikita Parmar who joined the research team from the start and shouldered the responsibility of leading it. She had joined as a critic of Modi but, after the research, became his ardent admirer. She and the team worked while I continued with my job in the NewsX. For almost a year, she kept aside the legal profession to help in the writing of this book.

Surajit Dasgupta, a journalist friend and compatriot in political and social activism, joined a little late but soon became an integral part of the team and added a lot of value through helping in the research, content and editing. The discussions over coffee sips became more exciting and helped in paraphrasing of a few chapters.

Ravi Ranjan Mishra, another friend from JNU, with long experience in banking and infrastructure development organizations, helped with some crucial chapters on development. He made me more comfortable with the statistics and gave me the confidence that I was on the right track while dealing with economic issues.

The book would not have made sense, if Narendra Modi had not given time for the various interactions at short notices. He had a very tight schedule after being projected as the BJP's candidate for the prime minister's post. Yet he managed time to speak to me and never made me feel that I was talking to the PM candidate. I am indebted to his elder brother Sombhai for sharing stories about Modi's early years and for being available whenever I or any member of my team wanted.

It is fashionable to thank one's wife. But my gratitude to Renu is heartfelt since she kept reminding me that the book must be a quality product and not a copy paste job. She also did not mind the elbow room I created for myself and stayed out of home from 7 am to 11 pm almost daily for more than 10 months.

In the process of growing up, I have earned the trust of a number of Muslim friends. While Seraj Ansari agreed that there was a need to remove misgivings against Modi; Faiza, after reading a few relevant chapters, felt that Modi was more sinned against than sinning.

Zafar Sareshwala is a great human being. His positive energy was inspiring and he helped me get a peep into the Muslim outlook on Modi and development.

My very special thanks to Mr Kartikeya Sharma for reposing trust in me and for giving me a liberal study leave without pressuring me to reveal my exact intent, which was a secret, till the book came out.

Pavani Sinha was very helpful through her comments and suggestions that shaped the flow. Papri Sriraman was very critical of Modi and she provided me the challenge to present facts in a convincing way. Antonia Filmer was kind to suggest a headline for one of the chapters which the entire team found powerful. Aastha Sharma edited the raw manuscript and made the book more presentable.

Special thanks are due to Ram Kaushik, Sanjay Verma, Seshadri Satyanarayanan, Gautam Hore, Sharad Gupta, Vijay KBK, Nilesh Shukla and Anu Kapoor for inspiring me in various ways, knowingly or unknowingly.

Rabinder Kaul's suggestions after reading the final blueprint, helped to further improve the book. Santosh Verma helped me to assess the contents of other books and their shortcomings.

Special thanks, are due to Harishankar Lal, Rakesh Tiwari and Kunwar Shyamendra Singh for their invaluable suggestions. Shri Ajay Kumar was always encouraging.

The biggest source of inspiration has been my parents who have lost all hopes in the government system. I want them to see a better India before they complete their journey of life.

I was surprised when my 8-year-old son Aankush wrote a letter to Narendra Modi giving best wishes for his prime ministerial bid. In return, a letter came from the Gujarat CM with his blessings. I was surprised by this exchange that had happened without my knowledge. Also impressive was the curiosity of my 12-year-old son Aryan about the book.

I thank my publisher for bringing this book with the urgency that was needed. In particular, I thank Veena Batra for last minute editing and proof-reading that made the book tidier, Alok Saini and Geetali Baruah for production, Sandeep Singh for cover design, and Megha Parmar for her infectious enthusiasm and timely feedback. Ruth, Kanhaiya, Shesh, Preeti and Dharam contributed in their own ways.

Preface

During my numerous debates with officials of the government of the United Kingdom in India, I used to get quite baffled by a paradox. They would find a lot of weight in my arguments that Gujarat should not be treated as a pariah, and that they had no choice but to deal directly with Narendra Modi. Yet they would go with the rival opinion of no relations with Gujarat.

The British officials would take a call after giving an impression that the entire house was one. But the decision would always be one that suited the NGOs based in London as these NGOs exercised tremendous clout in the British administration. If anything untoward ever happened in any part of India, they would rush to the foreign office to complain to the India desk! The India desk would then ask us to send a report on the situation. The phraseology of the directive suggested we should only tell them what they wanted to hear.

There was reportedly an attack on a church in Rajasthan. One of these NGOs in London complained that no FIR was lodged by the State government. I was on an official visit to London then. I told them I would send something after I returned. When I came back, I dug deep into the affair but could not find any reference to this incident in any of the newspapers. Then I discovered a photograph of the Archbishop with the then chief minister of Rajasthan, Vasundhara Raje, only two days after the incident in question. With that photograph, I approached the Raje administration and the neighbourhood around the church. The officials and the people informed me that nothing unpleasant had transpired and that the Archbishop was happy with the meeting.

Most such complaints came from the States that were ruled either by the BJP or its allies. The pattern was understandable. Paint these governments negatively and the BJP as intolerant. A British bureaucrat told me privately over two pints of beer in a London pub that it was not easy for anyone in the UK or the US "to accept a government or party that sought pride in nationalist resurgence".

Once a 'secular' friend, in a bunch of 'seculars' from the Jawaharlal Nehru University, disagreed with the opinions they used to express publicly. He conceded that "Modi definitely did not give swords in the hands of Hindu rioters to slay Muslims." "At the most, he might have been sympathetic to the 59 Hindus burnt alive in S-6 coach of the ill-fated Sabarmati Express in the morning of 27 February 2002," another 'secular' chap in the group said. They all agreed that the chief minister did not utter anything that justified the killings; he actually denied having issued all the statements attributed to him.

When Godhra happened, I was working with *The Statesman* and was reporting on the BJP. The budget was to be presented the next day; two of my colleagues and I were at the BJP's Ashoka Road headquarters. A lady journalist laughed sarcastically when the news of the burning of two coaches of Sabarmati Express and charring to death 58 *Ramsewaks* came in (a victim succumbed to the burns later, making the toll 59). She said, "This would be a lesson to these rowdy '*Ramsewaks*'."

I was aghast. I could not restrain myself from asking her point blank, "Do you think it is an ordinary incident like a few people getting killed? Do you know what kind of repercussions it may produce in Gujarat?" She retracted, realising I was not ready to play her game.

Given the precedence of frivolous incidents in Gujarat escalating into full-fledged riots, the Godhra incident was not to be taken lightly. Why was there not enough condemnation of the incident to cool down rising tempers? Why was the budget allowed to be tabled without any mark of respect to the victims? What would have been the reaction of the country if the victims had been Muslims? Why did the country fail to take the incident with the seriousness it deserved? Was this then not our combined failure? These thoughts kept me occupied for a long time.

The other experience I'd had is of the present scenario in the newsroom of *NewsX*, an English news television channel, where I am still working as the news editor. When I joined the channel in early 2013, I was taken aback by the bias that existed against Modi. Those who claimed to be 'secular' would beat their chest every time Modi spoke of development. One of the editors went to the extent of saying that Modi would kill all Muslims. "He is a mass murderer." When I asked how, he said, "You see this is what people are saying". When I said nothing had been proved, he said, "What about the image?" I argued, "You create an image and then use the same image to paint someone as a villain." He shut up.

When I asked the newsroom staff to show Modi as much as possible because people wanted to see him on screen rather than follow the run-of-the-mill stories we would dish out as news, there were many who disagreed with me. I insisted on having my way and succeeded eventually. Soon we were on top of the Television Rating Point (TRP) chart. This was because people saw hope in Modi which we as journalists were unable to understand.

So much of bias! So much of antagonism! When I entered into debates impromptu with my colleagues in the newsroom on Modi, I would often ask them to talk with facts. In return, they would bombard me with opinions and chicken out of every debate. Ignorance is bliss, more so for those who prefer to stay ignorant because knowledge breaks their long held assumptions and forces them to take positions that might make them uncomfortable in certain milieus.

It was then that I thought of writing this book. The purpose is to attempt to clear the cobwebs and appeal to reason. The nation is waiting to take a turn. We must all witness this phenomenon with an open mind. Narendra Modi is an inspiring story. He is a symbol of discipline and self control — two virtues that we all try to cultivate. Hence, most people admire the man. The fact that he had a humble beginning makes his story compelling in a democracy. Every Indian, irrespective of love or hate for him, will find a part of his or her life reflected in this story.

After more than a decade of the 2002 riots in Gujarat, the ghost of Godhra is refusing to die. Certain vested interests are not ready to allow Modi to come out of the image they have created of him for their own consumption and for that of their diehard followers. Why so? Why is Modi not being rated on the basis of his performance? The 'secular' fundamentalists have got blinded by their own blinkered vision. While they were busy attacking Modi and Gujarat, the State took a giant, unprecedented leap forward.

I have tried to delineate initiatives that have helped Gujarat evolve as a model state of development. I strongly believe that other states and the intelligentsia failed to notice the advancement and appreciate the factors that helped it grow because they got their vision impaired by adverse propaganda. Perhaps things are changing. It is time to make a fresh assessment and bury the past.

While writing on development, I thought I would make it clear that I am not an economist, but I have reported a lot on issues of development as a journalist. Critics say Gujarat was already a developed State. They forget the State's pitiable condition following the earthquake of 2001 or after the droughts and floods that had struck Gujarat before. My effort has been to extricate the success stories from the labyrinth of jargon of economics to make sense to the common man.

I was immensely impressed seeing the rural people in Gujarat benefit from the steps taken by the government. They have become possessive about their land because Modi made policies that turned agriculture profitable. The farmers say so. It is difficult to sustain the growth story for a long time if a state is already on a higher growth trajectory. But Gujarat has done it. And there is no reason to believe it would not do so in future.

Whether one likes it or not, one cannot escape appreciating the development of Gujarat. International agencies such as the United Nations do not confer awards on the basis of hype generated by the media. Chief Ministers of other Indian states are beginning to learn that divisive issues may prove counterproductive. They may like to emulate some of the best practices from Gujarat's progress.

What is it that critics of Modi fear? Is it that they cannot imagine a visionary coming from the RSS stock since, to them, it represents an ancient philosophy that would not allow the State to grow beyond the proverbial Hindu rate of growth? Or, is it their combined shame that this man has marched ahead despite all their efforts to pull him down? Or, is it something else which most vested interests have: Modi is not used to co-opting those who are unproductive. Do they fear being left out of the race if Modi comes to power?

The case is worse than one of 'more sinned against than sinning.' I have always held that Narendra Modi has been sinned against;

he has not sinned. He is evidently a victim of a bunch of 'secular' fundamentalists who, though a handful, are so shrill that they can make or break anyone. Most of the time they do not have the voices of reason, but they shout so loud that others tend to succumb to their rants. When they get exposed to one group of people, they catch hold of another in the name of 'secularising' them. Otherwise, why has he been singled out for the combined failure of the Gujarat State's law and order machinery during the riots?

Modi also appears to be an experiment the BJP once dwelt upon — to have a presidential form of parliamentary democracy in place of the Westminster model. When the NDA came to power, it set up a commission to explore this possibility. The Commission concluded that the present system was the best.

Modi has revived that hope once again. It remains to be seen if people will vote on his agenda and for his leadership. If they do, it might usher in a Presidential form within parliamentary democracy. Having suffered for so long, the country perhaps needs one leader who can bring hope to the system that is rotting due to corruption and inefficiency.

There is always a question: What happens if he becomes despotic? The answer is simple. What happened when Indira Gandhi became despotic and imposed the Emergency in 1975? She was defeated. Then, the same people who voted for Rajiv Gandhi, who rode a sympathy wave after the assassination of Indira Gandhi, his mother, to power with a three-fourth majority, brought him down after five years. People are larger than any individual. They know who is right and who is wrong.

As the author, I have tried to present Modi and his vision for the common man so that they can judge him better. This is not a book on Godhra or the riots. Neither is this a book about development alone. This is a book that puts Modi at the centre and looks at him from all angles possible.

While reading this book, one may ask why some aspect of the riots have not been covered, or why some other topic has not been dealt with in more detail, or why the opinions of critics have not been taken into account. The answer follows.

There is a plethora of material on the Internet and in many other books. There was no need to have another book in the genre of cynicism.

Most criticisms are based on opinions and hearsays. Someone quotes something and that goes viral, with no one trying to verify the claims with the original source. I have relied only on aspects that are verifiable.

Modi is a human being like anyone of us. He aspired to do bigger things in life. What is important is that he used hard work and determination to meet his aspirations. Inspired by Swami Vivekananda and trained in the RSS, Modi's never say die attitude has helped him surmount difficulties one after another.

Modi is a man fighting the battle alone. He has been facing attacks from all sides. Yet the people of Gujarat voted him to power thrice. It forces us to ask if those fighting against him with barbs laced with poison have a score to settle with him. He talks of development, his critics talk of riots; he talks of democracy and his critics talk of those people who claim to be sidelined by him; he talks of building a modern India, people say he is arrogant.

It is time the critics re-evaluated him. Indian voters have proved time and again that they are smarter than those who claim to read them. This explains why most analysts and psephologists go wrong. He is getting crowds very few other leaders before him got in the history of India's independence. It is time to apply self correction and study the phenomenon by jettisoning the old beliefs.

I have one caveat for friends who may feel bad or hurt by this effort of mine. They need to come out of illusions created due to propaganda by vested interests. My appeal to them is—if governance becomes more transparent, more accountable and less corrupt, we all as citizens would stand to gain more. The police then cannot claim innocence for looking the other way when riots happen.

I must admit that I do not claim to have propounded a new theory. As a journalist I have always reported and commented on events. The effort is just that — to present what exists in a way that the reader finds interesting and, after the reading, enlightening.

I hope this book leads to a better understanding of Modi, now that he is trying to connect to India as the prime ministerial candidate of the National Democratic Alliance.

sudeshpersonal@gmail.com
www.sudeshverma.com

Abbreviations

3D- 3 Dimensional
AAP- Aam Adami Party
ATVT-Apno Taluko Vibrant Taluko
AWH- Anganwadi Helpers
AWW- Anganwadi Worker
BCM- (unit) Billion Cubic Metre
BHADA- Bhuj Area Development Authority
BJP- Bharatiya Janata Party
BKS- Bharatiya Kisan Sangh
BMS- Bharatiya Mazdoor Sangh
BPL-Below Poverty Line
BRTS- Rapid Bus Transit System
BSP- Bahujan Samaj Party
CAG-Comptroller and Auditor General
CEC- Chief Election Commissioner
CII- Confederation of Indian Industries
CISF- Central Industrial Security Force
CMO- Chief Minister's Office
CPI (M)- Communist Party of India (Marxist)
CSC- Common Service Centre
CSR- Corporate Social Responsibility
DCC- Department of Climate Change
DIC- District Industries Centre
DMIC- Delhi-Mumbai Industrial Corridor
EIA- Environment Impact Assessment
EMRI- Emergency Management and Research Institute
EMRS- Eklavya Model Residential Schools
EPH- Environment Public Hearing
ERP- Enterprise Resource Planning

FICCI- Federation of Indian Chambers of Commerce and Industry
GCVT- Gujarat Council for Vocational Training
GDP-Gross Domestic Product
GEB-Gujarat Electricity Board
GIDB- Gujarat Infrastructure Development Board
GIDC-Gujarat Industrial Development Corporation
GLSS- Gujarat Lok Sangharsh Samiti
GMB-Gujarat Maritime Board
GPCB- Gujarat Pollution Control Board
GSDMA- Gujarat State Disaster Management Authority
GSDP-Gross State Domestic Product
GUVNL- Gujarat Urja Vikas Nigam Ltd.
GWSSB- Gujarat Water Supply & Sewerage Board
HVC- Himachal Vikas Congress
HVP- Haryana Vikas Party
ICT- Information and Communication Technology
IMR- Infant Mortality Rate
INLD- Indian National Lok Dal
ITI-Industrial Training Institutes
JDU- Janata Dal United
JSK- Jan Seva Kendra
KHAM- Kshatriyas, Harijans, Adivasis and Muslims
MCM- Million Cubic Metre
MMASY- Mukhya Mantri Awas Samruddhi Yojana
MMR- Maternal Mortality Rate
MoU- Memorandum of Understanding
MSME- Micro, Small and Medium Enterprises
NCM- National Commission for Minorities
NCVT- National Council for Vocational Training
NDA- National Democratic Alliance
NGO- Non-Governmental Organisation
NH- National Highway
NHRC-National Human Rights Commission
NIC- National Integration Council
NRHM- National Rural Health Mission
OBC- Other backward Castes

ONGC- Oil and Natural Gas Corporation
OTC- Officers Training Camp
PDP-People's Democratic Party
PIL- Public Interest Litigation
PNDT- Pre-Natal Diagnostic Technique
PPA-Power Purchase Agreement
PPP-Public Private Partnership
PURA- Provision of Urban Amenities for Rural Areas
R&B- Roads and Buildings Department
RSS- Rashrtiya Swayamsevak Sangh
RTI-Right to Information
RTO- Regional Transport Office
SAD- Shiromani Akali Dal
SCA- Sickle Cell Anemia
SDC- Skill Development Centre
SEWA- Self-Employed Women
SEZ-Special Economic Zone
SHG- Self Help Group
SIR- Special Investment Regions
SIT – Special Investigation Team
SP- Samajwadi Party
SRFDP- Sabarmati River Front Development Project
SVPRET- Sardar Vallabhbhai Patel Rashtriya Ekta Trust
SWAGAT- State-Wide Attention on Grievances by Application of Technology
TDP- Telugu Desam Party
TERI- Tata Energy and Resources Institute
ToF- Trees outside Forest
TVET- Technical Vocational Education & Training
UPA- United Progressive Alliance
USD-US Dollar
VCE-Village Computer Entrepreneur
VHP- Vishwa Hindu Parishad
WASMO-Water and Sanitation Management Organisation
XGN- Xtended Green Node

Introduction

I came into politics because I wished to change things. You can't do that by lying to people; you have to educate, and persuade, and carry them with you — and it's often a long haul.

— Kenneth Robert Livingstone,
First Mayor of London

It's a victory of Indian democracy that even a *chaiwala* can think of becoming the country's prime minister. It is possible because our institution of democracy has become reflective of the aspirations of a common man to dream big and realise the dream as well. In that sense, Narendra Modi represents the aspirational India away from dynastic politics and feudal order.

Modi's prime ministerial bid is backed by performance and the abilities to deliver good governance. He represents a growth model that is inclusive, environment friendly and job oriented. But how did he get this vision? He did not have a background that could help him learn governance. How did he reach this position from where whatever he says appears logical and possible?

This book tries to trace the transition of Modi from a *chaiwala* to the man he is today. His trials and tribulations, his influences and his struggle have been captured through the eyes of the people who were witness to the transition. The growing period of Modi was also an eventful period in India's political history. The reader may want to meander through events and would want to know more. But this is a book on Modi. The events are important only insofar as they influence the personality of the man and his achievments.

His early life till he becomes a full time *pracharak* in the RSS has been depicted in *Chapter 1*. Vadnagar has a social fabric that has not been disturbed till now. Modi is a product of that background where

Hindus and Muslims lived together as part of the mosaic of society. When his peer group tried to learn alphabets and numbers, Modi also tried to learn how to sell tea to passengers in the trains that came at frequent intervals. This was essential to supplement the family income. Struggle makes one tough. Modi emerged a natural leader in his group and everyone in Vadnagar talks of him as a hardworking boy who wanted to make big. His associations with the RSS as a *bal swayamsewak* (child volunteer) and training at National Cadet Corps (NCC) made him more determined to succeed. Even his years of wandering as an ascetic to find the meaning of existence added to his strength. He realised much earlier in life that for a larger impact on society one must become a part of an organisation and he came under the guidance of his guru Vakil Saheb.

This chapter is based on Modi's interview and interviews of his childhood friends, his teachers, those who interacted with his father, about half a dozen RSS people, some media persons and Modi's elder brother Sombhai. Modi has been addressed as Narendra, ND or Kumar here most of the time. Many of the people did not wish to be quoted.

Chapter 2 deals with Modi's trials and tribulations during the Emergency. Even before the Emergency, Modi had initiated the process of setting up a media wing at the RSS headquarters in Ahmedabad. This proved helpful during the Emergency. This chapter is based mostly on Modi's own book *Apatkal Mein Gujarat* which came originally in Gujarati language in 1978.

Chapter 3 deals with Modi's induction into the BJP in 1987 and his emergence as a strategist and *yatra* expert. He organised *yatras* locally to expand the party's support base and later got involved in LK Advani's Ram Rath Yatra in 1990 and Dr Murli Manohar Joshi's Ekta Yatra in 1991-92. The massive mass contact that the party launched helped it increase its mass support and dethrone the Congress on its own in the State in 1995. Keshubhai became the chief minister of Gujarat.

But the taste of victory was short-lived. Shankersinh Vaghela led the banner of revolt and split the party in 1995. Both Keshubhai and Vaghela blamed Modi. He became a thorn in their eyes because he was not ready to become part of any group and was forthright in working for the organisation. Destiny has its own way of playing its role. Modi was banished to Delhi but this was, perhaps, needed for his own growth and to enable him to think beyond Gujarat and link with the entire country.

Within six years, Modi became the chief minister of Gujarat. He had never imagined that he would become the chief minister one day. He had seen senior RSS leaders wielding immense influence on politics because of their ideological moorings and simplicity and he would have preferred to lead such a life. But fate had willed otherwise.

Chapter 4 deals with his Delhi years. How, a person who was alien to Delhi made a mark as the party's organizational man. Wherever he went, he earned plaudits for his commitment and organizational acumen. He stayed in a one room accommodation and people liked his spartan existence. This chapter documents his actions as in-charge of the party's organization in Himachal Pradesh, Punjab, Haryana, Jammu and Kashmir and the Union Territory of Chandigarh. This also talks about his contribution to bringing Keshubhai Patel back to power in Gujarat in 1998 even as he excelled as the BJP's national general secretary. The circumstances that forced the BJP to send Modi as the chief minister are also described in detail.

Chapter 5 deals with how he organised the mammoth relief and rehabilitation task and enthused the same administration with a sense of new purpose. This was the time when he would come early at 9 am to the office and go back very late at night. He had nothing else to do hence he stayed most of the time in office. We see how Modi immersed himself in the task and produced a miracle of sorts. The affected areas of Kutch have become new modern cities.

Chapters 6, 7 and *8* relate to Godhra and its aftermath. The historical context of riots in Gujarat has been outlined in *Chapter 6*. This gives us an idea about the volatility of the society where smaller incidents led to riots that would continue for months. Many Commissions set up to probe riots earlier questioned the role of the police and spoke about developing a broader outlook in the youth. *Chapter 7* details the Godhra train burning incident of 27 February 2002 and the riots that followed after that. While what happened at Godhra is based on the findings of the Nanavati Commission report, the incidents of post-Godhra riots are based on various sources such as the Supreme Court appointed Special Investigation Team Report by former CBI Director RK Ragavan, media reports and deposition of the chief minister before the SIT. *Chapter 8* raises the main issue whether Modi was personally responsible for the riots other than being the administrative head of the State then. An honest attempt has been made to put the debate over Modi's role in perspective. Till proved wrong through contrary facts, there is no reason to doubt the version of the chief minister, the report of the SIT and the various reports that point to the truth outlined here. Insinuations and untruths cannot be the basis for condemning a person. Has he been condemned without sinning?

Chapter 9 deals with Modi's resignation that came amid finger pointing from all directions, including some from within the BJP. This was Atal Bihari Vajpayee's way to tell the world that he was not impervious to criticisms. But many in the BJP including LK Advani felt that resignation was not the solution. When Modi offered to quit at the Goa national executive in 2002, everyone rose in one voice saying "No". Even Keshubhai said this would be wrong. Modi was then asked to seek a fresh mandate.

Modi's three successive victories have been depicted in *Chapter 10*. Events have been given in detail to help understand their impacts. There was almost a rebellion in the BJP in 2007 which got crystallised in the formation of a separate political party by Keshubhai Patel in 2012. Despite all odds Modi pulled out victory from a situation that had made the Congress look victorious till the results. In his thanksgiving speech Modi asserted that people had voted for development and they had risen above, caste, communalism and regionalism. More people came out and voted for Modi. It was a positive vote for development.

Chapter 11 highlights the problems of development that Modi faced when he became the chief minister for the first time. Hence it has been named *development challenges*. It included infrastructure challenges—power, water and roads, fiscal consolidation and better governance. *Chapter 12* gives details of how these problems were tackled. How the State resolved the power and water issues and what steps it took to attract investment so that the government could focus on social sectors? Modi would be seen everywhere since he worked with a missionary zeal in all spheres.

Governance comes out of logical thinking, simplification of procedures, putting up systems of checks and balances and preparing the mindset of the implementing agency to accept changes. *Chapter 13* deals with governance and shows how Modi used a rational mind and discipline to help bureaucracy deliver. Gujarat has already met demands by citizens that government services should be available to them without any hassle. It would be interesting to see how he made this possible.

Chapters 14 to 22 describe the impact of good governance on development. Anecdotes and stories will show the development that the State has witnessed under Modi's leadership. Some sectors that have maximum impact have been chosen. If Gujarat has had about 10 per cent agriculture growth for about a decade, it deserves notice not only in terms of growth but also in terms of village empowerment it has brought about in rural areas.

How agriculture became profitable has been outlined in Chapter 14. One is surprised by the agriculture consciousness that exists in the State. *Chapter 15* highlights how Gujarat has become a favoured destination for industries. It is not just the Nano story at Sanand but also the G-Auto that were not possible without the personal intervention of Modi. *Chapter 16* details how the chief minister showcased Gujarat to investors. Beginning with Gujarati NRIs, Vibrant Gujarat summit held every two years since 2003 is the biggest Indian success story in terms of attracting investment.

Urbanisation and its challenges have been described in *Chapter 17*. Gujarat is the most urbanised state of India and Ahmedabad is the fastest growing urban city. But the story is not just about Ahmedabad. Even villages look urban with *pucca* roads, 24-hour electricity and water. The immediate thought that comes to mind is--what about Environment? *Chapter 18* deals with Green consciousness. The chief minister has written a book on climate change highlighting his green vision. This chapter is based mostly on this book. "*Khushboo Gujarat Ki*" which is *Chapter 19* shows how a determined state can convert its opportunities into advantages and reasons for economic growth. Modi's role in making tourism attractive and the passion with which he does everything has been highlighted here.

Chapters 20, 21 and 22 are about the social issues the State has been trying to tackle on a war footing. Every citizen needs dependable healthcare. The chief minister has been articulating in almost every meeting that in absence of proper healthcare a family gets ruined. *Chapter 20* shows what steps the State has taken steps to attack malnutrition. The success of 108 Service is an interesting case study. It has emerged as a dependable medical emergency service for everyone. *Chapter 21* 'Making Women Count' talks about various steps of women empowerment including waiver of registration if a property is registered in their name, reservation in government jobs and making loans easily available to them for business. The sex ratio is also improving due to targeted measures undertaken. The chapter on 'Education and Skill Development' (*Chapter 22*) highlights the steps taken to increase enrolment in schools, more so for the girl child. Even in skill enhancement women are moving ahead. The State is far ahead of the Central government in adopting measures for skill development.

Chapter 23 showcases the 'Statue of Unity' that shows Modi's grand vision in everything he does. Lakhs of boxes have been dispatched in 1000 trucks to collect used iron pieces of farm implements and soils from about 6.5 lakh villages. The boxes have been fitted with micro chips to track their movement.

The events that led to Modi becoming the BJP's PM candidate have been underlined in *Chapter 24*. If Modi had not been there, the BJP did not have any chance. He is the party's winning decision. The tension and the triumphs are captured in this chapter.

Chapter 25 could have come after the Godhra chapters but it is prudent to talk about this here when we are talking about his candidature for the prime minister's post. Those who cannot debate on development jump to Modi and Muslims. Facts about Muslim empowerment such as 12 per cent Muslims in the police force and better economic conditions than their counterparts in other parts of the country have cut through this vilification campaign.

Muslims have started realising that Modi is their best bet. One of his bitterest critics, Mahesh Bhatt, feels Modi is a genuine person who wants peace to return. Salim Khan wants Muslims to realise this truth. People are against Modi because he has been winning elections, he argued.

Chapter 26 depicts the hollowness of the USA and the UK in dealing with the issue of VISA to Narendra Modi. *Chapter 27* is the conclusion and justifies the title — why he is being described as a gamechanger. Modi has played by his own rules whether it is governance or politics. In politics he was straight and knew what he wanted — to bring the party to power. In governance he knew how to deliver services to people. He perfected bureaucracy as an instrument and launched massive development initiatives in all spheres of economic and social activities. People tried to pin him down on 2002 riots, yet he did not get deterred from his task of making the State prosperous. In mass mobilisation, his rallies are the best attended. He is articulating the vision of the country that touches the common man. He has a massive youth following and is one of the most popular leaders in the social media as well. This is indeed very rare in the county that young people have actually paid to listen to him. He is redefining old concepts and is emerging as India's leader who will restore the pride of being an Indian. This chapter also outlines his Rainbow Vision for India.

Rebellion and Direction

A Peek into Modi's Growing Years

Do not be afraid of a small beginning, great things come afterwards.
Be courageous. Do not try to lead your brethren, but serve them
— **Swami Vivekananda**

A young child of 12 years took the train to Mehsana to respond to his patriotic call. He used to serve tea to passengers in the trains, but had never dared to go inside the coaches with an intention to travel. He did not even inform his father for the fear of being stopped. He had come to know that smartly dressed soldiers of the Indian Army had come to Mehsana to board trains to the borders. He just could not stop himself.

At the Mehsana railway station, which is a junction, he was excited to see Army personnel transiting and doing one thing or the other. He became a part of the NGO that was honouring the *jawans* going to the India-China border. China had attacked India and soldiers were being rushed to the borders to fight the enemy. The young boy did not know what to do; so he took the task of serving tea and snacks to the soldiers. This boy was none other than the present chief minister of Gujarat, Narendrakumar Damodardas Modi.*

Like any other child, Narendra too had many aspirations. One of these was to join the Indian Army. But like many poor children of his hometown, he could not do anything except dream about it.

Poverty came in the way of his dreams and he could not travel to take the examination for the Sainik School in Balachadi, Jamnagar. He had somehow managed to collect Rupees two for the money order that was to be sent to the school as the examination fee. For the first time in his life, he visited the local post office and got the form filled with

---

* Name as per college record available with the author.

the help of people present there. He sent the money order. Immediately came the admit card, but he could not go. His father told him that the family had no money to send him to Jamnagar to take the examination and asked him to complete his studies at the local school. Narendra was a student of the fourth grade back then.

Narendra or ND, as his school mates addressed him, was born at 11 am on 17 September 1950 in a poor family of Ghanchi caste that fell in the category of Other Backward Castes (OBCs). His moon sign is Scorpio, and sun sign is Virgo with star constellation called Anuradha.

The school record carried over to the college at Visnagar shows his date of birth as 29 August 1949. His associates say this was a mistake since people those days did not maintain birth certificates and the date of birth reached the records through the word of mouth. However, after proper calculation by his mother and other family members, the date of birth accepted by one and all is 17 September 1950 and Modi has been celebrating this date as his birthday.

His father Damodardas ran a small tea shop adjoining Vadnagar railway station close to the main entrance. Young Narendra was assigned the task to take tea in an aluminium kettle to serve passengers in the trains that came to Vadnagar and left for either Mehsana or Taranga Hill. This was his way to supplement the family income. He would sell tea in earthen *kulhads* (small container made of baked earth). One cup of special *chai* (tea) cost two *annas* (One *anna* was equal to six paise) whereas the *chalu chai* (normal tea) cost one *anna*. There used to be coins of one paisa, two paisa, one *anna*, two *anna* and four *anna*.

Alongside the platform and in front of the ticket counter is open space with half walls on three sides and a tin roof. *Sadhus* used to stay here for months and Narendra would often spend time with them while serving tea.

Now, the town has a population of 30,000-35,000. During Modi's formative years, the town was a *panchayat* with a population of 18,000-20,000. The place is now connected by well-laid roads besides the railway station that serves as a link with Mehsana on one side and Taranga Hill on the other. It had a metre gauge line that is still a metre gauge.

Earlier, the station served as the nerve centre for the town's activities. Thousands of people could be seen going to the station with their lunch boxes in hands so that they could catch the train to go to other places for their respective jobs. Students from Vadnagar used the trains to go to Visnagar College, about 14 km away towards Mehsana. The morning and evening trains, in particular, would bring lots of crowd; the crowd brought with it a plethora of activities and stories discussed over sips of piping hot sweet tea.

At present, three local trains ply between Mehsana and Taranga Hill, making it six trips in all. There is no train on Sunday. There is only one counter to sell tickets. There is no tea shop closer to the railway station. A bicycle servicing shop and an irrigation oil shop have come up at the place earlier owned by Damodardas. A concrete structure now stands where once semi-permanent structures made of mud and wood stood. There used to be a canteen inside the railway station that is closed now for many years. The trains have lost their importance and road transport has became more efficient.

During Modi's childhood, there were eight passenger trains that passed through Vadnagar, of which the first one from Taranga Hill to Ahmedabad passed at six in the morning. The train from Mehsana to Kheralu came at 8 am and the one from Kheralu to Mehsana at 9 am. There was another train from Patan to Kheralu at 11 am. Two trains — one from Kheralu to Vadnagar to Mehsana and the other one from Palanpur to Taranga — crossed at Vadnagar at 12-30 pm. This was followed by the Taranga to Palanpur train at 4 pm and the one from Ahmedabad to Taranga at 8 pm. So the town was abuzz with activity till 8 pm. Sikander Khan Qureshi remembered that all trains used to be of 10 to 12 coaches.[1]

The trains spruced up activities and generated jobs around the station. The timing of the trains was important for young Narendra since he would have to leave the class and run to the tea shop. He needed to reach the railway station before the train entered the platform. After the train left, he would rejoin his classroom sessions. Since Narendra had no watch and also that the trains often came late, he had to depend on the whistle of the trains. His primary school and even BN High School, where he studied, were hardly a kilometre from the station.

Modi's associates remembered him walking to the railway station at about five in the morning to open the shop and prepare for the day. He would take along the essential items that were needed to make tea. Later, his father would come and prepare tea. Towards the side of the railway station, where Narendra's father ran the tea shop, is one of the six gates that once dotted the Vadnagar outline. Closer to this gate are three shops vending tea and food items; all owned by Muslims.

One of the shops belongs to Babubhai Amirbhai Khan or Babu *chacha* as he came to be addressed with the passage of time. The shops wore the same look that they did some 40 years ago. Babu *chacha* was once very close to Modi. The young Narendra would cross his shop daily everytime he would go to the railway station or return. He would warmly greet other Muslims who would gather at the tea shop. Babu *chacha* fondly remembered him as a very hardworking and humble boy.

Another person who stayed in the locality, Firoz Khan, recalled how Narendra used to rush to the station early morning every day. He appeared committed and sincere to everyone he interacted with. Muslims of the area knew Modi also because his residence was at Kalavasudev Chachar, a neighbourhood of Muslim-dominated Sembhavada to the west of Vadnagar. There are two Muslim-dominated areas: one is in the west and the other in the east called Chakla near Amtol Gate, which is closer to the railway station. The Muslims who stay at Amtol Gate are poor, whereas those staying at Sembhavada are relatively rich. Most people remembered Modi as affable and courteous. He grew up playing with young Muslim boys.

There was never a communal discord in the town. "We lived as one, never mindful of being a Hindu or a Muslim," said 74-year-old Maqbool. Hasan Ali, who was involved in carpentry, said that Modi had done a lot for the development of the state and so should be given a chance at the Centre. Including Vadnagar, there are seven villages that have a sizeable Muslim population. These villages— Badalpur, Maulipur, Kesimpa, Sekhpur, Rasulpur, Sadiqpur and Vadnagar—together have a population of about 40,000 Muslims. No untoward incident happened in Vadnagar during the 2002 riots, Hasan Ali recalled.

Some Muslims in Vadnagar pointed out to the secular tradition of the Modi family. They fondly remembered Modi's father Damodardas providing shelter and home to a Muslim boy Abbas Mohammad Ramsada (Momin). Abbas' father was a farmer from Kesimpa village who would come to the APMC market in Vadnagar on a regular basis and stop at the tea stall owned by Damodardas. They became friends. His son Abbas used to study in BN High School and had to come daily from the distant village. In 1973, when Abbas was in matriculation the family ran into financial difficulties. His father had already expired in 1970 and there was no way he could raise the resources and continue his studies. When Damodardas came to know of this, he brought Abbas home and asked him to complete his studies. Abbas recalled his stay at Modi's home for one full year and how well he was treated by the whole family. He testified to the fact that the family never discriminated between Hindus and Muslims. He was treated as an integral part of the family and accompanied them on social visits. Abbas later studied M.Com and LLB and is now employed with the Gujarat government.

The Modi Family

Narendra's family originally came from Navdotra village in Gujarat's Banaskantha district, which is closer to Rajasthan. His great grandfather Maganlal Ranchoddas decided to settle in Vadnagar and set up a grocery there. Narendra's father Damodardas was the grandson of Ranchoddas.

The family belonged to the extremely backward *Ghanchi* caste that specialised in the occupation of oil pressing (*teli* caste). The same caste is found in areas of Rajasthan.[2] Oil pressing people came to be referred to as Ghanchis because the traditional name for the oil pressing machine is *ghanch* or *ghani* in Rajasthan.

But how can the surname 'Modi' belong to an other backward caste in Gujarat or Rajasthan? Modis are normally *Marwaris* of Rajasthan, but they are not backward. They are a business community and there is no trace of Modis in Rajasthan in the oil pressing trade. The oil pressing community bearing the Modi name is found in Bihar. Their women used to go house to house selling oil and they were referred to as *Modiyayin* (ladies of the Modi caste). They are an OBC spread over areas of Bihar bordering Jharkhand, such as Gaya in Bihar and Kodarma and Ranchi in Jharkhand. It is quite possible that some Modis of Bihar moved away to Gujarat some 200 years ago and settled there.

BJP MLA from Chapra Vishwanath Bhagat did his own research and found out that such a migration took place about five generations back. Former president of the BJP's Bihar unit, Professor Gopal Narain Singh, and Bhagat tried to trace the origin but they could not say anything with authenticity.[3]

The Modi clan claims descent from the Kshatriya community in Rajasthan. Some 700 years ago, they were close to the Kings and used to ensure that people involved in oil pressing were doing their job well. As the story goes, the oil pressing people fled the occupation since they were subjected to a lot of physical pressure and confinement. Thereafter, the Kshatriyas took up the profession and gradually emerged as a new offshoot called Ghanchis.

Now, due to intense caste consciousness, various members of the community have come under the Sahu *samaj* and their number is close to 16 crore. Modis from Gujarat are also members of this larger grouping.

Damodardas was born in 1915. He had five brothers. One of the brothers, Narsinhbhai used to run the railway station's official canteen. A blue-coloured stall made of tin stood at the same place—closed and locked. It looked old, dilapidated and dusty, having fallen to disuse. It looked like any tea stall that one normally finds at any small railway station. Outside, opposite to Damodardas's shop on the other side of the radial road was another tea shop run by another brother, Narottambhai. This tea shop catered to the passengers at the bus stand that brought people from different places and connected them to the railway station. Now, some construction has taken place at the old bus stand. The new bus stand has come up at a site opposite the railway station. Another brother, Jagjeevan owned a shop that sold *bhajia* (fried Gujarati snacks) relished by people with tea.

There were two more brothers, Jayantibhai and Kantibhai, who later became teachers at Durbar. Sombhai (elder brother of Narendra) said that Jayantibhai became a teacher in 1960 whereas Kantibhai got the job in 1965. Narendra was not taught by any of his uncles since he had already left the Durbar when they joined.

Narendra was Damodardas' third child. His father lovingly called him Kumar. He had five more siblings. His eldest brother Sombhai was born in 1944, second brother Amritbhai in 1946 and sister Vasanthi in 1955. Later, Prahlad and the youngest brother Pankaj were born.

All of them are happily settled. Sister Vasanthi is married and lives in

Visnagar. Amritbhai has his own small business and stays aloof from the family. Sombhai retired from the State government's health department and now he runs an old age home in Vadnagar on behalf of a charitable trust. He spends at least two days a week in Vadnagar and the rest of the time in Ahmedabad. He has a busy social life. Prahlad used to run a kerosene business; later, he became an office bearer of the union of Fair Price Shops.

Pankaj, the youngest brother, is employed with the Gujarat Information Department. He moved permanently to Gandhinagar after he was transferred there. Narendra's mother Hiraba stays with Pankaj. Pankaj sold the Vadnagar house in 2003, much to the dislike of his mother. But since no one was ready to stay there, there was no point in hanging on to it. The house is still known by its once illustrious occupant, the Gujarat chief minister.

The house was like a train compartment with 12 by 40 sq ft dimensions. It had an entry from the front into the room that acted as the living room. From this room, one could enter another that had a half partition wall to make a closet for kitchen and another for worship. The last room was small, almost half the size of the first room. The floor was not cemented and would be plastered with cow dung paste on a regular basis. On the first floor, there was a room that catered to guests who visited the family quite frequently. Imagine such a big family living in such a small accommodation! The two neighbouring houses adjoining that house sported a pristine look in wood and concrete. The original Modi house has been renovated by the new occupant and looked modern.

All of Narendra's brothers have now shifted to either Ahmedabad or Gandhinagar. Modi keeps minimal contact with the family. He has told all his kin that none of their activities should sully the name of the family. All the brothers have ensured that they do not indulge in any activity that can be damaging for Modi's image. This self-censorship has continued and has stood the test of time. No charge of nepotism has ever been levelled against Modi. None of the family members have ever gone to the CM house for any work.

Modi did not attend wedding of any of his brothers except Sombhai. The family was so poor that they could not make arrangement for photographs. This explains the reason for absence of photographs of Most social functions.

Modi visits his mother occasionally to receive her blessings; he makes sure to visit her on his birthday. When he became the chief minister for the first time and went to seek her blessings, she said: "*Beta kadi lanch na leis*" (Son, never take bribe). This lesson has stayed etched in Modi's mind very strongly and may have contributed to the zero tolerance for corruption at the chief minister's office (CMO).

His mother Hiraba* is a simple housewife who stays in a 5 × 5 ft room and wears a bathroom slipper. Modi has developed immense respect for his mother for the way she took care of the entire family. The family was very big and it lived on modest means. It was not an easy task to keep all the members well-fed and well-clothed.

His mother used to work at houses of others to earn extra money. There was an office of an oil miller right opposite their residence. The documentations of the mill and accounting was done from that office. Hiraba would get up in the morning and go to village-well to fetch water for the office. Even before others would come she would fill water in the pitcher and the iron bucket for use by the office. She would also clean the utensils. There was another house in the neighbourhood where she would do the same. That way she had to go to the well thrice—the third time for her own family. There was no water supply in Vadnagar that time and everyone depended on water from the wells. It is no wonder that Modi's eyes well up with pride for his mother who tended the family this way. Modi referred to a part of this at the meeting of the BJP's national council in Delhi on 19 January 2013.

Even now the blessings of his mother mean more to him than other things. "I came for my mother's blessings; there is no bigger privilege than that," Modi said while touching the feet of his mother on his birthday in 2013.[4]

Modi's mother has no complaints about her son, who could have made her stay at the chief minister's residence and provided her with all

---

*   In Gujarat, a lady is addressed as 'ben' such as Hiraben. But if the lady is elderly, she is addressed as 'baa' to denote mother such as Kasturba. We have chosen to address Modi's 94-year-old mother as Hiraba

the luxury at his office's disposal. Her son has made a great sacrifice and she does not complain. She derives happiness from the fact that Modi has brought laurels to the family. She is proud that her son is a person of commitment, who does what he says and works very hard to realise his dream. "He has won (over) Gujarat. My chest swells with great pride. He has to do (a) lot more. Narendra will not stop here," she said after Modi's victory in 2012.[5] This was a rare statement from a proud mother for an emotional son who is unable to do anything for her because of his commitment to serve the nation.

Umpteen times Modi has expressed his love and devotion for his mother to his close friends, but has never done this in public to avoid the charges of using emotion to further politics. He has kept his family away from politics. His mother stays in one room and lives an average existence. Whenever the issue of his mother not staying with him is raised, his eyes moisten: "I had taken the decision to stay away from family and this has continued... I have to think of the entire country."

This is one way to keep the family away. The decision is tough indeed but if you try to set high standards in public life, you have to walk the talk first. "*Jab aadmi bada hota hai to maa zyada yaad aati hai, lekin kya kare bechara. Bandha hua hai apne pran se,*" one of his friends said. (When one grows older, one remembers one's mother more. But a man wedded to his vow to keep the family away cannot do anything).

The unity with which Narendra's father and uncles lived in the family was highly commendable. His father was a handsome man; tall and well-bodied like Narendra. While the family was poor and struggling and not many noticed their activities, Damodardas commanded respect and adoration. His word was the last and no one in the family could refuse him. He wanted his Kumar (Narendra) to join the family business since he was not doing well in studies. But the young man was keen to follow his own dream. His father wanted him to be stable but Kumar was keen for action and movement. His father did not like it when he left home for spiritual pursuit.

One of the controversies surrounding Kumar is about his marriage. In backward Ghanchi caste, to which Kumar belonged, the concept of child marriage is still prevalent. This was more so in the 1950s and 1960s. Damodardas got Kumar engaged to Jashodaben when he was merely six.

This was a sort of engagement ritualised through word of mouth and some gifts. The young child was not even aware of what was happening. The second stage came when Narendra had turned 16. According to one of his close friends, he told his bride immediately after marriage that he was not the right person for marriage and that she would not get anything from this marriage. He also asked her to get remarried since he had decided to take a different course. This was the only brief interaction he had with her, his friend asserted.

The third stage is 'aana' (term used in Gujarati for bringing the bride to husband's place for cohabitation to formalise the marriage. This is referred to as 'gauna' in other parts of India) when the bride is called home to cohabitate with the bridegroom. The two families did not keep any interaction with Jashodaben's family after the second stage, since Narendra had clarified that he was not interested in the marriage. Hence, the third stage never happened. Narendra stayed at home only about one year after the second stage. He had already started contemplating deep and was on course to becoming a recluse.

Dasrathbhai Laxmandas Patel, better known as DL in close circles, was an RSS insider and knew everything about Modi. His so-called marriage never came in his way of becoming a *pracharak*, he said. While *pracharaks* are supposed to be unmarried, there would not have been a problem even if he was married. There were examples where married people worked as *pracharaks*, he pointed out. In ND's case, they all knew that the marriage had not got formalised. "We respected him for taking the bold decision and rather thought of him as a social reformer."

Continuing with the story of his marriage, DL said that it created an unspoken rift between ND and his father. The son, when six, had surrendered before the wishes of his father since he did not know what really was happening. At the time of the second stage of that child marriage, he could not muster courage to refuse to sit for the ceremony and was awed by his father's authority. Mahendra Darji, Narendra's other childhood friend, also testified that Damodardas was feared by his sons. In those times, young people seldom opened their mouths in front of their elders. His father did not like this defiance that he thought was making his son unstable.

Marriage was a way his father wanted to chain Kumar to worldly life. But ND was a social worker at heart and would stand up for anyone in adversity. Due to family pressure, he could not say anything but was deeply unhappy, DL said. He also wanted to play a big role in society and thought that worldly life would come in his way.

This perhaps helped him to take the decisive step of leaving home forever and he left Vadnagar in 1970. He briefly visited the place during the Emergency in 1975 and mobilised people in villages against the Congress. He went there disguised as a Sikh for the fear of getting caught. He visited the town again in 1997 to lay the foundation stone of a school. During the same time, he inaugurated the computer lab at BN High School.

Despite a few bumps, both father and son respected and loved each other. Jagdish Prajapati, who bought the tea shop from Hiraba after Damodardas's death, said 'Damodarbhai' had often told him that he knew Narendra wanted to do something big and that he would not stay in the family. In private conversations, he always referred to his son as a *sannyasi*, though he publicly expressed his worry that his son might end up being unemployed and a wanderer.

Narendra was able to defend his action by remembering Gautama Buddha. Narendra's friends recalled his explanation in private talks that even Buddha had left his wife, son and all pleasures and luxuries of a royal life in search of Truth. Vadnagar was once under a strong Buddhist influence and Narendra had read a lot about this. He used to vist the library at Sharmishtha lake and read about Buddha.

He did not leave home in a huff. He gave time to his family members to reconcile since he did not wish to be seen as a vagabond. One fine evening, in 1967, he told his mother that he wanted to leave home in search of truth. Hiraba laughed at him. After all, this was not the age to talk of such spiritual matters. She asked him to focus on studies instead. He persisted and one day he finally told them that he had made up his mind to leave his house but he did not want to run away.

A meeting of the entire extended family was convened to discuss the situation and to persuade him to lead a normal life. Sombhai remembered that everyone in the family attended the meeting. Kumar told everyone present at the meeting that he wanted to pursue a different path and that he could no longer stay in the family. Everyone tried to reason with him that he was too young to think of renunciation and that the right course was to lead a family life and think of earning a livelihood. Young Kumar clarified that he did not wish to lead a normal existence. He even quoted Lord Buddha to justify his decision.

"I will go only if you are all convinced and you allow me to go. I won't run away from home, but then if I stay, I will live life on my own terms," Modi told his family members. Sombhai recalled that Kumar had already become a recluse. He would stay distant and not talk much, go to the library and read books, come back home and sleep. He was always deep in thought.

The family finally decided that he be allowed to do what he wanted. After all, it was his life. When he embarked on this journey for the first time, he was in his pre-university days. Hiraba prepared *laapsi* (a sweet dish made of ghee and jaggery and considered auspicious) for ND, put a *tilak* on his forehead and the entire family was at the door to see him off. Everyone was sad to see him go, but they were not angry with him. Ever since then, ND became a *sannyasin* who came home only briefly to meet his mother and left for wandering again.

Modi had deep respect for his father. This was evident when his father fell ill in 1986. Sombhai took Damodardas to Ahmedabad and got him admitted to a government hospital. Modi met his father and ensured that much better treatment was given to him. His father returned to Vadnagar but he could not recover fully. Later, he was diagnosed with bone cancer. He became sick again in 1988.

Modi used to apply every year to the government to include him in the list of pilgrims for Kailash Mansarovar. Every time his application would get rejected. However, he got the clearance to go on the pilgrimage in 1988. He spoke to Sombhai whether or not he should go ahead. Their father was critical. He could always take time out from his political routine in Ahmedabad to visit his father. But if something happened when he was away at Mansarovar, he would be unable to come at a short notice. Sombhai advised him to go ahead with the journey. Modi gave his elder brother the contact number of the RSS headquarters in Delhi where Sombhai could drop a message in case of an emergency.

Modi went on the pilgrimage and completed the journey but when he was returning, he got news from the RSS headquarters that his father had fallen seriously ill. He took a flight from Delhi to Ahmedabad and then hired a car from Ahmedabad to reach Vadnagar in the shortest possible time. The ailing father had asked incessantly, "Kumar *Kyan chhe? Kumar kem nathi aavya?*" (Where is Kumar? Why has he not visited me?) He would be told that Kumar had gone to Kailash to get holy water of the river Ganga for him. When Kumar reached home, he was wearing a saffron *lungi* (cloth wrapped around the waist) and *khadayun* (wooden slippers). He offered Ganga water to his father to drink and *prasad* (religious offering of food) that he had brought from Kailash Mansarovar Shiva temple.

When Kumar reached home, the house was jam packed with relatives and well-wishers. He was very tired and did not wish to meet other people. Also, he was unhappy and disturbed because of his father's suffering. Sombhai took him to his residence in Mehsana. The next morning, Narendra left for Ahmedabad to attend some pressing political work. At 3 am the next day, he received the news that his father was no more. He then immediately rushed to Vadnagar.

Narendra and his brothers took their father's body to the cremation ground. Some of the close friends of Narendra were surprised to see him arrive unannounced but understood the situation when they saw him holding the bamboo-stretcher that carried his father's dead body. It was a touching moment for everyone close to Modi. He returned to the Vadnagar home, comforted his mother and left for Ahmedabad.

Modi said he felt he was lucky to have met his father at the last moment. In an interview to the author, he remembered his father as a sensitive soul. "Whenever my father would go to attend any funeral procession in the neighbourhood, he would fast the whole day."

Growing Up

When Narendra was 14, an astrologer predicted that he would do very well in life. However, at that time, he was in a pitiable condition. He had no idea what he wanted to do in future and the fact that he was not the best of students was no help. According to Mahendrabhai Darji, a close friend of Modi, the astrologer said: "*Ye ladka ya to bada tapasvi, ya sadhu purush, ya rajkarani hoga. Aisa hoga ki pura vishwa unko janega.* (This boy will either become a big saint or a big political leader. The whole world will know him). Darji said, *"Aur tab to baju wale bhi nahi jaante the."* (And at that time, even the neighbours didn't know him).

Narendra's friends were worried with his constant exploration of life. The family naturally wanted to know if there would be an end to the cycle of poverty and if any of the sons would do well in life. They were more particularly worried about Narendra who was not very keen on studies. Even his friends wanted to know what was in store for him.

The prediction made by the astrologer gave the family more reasons to worry. The family was facing some really bad days, and they could not even imagine Narendra getting involved in politics. His father did not want him to become a wanderer. Surprisingly, both predictions proved to be correct. A teenage Narendra ran away to the Himalayas in search of truth and later, he entered public life and rose through the rank and file to become one of the tallest political figures in the country.

Ascetics used to be treated with reverence when they visited the family. This must have impacted young Narendra's impressionable mind. The family would give whatever was possible to those hermits. The Vadnagar railway station had a shade where the *sadhus* used to stay for the night and at times stayed there for days. After completing his chore of serving tea to the passengers of whichever train was standing at the platform, Narendra would spend his time with the *sadhus*. The sound of trains coming and then leaving the station and associations with *sadhus* produced a deadly combination of longing for movement and action and spirituality.

He left college mid-way in 1968 (before completing graduation) and wandered for about two years. He had become too contemplative and turned a recluse. Amongst his close circle of friends, he always spoke of higher things. "What should we do and what is our position in this vast world, he always asked," DL said. He wanted to make sense of his poverty and existence. He had the option to complete pre-university in college and get jobs like his elder brothers and friends. But he chose not to.

During this time, he visited the headquarters of the Ramakrishna Mission Ashram at Belur Math near Kolkata and then went to the mission's office in Rajkot. It was only after these two visits that he set off for the Himalayas. He wanted to do something, but could not clearly choose which path to take. Nothing much is known about what he did and whom he met with during those wandering days.

When Modi visited Belur Math in April 2013, an exception was made for him by opening the room where Swami Vivekananda stayed. Modi was allowed to be alone in the room where he meditated for 25 minutes. This was reminiscent of his previous visit to Belur Math as a teenager.[6] During that visit, he had met the then president of the Mission, Swami Madhavananda Maharaj, and asked for his permission to become a monk. He had advised the boy to first complete his studies.

Narendra had also met the chief of RK Mission at Rajkot, Swami Atmasthananda, and spent some time there. He had requested that he be taken into the *ashram* as a disciple but the swami politely refused. He had seen something in Narendra that made him persuade the young boy not to become a monk. He had told Narendra that he was meant to do something spectacular in worldly life. A dejected Modi left for the Himalayas. The Swami advised him to keep a beard, something that has stayed with him ever since. Swami Atmasthananda is now the president of the Math and the Mission.

Modi still remembers the incident: "Yes, the swami did not allow me to become a monk". He had fond memories of the time he spent with the Swami at Rajkot.

After his visit to the Belur Math and the Rajkot *ashram*, Narendra visited Vadnagar, met his mother, and after spending some time with her, he immediately left for the Himalayas. During this journey, he spent time at the Vivekananda Kendra at Almora. After more than a year of wandering and meeting wanderers of different kinds, he returned to Vadnagar in 1970. But this too was a short visit and he soon left Vadnagar for a life of struggle and action that was to keep him away from his birthplace for almost 30 years.

Some people claiming to know him said that the visits led him to the realisation that the life of a wanderer was not something that would give him inner satisfaction and peace. His interaction with *sadhus* and religious teachers gave him a new insight, and gradually helped him to come out of his exile and enter the life of action. This brought in him new determination to be meaningful for the society.

He discovered that those who claimed to be saints were involved in the same mundane calculations of daily existence as anyone else. He often wondered if he was running away from the responsibility towards society. The life and teachings of Swami Vivekananda which he had learnt during those days had started exercising immense influence on him.

Swami Vivekananda had popularised the concept of Sri Ramakrishna Paramahansa's "*nar seva narayan seva*" (service to man is service to God). Narendra was immensely impressed by this philosophy that helped him to realise the truth of existence and return to his *karmabhoomi*. In all his life thereafter, he tried to act as per the Vedanta philosophy enunciated by Swami Vivekanand.

During this phase of life, Modi learnt the value of isolation and contemplation, something that stayed with him forever. This helped him appreciate the beauty of lakhs of eggs of flamingos laid in the Rann of Kutch near the creek (when he became the chief minister). During every visit, Modi would sit there for hours in isolation, appreciating the Creator and his design. "Can you imagine lakhs of white eggs laid at equal distance from each other?" Then he answered, "This is God and his design." People are not allowed to go there but the State government has made plans to show these images to people live through satellite and 3D technology.

For years Modi used to burn his belongings or anything associated with him. He would think why to keep things that would create attachment. He did not wish anyone to remember him with those signs. "People should remember me by my work and not through these signs", he had told one of his friends. This was his way to disconnect with the past. He used to read a lot about history. After reading he would contemplate for hours on the meaning of existence. Everything that existed would vanish. He thought burning his belongings was the best way to disconnect with past life.

One thing that always remained with him during his days of wandering was a photograph of his mother. This discovery was made by Hiraba when she once checked the bag when he came back from the Himalayas. Besides one pair of clothes, shorts, half-sleeve garments and a shawl, there was a photograph of his mother. He used to carry a cotton bag. Almost the same items continued to occupy the bag when he later toured entire Gujarat to spread the ideology of the RSS.

The desire to be a part of the outer world and to be meaningful had already manifested in his participation in RSS activities in the *shakhas*. These *shakhas* provided an environment to play games, sing patriotic songs and get involved in more responsible activities. Some of his peers remembered him participating in the *shakha* activity as early as eight years. His friend from childhood Dr Sudhir Joshi remembered him joining the *shakha* when he was a fifth grade student. A new teacher had come to Bhagvatacharya Narayanacharya High School (BN High School) and started the *Bal Shakha*. Some students from primary schools also attended the *shakha*. About 20 children attended the session held near the Vishnupuri temple complex every evening at 5 pm.

Dr Sudhir Joshi was studious whereas Narendra excelled in fitness. "We were under constant pressure to perform well, but Narendra had some other things to do as well, such as fending for the family." DL Patel came to know Narendra from the *shakha* days and developed an emotional bonding with him. Narendra was not an exceptional student in the class in terms of scoring marks, but he always figured among the top ten students, he said. A batch usually had 35 to 40 students.

His friends found him to be extremely brilliant in terms of grasping the issue, action points and social behaviour. When asked to comment on him being an average student, Modi said he did have enough motivation. "I was not extremely brilliant, but I understood everything. When others attended the class, I had to listen to the whistle of the train so that I could run before the train arrived."

Their English teacher Bijlibhai Chowdhary once told Damodardas that Narendra was very talented and that the family should give him time to study rather than make him work at the tea stall. Narendra's father said, "I have given my son to you and you should take care of him." However, the little money earned from the tea stall was indispensable for the family, and hence, Narendra also had to put in his efforts to run the shop.

Young Narendra's routine would run something like this: He got up at 4:45 am to reach the shop at 5 am; after cleaning up and serving tea to passengers of the first train that came around 6 am, he would go back home and, at about 7 am, he would reach Sharmishtha Lake for a swim. He would swim and reach the temple in the middle of the lake, touch the flag on top of it and come back to the bank. He repeated this three times. This was perhaps the only luxury he had. It helped him develop stamina and a good physique.

Once, Narendra was badly injured when a crocodile hit his left foot with its tail. A croc's tail is strong; a hit by it can be fatal. It is like you are struck with a sword. Villagers say there used to be 29 crocodiles in the lake. Narendra was an eighth grade student then. He got nine stitches on his left foot near the ankle and was bed-ridden for more than a week. The cut marks are still there on his left foot. This incident would have scared any other child for the rest of his life, but not Narendra. Within a month, he was back in the lake. "I never bothered about my life and was ready to do any daring act," he told the author.

After the swim, he would return home, get ready and go to school with his friends. From school, he would go to attend the evening *shakha*, and from there to the railway station to cater to the passengers of the last train. Since he also joined junior NCC at the BN High School, and later senior NCC in college, this kept him preoccupied with NCC activities too. The refreshment given at NCC was a big attraction. The NCC helped inculcate discipline, punctuality and leadership at a very young age.

The much written about flag changing ceremony at Sharmishtha Lake happened after his near-fatal injury, when hurt by the crocodile. The lake dates back to the Solanki period. Now, it is at the centre of Vadnagar. In the middle of the lake is an old temple on which a saffron flag flutters with pride. It has been customary to get the flag changed during the Bhadra Paksha (an auspicious fortnight for Hindus) that falls in May-June during the peak of the monsoon. It was almost taken as a ritual and a game. The tradition stays even to this day, said Valimikbhai, who lived near the lake.

As swimmers would try to reach the top of the temple in order to change the flag, coconuts would be thrown on the sides of the swimmers to prevent crocodiles from coming closer. Crocodiles normally did not harm anyone, but during the peak of monsoon anything could happen.

On one such day, when the Monsoon was on a high and the waters of the lake looked dangerous, few young boys started swimming together but could not go to the temple top. Elders advised them not to, but they took this as a challenge. Three swimmers finally came back after the water swelled dangerously high. But Narendra continued, went to the top of the temple, changed the flag and then returned. Everyone looked at young Narendra with disbelief.

There is another story of Narendra and crocodile when he was just 12 years old. While coming back from his swimming routine, he found a baby crocodile lying alone at the side of the lake. It was more than a foot long. ND took the baby croc to his residence to nurse it, Dr Joshi recalled. His mother got angry and asked him to drop the crocodile back in the lake. Narendra followed her instruction obediently. However, the naughty boy in him thought of rearing the crocodile without knowing that it was not possible. Mahendrabhai Darji recalled that Damodardas used to scold Narendra to prevent him from swimming in the lake for the fear of anything untoward happening to his Kumar.

Narendra's bravery has made it to Vadnagar's folklores. There is a consensus in Vadnagar that Modi was adventurous, fearless, laborious, determined and keen to change his destiny. But there is also a consensus that he was naughty and mischievous but without offending anyone.

The evening *shakha* provided him opportunities to learn higher ideals and helped to imbibe in him a heightened sense of patriotism. Whatever happened at the national and international arena, such as the Indo-China war in 1962, figured prominently at the discourses in the *shakhas*. Narendra spoke of undiluted patriotism at those *shakhas*. This explains why he went to Mehsana to meet the jawans of the Indian army.

Even during his school days, he participated in extra-curricular activities. Dr Prahlad Patel, who taught Sanskrit and Gujarati in BN High School, fondly remembered young Narendra coming to him with a request that his name be included in every debate. Every Thursday, the last two classes were earmarked for debate. The topics would be 'doctor or lawyer: whose role is better for society?', 'whether students should participate in politics', 'the role of men and women in society' etc. The topic would be announced in the first period and students were asked to give their names by 2 pm. Then the students would be asked to speak one by one. Patel, who taught Narendra in Class X and XI, recalled that Narendra could speak on any topic and students clapped at his articulation. "I cannot but be proud if my student becomes the prime minister of the country," he said.

During those days, there used to be a junior primary level for classes I to IV, upper primary for classes V to VII and higher secondary for classes VIII to XI. This was followed by senior secondary school beginning from class XII, culminating into a three-year graduation course. Narendra along with friends studied junior primary in *Gamthi Shala* run by one Jethalal Joshi as a charitable work. This was a proper school close to his residence. Narendra studied the upper primary at Durbar. He joined the BN High School for higher classes where he continued till class XI. For senior secondary and graduation, he joined MN College in 1967-68.

Dr Sudhir, who shifted to BN High School along with Narendra, was five days junior to him in age and one of the few who addressed him as *'tu'* (you). Sudhir's father was a medical practitioner and Narendra's father used to visit him often. This developed into a friendly bond that also helped the two children to come together and become good friends. They would sit on the same bench in the classroom.

Besides broadening of minds at the *shakha*, Narendra learnt the qualities of leadership including camaraderie and brotherhood. He also learnt the art of keeping communication alive since he was always asked to give information to people as a part of the *shakha* training. The NCC taught him discipline of a different kind that focused on working hard without complaining, telling no lies and making no excuses, and obeying with a smile—the four cardinals that were taught to all those who joined the NCC.

DL Patel was senior to Narendra by two years but a friend at the *shakha*. He described an incident of Narendra filling the nomination for class representative, which then used to be an elected post. This was in the ninth grade. He did not ask or tell anyone, he just filled the form. He then came and informed his friends at the *shakha*. Everyone said he should not have filled the form as this would distract him further from studies, but he said he would go ahead with the nomination. He worked very hard, persuaded students with his arguments and won handsomely.

Modi did not want to become the class representative to show his power, but to do something constructive for the class. The students had problems with a particular teacher since he did not teach well and this impacted the performance of the students. They complained that the teacher must be changed. Students' rating also mattered in evaluation of a teacher's performance. But no one dared to tell this to Ras Behar Maniar, the principal, who had a reputation of being very strict. Narendra took up the challenge, spoke to the principal and in just one sitting he convinced him that the teacher was not up to the mark. The teacher was finally replaced, recalled Dr Joshi.

Once in 1965, a PT (Physical Training) teacher slapped a boy mercilessly without provocation. Narendra and his friends decided to boycott the class to oppose the corporal punishment. The boycott continued for three days. Students came and sat at the ground but did not go inside the classrooms. Seniors such as DL Patel ensured that the students did not suffer and organised special classes by brighter students. Finally, the PT teacher had to apologise. After this, no teacher dared to give such a punishment to any student, recalled DL.

Narendra was a disciplined child, Sombhai recalled. He would often wash his clothes and keep things ready. Since they could not afford to pay for ironing of clothes, he would keep the shirt and pant under the pillow or mattress. When he would get up in the morning, the clothes would look fresh and ironed. Modi made sure that his clothes were always clean.

Once, Narendra was caught on the wrong foot when he was a student of class VI at the durbar. He had climbed a tree in the school compound. Students were not allowed to climb trees and this was a part of the school discipline. Some students complained to the teacher, who caught him red-handed and asked him to come down and scolded him loudly. Narendra did not utter a word and kept looking at the ground. When the teacher asked him why he had done that, he pointed out towards the tree and said that a bird had got stuck in the tree and he was merely trying to set it free. The teacher felt really bad and apologised to Modi then and there.

Modi's leadership qualities had started getting recognised by his friends. Whenever there would be a fight, his friends would wait for him to come. He always tried to broker peace. Once he went on a picnic with select friends at DL's farmland. The friends had put a condition that they would go only if ND would cook *Undhiyu* (Gujarati mix-vegetable dish). While coming back, they had a verbal argument and one of them used abusive language. Modi was quick to point out that such language should not be used among friends. Everyone realised the mistake and shook hands, recalled DL Patel.

Modi's *bhabhi* spoke high of his culinary skills. During his visit to Sombhai's Mehsana home, Modi would get up in the morning, go to the kitchen and cook *Saboodana khichdi*. He knew almost all Gujarat recipes, she said. But he was very simple even in his eating habits. His favourite was tea and bajra bread. He would not demand anything else.

A very good peer group had emerged at the secondary school level. Besides ND, the group included Dashrathbhai, Dr Sudhir Joshi, Harishbhai Patel, Bharathbhai Thakkar, Mahendrabhai Darji, Badarkhan Pathan, Pravinsinh Thakur, Bhalabhai Satwara, Ishwar P Patel, Madhusudan Seth, Pravin Bhatt, and Trilok Nayan. All of them were invited with their families for a get-together at the CM house when Modi became the chief minister for the first time in 2001.

This peer group became strong when Narendra joined the Maneklal Nanchand College (MN College) at Visnagar in 1967. He joined the pre-university and took up science course but was soon shifted to arts due to shortage in attendance. Visnagar College was then called "Princess of the Desert", said Dr Prahlad Patel. This was the only college between Ahmedabad and Ajmer and was rated among the top few colleges of the state. More than 4,000 students studied there. Other eminent political personalities who studied at Visnagar College were Shakersinh Vagehla and Anandiben Patel (minister in Modi Government).

Professor KM Joshi, principal of MN College, who has been in the college since 1995, held that Narendra finally dropped out of the college because of personal reasons. Narendra and his friends would take the train from Vadnagar to go to Visnagar to attend college.

DL showed the room at his residence where Narendra used to come and rehearse for the play *"Pagrakha no Padiyo"*. This play was a telling commentary on the ruler of the time, who lived a luxurious life, and did not bother about sufferings of his people. The king was from Saurashtra.

Modi and his friends used to rehearse regularly and the drama was so good that DL formed a company by the name 'DL Patel and Party'. The idea was to show the play to people in various villages. The play was rendered in a hilarious way. The tall and handsome Narendra played the role of the king. Darji said that Narendra delivered the dialogues powerfully and was therefore given the lead role. This group of RSS workers was also active in social mobilisation and used theatre to achieve their end.

Narendra used his acting skills to further his social commitment. He staged the social drama *Jogidas Khuman* to raise funds for the boundary wall of BN High School in 1967. The school did not have enough funds. Narendra came up with the idea of a charity show. This was his last year in school. He played the lead role. It helped the school to collect Rs 25,000, a large sum in those days.

Dr Prahlad Patel remembered that Narendra had rehearsed a lot for the play and everyone appreciated the drama. The entire Vadnagar seemed to have converged at the school to watch the play.

The rebellion was more pronounced in the play *Piloo Phool*, which was written and directed by Narendra in the last year of School. It was a one-act play of about 15 minutes involving only one actor. Narendra acted in that play, which revolved around the theme of untouchability. A Dalit child fell ill, and his mother, who was a widow, had no money to take him to a doctor. People did not give her any money, but someone told her that she should offer a yellow flower at the temple to get her son cured. When she visited the temple that had plants with the kind of flowers needed, she was not allowed to enter the premises because of her so-called low caste. Dejected, she came back home and discovered that her son had died when she was away. Narendra would render it so powerfully that tears would roll down the eyes of the audience.

The play *Piloo Phool* (yellow flower) must be seen in the context of his friendship with a Dalit (manual scavenger). Even now, one can see scavengers and other Dalits living in the outskirts of a town or village or at least in an exclusive area so that their presence do not disturb the so-called higher caste people. Narendra used to get agitated by the plight of the downtrodden. He empathised with his friend. The relationship was so close that if he did not eat food at his home, Hiraba would know that he had taken food at the house of his Dalit friend.

Hariyali no Hatyaro (Killer of greenery) was another important play in which he acted. The theme was "the importance of trees and the need to protect them".

Modi explained that theatre was a powerful medium which helped in giving vent to his passion for social change. "I found this to be a powerful medium to communicate." He was disturbed with the social inequalities and spoke of this even at the *shakhas*.

The ordeal of Dalits was close to his heart. Young Narendra questioned the discriminatory caste regime and did not surrender to the oppressive social order. In that sense he was a social rebel as well. Once he tried to expose Congress Seva Dal people who had come to Vadnagar to visit the houses of people to demonstrate that everyone was equal. The practice was to display names of people, whose houses they would visit, on the public display board at the library. Modi wrote the names of four Dalits with addresses as priority visits. All Sarvodaya leaders went back without visiting the Dalit houses and this exposed their claims of trying to remove untouchability or treat everyone as equal.

When Sombhai was working in Mehsana, they used to feed students on nominal payment. Once Modi visited them and came to know of this. He asked them to include some Dalit students also in the list, even if they were unable to pay. "We must try to take all sections of society together," Modi told them. His *bhabhi* informed him that the list already had some Dalit students.

She remembered Modi as very friendly with children. During his visits, he would play with children in the neighbourhood. He liked to interact with children and was very natural with them.

One of the early influences on Narendra was that of Rasikbhai Dave whose office was close to Damodardas's tea stall. Dave was the local coordinator of Maha Gujarat Janata Parishad, which was fighting for separate Statehood for Gujarat. Rasikbhai was of the age of Narendra's father and both were part of the Congress Seva Dal in the early days. There was no organisation other than that and the Congress Seva Dal was respected. Damodardas even wore the prestigious Gandhian cap during that time, DL Patel said.

Narendra would visit Dave's office regularly to collect the badges that proclaimed support for Gujarat's separate statehood. Rasikbhai trusted his honesty since he was among the few boys who distributed the badges with full sincerity. He spotted the strong leadership quality Narendra possessed as a child. The first thing he learnt from Dave was the art of political slogan shouting.[7] This gave him a sense of being a part of what the elders were doing. He was unaware that this political participation was giving him a unique experience. In 1960 when Gujarat was granted separate statehood, Narendra led the celebration in his primary school and few could miss the enthusiasm of the young boy of ten.

Formal Induction in the RSS

With a desire to find his own feet in the vast world, Narendra shifted to Ahmedabad in 1970. After his return from the Himalayas, he had decided to struggle hard and not complain about his state of affairs. He touched the feet of his mother, took a few of his belongings in his cloth bag and reached Ahmedabad via Mehsana. The train that used to entice and challenge him to movement had finally ensured his arrival in the city of his dream — 102 km south of Vadnagar.

His elder brother Amritbhai was already in Ahmedabad, but Modi did not wish to disturb his arrangement by staying there. He also did not want the struggle to be easy. So, he made the canteen of the State Road Transport his home. This was run by his maternal uncle Babubhai. Modi would serve at the canteen and at times perpare tea for customers. He also assisted his uncle in maintenance of accounts.

When he visited Ahmedabad, he was keen to meet his mentor Vakil Saheb. While the stay in the canteen was okay, this was not the life he had longed for. A chance meeting with Ambalal Koshti, general secretary of the Jana Sangh's Kankaria ward, brought about the turning point he was looking for. Koshti and others were protesting against fare hike in the State transport. Narendra sat in the canteen opposite the venue of the protest. Impressed by their slogans and posters, he walked up to them and shared his own thoughts. Koshti, then 31, was impressed by the young boy.

"At that time, Jana Sangh was not a strong force and we kept on looking for people who could join us and lead. I was immensely impressed by the spark in Narendra. I visited his canteen regularly to be in touch with him. Narendra was politically very conscious. Whenever I visited the canteen I found him reading one or the other book, mostly either history or political science. If only we could get him in the group, I thought," said Ambalal Koshti.[8]

He then offered Modi his own position of general secretary of the ward. This was his way to entice the young mind that he could do something big, if he wanted. Modi took up the challenge, but could not continue for long since destiny had something else in store for him. He had established a rapport with the RSS headquarters. He used to attend the *shakhas* too, but had to wait till 1971 to have a one-on-one meeting with Laxmanrao Inamdar, the *prant pracharak*, who was more popular by the name of Vakil Saheb (Laxmanrao Inamdar). Modi was nearing 21 when he met Vakil Saheb in Ahmedabad

He had met Vakil Saheb when the latter had visited Vadnagar in late 1950s. At that time, Modi was merely seven and he was asked to take a vow to become a *Bal Swayamsewak*. Under Vakil Saheb's influence, he had taken the vow to dedicate more time to RSS activities. This was on Diwali. The young child was so impressed by Vakil Saheb that he spent the whole day moving around to get to know him more and more. This angered the family since Modi was away from home on the festive day.[9]

Fascinated by Inamdar's personality, Modi wondered how he could always look cheerful whereas most *pracharaks* looked thoughtful and serious. Modi thought that perhaps Vakil Saheb was practicing meditation to get a persona that impressed one and all.[10] After this meeting with him, RSS *pracharaks* started visiting the family on a regular basis. The mentorship of the RSS had begun without anyone realising it.

Thus, when he met Vakil Saheb in Ahmdabad, it was not difficult to reconnect. Although the images had blurred, Vakil Saheb had a sharp memory. Modi re-introduced himself and told him about what all he had done till then. When he asked him for guidance, the RSS *pracharak's* first reaction was to ask him to continue with his studies so that he could know the world better.

The person, who was to turn Modi's mentor, appreciated his grasp of knowledge and curiosity. Modi said that he did not wish to pursue higher studies. Doing graduation could land him an easy government job, but he was not interested in any job; he was keen to devote his life to social service. He pleaded with Vakil Saheb to induct him into the RSS, and his mentor invited him to stay with him at the RSS headquarters at the Hedgewar Bhawan. The pupil's determination moved Vakil Saheb, who decided to mould him for the RSS journey ahead. In deference to his mentor's wishes, Narendra decided to pursue further studies along with Sangh's activities.

He completed his graduation from the University of Delhi through correspondence. Political science and history were his favourite subjects. He joined the course in 1971, but completed it during the Emergency days. In 1977-78 he completed his Masters in Political Science from Gujarat University. Sombhai said that he completed both graduation and Masters as an external student.

Modi insisted on washing the clothes of Vakil Saheb along with his own. Vakil Saheb did not allow him to do so initially, but later relented when the young man persisted with folded hands that he wanted to do so out of respect for him. He performed these duties with complete devotion. Modi proved to be a true disciple of Swami Vivekananda who had taught that one must learn to serve well.

While he was happy that he got a chance to live with his guru, Vakil Saheb was not going to accept his disciple without a test. Modi was put through a rigorous routine. He would get up early in the morning at about 4:30 am, get ready and fetch milk from the cowshed, wake up the other inmates and make tea for them.

The Hedgewar Bhavan had nine rooms and there would be at least 15-18 inmates at any given point of time. He made and served morning tea to everyone. After this, he washed the utensils and participated in the morning *shakhas*. He also made snacks and served breakfast to the inmates. For full two years he worked like this. He also swept the floors of the nine rooms. He befriended a 7-year-old boy Premchand who also served tea there. Later, Premchand became a peon. A chance meeting after he became the chief minister, Modi identified Premchand and called him to the chief minister's office. Nobody treats Premchand with disrespect as he is Modi's first friend in Ahmedabad. Both the *chaiwalas* now work at the CM office though in different capacities. They share a bonding without speaking about it.

As time passed by, Modi was given more responsibilities such as looking after correspondences of RSS workers at the level of Prant (division of RSS organisation above district). He would also be responsible for making railway reservations for various *swayamsewaks* who travelled on a regular basis. After finishing the work at the headquarters, Modi would visit railway officials and befriend them. Soon they all began to like the jovial Modi and readily obliged the requests for tickets and reservations. Modi learnt that personal relations counted so much for job delivery.

His role was further enhanced when he was asked to look after the families of the *swayamsewaks* who visited Ahmedabad for various needs such as medical treatment, organisational get together etc. He would make arrangements for their stay at the residences of other *swayamsewaks*. He had learnt from Vakil Saheb that for the organisation to grow, family members of the *swayamsewaks* must be given due respect. Modi lavished high praise on Vakil Saheb for inculcating family values in *swayamsewaks*.[11]

The year 1971 was tumultuous for Indian politics. When Modi came under the internship of Vakil Saheb, already there were sporadic agitations all across the country on the issue of the US support to Pakistan in the Bangladesh war. Modi had visited Delhi to inquire about admission in Delhi University. It is here that he had his first brush with politics. He participated in a demonstration of angry Jan Sangh workers against the US embassy to protest arms aids to Pakistan. The Jan Sangh supported liberation of Bangladesh from the Pakistani occupation.

The RSS had organised protests to express solidarity with Bangladesh. People cutting across all sections of society appealed to the government to oppose the US stand and to teach Pakistan a lesson. Workers of various organisations came on the streets asking the government to recruit them in the army and to send them to the war front. At one such protest that was joined by people such as George Fernandes and Madhu Limaye, Modi was arrested and sent to Tihar Jail. They were protesting outside the residence of then Prime Minister Indira Gandhi.

After release from Tihar, he went straight to meet Vakil Saheb and requested that he be allowed to stay at the RSS headquarters. He knew that he must become an integral part of the organisation to make a bigger impact. Modi was enthused with politics, but allowed himself to be tamed by the RSS. When the entire country was celebrating the victory of India over Pakistan and creation of Bangladesh, Modi was sweeping the floors of the Hedgewar Bhavan.

Everyone in the RSS had started taking Modi seriously due to Vakil Saheb who had seen great promises in Narendra. He soon grew into a natural organiser of men and resources. When asked to coordinate a work, he would do it so meticulously that even Vakil Saheb would be surprised. A senior RSS worker of that time said, "we had already heard that a very sincere young man was going to become a RSS *pracharak*," he said.

Modi became a full time RSS *pracharak* in the early months of 1972.[12] What were needed for this was to understand the ideology of the RSS, a commitment to lead a life full of restraints and dedication to the cause of the nation. Modi already had all those. It is pertinent to mention here that a three year OTC training to become a *pracharak* is desirable, but not mandatory. When one becomes a *pracharak* the organisation checks all his antecedents. Entire track record of Modi was checked before he was given any major role.

He completed his first and second year of OTC between 1973 and 1974. The RSS used to call its training of workers as Official Training Camp (OTC) since it aimed at producing leaders wedded to patriotism. Later, it started calling it Sangh Shiksha Varg (RSS Training Classes). The training is classified as First Year, Second Year and Third Year. A RSS *pracharak* is supposed to have undergone all three trainings. Modi completed his third year OTC in 1978. Those who were his colleagues at the course in Nagpur were Pravin Togadia, Kaushik Mehta, Dashrathbhai and Shankersinh Vaghela.

Sometime between 1978 and 1980, Modi called Sombhai on phone requesting him to send documents related to his birth, school certificates etc. When the elder brother asked for the reason, Modi told him that he had got an invitation from Ohio University to do a Doctorate in Political Science. Modi had to get a passport made. But within a month, when Sombhai sought to know the progress, Modi told him that he had shelved the plan. He explained to Sombhai that on second thoughts he had decided not to leave the country for a Doctorate degree. He did not wish to lose three years of serving the country particularly since he did not plan to take up any job.

Vadnagar

A chapter on Modi's early life would be incomplete without describing the Vadnagar town. People say this is one of the oldest cities in the state, about 2,500 years old. It was referred to as Anartapur during the time of the Mahabharatha. Situated about 100 km north of Ahmedabad, the town with a population of more than 30,000 has a *nagarpalika* now. The city is on top of a hillock and was surrounded by six gates that guarded it from invasion. The gates are still there. One of the gates is called the 'nose of Vadnagar' since a human face with a prominent nose is inscribed on this gate. Legend says that the city had 365 temples and 365 lakes and ponds.

The city has traces of Buddhism. Recent excavation carried out on suggestion of Modi has discovered a Buddhist shrine that used to house Buddhist monks. The Chinese pilgrim Hiuen Tsang visited the city in 11th century AD and found about 10 Buddhist monasteries.

The city is full of ancient legends that border on myth, but the stories have been carried forward through the oral tradition. One such story is that of Tana-Riri. They were two sisters who knew how to sing Rag Malhar that brought rains. Once, Tansen was forced to sing Rag Deepak at the court of Emperor Akbar which led to immense heat in the singer's body. He finally landed up at Vadnagar where the two sisters sang Rag Malhar and brought peace to Tansen's body.

However, this brought trouble to the two sisters when Akbar came to know of this and wanted them to be brought to his court. Akbar was keen to marry them. He sent his army to get them to the court, but the two sisters resisted the move and committed suicide. Ever since then, Tana-Riri festival in Vadnagar has come to symbolise celebration of music.

After becoming the chief minister, Modi made Tana-Riri festival popular by constructing an amphitheatre close to Sharmishtha Lake. He also ordered development of Vadnagar by renovating the lake, making concrete structures and getting a ring road around the lake that also covers the city. The street lights in Vadnagar are lighted using solar panels.

A major food processing company's plant has been set up close to the city giving employment to about 1,500 people. It deals in food products and processed mushrooms, potatoes, appetizers and dairy products. Some more industries have come up around the city at a distance. The city now has better education and more schools than the time of Modi's childhood.

***

Political Baptism by Emergency Fire

Change does not roll in on the wheels of inevitability, but comes through continuous struggle. And so we must straighten our backs and work for our freedom. A man can't ride you unless your back is bent.

— Martin Luther King, Jr.

Modi had some sort of political grooming without anyone planning it. This was by way of listening to discussions seniors used to have at the tea stall of his father, mentorship by Rasikbhai Dave during the Maha Gujarat agitation, and participation during the anti-US agitation on the issue of the Bangladesh War in 1971. All these were nothing compared to the role he was forced to play during the Emergency imposed by then Prime Minister Indira Gandhi in the early hours of 26 June 1975. The Emergency is often described as the darkest era in Indian democracy because it sought to muzzle dissent and impose a totalitarian regime.

He gradually rose to handle the protesters' communication system with almost all top leaders during the Emergency. This gave him a first-hand experience of political mobilisation — something that was to come in handy in subsequent years.

Most political leaders in India today, who do not come from the Congress stock, had played crucial roles during the Emergency. They all came under the influence of the towering personality of Loknayak Jayaprakash Narayan (JP), participated in the political struggle that shaped their destiny and acquired significant positions in politics that the energy unleashed. But they failed to live up to the expectations and lost direction midway when they got opportunities to govern and implement the ideas of JP. Some of them are faced with serious corruption charges.

Modi in that way is an exception. The anti-Congress feeling that was ingrained in him during the Maha-Gujarat agitation got further strengthened during the Emergency. He empathised with the sufferings of people due to the callous state and, when the time came, he used the administration to deliver the greatest good to the largest numbers going by the Hindu spiritual lesson "*bahujana sukhaya*".

Gujarat was the first State to raise the banner of revolt against the Congress and corruption. It began in the form of demonstrations by a handful of students from Morbi Engineering College over their spiralling mess bills. This happened in December 1973. Other colleges such as LD Engineering College joined in January 1974. It culminated into opposition to the Congress since price rise was attributed to the State government's inability to check corruption. Cases of corruption involving Congress leaders added fuel to the fire. Gujarat was in a serious political crisis with the Navnirman Movement (a movement for rebuilding the nation) turning into a rage. Jayaprakash Narayan supported this movement and provided ideological muscle to the momentum of change.

Narendra was assigned the task of helping the anti- Emergency agitation by staying underground. By virtue of his being a young student, he had already become an integral part of the movement. The ABVP was on the forefront and the RSS was fully supporting the movement.

Modi's understanding of the Congress during that time could be seen in the following words·

"The love for power, like the flow of water, comes from top to bottom. This is evident at every level of Congress. It is like an epidemic... From a village *mukhiya* at a far flung village to top officials in power, corruption has become an integral part of life. No paper or file would move unless adequate weight was added to it..."[1]

Modi had a significant meeting with JP when the latter visited Gujarat during the Navnirman agitation. He met JP as a representative of the RSS and had several rounds of discussions with him. He was inspired by JP's charismatic personality and held the experience to be very precious. He had given his own briefing to JP about the agitation. JP never allowed age to come in between and young Modi did not feel uneasy talking to the country's tallest political personality of that period.

Inspired by the Navnirman Movement, JP launched a similar agitation against Bihar's corrupt Congress regime. Later on, he became the symbol of the movement that spread all across the country.

The Emergency was a great learning experience for many Indian leaders of today. It had far reaching impact on the personality of Narendra Modi, who was just 25 and an integral part of the RSS. Already in 1974, Modi had founded the media cell at the RSS headquarters. Praful Raval, a former RSS *pracharak* who has worked with Modi, said that this was Modi's innovation. Modi's vision was "*saru sav jane*" (good things should be known to all).[2] This was a changed attitude since the RSS normally shunned publicity. Vakil Saheb had given a free hand to Modi. The technique and network he established proved useful during the anti-Emergency upsurge in the country.

Modi was an active participant as well as chronicler of events during the Emergency. He brilliantly described the role played by numerous RSS workers in his book "*Sangharsh ma Gujarat*" published in 1978. He described in detail how most leaders and organisations vowed to oust the Congress from power. Then Chief Minister Babubhai Patel had launched the book.

Modi had concluded that if the Gujarat assembly could be dissolved, it could act as a catalyst for an anti-Congress agitation across India. Indira Gandhi in that sense committed the blunder Modi highlighted it.[3] Modi had begun to understand the finer nuances of politics and the strategy behind any move.

He played the role of a backroom manager for underground mobilisation of RSS workers. In the elections that ensued in the State, the Janata Morcha, comprising forces opposed to the Congress, came to power, and on 19 June 1975 Babubhai Patel took oath of office as the chief minister. This ensured that Gujarat had a non-Congress government when the Emergency was imposed on 26 June 1975. This helped the State to emerge as the main centre of support to anti-Emergency forces.

The country was unprepared for the Emergency. It was like a bolt from the blue. Curtailment of freedom led to arrests of individuals in the name of controlling rebellion. What shocked the nation was the arrest of prominent leaders such as Jayaprakash Narayan, Morarji Desai, LK Advani and Atal Bihari Vajpayee.

The RSS swung into action overnight. In Gujarat, under the chairmanship of Vakil Saheb, who was the RSS's *kshetra pracharak* (the Sangh's chief campaigner for a region) then, the Gujarat Lok Sangharsh Samiti (GLSS) was formed to carry forward resistance through underground movement. Some key RSS workers had to avoid arrest and carry forward a non-violent struggle against the undemocratic government.

During the entire period of underground activities during the Emergency, Modi operated under the fictitious name of Prakash. Very few people knew this identity. On one occasion, the police came to know that there was someone operating under the name of Prakash and that he was influential. They tried their best to know who the real person was, but none of the arrested RSS workers revealed Modi's real identity to the police.[4]

Vakil Saheb had insisted that he should study further. As a result of this Modi became a student of political science (honours) at the University of Delhi through distance learning. This came as a boon during the Emergency. Modi could easily go to Delhi under the pretext of taking examinations or buying books, and no one would doubt him. He could then pass on the information to anti-Emergency leaders in Delhi.

Modi described in detail how he saw the entire police force land at the RSS headquarters in Ahmedabad after the imposition of the Emergency. *Prant pracharak* Keshavrao Deshmukh had come to visit the office. Modi and Nathabhai Jhagda, a Jana Sangh activist, were going to the RSS office on a Bajaj scooter (two-wheeler). They saw the police and some construction workers, who were employed to do repair work, standing outside. Modi anticipated the danger and sped the scooter away.

He had instructions to avoid arrest at all cost. He was not scared. When he came to know that during the time of arrest, Keshavrao had some classified documents with him that contained the names of RSS workers and other details, he roped in a woman activist to visit the jail. Finally he got those documents smuggled out right under the nose of the police.[5]

Modi described in detail his dramatic meeting with George Fernandes. The ex-Governor of Tamil Nadu Prabhudas Patwari, who was also a prominent lawyer and activist, within days of acquaintance invited Modi to his residence. Patwari introduced him to Fernandes. George was a towering personality of that time and had become a well known name due to his role in the railway strike of 1974.[6] He had come disguised as a *fakir* (see the anecdote given below). George argued in favour of a violent armed protest saying this was the only form of protest that would bring the government to its senses. Modi told him that the RSS was for a non-violent and democratic form of protest.

Later, George visited Ahmedabad on 31 December 1975 to attend a secret all-India meeting of the Lok Sangharsh Samiti. George did not attend the meeting but the agenda he set through trusted leaders wanted the meeting to consider sanctioning the use of violence in the resistance struggle. The meeting discussed the issue but rejected the use of violence.

Modi was enamoured of George Fernandes. He described both Nanaji Deshmukh and Fernandes as two towering personalities whom Indira Gandhi feared. Despite her best efforts, she was unable to get them arrested. Modi had arranged the meeting between Fernandes and Deshmukh in August 1975 in Ahmedabad.

Modi described the incident that brought Deshmukh closer to JP. Loknayak had taken a massive procession in Patna towards late 1974 and the police resorted to *lathi*-charge. It is said that JP was the target. But one person sprung to JP's protection, covered him with his body and took all the blows on himself. This person was Nanaji Deshmukh.[7] When JP was arrested, he made Deskhmukh the national secretary of the Lok Sangharsh Samiti.

The Lok Sangharsh Samiti was formed much before the Emergency in 1974 as a resistance force against the Congress's corrupt rule. This body was to coordinate with several parties and movements that supported JP's *Sarvodaya Movement*. The RSS had hailed JP as a *sannyasi* and JP termed the *swayamsevaks* "true patriots".[8] Therefore, there was nothing for which JP could doubt a member of the RSS.

Towards the end of 1975, when Nanaji Deshmukh was arrested in Delhi and sent to Tihar Jail, veteran Congress Leader Ravindra

Varma took over as secretary of the Sangharsh Samiti. The veteran Congressman had decided to throw his lot against the Congress. When Varma reached Ahmedabad he spoke to Modi over the phone and expressed the need for an urgent meeting. Modi was a part of the meeting that had decided that the news about Nanaji's arrest should be kept a secret to prevent its negative impact on the cadre and other members of the anti-Emergency movement. Later, Modi was among the top five leaders that planned *satyagraha* (peaceful agitation) across Gujarat. Besides Modi, the other four leaders were Vasantbhai Gajendra Gadkar, Ravindra Varma, Radhakrishna and Keshavrao Deshmukh.

Varma was a famous personality, and meeting and interacting with him was a rewarding experience for Modi. They developed a good rapport. Varma would speak to him to share information or disseminate it to other people in Gujarat.

Modi had emerged as the pivot of underground activities and it was his job to keep RSS workers posted on what was happening, more so because newspapers did not give factually sound reports about the real happenings. Newspaper reports were screened by the nominees of the government, thereby, preventing dissemination of any anti-Union Government reports.

A meeting of parliamentary representatives from Commonwealth countries was organised in Delhi in October 1975. In her address, Indira Gandhi was supposed to justify her decision to impose the Emergency. She had even prepared reports that said that ordinary citizens were supportive of the move. She wanted to prove herself to be a saviour of democracy. Leaders of the Lok Sangharsh Samiti decided to bring out booklets on various aspects of Emergency and expose Mrs Gandhi's misdeeds.[9]

The task of preparing the publicity material, getting them printed and sending them to Delhi and also to get the same distributed had fallen on the Gujarat unit. Modi played a prominent role in this. Five booklets were prepared, namely: *Indian Press Gagged; Facts (Nail Indira's lies); 20 Lies of Indira Gandhi; When Disobedience to Law is a Duty;* and *A Decade of Economic Chaos.*

To get them printed was not easy. The government would conduct raids on printing press to prevent any such publication and keep tabs on what was being printed. Modi got help from the Jana Sangh office secretary Bachubhai Thakur to get these printed. The next big task was to get these booklets transported to Delhi. Some RSS workers were identified and sent to Delhi by train. These booklets were hidden in the beddings of these workers.

However, the biggest challenge was to distribute these among the representatives without getting caught by Indira Gandhi's secret agents. Many leaders in the conference were representing the Congress-ruled States. The Gujarat assembly was represented by Suresh Mehta who was an MLA from the Jana Sangh, a constituent of the Janata Morcha. Mehta took the risk and got the material distributed to every member without anyone's knowledge. The government was caught completely unawares, Modi writes.[10]

Modi describes how Subramanian Swamy was assigned the task to contact and talk to those people who had come for the Commonwealth meeting. A room in the same hotel where these representatives stayed was booked for Swamy. Some of the leaders whom Swamy met at the hotel said they were surprised by his guts and determination.

Swamy and Modi got many opportunities to bond together. Modi was a young student leader and Swamy was an established name in the Jana Sangh. Together they went to Bhavnagar. Swamy had visited Ahmedabad in the second week of October 1975 to attend an underground executive meeting of the Jana Sangh. Swamy briefed RSS workers about activities of the underground movement and appealed to them to have faith in an inevitable victory of democracy instead of despairing. Later, when Swamy was sent abroad to present facts about the Emergency, Modi stayed in constant touch with him as a part of his work. Swamy wrote letters to Modi detailing the situation.[11]

That Modi was an important youth leader during Emergency was evident during a youth conference in Ahmedabad on 21 November 1976. The conference that was to be addressed by Babubhai Patel and Piloo Mody was banned by the government. The organisers decided to hold the conference outside the city. The students and youth who came to attend the conference were redirected to the new site at Barejhadi. Patel, Mody and KD Desai dodged the police and reached the venue. Raval recalled that Modi sat the whole night to prepare message on stencil and get as many copies as possible. The message regarding the change of venue was secretly distributed to all the main people who were to attend the meet.[12]

The message sent by Modi was read out at the youth conference and copies were distributed. The message exhorted the youth to participate in the movement as "history makers". The high sounding letter showcased Modi's public speech at his best. "Youths have never submitted before authoritarianism. Let us participate in the second struggle for India's freedom", he said.[13]

Modi, Keshavrao Deshmukh, Nanabhai Jhagda, Shankersinh Vagehla and Vishnubhai Pandya used to meet quite frequently to keep tabs on the underground movement till the fall of the Janata Morcha Government in March 1976. The police crackdown later made such meetings difficult.

Modi played a very active role in organising the campaign against the Emergency in foreign countries. This became more pronounced after the Morcha appointed Makrand Desai to go abroad to counter the government's propaganda there and spread awareness about the methods Ms Gandhi was adopting to stifle democracy. Modi was very appreciative of the sacrifice of Desai. "He left for a foreign land without knowing when he would return and did not inform even his father," he noted.

Desai stayed in touch with Modi. The former used to communicate to top people through the latter. In a letter, Desai briefed Modi about the news that had appeared in the foreign media outlets, and explained how to coordinate for better reports. In another, he asked Modi to talk to then chief minister Babubhai Patel and request him to write letters to some important people in the Patel society abroad. Desai wanted Babubhai to give the true details of the Emergency and seek their support for the Friends of India Society. Desai also asked Modi to persuade Keshubhai to write a letter to him.[14]

During mobilisation against the Emergency, Modi learnt the importance of building public opinion in foreign lands. The NRIs, particularly Gujaratis, wielded a lot of influence and they were keen to work for the country. Modi knew about the intricacies and impact such campaign would bring to the movement. Modi's natural positive attitude towards the NRIs now must have been influenced by those experiences.

Many leaders from various political shades were put behind the bars and the administration had not taken care to keep people of one ideology separate from the other. These activists, arrested under the Maintenance of Internal Security Act (MISA), were opposed to the Congress, but they were also mutual rivals. Jails provided them an opportunity to debate their ideologies openly, clear misgivings about each other and come closer. This created a platform for them to come together when the Emergency was lifted. Modi learnt his lesson that, in politics, none should be considered an untouchable.

It particularly helped in clearing misconceptions about the RSS, said Modi in his book. The attempt by the Congress to paint the RSS as an enemy of Muslims was exposed too. Activists and leaders of the minority community were pleasantly surprised to find these workers so cooperative and humane. Modi writes about an event in the jail thus:

By watching the conduct of RSS workers inside the jail, Muslim activists realized that they were misguided due to the propaganda outside. During Namaz, RSS workers would cooperate with them with full devotion. In the holy month of Ramzan, they would get up at 2 am and make food for *sehri* for jailed Muslim activists. Jamat-e-Islami workers also participated in all events organized inside jail.

Christophe Jaffrelot noted the same thing. He observed that members of the Jamaat-e-Islami and RSS were imprisoned together. Demolition of Muslim houses and old Delhi's Turkman Gate had enraged Muslims. The Shahi Imam of Delhi's Jama Masjid favoured lifting the ban on the RSS.[15]

Giving correct information to the rank and file was important in view of the press censorship. The Gujarat Lok Sangharsh Samiti decided to publish an underground weekly by the name *Janata Chhapu* (*Janata Akhbar* or *Janata* newspaper). It started getting published from 2 July onwards under editor Bhogilal Gandhi who was a secretary of the Gujarat Lok Sangharsh Samiti (GLSS). The job of bringing authentic news was given to the RSS. Within a month of imposition of the Emergency, that is, by the end of July 1975, the RSS had created a dependable network for collection, printing and dissemination of news. Modi, being the RSS's main man for communication, played a crucial role. But the newspaper closed down under pressure from different quarters.

The *Sadhna* magazine, published locally, had more than adequately replaced the *Janata Akhbar*. It started publishing news about the rebels' underground activities. It took all the risk of getting exposed. But it closed down under pressure of the government. The administration sealed the premises of *Sadhna* and all its key personnel were sent to jail in July 1976. It was then that an underground magazine *Muktavani* was launched. Modi edited the magazine under the pseudonym Khabardar.

The Emergency strengthened Modi's belief in non-violence. During the entire agitation, RSS workers and other activists were told not to resort to violence, whatever be the provocation. This resolve was tested when Maniben Patel, Sardar Patel's daughter, led a protest march from Ahmedabad to Dandi. The police arrested those who joined the protest on the way. But they did not arrest Maniben, fearing negative consequences. Modi says that the police tried to foment trouble by resorting to baton charge on the demonstrators. The police clearly wanted people to turn violent to get an alibi for use of brute force, but it failed and the march went all the way as intended.

A sense of upholding Gujarati pride was ingrained in Modi even when he was a young man. This got more pronounced during the Emergency. The fact that the anti-corruption Navnirman Movement had started in Gujarat, eventually leading to the state becoming the fulcrum of the anti-Emergency movement, brought a sense of great pride in Modi. The sense of participation in history and the huge responsibility that it brought about always shaped his thoughts.

An all-India meeting of the Lok Sanghrash Samiti was organised on 31 Dec 1975. The organisers, including Modi, got information that some participants at the meeting could be moles of Indira Gandhi, and vital information about the activists could leak out. They decided to keep the venue and the agenda secret till the end even from the participants. Fernandes, who had come to attend this meeting, was kept in a separate room and briefed before and after the meeting. Modi said, "The moment we got this information, we felt that a small mistake could invite big trouble for the movement... it could have been a blot on the name of Gujarat."

After the Emergency when many people he assisted got elected to the government and became ministers, Modi took the opportunity to complete his third year Officers' Training Camp (OTC) programme of the RSS at Nagpur with other colleagues. During the 1977 Lok Sabha elections, Modi's role was confined to mobilising support for the Janata Party through the vast network of the RSS in areas under his charge. He submitted completely to the wishes of Vakil Saheb who had asked him to work for the success of Janata Party candidates from behind the scene.

By the age of 28 in 1978, Modi became a *vibhag pracharak* (looking after a division larger than a district). The *vibhag* consisted of six districts — rural Vadodara, Panchmahal, Dahod, Anand, Kheda and the Vadodara city. He also became a *prant padadhikari* (office bearer at the level of a region). He was, in effect, a joint *vyavastha pramukh* (operations head) at the regional level.

Within two years, he was appointed the *sambhag pracharak*, (a *sambhag* is bigger than a *vibhag*) and was given jurisdiction over the *vibhags* of Surat and Vadodara. Modi's organisational skills were on display once again in 1979 when the Morbi Dam over the Macchu River at Morbi (now a district) collapsed. The RSS launched a massive relief operation that went on for more than a year. Modi led the operations from the front. Senior RSS leaders were impressed. The Sangh's role was lauded by the media. Relief camps were organised for more than 10,000 displaced people who had moved to Rajkot. Vakil Saheb reached the spot to personally look after relief and rehabilitation and guided *swayamsevaks* to work with full dedication.[16]

Although Modi's role was confined to the State, he had developed good rapport with many senior RSS leaders at the national level. This included the chief of RSS intellectual wing (All India *Bauddhik Pramukh*), Bapurao Moghe, and Dattopant Thengdi, founder of the Bharatiya Mazdoor Sangh (BMS). The national level organisation brought Modi into the team that produced a book outlining the RSS's role during Emergency across the country. Dattopant Thengdi was to anchor this book.

This project brought Modi to the RSS headquarters in Delhi, where he stayed in 1979. He interviewed a number of people who had fought against the Emergency in other States as well. When he returned to Gujarat, he was a matured person with varied experience of political happenings in Delhi. The first volume of the book was published. The RSS then shelved the plan to release the full compendium as it could have led to severe embarrassment to many people.

When *prant pracharak* Keshavrao Deshmukh died in 1981, Modi was instructed to be present at the headquarters at Ahmedabad to coordinate with various Sangh affiliates such as the Bharatiya Kisan Sangh (BKS) and Vishwa Hindu Parishad (VHP).

Anecdotes

Meeting Fernandes, the *fakir*: Prabhudas Patwari, ex-Governor of Tamil Nadu, during a morning walk, invited Narendra Modi to his residence. Modi was surprised since he had known the governor only for a month. But Patwari knew that Modi was an RSS *pracharak* who had access to vital information about underground activities during the Emergency. When Modi reached Patwari's place at 10:30 am, Patwari whispered meaningfully into his ears that George Frenandes would be visiting them anytime. Fernandes was a famous personality and this was the first time Modi was to meet him. The firebrand trade union leader appeared in an un-ironed old kurta, a check-*lungi* and a green cloth over his head. Fernandes had grown his beard and looked like a Muslim *fakir*. He could not be easily recognised. Modi knew that Fernandes wanted a safe place of stay in Ahmedabad and had requested the RSS to make such an arrangement as he could trust no one. But Fernandes was more keen to know about the agitation and involvement of the people. Modi and he had a long discussion in which Modi gave all the information he had about the ongoing activities of the RSS to him.

Getting secret documents out of jail: At the time of arrest by the police, Keshavrao Deshmukh was in possession of some important documents that could disclose information about the involvement of RSS workers in the agitation. Modi enlisted the support of a lady worker and sent her to meet Deshmukh at the Maninagar Police Station. She took along with her snacks and other edible items in a bag and some books and newspapers in another. Modi explained to her the importance of the documents that needed to be taken out of the jail. She left the edibles with Deshmukh, got the documents placed in the bag with books and newspapers and got out of the Police Station premises. The documents contained important addresses of underground activities and the message from RSS chief Balasaheb Deoras that exhorted workers to support the anti-Emergency movement.

Modi visits jail as a swami: Modi visited Bhavnagar jail in September 1976, when it became extremely important for him to have one to one interaction with Shakersinh Vaghela and Vishnubhai Pandya. Secret communication could not serve the purpose. For an underground worker, this was dangerous and akin to embracing death. He roped in a local female worker and they together visited the jail. Modi had donned the garb of a saffron swami. After spending an hour in the jail and meeting the people there, Modi as swami emerged out of the jail without creating any suspicion.

'Sardarji' Modi: Modi had once played the role of a Sikh in real life when he stayed at the house of a *swayamsevak* in Ahmedabad during the Emergency. During this period, he would often hear children cracking 'Sardarji' jokes. They would talk aloud to ensure that he heard the jibes. Often, children of known families would call other friends and ask him (a Sardar) to tell jokes about Sardars. The way innocent children would come asking for jokes presented a very interesting situation, Modi said. Once he visited Vadnagar as a Sikh to mobilise public opinion. None, except the senior RSS workers who knew he was coming, could identify him.

Happy New Year Ravindra Varma: On 1 January 1976, Modi went to meet Ravindra Varma who had come to Ahmedabad. It was early in the morning. He was waiting at the residence of Ramlal Parikh, then vice chancellor of the Gujarat Vidyapeeth. Modi greeted him by saying, "Happy New Year," in place of traditional greetings such as *namaskar*. Varma said, "Narendraji, I wanted to say Happy New Year to you. But I was hesitant and thought you would feel bad since you are a Hindutvavadi. But you are…" Modi stopped him midway and told him that this was the greatness of Hindutva that it did not allow the adherents of Hindutva to be narrow-minded.

Modi as swami faces a real swami: Modi was an expert in changing appearances. So much so that even close acquaintances would fail to identify him. Once he worked under the disguise of a swami. He wore saffron robes and stayed at the residence of an RSS worker. It became quite a challenge when a preacher from the Swaminarayan sect visited the house. Modi (in the disguise of a swami) was introduced to the priest as a swami who had come from Udaipur. After exchanging pleasantries, an intense debate began between the two swamis. It lasted for an hour. Somehow Modi saved the reputation of the Swami from Udaipur and breathed a sigh of relief.

***

Delhi Calling

Great work requires great and persistent effort for a long time...
Character has to be established through a thousand stumbles.

— Swami Vivekananda

Modi continued to work actively for the RSS. He was determined to mobilise support for the organisation and ensure its expansion at a faster pace than before at the political level, Indira Gandhi staged a comeback at the national level in 1980. The Congress had struck a powerful caste alliance in Gujarat that delivered it an unprecedented electoral victory at the state level both in 1980 and 1985.

Indira Gandhi's handpicked person Madhavsinh Solanki, who was made the chief minister of Gujarat during the latter part of the Emergency, had to bow out once the Janata Party formed the government at the Centre. He was a non-descript personality at the time of his appointment. His name was proposed to Indira Gandhi by Zinabhai Darji, a backward caste leader who came with the concept of KHAM as the Congress's main political support base which ensured creation of a vote-bank for the party. KHAM stood for Kshatriyas, Harijans, Adivasis and Muslims that together formed about 60 per cent of the state's population.

Solanki and Darji worked together but the latter refused to join the government. He was happy working for the party and social combination. However, this led to alienation of the other castes that were formerly a part of the ruling structure. This was particularly true of the Patels who formed about 20 per cent of the state's population. Under the leadership of Keshubhai Patel of the BJP, the party drew the Patel community towards itself. Modi could work silently since the RSS and the BJP were not taken as a major force then. Founded on 6 April 1980, the BJP was considered a newcomer.

In Gujarat, the media and political experts declared KHAM and the Congress as invincible. The Congress under Solanki-Darji won 141 of the 182 assembly seats in 1980, and the BJP could win only 9. In the assembly elections in 1985, the Congress improved its tally to 149. The BJP won only 11 seats, two more than its tally in 1980.[1]

The state of Gujarat was disturbed in the 1980s. On the eve of the assembly elections in January 1985, the Solanki government decided to increase reservation for the backward castes from 10 per cent to 28 per cent.[2] This led to an anti-reservation stir by people not falling in the reservation category. Caste riots that ensued further consolidated the Congress's KHAM strategy. Students rose in revolt and riots spread everywhere. The RSS clearly did not want such a thing to happen since it divided Hindus and created social disharmony. Modi, a leader from a backward caste, was at an important position in the RSS at that time.

In order to stress the need for Hindu unity and to apply salve on the fractured social fabric, the RSS made a plan to organise a *sadbhav yatra* comprising godmen from different religions. The *yatra* witnessed participation of about two dozen *sadhus* who visited 20-25 villages without discriminating between Kshatriyas, Harijan, Patel and the forward castes. They discussed the issues facing Hindu society and asked people to undertake a pledge of peace and unity. This had a salutary effect in those villages, stated Modi.[3]

Although the Congress won 149 seats in the assembly elections of 1985 because of caste polarisation, its hold seemed to be loosening once the reservation policy was implemented. The BJP, which looked lost and struggling once the assembly election results were declared, surprised everyone by winning the prestigious corporation elections that followed in Ahmedabad, Surat and Rajkot. Senior leaders in the BJP and RSS appreciated the way Modi involved himself in ensuring this victory. Modi was clear that these were the building blocks that would help the BJP capture power in the state. "I was asked to look after the campaign. Everyone was surprised—there had been a debacle in the country (1984 Lok Sabha elections) but we won the corporation elections. Even though we had only 17 councillors earlier, we won a two-thirds majority. Throughout the country, we developed some kind of a confidence that we can win again."[4]

BJP Beckons

Honest work never fails to get recognition. Gujarat was warming up to the BJP and LK Advani had become the national president of the party in May 1986. Around the same time, the Congress, led by young Prime Minister Rajiv Gandhi, in May 1986 upturned the Supreme Court judgment that had upheld the validity of maintenance to 70-year-old Shah Bano. The apex court verdict was taken by many Muslim leaders as an affront to the Muslim Personal Law. This gave fodder to the BJP that had been raking up the issue of Muslim appeasement. The civil society was clearly in favour of the apex court judgement. A young cabinet minister in Rajiv government, Arif Mohammad Khan, resigned to protest the government's decision to nullify the Supreme Court judgement.

Advani wanted to strengthen the BJP in Gujarat where the party was steadily gaining ground. On the one hand, he encouraged Patels to come closer; on the other, he decided to strengthen the organisation so that it could hold on to the increasing support base. The RSS's Ramjanmabhoomi movement had started peaking. Advani looked for someone who understood the RSS's philosophy well and was also a good organiser. The choice fell on the then 37-year-old Narendra Modi. So, in 1987 he was asked by the RSS to work for the BJP. In 1988, he became the organising secretary of the BJP's Gujarat unit.

Prior to Modi, Nathabhai Jhagda was the RSS's organising secretary. Modi used to accompany him on scooter to some of the meetings of the BJP. Modi had immense respect for Jhagda and was reverential to the extent of carrying the luggage of the latter while receiving him at the Ahmedabad railway station after every tour. When Jhagda fell ill, he wanted someone younger to keep the momentum going. He spoke to Atal Bihari Vajpayee and LK Advani and started sending Modi to BJP meetings. Modi had instructions not to speak but to listen and observe. As the organising secretary, his role was to act as a link between the RSS and the BJP. Modi continued to stay at the Hedgewar Bhawan even when he formally became part of the BJP structure.

Roadshows: Modi's Brainchild

Immediately after getting into the BJP, Modi conceptualised two roadshows, the Nyay Yatra (Journey for Justice) and the Lok Shakti Rath

Yatra (a journey to awaken people about their strength). Both these *yatras* made it clear that Modi was determined to broaden the BJP's support base. There was no doubt that Advani had made the correct choice.

We have seen that Madhavsinh Solanki's reservation policy had led to large-scale social conflict. It had also degenerated into communal riots. More than 200 people died in the riots in 1985. Violence continued for more than six months after which the Congress bowed down to the popular belief that Solanki had failed to control the riots and the party replaced him with Amarsinh Chaudhary, the first and the only chief minister of Gujarat who belonged to the tribal community.

Nyay Yatra

The Amarsinh Chaudhary government reduced the quantum of reservation from 28 to 10 per cent.[5] This strengthened the RSS perception that the original Solanki plan was just to divide the Hindu society. The *yatra*, in that sense, was an expression of this anger.

The formal agenda of the Nyay Yatra was, however, a way to seek justice for scarcity in relief works for the drought-affected areas of Gujarat. The *yatra* was undertaken in jeep and *raths* drawn by party workers. Modi stated: "Lakhs of rupees are being siphoned off daily by officials in the name of scarcity. The BJP is committed to exposing this."

Four Nyay Yatras from different parts of the state began in December 1987 to cover 115 of the 182 *talukas* over 40 days. BJP workers submitted a memorandum about the plight of the people to the chief minister through the district collectors.[6]

Lok Shakti Rath Yatra

Towards the beginning of 1989, Modi launched the Lok Shakti Rath Yatra in five phases. In Ahmedabad, it was planned so as to initiate action against the city's liquor mafia. Modi utilised this *yatra* to interact with BJP workers at local level and to strengthen their resolve to organise themselves better. The *yatra's* main aim was to project the BJP as the only alternative to the Congress.

Ram Rath Yatra

Modi's real challenge came when Advani asked him to organise the Gujarat leg of his Ram Rath Yatra that began from the historic Somnath temple on 25 September 1990. It had to culminate at Ayodhya.

A look into that time would put things in perspective. The VP Singh government had come to power riding an anti-corruption wave against the Congress in 1989. The Bofors kickbacks enraged the nation and VP Singh became the symbol of opposition to the Congress. The National Front led by the Janata Dal had managed to make some seat adjustments with the BJP and the Left against the Congress. This resulted into the Congress falling down to a mere 197 Lok Sabha seats from the glorious mark of 404 it had secured in 1984. The Janata Dal won 143 seats and emerged as the single largest party in the opposition camp. The BJP won 85, which were 83 more than its tally of 1984. The Left parties managed to win 52 seats. VP Singh became the prime minister with the outside support of both the BJP and the Left.

VP Singh unearthed the ten-year-old Mandal Commission report and announced its implementation in August 1990. The commission had recommended 27 per cent reservation for the Other Backward Classes (OBCs). The situation witnessed in Gujarat in the early 1980s under the Madhavsinh Solanki government was replicated across the country. VP Singh's announcement led to a massive anti-reservation stir and violence across the country.

The RSS believed that this was an attempt to divide Hindu society for political reasons. The BJP did not oppose Singh's move, but it felt bitter. Advani said, "Mr VP Singh is like an old style princeling. He is all courtesies and conspiracies."[7]

BJP president Advani, with full blessings of the BJP and the RSS, launched Ram Rath Yatra to create awareness about the need for construction of a grand Ram temple at the disputed Ramjanmabhoomi-Babri Masjid site at Ayodhya. The real aim was, however, to prevent division of Hindu society in the name of caste.

In the meantime, Modi had acquired an important position in the BJP when the state assembly elections took place towards the beginning of 1990. He had opposed coalition with the Janata Dal led by Chimanbhai Patel. He wanted the BJP to contest the elections without any alliances. He calculated that most activities of the RSS and the VHP in Gujarat had created a mass base for the BJP. Chimanbhai Patel was considered a rank opportunist in politics, whereas Modi was young and righteous. During the negotiations, Modi suggested to Patel that they should contest on equal number of Lok Sabha seats, which meant 13 seats for the Janata Dal and 13 for the BJP. The senior leader sought a larger share. Finally, the JD contested 14 seats and BJP 12. The BJP won from all while the Janata Dal won from only 11.

Everyone in the BJP and RSS was forced to recognise that Modi had a better ear to the ground. This eventually increased Modi's say during negotiations with the Janata Dal for the assembly elections in January 1990. He insisted on fair play and demanded that both the parties contest an equal share of the 182 assembly seats. Chimanbhai Patel disagreed and the alliance broke. At the last minute, it was resolved that the BJP would contest from 80 seats and the Janata Dal from the rest. Many candidates withdrew their names at the last minute, creating a lot of confusion. The BJP won 67 seats and the Janata Dal won 70. There were many constituencies where the BJP and the Janata Dal contested against each other and contributed to the defeats.

The war of attrition created bitterness between Patel and Modi. A young Modi told Patel that he had ruined the spirit of the partnership and criticised the latter for being rigid. To mollify the *pracharak*, Patel visited Modi to seek support. Modi assured him that he would not attack him at the personal level so that they could have a working political relation. Patel knew that it would not be possible to form a government without the two coming together. But when the two joined hands, he refused to accommodate BJP's nominee Keshubhai Patel as the deputy chief minister. Modi ensured that Keshubhai was recognised as the formal number two in the government.

Modi was unhappy with the arrangement as he wanted the BJP to come to power on its own. He knew it had developed the capabilities but was forced by the situation to align with the Janata Dal. In his assessment, the BJP had developed enough muscle to throw the Congress out.

It was during this time that Advani asked an energetic Modi to look after the Gujarat leg of the Ram Rath Yatra. In fact, it was Modi who suggested to Advani that the *yatra* should begin from Somnath (in Saurashtra). Somnath was symbolic as it was attacked and destroyed by Mahmud Ghazni many times before it was finally rebuilt post-independence. Sardar Vallabhbhai Patel and India's first President Rajendra Prasad played prominent roles in its reconstruction.

Modi accompanied Advani up to Mumbai. The *yatra* received tremendous response in Gujarat, thereby generating curiosity about it across the country. It passed through about 600 villages; people came in large numbers just to catch a glimpse of Advani.[8] The route was chalked out by Modi who knew the organisation well and had anticipated the response. Advani was so happy that he asked Modi to accompany him up to Mumbai. There were some reports in the media saying that a member of the Bajrang Dal applied *tilak* of his own blood on Advani's forehead. At Jetpur (near Rajkot), about a hundred more offered him a jar full of their own blood.[9]

Advani was impressed: "I was truly overwhelmed by the response to the *yatra* within the first few days of our journey in Gujarat. The Rath was received by tumultuous crowds everywhere—in villages, towns and even along roads where people from nearby hamlets would gather under trees, eagerly waiting for the *rath* to arrive. The response reached a crescendo in bigger towns and cities, where it would take hours for us to reach the venue of our meetings."[10] The details of the *yatra* were announced in Ahmedabad by Modi who had already become the general secretary of the BJP's Gujarat unit in 1988. While addressing the media, he expanded on his idea of cultural nationalism and justified the BJP's agenda of promising to construct a grand Ram temple at Ayodhya. According to him, this was essential for India's national identity. He warned the Union government ruled by the Janata Dal and the state government of Uttar Pradesh ruled by the same party that if Advani's *rath yatra* was stopped, the BJP would not think twice before withdrawing support to the VP Singh government. With this *yatra*, Modi had clearly arrived on the national scene. Needless to mention that Advani's *yatra* got halted on 23 October 1990 when then Bihar Chief Minister Lalu Prasad Yadav got him arrested in Dumka district and, subsequently, the BJP withdrew support to the VP Singh government, leading to its eventual fall.

Ekta Yatra

After the success of the Ram Rath Yatra, Modi's skills at organising the *yatra* received wider acknowledgement within the RSS and BJP. Later, BJP president Murli Manohar Joshi (1991-93) gave Modi full responsibility for organising the Ekta Yatra from Kanyakumari to Srinagar. This was dubbed "the march for unity". Modi acted as the charioteer from beginning to the end—the role Pramod Mahajan had played for Advani.

Prior to that, Modi was inducted into the BJP's national executive that met at Thiruvananthapuram in November 1991.

The BJP had made substantial gains due to the temple agitation and could have been in striking distance of power but for the assassination of then Prime Minister Rajiv Gandhi. The elections that took place after his tragic death gave a new life to the Congress. PV Narasimha Rao had become the prime minister and he successfully ran a minority government for full five years.

Joshi launched scathing attack on the Rao government. The focus of the Ekta Yatra was to oppose divisive forces and violent politics and to put an end to the menace of terrorism that had raised its ugly head in Kashmir.[11] The task of organising the *yatra* was difficult since Modi did not get much time. The *yatra* had a clear aim to hoist the National Flag at the Lal Chowk in Srinagar.

Modi visited every state the *yatra* would cover, met party workers there and made elaborate arrangements for reception, public support mechanism and other logistics. Since he was given the responsibility of the *yatra* in August 1991, he had only about four months to prepare for it. The *yatra* commenced on 11 December 1991 and covered a distance of 15,000 kms (9,000 miles). When Modi announced the details of the *yatra* and the route it would follow, everyone could understand the groundwork that had gone into the minutest details.

The Ekta Yatra created a patriotic fervour and galvanised the BJP's rank and file. Joshi had to be airlifted to the Lal Chowk at the last stretch of the *yatra* due to landslides.[12] Many critics felt that 67 BJP workers were air lifted to Srinagar because of the militants' threat. Modi, disagreed with this and held that if they had waited for the landslides to clear, they would never have made to the Lal Chowk in time. Finally, the efforts of both Joshi and Modi paid off when the tricolour was hoisted at the Lal Chowk on 26 January 1992, braving continuous warnings from separatists. Pakistan-based terrorist groups had warned against the unfurling of the Indian flag at Lal Chowk. Joshi described the *yatra* as 'a big success'.

Modi made sure that the national media that accompanied the *yatra* was given all the facilities for a smooth coverage. Wherever the *yatra* would halt, media persons would get easy access to STD phones, fax machines and typewriters. He interacted with journalists and made them feel at home. Modi would not hide anything from them. Even if a junior reporter wanted to know the details of a particular event, he would share all necessary information with the scribe. This made him very popular with all the journalists who were reporting on the *yatra*.

This *yatra* saw active participation of Modi; he gave speeches and interacted with the people. Joshi was immensely impressed by Modi's patriotic speeches and the way he articulated them.

When Modi returned to Ahmedabad on 30 January 1992, he received a rousing welcome wherever he went. The Ekta Yatra had marked his emergence as a public figure. But if you rise very fast, you create envy among others. And in Modi's case, some of his colleagues were already considering him to be a threat.

When veteran politician Shankersinh Vaghela became the new president of the state unit, he kept Modi out of his new team. Apparently, Vaghela was peeved that Modi had supported Keshubhai Patel to become the formal number two in the Chimanbhai Patel government. Vaghela always thought of himself as the most deserving since it was he, a Kshatriya, who had successfully weaned his caste group away from the Congress. Modi with full backing of the RSS and Advani concluded that Keshubhai was more wedded to the RSS ideology than Vaghela. But Vaghela took his revenge and no one could do anything. Modi was steadfast in his approach; he knew that he had done no wrong. He believed that the situation would change for the better. Modi decided to devote himself to constructive social work and not to let these matters affect his zeal for working for the party.

Sanskardham

Modi's closeness to Murli Manohar Joshi during the Ekta Yatra led many in the BJP to believe that he had moved away from Advani. However, Modi's conscience was clear. He knew that he was merely delivering a job. He was very supportive of Advani when the latter decided to contest the Lok Sabha elections from Gandhinagar in 1991. It was actually Modi who had suggested to Advani that he should contest from Gandhinagar, the capital city.[13]

Since then, Gandhinagar has been Advani's home constituency. Whenever Advani would visit Gandhinagar, Modi would be there in attendance. Advani trusted him completely. Modi had emerged as one of the key players in Gujarat to have planned BJP's electoral strategy in 1991 Lok Sabha elections. The fact that Advani contested from Gandhinagar revived the fortunes of the BJP in Gujarat by bringing in a new political energy in the state unit.

Sanskardham is a modern co-educational Gujarati medium school spread over 125 acres of lush green landscape. The school is located near Sanand on the outskirts of Ahmedabad. It practices the *gurukul* system of education. Modi loves to visit this school even now whenever he gets time.

Modi was considered a *manas putra* (foster son) of Vakil Saheb. When the RSS decided to set up a school in memory of Vakil Saheb, Modi volunteered to fully involve himself in that. It is also said that Sanskardham was Modi's brainchild. He was intrinsically involved with the school right from the laying of its foundation stone to its completion. He made sure that he was readily available to the staff and teachers regarding any matter for which they required his guidance. When the school was inaugurated in June 1992, students sang two inspirational songs that were composed by Modi.

Although Modi was not a part of the formal structure in the party, he wielded immense influence because of the network he had built when he was the organising secretary. The RSS had full faith in him. Modi helped mobilise *karsevaks* for the Ramjanmabhoomi temple agitation and ensured that Gujarat had one of the largest contingents of *karsevaks* in Ayodhya. The entire machinery of the sangh parivar was involved in building public opinion on the construction of the proposed/promised grand Ram Temple in Ayodhya. The VHP had announced *karseva* from 6 December 1992 onwards. The controversial Babri structure was demolished on the same date. This led to communal riots across the country, with Gujarat being the worst affected state along with Maharashtra. The RSS was banned immediately and the ban continued till 1993 when the courts declared it illegal. During the ban period, most workers of the RSS, VHP and the

Bajrang Dal continued their activities under the banner of the BJP. Most of their programmes or activities were conceived by Modi.

Unprecedented Political Success

Modi could not be kept out of the party organisation for long. When Kashiram Rana became the state BJP president in 1993, he too wanted to keep Modi out. But this time the RSS put its foot down. Then party president LK Advani also supported Modi and eventually he was appointed as general secretary with the task of organising secretary. He had to prepare the party for the assembly elections in early 1995.

During that time, BJP leaders were not as well-known as Congress leaders. Hence, elections could not have been won on the credibility of any one leader. Modi concluded that the elections would have to be fought on the basis of party organisation. The Ramjanmabhoomi temple agitation had charged up the atmosphere. What the party needed now was a political structure that could sustain the campaign. It was for the first time that the BJP was going to contest the elections completely on its own.

Modi focussed on training workers and preparing them to face polls in a calculated way. More than 1.5 lakh workers were trained to man 28,000 polling booths for the 182 assembly seats. Based on these calculations, nearly five workers were allocated per booth. In the BJP's scheme of things, it needed a team of volunteers to check bogus voting and impersonation. The workers were, therefore, trained on how to handle voter's list, how to prevent impersonation and rigging and how to bring voters to the polling booths.

When elections came closer, the party coined the election slogan of removing "*Bhay, Bhook aur Bhrashtachar*" (Fear, Hunger and Corruption). Things were looking favourable for BJP and the Congress camp was divided. Chimanbhai Patel's widow Urmilaben, then chief minister Chhabildas Mehta, Madhavsinh Solanki and Prabodh Rawal were leading various factions of the Congress. As against this, the BJP appeared united and more organised.

The hard work paid off and the BJP headed for a landslide victory, bagging 121 of 182 seats. The Congress could win only 45 seats. Keshubhai became chief minister of the first BJP government in Gujarat on 14 March 1995.

Long ago, the BJP and RSS strategists with the concurrence of LK Advani had planned that Keshubhai should be projected for state leadership, whereas Shankersinh Vaghela should play a role at the Centre. Vaghela had got national exposure when he was elected to the Lok Sabha in 1977 on a Janata Party ticket. Prior to the merger of Jana Sangh with the Janata Party, Vaghela was a senior Jana Sangh leader. When the Janata Party government collapsed, the BJP sent Vaghela to the Rajya Sabha for a six-year term. Later, he got elected to the Lok Sabha in two successive elections; first from Gandhinagar in 1989 and then from Godhra in 1991. Vaghela had vacated the Gandhinagar Lok Sabha seat in 1991 for Advani.

Vaghela was 10 years junior to Keshubhai and 10 years senior to Modi in age. He wielded considerable influence in the party. He wanted to contest the assembly elections in 1995 to be in the fray for the post of the chief minister, should the party win. The BJP, however, applied the principle of 'one man one post' and persuaded Vaghela not to contest an assembly seat when he was already a member of the Lok Sabha. The party argued that it would send a wrong signal to the masses.[14]

However, Vaghela was not going to yield so easily. He agreed not to contest, but ensured that many of his loyalists were given party tickets. Keshubhai, therefore, emerged as a clear choice. Vaghela always thought that he had the rightful claim to be the chief minister and nursed a grudge against Modi for promoting Keshubhai. He waited for his time.

The BJP's juggernaut in Gujarat was unstoppable. It demonstrated the groundwork that the party had done. In the local elections held in August 1995, it swept the polls by winning 18 out 19 *zila panchayats* and 154 out of 183 *taluka panchayats*. This was enough proof for the critics that the assembly victory was no fluke. Out of total 811 district *panchayat* seats, the BJP secured 624, almost 82 per cent. In contrast, the Congress won only 161 seats. Later in the *taluka* elections, the party repeated the performance, and of the 3,785 seats that went to the poll, the party won 2,567 seats while the Congress managed a poor tally of 902 seats, constituting only 24 percent of the total seats.[15] The entire political class and media gave the credit of the massive victories to the astute organisational work of Narendra Modi. This gave him an upper hand and everyone started believing that he was behind most decisions of the Keshubhai Patel government. Vaghela thought that he was first ignored in the ministry formation and then in the appointment of chairpersons of various boards and corporations under the State government. He put the blame on Modi. Vaghela wanted to be consulted on all these appointments. This further strained the relationship between Keshubhai and Vaghela.[16]

Banished to Delhi

Modi was, however, not much interested in running the government. He wanted to utilise the opportunity to strengthen the party at the grassroots. He was basically an organisational man. Also, he could not have done much in governance as Keshubhai was senior to him in age as well as a reverential figure in the BJP and the RSS. Any action by Modi in matters of governance could have been construed as disregard for the veteran leader.

The Keshubhai government came to power in March 1995. In the following months, Modi got busy in training party workers for the local elections. When elections were held in June 1995, the BJP won all the six municipal corporations. The party had won all the seats in Surat municipal corporation.[17] The *panchayat* elections that followed in August continued the BJP's winning spree.

In September 1995, Keshubhai left for a foreign tour (the US and the UK) to mobilise funds for the development of Gujarat. Before leaving, he appointed chairpersons of various boards and corporations. Vaghela was upset because he was not consulted for any of these appointments. These posts were considered prized postings as they gave control over state-run corporations and sustained the culture of political patronage.

Vaghela raised the banner of revolt, consolidated MLAs loyal to him and took them to Khajuraho in Madhya Pradesh, where Digvijaya Singh of the Congress was the chief minister. That the BJP was on the edge was clear when only 60 MLAs attended the official convention of the party on 26 September 1995. This indicated that Vaghela had gained support of a substantial number of MLAs and was ready to take a shot at the top job.

Vaghela mobilised other BJP leaders in his support and put the blame entirely on Modi since he wanted a convenient excuse to justify his rebellion. Modi thought that his resignation may save the party and the government. As a last ditch effort, he tendered his resignation to then president Kashiram Rana on 28 September 1995.

In his resignation letter, he gave a very moving example to describe the situation.

"... I remember a story. A fight was going on in a court between 'a real mother' and 'a stepmother' over a child. The judge suggested that the child be cut into two so each claimant can have one part. At that, the real mother pleaded against the child being cut into two. Yes, on the same premises, I have come to this decision....

To be bali for the sake of the party means to resign from the post of the general secretary. I shall always work for the party as a worker...

... I am earnestly requesting you to accept my resignation, unlike in the past when you have refused it..."[18]

Vaghela took the 48 MLAs supporting him first to Vasan (near Gandhinagar) and then he took them to Khajuraho in Congress-ruled Madhya Pradesh. All the MLAs who went to Khajuraho came to be known as 'Khajuria' and all those who stayed loyal to Keshubhai came to be known as 'Hajuria' (meaning loyalists). Once Modi was asked if he was a part of the Hajuria or Khajuria lobby. He said he was not a part of either. He described himself as 'Majuria'—one who works hard for the party without any fear or favour.[19]

Shankersinh Vaghela attacked Advani for not giving enough attention to Gujarat despite differences in the leadership. The role of being a peacemaker fell on Atal Bihari Vajpayee. A compromise formula was worked out by which Keshubhai was to step down as the chief minister, Modi was to be sent out of Gujarat and a compromise candidate, other than Vaghela, was to become the chief minister.

Consequently, Vaghela returned to the BJP with his supporters, Keshubhai resigned as chief minister after the confidence vote and Suresh Mehta was made the new chief minister. As a part of the compromise to save the BJP government in 1995, Modi was silently banished to Delhi. Modi rarely visited Gujarat after that and before 2001. When he did, he did not visit the RSS headquarters or the state BJP office. At the most, he would visit the Sanskardham school at Bopal and stay there.

In retrospect, it appears that his banishment was providential since it allowed him a far greater exposure to macro politics than what the leadership in the state could have offered. It gave him time to think what had gone wrong, apply correctives in his personal and professional life and prepare for the big battle ahead. Furthermore, he acquired a vision of development that proved helpful and made him what he is today.

Vaghela got his revenge on both Keshubhai and Modi but the truce was not going to last long. There were repeated pinpricks to Suresh Mehta government from both Khajurias and Hajurias. Finally, they settled scores in the 1996 Lok Sabha elections by working against each other. Vaghela could not even win his Lok Sabha seat from Godhra.[20]

Vaghela finally broke away from the BJP and became the chief minister in October 1996 with the support of the Congress.[21] At the Centre, the Congress was supporting the Janata Dal-led government under HD Deve Gowda. But the Vaghela government too did not last. He was replaced by Dilip Ramanbhai Parikh after one year in October 1997. The state witnessed assembly polls in March 1998. The BJP had its sweet revenge by winning 117 of the 182 seats. Vaghela's new party could win only four seats. Keshubhai became the chief minister again and Vaghela finally joined the Congress.

Modi always felt that he was being made a scapegoat by both Keshubhai and Vaghela for the sin he had not committed. Keshubhai blamed him for the fall of the government. Vaghela nursed vengeance against Modi for not projecting him as the chief ministerial candidate despite being a good friend, and later for sidelining him and his supporters when Keshubhai was in power.

Modi preferred to remain silent, but this did not mean that he had accepted the allegations. Much later in 1998, Modi gave his defence: "Look, I am a humble party worker with no political ambition. When Keshubhai was in power, I never visited him at Gandhinagar, did not phone him or his ministers and never interfered with the functioning of the government. I was busy with party work. Mind you, I have been in active party politics only for the last six years."[22]

***

Destiny Takes a Turn
Modi Sent Back as Gujarat CM

Everything is determined, the beginning as well as the end, by forces on which we have no control. It is determined for the insects as well as for the star. Human beings, vegetables, or cosmic dust, we all dance to a mysterious tune, intoned in the distance by an invisible piper.

— **Albert Einstein**

Narendra Modi was attending the funeral of photo journalist Gopal Bisht of *Aaj Tak* News Channel in Delhi. It was 2nd October 2001. Just a day before, Madhavrao Scindia* had died in a private plane crash along with special correspondent Ranjan Jha of *Aaj Tak*, Sanjeev Sinha of *The Indian Express* and Anju Sharma of *The Hindustan Times*. The entire nation was shocked at this tragedy. Modi felt sad and remembered Bisht as one who was simple and enjoyed a low profile.

In the middle of the funeral services, Modi received a call on his mobile from the Prime Minister's office. He went aside to take the call. The then Prime Minister of India, Atal Bihari Vajpayee, was on the line.

"Where are you?" asked the deep voice of Vajpayee.

Modi told him, "I am at a crematorium."

Vajpayee asked, "What are you doing there?"

When Modi told him the reason, Vajpayee went silent. After a while, he asked Modi to meet him at his residence in the evening.

When Modi met him in the evening, Vajpayee said, "You have become fat eating all this Punjabi food. Go away from here. Go to Gujarat. You have to work there." Modi did not get the sense of

---

* A former Union minister and senior leader of the Congress party who died in the same plane crash

Vajpayee's words. He thought he was being asked to look after the organisation of Gujarat as the national general secretary in-charge. So he asked whether Gujarat would be his additional responsibility along with other states.

Vajpayee said, "No, no. You will have to contest the elections. So far, you have helped others to fight, but now you will contest."

Modi realised Vajpayee was asking him to become the chief minister. He did not know how to react. He told him it was impossible for him to contest elections.

He said, "If you want, I can be in Gujarat for 10 days a month and look after the organisation."

He told Vajpayee that he had never stepped inside the Gujarat Vidhan Sabha or the Chief Minister's office.

"What will I do there?"

Not sure how to react to this sudden turn of events, Modi demonstrated his reluctance, saying that he was away from Gujarat for six years and was not aware of the issues there.

Vajpayee told him, "When I had come to Delhi, I did not know anyone."

Modi had never expected that his Gujarat calling would come this way.

Deep inside, he was a worried man. The way he was banished from Gujarat was still fresh in his memory. Although he had stayed in Delhi since his 'banishment', he had worked overtime through his network to ensure that Keshubhai came back as chief minister in 1998. In that sense, he had paid his debt to the veteran.

Now he was being asked to replace Keshubhai! What message would it send to the people of Gujarat? He was clearly uncomfortable. He looked for guidance towards Advani, the person who had brought him into the BJP.

Modi met Advani the same night. Advani straightaway asked him: "What did Atalji tell you?"

Modi said, "What?"

Now he could sense that the prime minister was not the only one who backed the plan to send him to Gujarat.

Advani explained to him that the decision was consensual. Modi realised that his going to Gujarat had become a *fait accompli*.

Advani was more determined than Vajpayee to send him there as chief minister. Modi shared his dilemma with Advani who explained that the state was in dire need of change. Being an organisational man, Advani knew that Modi had built the party in Gujarat; given a chance, he could do wonders there.

It was Advani who had proposed Modi's name as a replacement. He had spoken to Madandas Devi, who was the RSS general secretary looking after the BJP, and senior RSS leader Dattopant Thengadi and then RSS Chief KS Sudarshan. In that sense, when Vajpayee spoke to Modi, the former was merely articulating the decision that had already been taken.

The BJP had lost the Sabarmati assembly seat in the by-election; it seemed that the BJP was running out of luck. This assembly formed a part of the Gandhinagar seat that Advani represented.

It is not that Modi did not have an inkling that he could be asked to go to Gujarat, but he did not know that it would happen so soon and in this manner. It often happens that when you get something you knew was coming your way, you do not know how to react. Between possibility and reality lies a big chasm. This explains why Modi was not ready to believe what most people knew was going to happen. Narendra Modi was sworn in as the chief minister of Gujarat on 7 October 2001.

***

From banishment to Delhi to the chief minister's chair is an amusing turn of events and goes on to show that Modi had worked very hard to earn the trust of the RSS and BJP leaders; a hard-earned trust that allowed a *pracharak* to hold an elected office.

His hard work, dedication and conviction to work for the greater goal of making a strong base for his party while keeping his individual growth secondary, separate him from other politicians. Whatever came his way—be it praise or reproach, admiration or envy—he accepted it all gracefully and did not allow anything to change the man that he was. His seniors recognised the drive and ability in him and allocated responsibilities to him gradually, and this nurtured him into a great political leader that he is today.

Modi was appointed as national secretary of the BJP in 1995 and given charge of five states. Towards 1998, he was promoted as general secretary (organisation). Advani asked him to look after the election campaigns in Gujarat and Himachal Pradesh. He was the key strategist for the BJP in 1995 and 1998 for the Gujarat state elections.

Modi had submitted his resignation from the state unit on 28 September 1995. He was to be banished soon. Some leaders tried to work out a compromise to enable him to continue as a general secretary, but there was stiff resistance to that. Keshubhai Patel proved the majority of his government and then resigned, enabling the installation of Suresh Mehta as chief minister on 21 October 1995. Keshubhai was made a national vice-president, but he preferred to stay mostly in Gujarat. Modi was sent to Delhi and he seldom went to Gujarat during that period.

After the announcement of his banishment, Modi had to wait till the conclusion of the party's plenary in Mumbai where Advani announced Vajpayee's name as the BJP's prime ministerial candidate. After this, on 20 November 1995, Modi was appointed as the national secretary with Delhi as his headquarters. Few gave importance to this announcement as everybody was debating why Advani had announced Vajpayee's name. This demonstrated Advani's determination to use the young man's energy to strengthen the party organisation. Modi was made in-charge of Chandigarh, Haryana and Himachal Pradesh.

In his initial years in Delhi, he did not have a place to stay. All the rooms at the rear end of 11 Ashoka Road, meant for full-time workers, were occupied. Modi was then a non-descript person for the dispensation in Delhi. He got help from Dilip Sanghani, BJP's Lok Sabha member from Amreli, Gujarat. Sanghani gave him a room that was part of his bungalow at 7 Harishchandra Mathur Lane. It was at a walking distance from the BJP's headquarters at 11 Ashoka Road. The room had a simple wooden bed, a thin green mattress and a few plastic chairs. There used to be a cylindrical copper container in a corner of the room to store drinking water. On one of the windows, three feet above the ground, was placed a cooler. He used to have a laptop on which he would surf the Internet. He did all his daily chores without any help. He would take his lunch at the party office and often skip dinner. At times when some BJP workers offered him dinner, he would refuse and say, "Dinner *karna zaruri hai kya?"* (Is dinner so essential?) This arrangement was extremely comfortable for Modi as he believed in simple living.

He spent most of his time interacting with younger members of the organisation. Sanghani had come close to Modi during the Ekta Yatra and was one of the main persons of the special force of volunteers that provided a ring of special security to Murli Manohar Joshi. Sanghani was active in the ABVP and was jailed during the Navnirman Movement. Modi's stay at Sanghani's place interspersed with his stay at Chandigarh and other places where he went on tour.

In the BJP hierarchy, a secretary works under—and reports to— the general secretary. Modi had relatively more freedom since he was a *pracharak* and already had years of organisational experience. Rather than sulk and complain about the treatment meted out to him in Gujarat, he took the assignment as a challenge. He knew that this was his test by fire that he must pass. For about three months, Chandigarh became his head office; he stayed at Panchkula near Chandigarh.

The BJP was unable to perform in Chandigarh that has a Lok Sabha seat, but assumes importance since it is a Union Territory. Being the capital of both Punjab and Haryana, the place also helps plan strategies for the two states. Hardly a two-hour drive from Chandigarh is Shimla, the capital of Himachal Pradesh. Modi's stay at Chandigarh was, therefore, a necessity if he wanted to actually get the pulse of the political situation in these state.

When Modi reached Chandigarh towards the end of 1995, he asked the party office to provide him with an accommodation. The party's Chandigarh unit had a one-room office called Kamalam in Sector 33. They had never received such a request earlier. Whenever senior leaders from Delhi came to meet important leaders of the state unit, they would address a press conference and go back. Modi's request was, therefore, strange. At that time, the state unit president was Gyan Chand Gupta.

Finally, all eyes turned to the local president of the Bharatiya Janata Yuva Morcha, Mahavir Prasad. He owned a plot adjoining his house in Panchkula. The plot had a semi-constructed, one-room outhouse with no air-conditioning. This became Modi's abode.

Modi would brave the mosquitoes and at times use incense to keep them away. He would sleep on the wooden bed but never complain, a party worker said. He had his own arrangement to cook, though his host at times provided meals that he would accept with all humility. He would fast a lot during those days, a BJP leader said. This continued to be his home during his entire stay, besides the office that he used liberally.

When Modi started his work in Chandigarh, no one believed the BJP had an electoral chance. The party's presence was marginal and the cadre had lost confidence that they could win. This explained why the earlier in-charges from the Centre did not bother much.

However, much against popular belief, the BJP achieved a miracle within months. It won the Lok Sabha election from Chandigarh in 1996. Young lawyer Satyapal Jain continued the winning spree in 1998. In December 1996, when elections took place for the first ever corporation of Chandigarh, the BJP-Shiromani Akali Dal alliance swept the polls, winning 19 of the 20 seats. The Congress could win only one seat.[1]

Everyone, from an ordinary party worker to the senior-most leader, gave full credit of the success to Modi. "The young *pracharak* had helped achieve the miracle," a worker said. When he started staying in Chandigarh, the move was resisted because this meant intrusion into the affairs of the local unit. It also meant more work. Soon, however, "we all realised that Modi was a no-nonsense man determined to produce results," he recollected.

Immediately after getting the accommodation, Modi sought to know details of those *karyakartas* (party workers) who could work on computers. The computer had yet to become fashionable those days. It was not easy to find someone who was an expert in information technology. Further, the one-room office was not very attractive for a young person to work. With great difficulty, a *karyakarta* was identified. Modi requested him to teach him how to operate a computer. Soon enough, he got a computer installed at the office and started working on that. He would search for news and store information in the computer.

Modi suggested that representation from all segments of society was a must to create a stronger electoral base and that the BJP could not be limited to just a few sections of the society. He identified women, the Schedule Castes, Sikhs, ex-servicemen, etc., as the party's targeted groups. Air Marshal (retd.) Randhir Singh Bedi was persuaded to contest the municipal elections; he won comfortably.

Gyanchand Gupta recalled the incident and said that Modi presided over a meeting for selection of Chandigarh municipal candidates; the meeting went on for 13 hours and was concluded at 7 am in the morning. Everybody was surprised how Modi convinced the (retd.) Air Marshal to contest such a small election.[2]

Some party leaders recalled the active membership drive launched by the Chandigarh unit before the 1996 Lok Sabha elections. About 500 people had registered to be active members. Modi ensured that he met each of them individually and spent full four days in the party office. All these active volunteers were surprised at Modi's commitment. They worked overtime to ensure victory of the BJP.

A BJP worker remembered Modi as a liberal *pracharak*. He narrated an incident of Chandigarh in 1998. The party had organised a function to host some local singers. The state unit president's daughter, an MBA from Bangalore, went to the stage and started dancing with the singers. Detractors of the state party president went to Modi and complained that this was very bad and that it was a cultural degeneration. Even before they could say anything further on this, Modi told them there was nothing wrong in that. The young girl had done nothing wrong and that the desire of the youth to express themselves must be appreciated.

A woman worker of the party remembered him for teaching her the first lesson of the need to be tech-savvy. Modi met a modern-day BJP worker and sought to know if she was well-versed with computers. When she replied in the negative, Modi was quick to tell her that she should learn computers. "After some years, those who would not know computers would be considered illiterate," Modi told her.

Haryana

When Modi was given the charge of Haryana, the BJP was seen as a marginal player. In the 1989 Lok Sabha elections, despite electoral adjustments with the Janata Dal, the BJP lost both the seats it contested. Suraj Bhan lost to the Congress from Ambala and Sushma Swaraj lost to the Congress from Karnal. The Janata Dal had won six seats and the Congress four.[3] One needs to recollect that in 1989 the BJP had won 85 Lok Sabha seats, and this was considered a phenomenal rise. Yet its veterans lost in Haryana.

The BJP's attempt to test its own independent strength came a cropper when it contested all the 10 Lok Sabha seats in 1991. It lost deposits in nine seats and Suraj Bhan was the runner-up from Ambala. The newly formed Haryana Vikas Party (HVP) had contested in four seats but it won only one. Jangbir Singh of the HVP won from the Bhiwani seat. The BJP's poor performance in Haryana should be seen against its overall performance in the country, which was quite good. It had won 120 seats.

In the assembly elections of Haryana in 1991, the BJP contested 89 seats, but won only two; represented by Khairati Lal from Shahabad and Ram Bilash from Mahendragarh. The party lost deposits in 70 assembly seats. The Congress won 51 seats.

The BJP's saving grace was its percentage of votes. In the 1989 Lok Sabha polls, it had 8.31 per cent of votes and was the third party after the Congress and the Janata Dal. In 1991, the party polled 10.17 per cent of votes. In the assembly elections in 1991, although the BJP won only two seats, it secured 9.53 per cent votes.[4] Most votes came from urban areas.

Thus, when Modi was made in-charge of Haryana, he had a clear-cut task to increase the BJP's political presence. He knew that the party would not be able to come to power on its own. There were two non-Congress parties trying to dominate the political scene. The Indian National Lok Dal (INLD), formed by Om Prakash Chautala, did not have a clean image. It had yet to recover from the image downslide Chautala had witnessed after poll-related violence in 1990.

Bansi Lal, who had walked away from the Congress, was making his presence felt. The HVP had won the Bhiwani Lok Sabha seat in 1991 and polled 5.35 per cent votes. This was the only seat won by a non-Congress party. In the assembly elections the same year, the HVP had contested 61 seats and won 12. The HVP polled a significant 18.26 per cent votes. The HVP, under Bansi Lal, was fast making inroads into rural Haryana.

Modi had to choose between Chautala and Bansi Lal. The latter clearly had a better image and his party had promised good governance and better administration. Modi put his weight behind BJP-HVP alliance, which had support of senior party leaders, including Sushma

Swaraj, who comes from Haryana.

The alliance helped the BJP make substantial gains. In the 1996 Lok Sabha elections, the BJP contested in six Lok Sabha seats and won four, whereas its alliance partner HVP contested in four and won three.

At the assembly elections, the BJP-HVP alliance contested together. The HVP contested in 65 of the 90 assembly seats and won 33, and the BJP contested in 25 and won 11. Both the parties joined a coalition government headed by Bansi Lal, who became the chief minister on 11 May 1996.

However, this alliance soon became unpopular. The main reason was Bansi Lal's decision to impose prohibition on sale of liquor in the state that was landlocked, which made implementation of the law difficult. It led to bootlegging by young people for easy money. They first learnt how to make fast money and then started consuming liquor themselves, leading to a different social problem. Also, some of them fell into the police net, leading to social unrest. Added to this was the government's decision to forcibly recover power dues from farmers.

The government's dwindling popularity was evident in the 1998 Lok Sabha elections. Although the BJP did extremely well by winning 182 Lok Sabha seats across the country, both the BJP and HVP won only one seat each from Faridabad and Bhiwani respectively. As against this, Devi Lal's Haryana Lok Dal had won four Lok Sabha seats.

The national political situation brought the BJP and INLD close. The former sought support of Chautala's four MPs during the confidence vote of the Vajpayee-led NDA coalition in April 1999. In exchange for support, Chautala wanted the BJP to withdraw support from the Bansi Lal government, a promise that was given by senior leaders of the BJP in private circles. Later, four members of Chautala's party voted in favour of the central government. However, the Vajpayee government lost the confidence vote on 17 April 1999 and the country had to go for fresh polls.

The BJP withdrew support from the Bansi Lal government on 22 June 1999 and joined hands with Chautala, who was the chief minister twice earlier—First as the leader of the Janata Dal and then as the leader of the Samajwadi Janata Party. This time, he became chief minister as the leader of the INLD. He was sworn in as the chief minister on 24

July 1999, a few days after the Election Commission of India announced election dates for the Lok Sabha polls.

Thus, the transition from supporting Bansi Lal to Om Prakash Chautala took place when the BJP-led NDA was already out of power at the Centre. Although the caretaker government continued, the preoccupation was to stitch together a stronger NDA alliance. Leaving Bansi Lal and joining Chautala was no easy decision, more so for Modi who was looking after the state.

Modi had established a good rapport with Bansi Lal. He found it extremely tough to persuade the rank and file of his party to shift allegiance to Chautala as the candidates had won their seats contesting against Chautala's party. On 11 July 1999, the Election Commission announced that the Lok Sabha polls would take place in September. The situation demanded quick decision making. Modi fast developed a working relationship with Chautala and tried to persuade the cadre about the necessity of the alliance.

The BJP-INLD alliance worked well for the NDA; it swept all the 10 seats. The BJP's urban, combined with the INLD's rural votes, produced this spectacular result.

In the assembly elections in February 2000, the BJP contested in 29 seats, but won only six. The INLD contested in 62 and won 47. The INLD did not need the BJP, but the latter extended outside support without any condition. This left the BJP in a quandary as the INLD was reported to have been dishonest in the alliance. At many places, it allowed rebel candidates to contest, leading to severe reverses for the BJP.

Manohar Lal Khattar was the state unit organisation general secretary of Haryana when Modi joined and they had both worked together in the period 1995-2001. He credited Modi with infusing new dynamism in the party that was working in "an archaic way." One day, Modi came to the party office in Rohtak and asked *peon* Deepak to get three boxes from the car. When he got them opened, Khattar thought it was a television set. "I had not seen a computer till then," he said. Modi asked if anyone knew how to operate a computer. Soon a worker was called to install the computer. Khattar then started working on computers.[5]

Modi always loved new technology. Once he took a session of the

Haryana state executive meeting in 1997 to teach them the use of the Internet. The RSS at that time did not quite appreciate the use of such modern gadgets, Khattar said, but Modi thought otherwise. He even had a satellite phone. He used to say, "You must catch-up with technology to stay relevant," Khattar remembered.

He credited Modi with scripting the BJP's victory in the 1999 Lok Sabha elections after the Kargil War. At a party meeting, state leaders were deliberating who should contest. Modi was listening to them quietly. At the end of the meeting, he said at least one seat should be given to Kargil widows. Modi's suggestion was received by stunned silence. Haryana's traditional culture does not allow women, that too widows, to come out in the open. Modi later told Khattar that this would send a good message to the people. Khattar thought Modi must have had some names in his mind. When asked, Modi laughed and told him that he had no candidate and that a candidate should be located through proper search.

The BJP unit then identified Sudha Yadav whose husband was a BSF commandant. She was teaching in a private school and had two children. When the proposal that she should contest was mooted, she was unwilling, but she clarified that the decision must be taken either by her father or her father-in-law. Her father-in-law agreed, and she was made the candidate from Mahendragarh.

Yadav did not have money to contest. To decide what to do, a meeting of party workers was organised in Gurgaon. About 700 workers attended the meeting. Modi was present too. He told every worker that since she was a Kargil widow, every worker would have to take the responsibility of her campaign, including arranging for the resources. Everyone was touched when he said: "My expense is borne by the party. When I go home, my mother gives me money in blessings. When I think someone needs it for good work, I give the money to him. When I think it is pure work, I give it. Now I am putting my contribution to this." And he put whatever he had in the *kalash* (metal ware) that was kept there, Khattar said. All the workers were visibly moved. Some eyes were swelled up with tears. They contributed whatever they had, including gold rings and chains. That meeting saw a collection of about six lakh rupees —enough to charge up the entire cadre and sustain the campaign. Sudha Yadav won the seat.

Himachal Pradesh

The BJP has remained a powerful political player in Himachal Pradesh since the Jana Sangh days. A Congress government was in power in the state when Modi was made the in-charge. In the 1993 assembly elections, the BJP could win only eight of the 68 assembly seats even when it polled a substantial 36.14 per cent of votes. It was a reversal of the situation of the 1990 assembly elections where the BJP had polled 55.78 per cent of votes and won 51 seats. The Congress had polled 37.64 per cent votes and won only nine seats.

The immediate challenge before Modi was to improve the BJP's performance in the Lok Sabha elections. Although the party improved its voting percentage to 39.62, it could not prevent the Congress from winning all the four Lok Sabha seats. The Congress's winning streak continued in 1996 where it polled 54.33 per cent. Modi took it as a challenge and started giving more time to Himachal Pradesh.

He decided to reorganise the party by bringing in fresh faces and roping in the younger generation. He addressed a number of local level meetings of students and young leaders and persuaded them to work for expansion of the BJP. He had become a craze among the youth.[6] Modi would stay either in Chandigarh or Shimla and personally supervise organisational preparedness for the elections. The assembly election in Himachal Pradesh took place along with the Lok Sabha elections in 1998.

The BJP won three Lok Sabha seats and polled 51.43 per cent votes, whereas the Congress polled 41.9 per cent. While the Congress vote percentage in the assembly elections remained almost the same at 41, the BJP's dipped to 35.38 per cent. This clearly showed that the BJP was the state's favourite for the Lok Sabha. The substantial dip in the assembly was due to the rise of the Himachal Vikas Congress (HVC) which polled 10.51 per cent and made a severe dent into the BJP votes.

Polling was held for 65 of the 68 assembly seats. The Congress won 31 seats whereas the BJP won 29. Sukh Ram's HVC won four. The remaining one seat was won by an independent candidate who was earlier in the BJP. Later, the HVC split and the new outfit Himachal Kranti Morcha (HKM), with two MLAs, merged with the BJP. Thus the BJP's tally became 31. But a BJP MLA died before he could take oath, bringing the number down to 30.[7]

Modi's mettle was going to be tested now. He had already identified a simple and dedicated Prem Kumar Dhumal as the party's best bet. Dhumal had represented the Lok Sabha in 1989 and 1991, but had lost his seat in 1996. Senior BJP leader Shanta Kumar was the chief minister after the Emergency in 1977. He became the chief minister again in 1990. Modi, after due consultations with Advani, concluded that Kumar should play a leadership role at the national level. For this reason, Kumar was asked to focus on the 1998 Lok Sabha elections and not contest in the assembly polls. He won the Kangra seat and was thus out of the chief minister's race.

Virbhadra Singh, who was the outgoing chief minister, became chief minister again on 9 March 1998. He secured the support of a rebel BJP MLA who had won as an independent candidate but was considered to be close to Shanta Kumar. Modi did not appreciate the fact that Kumar could not retain the MLA. The Congress justified its move of forming the government saying it had received the governor's invitation first. However, Modi was determined to prevent the Congress from proving its majority on the floor of the assembly. He persuaded Sukh Ram not to align with the Congress that had not treated him well. Within a fortnight, fortunes changed and Virbhadra Singh had to resign. Modi got Dhumal installed as the chief minister on 24 March 1998.

Striking a deal with Sukh Ram was not easy, particularly since the Congress was eyeing to either get his support or break his party, the HVC, without which it could not have achieved a majority in the Vidhan Sabha. Further, the BJP had taken a high moral ground on the issue of corruption and Sukh Ram's image had taken a beating nationwide. As telecom minister in the PV Narsihma Rao Government, he was caught in the telecom scam. Wads of currency notes of Rs 50, 100 and 500 denominations were found stashed in trunks and suitcases at his Delhi residence during a raid by the CBI. But his image did not come in the way of his winning, and this showed his popularity in his constituency.

The BJP, however, had devised a way out by which it could judge the coalition partner by the agenda of governance and allow them to face the consequences of their actions without diluting its own plank of opposing corruption. The BJP already had many controversial leaders from regional political parties in the National Democratic Alliance

(NDA). Modi applied the same principle to form the BJP-HVC coalition government under Dhumal. He persuaded Sukh Ram to join the government and become the virtual number two in the cabinet without being designated so. Sukh Ram had lost the race for the chief minister's post to Virbhadra Singh in 1993. In that sense, he took his revenge on the Congress by supporting Dhumal.[8]

But the CBI was catching up with Sukh Ram. Within months, the fast-developing situation forced him to quit the government. Then President KR Narayanan gave permission to the CBI to prosecute the former minister. The Dhumal government was now left with no option but to persuade Sukh Ram to resign. The Vajpayee government at the Centre had already adopted a policy to ask a minister to resign if his or her image came under the cloud due to corruption charges.

The task of persuading a reluctant Sukh Ram to resign fell on Modi. Persuasion was the only way out since Sukh Ram was a senior minister, and sacking him could project an image of the BJP as being opportunistic and untrustworthy. Besides, this could lead to instability as the government had survived on the support of two HVC MLAs. Modi met Sukh Ram and their meeting continued for hours. Modi told him about the policy that the NDA government had adopted. He made Sukh Ram speak to Vajpayee over the phone. Sukh Ram was unhappy, but he resigned from the ministry in April 1998 and saved a major embarrassment to the government.[9]

Everybody except Modi thought that the government would fall if Sukh Ram was forced to quit. Modi was confident that the government would last its full term. This was due to his understanding of Sukh Ram and the personal rapport he had built with him.

The Dhumal government became more stable later by winning by-elections to assembly seats. In the by-election to the four assembly seats, the BJP improved its tally and moved towards stability. Rebel BJP leader Ramesh Chand had already come back to the party fold.

But the BJP did not junk the HVC. Modi ensured on behalf of his party that the alliance stayed. The relationship with Sukh Ram was sealed by sending his son Anil Sharma to the Rajya Sabha on a BJP ticket. This proved beneficial and the BJP-HVC alliance swept the Lok Sabha polls in Himachal Pradesh 1999.

Punjab

Punjab and Jammu & Kashmir were subsequently added to Modi's portfolio. Thus, he had become the BJP's in-charge for all the states of north India.

After the 1984 anti-Sikh riots, the BJP emerged as a strong votary of justice to the Sikhs. The party advocated Hindu-Sikh unity that could also translate into political opportunities in Punjab. The Shiromani Akali Dal (SAD) led by Parkash Singh Badal had emerged as a political voice of the moderate Sikhs. In fact, both the parties realised big social and political opportunities; social unity of Hindus and Sikhs translated into political possibilities of sharing power.

Before the SAD aligned with the BJP, it experimented in coalition politics by joining hands with the Bahujan Samaj Party (BSP), which was making deep inroads among the Dalit voters. In the 1996 Lok Sabha elections, Akalis joined hands with the BSP and won eight out of the nine seats they contested, whereas its alliance partner BSP won three seats out of the four it contested.

The Akali-BSP was, however, not a natural or long-term alliance because of the contradictions that existed between the landed Jat-Sikhs and Dalits who worked mostly for them. The Akalis also realised that they were allowing the BSP to emerge stronger. If the BSP had contested on its own, it would have cut into the vote percentage of the Congress. Despite losing the Lok Sabha elections, the Congress had still polled a substantial 35.1 per cent votes. As per Akali's calculation, the Congress and the BSP would not join hands because they were competing for the same social base. Therefore, if the BSP would be left to contest alone, they would cut into the votes of the Congress.[10] They also realised that the BJP that had a powerful representation in the urban areas—and had begun to promote Hindu-Sikh unity—would be a much better option.

The SAD gave vent to its thoughts when it unilaterally announced support for the 13-day long Vajpayee government at the centre. This was a masterstroke. In the 1997 elections, the SAD and BJP joined hands and swept the polls. The SAD won 75 of the 92 seats it contested and polled 46.76 per cent votes, whereas the BJP won 18 of the 22 seats it contested and polled 48.22 per cent votes. The BSP that did not contest in alliance with the Congress but had joined the Akali Dal (Mann) cut substantially into the Congress votes. The Congress won 14 of the 105 seats it contested and secured only 29.87 per cent votes.

The effort to forge Hindu-Sikh unity articulated by the leaders of the RSS, Akalis and BJP got further strengthened. In the 1998 Lok Sabha elections, the Akalis won all eight seats it contested and the BJP won three of the three it contested. The other two candidates who won were supported by the Akalis.

Within two years, the coalition government became very unpopular and failed to live up to the euphoria it had generated. In the 1999 Lok Sabha elections that took place in the shadow of heightened nationalism over the Kargil war, when the entire nation seemed to be positive towards the NDA, Punjab delivered it a humiliating defeat. There was no explanation other than the poor performance of the State government. The SAD-BJP alliance won just three seats whereas the Congress won eight out of the 11 contested. The downslide was visible when the state went for assembly polls in 2002 and Congress staged a comeback.

"By 1999, urban Hindus were wholly disenchanted with the BJP, as many rural Sikhs were with the SAD. The reasons were simple. Corruption, poor administration and the absence of an agenda of development had stripped the government of the massive popular support it had received just two years ago. Hindu voters were furious with the BJP for failing to contain the religious right within the SAD, while some of those elements, led by Badal's key foe Gurcharan Singh Tohra, had split to form the revanchist Sarv Hind SAD. In the Lok Sabha elections that year, the SAD won just two of the nine seats it contested, and the BJP won only one of the three. While the BJP roughly held its vote share of 9.7 per cent, the SAD's share fell to 28.5 per cent, much the same as in 1996. The Congress's share of the popular vote, however, increased dramatically to 38.4 per cent."[11]

Despite the electoral performance, Modi never had any problem with the Akali leadership. He and the entire BJP leadership recognised Badal's electoral strength. When the NDA coalition was formed at the Centre in May 1999, the SAD was honourably accommodated in the cabinet. Raj Bhatia, who was secretary of the Punjab unit then, recalled that Modi used to camp in villages and interact with party workers and guide them on how to work. His tenure in Punjab was not long, but he proved to a powerful mobiliser of workers on ideological issues, he said.[12]

Jammu & Kashmir

Jammu & Kashmir has been India's only state with a Muslim majority. Because of the composition of its assembly, it has been very difficult for the BJP to expand its appeal beyond Jammu. The state is divided into three regions: the Valley with 46 assembly seats, Jammu with 37 and Ladakh with four in the 87 member functional assembly. The demographic composition of the state is such that the BJP is unable to make much headway in the assembly electorally other than in certain parts of Jammu. Its maximum strength was in 2008, when it won 11 assembly seats from Jammu.

The party, however, has been able to make its presence felt in both the Lok Sabha seats in Jammu. It won both Jammu and Udhampur Lok Sabha seats in 1998 and 1999.

Modi's links with Jammu & Kashmir were established during the Ekta Yatra for which he visited the state first as an organiser and then as the charioteer; both Joshi and he had flown to Srinagar to hoist the tricolour there.

As the national secretary in-charge during 1996-97 and then general secretary in-charge 1998-99, Modi frequently visited the state. The Lok Sabha elections in 1998 and 1999 were the best periods for the BJP. Chamanlal Gupta won the Udhampur seat on both the occasions. Vaidya Vishnu Datt did the same from the Jammu seat.

Manoj Singh Chauhan remembered that Modi had a penchant for minute details. At meetings with party workers, he would ask them to always come with a notebook and a pen. This prompted the workers to give him the nickname 'Masterji'. Chauhan was state secretary when Modi was in-charge of Jammu Kashmir.

Once Chauhan told Modi that the party office needed renovation. At this, Modi got angry and asked him, "Who will do it? We are all RSS workers and we have to learn to start building the organisation brick by brick. Why don't you start working on this?" Chauhan said he did not like Modi's comment then but soon realised that he had the recipe for a very good office. Then Modi told him and all workers to try at their respective levels and contribute in their own way—whatever would help prop up the party. The state unit, subsequently became a moden office with many high-tech facilities.[13]

In Lutyen's Delhi

In his initial days, Modi stayed in Delhi. The national capital continued to be his second home even when he stayed in Chandigarh. He was a member of the team that planned and executed Advani's Swarna Jayanti Rath Yatra*, this yatra sought to remind people of the value of India's freedom and the sacrifices made by freedom fighters.

This was the golden year of India's independence. Advani convened a meeting of the team in February 1997 to discuss how to celebrate the occasion. The party concluded that a *rath yatra* be organised to visit places associated with martyrs of India's Independence. Advani also wanted to showcase this as a way to create awareness about good governance and the need to graduate from *swaraj* (self rule) to *suraj* (good governance). Thus, the *yatra* had the twin objective of 'patriotic pilgrimage' and the need to graduate from '*swaraj* to *suraj*'.[14]

The task of fine-tuning the minor details of the *yatra* had come on Pramod Mahajan, M Venkaiah Naidu, Sushma Swaraj, KN Govindacharya, Narendra Modi and Sadhvi Uma Bharati. The *yatra* had to traverse 21 states and Union territories in 59 days from 18 May to 15 July, covering a distance of over 15,000 km. Advani described this as the "longest and widest mass contact programme undertaken by any political party since Independence".

Although Modi was a junior functionary, he was fearless. He would not mind giving his ideas about the nitty-gritty of the *yatra* even when his two senior colleagues were experts in *yatra* planning. Govindacharya, who also came from the RSS school, encouraged Modi to freely air his views. Pramod Mahajan was not very active in the *yatra* that was taken over by Govindacharya, Modi and Advani's aide, Sudheendra Kulkarni.

During the 1998 Lok Sabha elections, Modi's role was mainly to supervise election preparedness in the states under his charge. Kushabhau Thakre had taken over as the new party president at the BJP's national

---

* Advani described this as a patriotic pilgrimage to mark the golden jubilee of India's Independence.

council meeting in Gandhinagar in May 1998. On 20 May 1998, when Thakre announced his new team, Modi's name figured as one of the five general secretaries along with Govindacharya, M Venkaiah Naidu, Sangh Priya Gautam and Sumitra Mahajan.

Modi's elevation was in recognition of his contribution to building the organisation in several states. Being a *pracharak*, he was now at par with Govindacharya, the most powerful general secretary then. Also, Modi had contributed greatly to the BJP's victory in Gujarat in March 1998. In Modi's words, he was determined to bring Keshubhai back to the government. His stock in the RSS had gone up due to his commitment and performance.

The BJP national council meeting in Gandhinagar in the first week of May 1998 was significant for three reasons. The first was the obvious formal takeover by Kushabhau Thakre as the new party president; the second, which was quite visible too, was the massive security presence, BJP being the ruling party and most ministers with their retinues were there including Prime Minister Atal Bihari Vajpayee and Home Minister LK Advani; and the third, which had gone almost unnoticed by the national leaders and the media, was the attention Modi was getting from the party's Gujarat unit leaders.

By that time, news was already out that Modi was going to be elevated as a national general secretary, a post considered very important in the party. Many leaders met Modi to revive their past links. The common refrain in Gujarat was that Narendrabhai had staged a comeback and was the man to watch. Those who had thought he was down and out were proved wrong.[15]

When a party is in government, the organisation ends up defending the government's policies and also serving as a feedback mechanism for people's reaction to those policies. It also gives immense powers to party functionaries because of their proximity to power. Modi's position was no different. But he never tried to use his position to influence ministers to lobby for personal gains. Modi would not even visit government offices; he had clarified to all those who approached him: "Let the ministers do their work and we will do ours." As a party leader, he would not mind pointing out if there was something missing.

And the party would defend the government in case of need, as the party had better mobilisation capabilities and independent communication mechanism. A good example of this was seen when the party was asked to defend the government on the Agra summit, which was dubbed a failure by the media. The Agra summit had concluded a day before. Then Prime Minister Atal Bihari Vajpayee had a 30-minute meeting with BJP office bearers on 17 July 2001 to explain the government stand. Modi, who was the general secretary and spokesperson, was also present. The Agra summit did not get the results that the euphoria about it had generated. The government needed the party to explain to the people the whole episode.

Modi launched one of the sharpest attacks on the then Pakistani President General Parvez Musharraf. He said that the Agra summit was not a failure and projected General Musharraf as unreliable.

"The very fact that Musharraf had to go back without signing any agreement clearly shows that Atalji was not on the defensive, but on the offensive... Musharraf was the architect of the Kargil War. Atalji told him bluntly that India had the capacity to deal with terrorism despite Pakistan's presence. This was done to send a signal to the terrorist outfits in Pakistan that, when it comes to dealing with them, India will not hesitate to crush them."

He also criticised the General for interacting with the Indian media and trying to conduct diplomacy through the media:

"It was not proper on the General's part to have played games with the media. We have been told by some editors that they were not even aware that it was being telecast live on Pakistan television... When two heads of States hold talks, you do not go to the media to score a point or two. If General Musharraf thought he could solve the Kashmir problem through press conferences, then he is welcome to hold 1,000 press meets. He would still be at square one."[16]

Modi's anti-Musharraf feeling got strengthened during this phase. When he attacked Musharraf during the campaign for the 2002 assembly polls in Gujarat and addressed him as "Mian Musharraf", he was talking in the context of the failure of the Agra summit and Pakistan's support to terrorism. The bitterness over the Agra summit was fresh in his memory.

Modi Moves to 9 Ashoka Road

This bungalow was allotted to Union Minister Arun Jaitley when he became a member of Rajya Sabha in 2000 from Gujarat. Jaitley offered this residence to the party for use, while keeping a small unit of it for himself. During the same time, Dilip Sanghani was moving to Lodhi Estate, thereby necessitating that Modi look for some other accommodation. Towards the beginning of 2001, Modi was allocated a separate one-room accommodation at 9 Ashoka Road. This residence proved very lucky for Modi. From here, he moved straight to the CM House in Gandhinagar. He also earned a very good friend in Arun Jaitley who defended him tooth and nail when the entire world seemed to be pushing him to the corners over the 2002 riots.

Modi's ascendancy in the party had begun also due to the decline of the most powerful general secretary, Govindacharya. The latter got involved in a controversy due to some statements that were attributed to him. He was quoted as having described Vajpayee as the party's mask; a statement he denied. The British High Commission, whose officials were supposedly told this by Govindacharya, denied the statement too. Vajpayee, however, did not like it. Govindacharya got increasingly sidelined to keep Vajpayee in good humour.

When Bangaru Laxman became the party president in 2000, Govindacharya was forced to go on a study leave. Laxman made drastic changes in his team. He made Naidu, Modi and Maya Singh general secretaries along with Sunil Shastri. In this team, Modi had a formidable presence since he was the only one representing the RSS in the organisation.[17] He was made the party's general secretary in-charge (organisation).

Gujarat in Modi's Absence

Modi was really unhappy about being sent out of Gujarat in 1995, particularly since he had built the unit brick by brick and he did not see himself responsible in any manner for the crisis in the state unit. Many people close to him thought that he was used by Shankersinh Vaghela who knew how to play politics by pitting one against the other.

Keshubhai Patel had become national vice-president of the BJP and Modi was made the national secretary as part of the compromise that also saw Suresh Mehta become the chief minister. But Mehta could not survive the pulls and pressures of government, party and opposition. The compromise arrived at between those who rebelled and those who stayed loyal to the party could not last long as it had created hostility in the sangh parivar. The affiliates of the RSS, such as the VHP and others, had declared Vaghela as a traitor. They held that Vaghela was rewarded for indiscipline in a party that used to project itself as the party with a difference.

In January 1996, the names of Advani and other senior BJP leaders figured in the Jain Hawala scandal. Advani gave an unprecedented response by resigning from his Lok Sabha seat from Gandhinagar and declaring that he would not contest in a Lok Sabha election till he was cleared of the charges. On 9 March 1996, Advani tried to take the battle against corruption to the Congress by launching the "Swaraj se Suraj" *rath yatra* from Ernakulam.

Advani's decision had two fallouts for Gujarat. First, he vacated the Gandhinagar seat, which was contested successfully by Atal Bihari Vajpayee. It dashed the hopes of Vaghela who wanted to shift his Lok Sabha constituency from Godhra to Gandhinagar.

Second, when Advani's *rath yatra* entered Gujarat on 18 March, it did not receive the expected response. Advani's meetings at Pardhi, Navsari, Valsad and Surat were poorly attended.[18] The response was poor compared to the enthusiasm Advani's Ram Rath Yatra had generated in 1990. Many felt that, in the absence of Modi, there was no one to galvanise the organisation to welcome the Suraj Rath. Chief Minister Suresh Mehta and Vaghela did not turn up for any of the meetings Advani addressed in south Gujarat, which the *yatra* traversed.[19]

If response to Advani's *yatra* was an indication of the intra-party factionalism in the BJP, the fratricidal war was out in the open when the Lok Sabha elections took place in April-May 1996. There were reports that party loyalists and the RSS-VHP joined hands to defeat the 'Khajuria' candidates including Vaghela. Sadhus held meetings in Godhra and appealed to people to defeat 'Hindu-traitor' Vaghela.[20] The BJP could win only 16 of the 26 Lok Sabha seats. Vaghela lost his contest in Godhra and candidates affiliated to him lost their seats from Surendranagar, Banaskantha and Baroda (Vadodara).

Vaghela formally broke away from the BJP and formed his own party, the Rashtriya Janata Party, in October 1996. He became the chief minister the same month with the support of the Congress and continued to be in the chair for a year. This vindicated Modi's assessment that Vaghela's rebellion in the BJP was motivated by his desire to grab power and had nothing to do with ideological issues. Vaghela contested the 1998 assembly elections on his own but could not win more than four seats. Later, realising that it was difficult to survive in the state's bipolar politics, he merged his party with the Congress in July 1999.

During an interview in 1998, Narendra Modi absolved himself of any blame for the fiasco of 1995: "I was blamed for the Gujarat fiasco but kept quiet because one day the truth will come out. A recent popular survey showed that 82 per cent of the people in the state believed that Shankersinh Vaghela was responsible for the split in the BJP and the toppling of the Keshubhai Patel government. But the media targetted me."[21]

The assembly polls in Gujarat that happened simultaneously with parliamentary polls 1998 made the loudest statement for the BJP and Modi. Modi was very keen to clear himself of the accusations levelled by Vaghela, and he also wanted to prevent Vaghela from staging a comeback by any means. Due to political reasons, the party did not announce but sent Modi to work for the larger cause of bringing the BJP to power. He received a rousing reception in Ahmedabad when he went there to campaign for the party in 1998.[22] Whichever place Modi visited during the campaign, one would often hear the slogan "*dekho dekho kaun aaya, Gujarat ka sher aaya*". (Look, who has come: the lion of Gujarat!). The BJP won the assembly elections comfortably and Modi was credited with Keshubhai's comeback. Much before the polls, Modi had predicted that the party would sweep the assembly elections and win more than 20 out of the 26 Lok Sabha seats.[23] The party won 117 assembly seats of the 182 and 19 of the 26 Lok Sabha seats. He knew the state unit of the party like the back of his hand.

An interview prior to the election results described Modi as the man in complete control: "There is little doubt that Modi is running the BJP campaign in Gujarat. He helped choose the candidates, he laid down the campaign rules and he is among the party's most active campaigners.

He has also visited all the 26 Lok Sabha constituencies in the state. A favourite of the sangh parivar, Modi once again lords over Gujarat, from where he had been banished after the Shankarsinh Vaghela fiasco."[24]

Modi was formally given the charge of the party's campaign machinery in the 1999 Lok Sabha elections in Gujarat. He used his established network in the cadre and returned to the central office after the elections were over. This justified the party's growing trust in Modi and his integrity.

Keshubhai's Woes

Although Keshubhai got a strong mandate without any fear of dissidence, he failed to capitalise on the voters' trust. He was in the news for all the wrong reasons such as corruption, nepotism and ineffectiveness.[25] Even Nature seemed to be working against him. The state faced two successive droughts in 1998 and 1999. Before that, there was a killer hurricane in Kandla in 1998 that killed 3,500 people and damaged 200,000 houses.[26]

In 1999, as many as 998 of the state's 225 blocks received less than 50 per cent of the expected rainfall, and the same year, the state faced the worst drought of the past 100 years. About 7,500 villages spread over 145 blocks in 15 districts were severely affected by this drought. In 2000, Ahmedabad was reeling under floods that reflected poorly on the State administration; the preparations for the monsoon were grossly inadequate. Massive building activities by the city's builders had dealt heavy damage to the drainage system. Everyone blamed the Ahmedabad Municipal Corporation and the Ahmedabad Urban Development Authority (AUDA) for officiating over the mess.

As if these were not enough, Gujarat faced the worst earthquake on 26 January 2001. The state had not witnessed such an earthquake in the past 200 years. The earthquake with its epicentre at Bhuj proved Keshubhai's nemesis. The situation demanded a dynamic chief minister who could rise to the occasion and instil confidence in the people. Keshubhai tried his best, but could not infuse dynamism in the entire exercise.

The earthquake affected 21 districts. Around 18 towns, 182 *talukas* and 7,904 villages witnessed large-scale devastation. Four urban areas in Kutch district, namely Bhuj, Anjar, Bhachau and Rapar suffered near total destruction. About 450 villages were completely destroyed. More than 20,000 people were killed, 1,66,000 were injured, many people went missing, and property worth Rs 21,262 crore was destroyed.[27] The state was grossly under-prepared for such a tragedy.

The media flashed numerous reports of the government's inability to deal with the situation. There were charges of corruption, tardy relief and lack of imagination. One such report would give an idea of the situation:

"There were numerous reports about bungling in relief and rehabilitation of quake victims... Report of the Comptroller and Auditor General (CAG) came as a major embarrassment to the government. There was a controversy over expenses relating to the chief minister's foreign trip to garner Non-Resident Indian funds. The CAG report also highlighted several irregularities in the award of government contracts and purchases of items ranging from aircraft to fodder...

There were allegations that ministers in the govenment and their relatives were using personal contacts to dole out government favours at a price. Some of the ministers were themselves reported to be involved in land deals that proved embarrassing for the Keshubhai governemnt.[28]

The public image of Keshubhai Patel suffered due to the adverse media reports. No one believed that he could deliver. On top of that, the BJP was losing the confidence of the people. Results of the local elections were discouraging enough.

The district *panchayat* elections held in September 2000 had demonstrated public disenchantment with the BJP. The party lost 23 of the 25 district *panchayats* and the majority of *taluka panchayats*. Earlier, it held complete sway over 24 of these. In the urban areas too, the situation was no better. The party lost the Ahmedabad municipal corporation as well as Rajkot, both of which had been winning seats for the party for the last 15 and 25 years respectively. In other four municipal corporations, the party's victory margin was reduced drastically.

For the first time, the BJP had lost support at the grassroots, something which most RSS and BJP leaders considered a warning. That the downslide had not stopped was clear when assembly by-elections took place in September 2001. The BJP lost the Sabarkantha and Sabarmati seats to the Congress. Sabarmati falls in the Gandhinagar Lok Sabha constituency, which was represented by Advani. The BJP had lost the seat by a margin of 19,000 votes. This was the first time since 1995 that the BJP had registered a defeat there. It was clear to the party leadership that something must be done to reverse the trend if the BJP wanted to have any chance in the assembly elections due in 2003.

It was then that the central leadership of the party decided to send Narendra Modi to Gujarat as chief minister. The RSS, too, was keen for a replacement because its citadel was crumbling down. Who could have been better than Modi who knew the sinews of the party machinery? It was a big gamble since he had no experience of being in governance. But those who knew him were confident that he would turn the tables.

Two senior leaders of the party—Kushabhau Thakre and Madan Lal Khurana—were sent as central observers of the party to ensure smooth sailing. Thakre, who had relinquished the office of the party president in 2000, was sent due to his seniority and the respect of the rank and file he commanded.

When asked what would happen in Gujarat and whether Modi would be accepted by legislators, party president Jana Krishnamurthy said that there would be no problem. "You see there will be a smooth sailing. There is nothing against Keshubhai. The party is trying to experiment with someone who is younger and who would work under Keshubhai's guidance."[29]

Despite a few initial hiccups that happen every time such a change is attempted, the sailing was smooth. Keshubhai proposed Modi's name for the leader of the legislative assembly and senior leader Suresh Mehta seconded the proposal. He had to be elected as the leader of the house before he could stake a claim before Governor Sundar Singh Bhandari to be sworn in as the chief minister. These formalities were completed on 4 October and Bhandari asked him to take the oath on 7 October. For the RSS and BJP, it was a rare moment. An RSS *pracharak*, Modi, was sworn in by another RSS *pracharak* Bhandari. This was the first time a *pracharak* had become the chief minister of a state.

***

Expediting Relief and Rehabilitation

The real story is about how a determined community extricated itself from the debris and created a better life for themselves.....

— **Narendra Modi**

Immediate Challenges as CM

When one becomes the chief minister, it is generally expected that there would be a honeymoon period so that the person can understand his job and start delivering. This applies more when someone becomes the chief minister without any prior experience of being in government. To acclimatise with governance, understand the issues and make the administration move need humongous efforts. Modi was given a herculean task, and he knew this was his big test. On top of this, the state unit of the party and the government had many people who would not listen to him so easily.

Before being sworn in as the chief minister, Modi clarified to his party colleagues that he wanted an administration that would deliver. He identified efficiency, discipline and integrity as the government's main objectives and delivered his famous statement: "I am here to play a one-day international and not a five-day test match."[1] Taking his cricketing analogy further, Modi said 'it would not be the number of balls that have been bowled, but the number of balls in which the batsmen score that matters.' He clearly sent a strong message that he needed people who would deliver. He also knew that he had a clear mandate of the party leadership to perform, and he used this mandate to bring a sense of purpose in those who were running the government.

The first big challenge was to speed up relief and rehabilitation for the earthquake victims. Tardy relief had put a big question mark on the government's ability to deliver. The State officials seemed to be under-confident and political leaders were failing to give them a sense of direction. Keshubhai Patel had also tried his best. The Gujarat State Disaster Management Authority (GSDMA) was established on 8 February 2001, to coordinate between departments for the rehabilitation and reconstruction programmes. But apparently, everybody was in a state of shock. What was missing was a strong leadership and direct communication with the people.

When the earthquake hit Gujarat on 26 January 2001, Modi was in Delhi. He was so worried that he requested Parimal Nathwani of Reliance Industries to fly him to Kutch in their private aircraft. He wanted to be the first to reach the region, see and analyse the situation and prepare a report so that the Vajpayee Government could rush immediate help.[2] Thus, when he took charge of the office, he was already aware of his immediate task. Now, he had an opportunity to address the issues that agitated him.

On 27 January 2001, the central BJP had formed a relief committee in Delhi called the Gujarat Earthquake Relief Committee. Party Vice President Jana Krishnamurthy, senior leader JP Mathur, Amitabh Sinha and Sardar RP Singh were members of this committee. The committee reached Radhanpur on the evening of 28 January. According to Sinha, all administrative offices had collapsed and there was no semblance of administration.[3] However, Modi reached there and the team swung into action. The BJP had become so defamed by then that the people would refuse to accept help if they came to know that the relief was coming from the party. Modi immediately took charge and mobilised local workers for distribution of the relief material. He suggested to the administration that a reconstruction committee be formed. He had to wait to become the chief minister to form this committee.

Within a fortnight of becoming the chief minister, Modi handpicked bureaucrats who were experts in relief and rehabilitation. He appointed PK Mishra, the CEO of GSDMA, as his principle secretary and Anil Mukim as additional principle secretary in the chief minister's office (CMO). Mukim, who was collector of Kutch when the earthquake hit, was promoted and shifted to Gandhinagar. This move by Modi was considered a clear indication of what his priorities were. It was clear that while the GSDMA would play its role, the CMO would be actively monitoring all the developments.[4]

From day one, he started going to office early in the morning and left quite late in the evening. Since he did not have any experience in governance, spending more time proved to be beneficial. Officials did not know how to deal with him. A chief minister who spent more time in office could not be taken lightly by any official. He called officials at will and interacted with them to understand the extent of problems and also give possible solutions. He started judging the bureaucrats by their actions in the field and not by their conceptualisations. Step-by-step monitoring was introduced to bring in more accountability.

During his initial months in office, he did not go to public functions for felicitations. He focussed on monitoring relief and rehabilitation. The process also helped him to identify the bureaucrats who were sincere and hard-working. People started talking of Modi as a man who meant business. The bureaucrats who were not used to this culture were surprised initially but learnt soon enough that there was no escape.

In the very first month of being in power, Modi decided that all the ministers, MPs and MLAs would spend Diwali (the festival of lights) at the residences of earthquake-affected families to gain their confidence. The chief minister had decided to lead from the front. Thus, on 14 November 2001, he and his cabinet colleagues visited earthquake-affected regions. Modi spent the whole day at the Chaubari village in Bhachau. In another village Trumbo, he lit lamps in memory of those who had lost their lives. On the request of a Dalit woman who had lost her 18-year-old son, he visited her shattered house and had *rotla* (Indian bread) and *chhas* (buttermilk) with her family.[5]

These gestures helped create a good impression about the administration. The chief minister urged his supporters not to flood newspapers with congratulatory messages but donate the money for relief. All these steps helped him to emerge as a no-nonsense leader.[6]

He took two radical decisions that changed the pace and face of relief and rehabilitation. The first was the massive involvement of civil societies with transparency, accountability and full authority; the second was to invite private companies to invest in the Kutch region.

Gujarat is fortunate to have a large number of functioning NGOs. Modi realised that the government alone was not enough to provide effective relief. The effort of the RSS and its network of NGOs came in handy. Modi knew that the RSS had a dedicated cadre with experience of working in such situations. Other private NGOs were also encouraged to participate. He left decision making on relief and rehabilitation to the NGOs and private individuals. The government's job was limited to part funding and monitoring.[7]

Private companies came in hordes to help after the Union government declared a five-year excise exemption and the State government announced sales tax exemption to make private investment attractive. This was needed to revive economic activity in the region. Investment above Rs 50 crore was given sales tax exemption for 10 years. Companies could now plan long-term investments. Other benefits were also given to companies that made higher investment. The chief minister was confident that such concessions would help the Kutch region grow faster.[8]

Soon industrial giants such as ESSAR, Adani Group, Suzlon, Sanghi Group, TATA power, Surya Group, JP Group etc., were making a beeline for Gujarat. All these companies started a chain of projects leading to Bhuj and the adjoining *talukas* of Kutch. Soon the region witnessed unprecedented prosperity. Many big corporate and public sector undertakings adopted clusters of villages for relief and reconstruction; they were given tax concessions for undertaking the task. In 10 years, the scenario changed completely.

"It has also helped to revive the local economy by providing assistance for agriculture, industries, small businesses and handicraft; this has led to the regeneration of livelihood for the people," said a report prepared by the government of India.[9]

A news report after 10 years of the tragedy told the success story albeit differently: "My flat that cost me Rs 500 per square yard in 2004 could now fetch me Rs.15,000-20,000 per square yard," says Chhabil Patel, a dates farmer. Prices of land crashed following the quake, but the way they have skyrocketed in recent years has taken everyone by surprise. Residential areas such as Revenue Colony or Bankers Colony, where earlier bungalows could be available for Rs 15 lakh, now cost Rs 2 crore.[10]

The rehabilitation in Kutch won international acclaim. M Greene, a rehabilitation expert from the United States, described the Bhuj reconstruction as commendable. "Even a country like America would have had problems with rehabilitation given the magnitude of the challenge," he said. Greene has worked in restoring quake-affected settlements in Japan, US, Turkey and Iran.[11] The UN was so impressed with the relief and reconstruction that it gave the coveted Sasakawa Award to the GSDMA in October 2003. The UN deviated from its own norm and, as an exception, the award was given to a government organisation.[12]

To mark a decade of its formation, the GSDMA organised an international conference on "Post-Earthquake Reconstruction—Lessons Learnt and Way Forward". Held in April 2011, the conference was inaugurated by none other than the Gujarat Chief Minister. Modi summed up the decade long experience of disaster management in the following way:

"The real story is about how a determined community extricated itself from the debris and created a better life for themselves..... The reconstruction program was also conceived with a clear vision in mind i.e. to Build Back Better. It is said that disasters create an opportunity to 'build back better'. Gujarat understood this and organized the entire reconstruction program towards converting the crisis into an opportunity. If you go to Kutch today you will find that the four urban towns of Kutch which were totally devastated has emerged into scientific ultra modern towns which showcase our efforts. We proved that adversity could really be translated into an opportunity."[13]

The credit for the complete makeover of Bhuj, Anjar, Rapar and Bhachau goes to the able leadership of Modi and the GSMDA. People remembered the devastation but they also remembered the way the government came out and helped the inhabitants build their lives afresh. Compensations were paid on the basis of three criteria: how big the house was; the extent of damage; and whether or not the owner/applicant was rebuilding his/her house strictly on the basis of the new designs given by the government's engineers. In Bhachau and Bhuj, people said that though minor tremors continue to shake the ground once in a while even now, the houses are so strong that people feel safe. Bhuj resembles a modern city with meticulous roads and buildings.

Except the old multi-storey buildings that did not collapse, no multi-storey structure were allowed to be constructed after the earthquake, said Chirag Bhatt, the surveyor of the Bhuj Area Development Authority (BHADA).[14] The Gamtal area in Bhuj was completely destroyed in the quake since the houses were old and weak. After recostruction, the area looks nothing like it did a few years ago. The lake in the middle of the town has become the centre of activity.

Once Kutch was supposed to be a punishment posting for officials. This was a way to threaten the officials and also to shunt them out of main centres of bureaucracy. There would be no activity or typical hustle-bustle of a city after 5 pm. Now the city has completely changed. The Kutch festival has made Bhuj attractive to tourists. 'Many modern hotels have come up to take care of tourists and the hotels are almost fully booked', said Shakeel Ahmed who was employed in one of the hotels.[15]

As one drove through Bhachau, one could see a four-lane state highway being laid using modern technology. The stretches that were already constructed could match any of the national highways. It hardly took five hours to reach Bhuj from Ahmedabad through the Bhuj-Bhachau highway which covers a distance of about 400 km. About 80 km north of Bhuj is the Dhordo village from where one can go and enjoy the vast white sheet, also known as the White Rann of Kutch. Every tourist has to pay a fee and those with private cars have to pay more.

Between Bhachau and Anjar areas, a large industrial belt dots the landscape. Many industries have mushroomed in this region. One could see smoke billowing into the skies to depict the new activity that has overtaken the region. Wellspun Group, a textile leader, has its 1,000 hectare township at Anjar. The population of these small towns of Kutch has increased and so has their economic activities. Ghulam Ali of Bhachau town said that there were more activities, more money and faster life.[16]

Separate town planning authorities were set up in 2002 for Bhachau, Rapar, Anjar and Bhuj with facilities including earthquake-resistant houses, wider roads, parks, etc, to make town living attractive and comfortable. A compensation package was also prepared for different categories of devastation. A quick word with those who were affected testified that the compensation was quick and adequate. There were no complaints.

An appreciation of the State government's effort came from the government of India: "By the end of the January 2004, 901,150 out of 928,369 houses were repaired and almost 87 percent of houses were reconstructed. The 42,678 classrooms of primary schools were completed almost by the first year itself. All hospitals and health facilities were also made functional within a small period after the earthquake."[17]

Tackling the aftermath of the earthquake helped Gujarat acquire capabilities in disaster management. This knowledge came in handy in times of disasters in other states. In December 2004 when a devastating tsunami rocked the shores of Tamil Nadu, Pondicherry, Andaman & Nicobar Islands, Odisha and Andhra Pradesh, Gujarat was among the first States to send trainloads of relief material to these places. The State also supplied drinking water to Andaman & Nicobar Islands. In addition to the relief, the government of Gujarat announced a relief package of Rs 10 crore the next day from the CM relief fund.[18] It is said that Modi had a meeting of the State's Crisis Management Group (CMG) even before the Centre could have a meeting of it own CMG.

Armed with the expertise and compassion that motivates one to help, Modi reached Uttarakhand with his officials. Rather than trying to learn from the expertise, the State government allowed politics to dominate relief. Modi was painted in a negative light in a news report that had no basis. *The Times of India* on 23 June came out with headline saying "Modi in Rambo Act Saves 15,000".[19] Modi had rescued 15,000 people from Gujarat who were stranded in different locations due to flash floods, the report claimed besides making other interesting reads. On 14 July 2013, the newspaper came out with an explanation denying the content of the report. But the damage was already done. The Congress went overboard and the reaction to an action that did not happen became a much bigger news.

It is surprising why the reporter as well as the staff at the desk did not bother to find out that rescue operation is handled by the army and paramilitary personnel. And the report did not mention the source. This was not a story that could go without quoting the source. If the reporter was describing the event based on what he had seen, then one can imagine the length to which one's imagination can go.

In all fairness, Modi had left an important State function of inaugurating five new flyovers in Surat to rush to Dehradun.[20] Learning from the Gujarat experience could have helped mitigate the sufferings. One needs to recall that Iran, Afghanistan, Bangladesh, Sri Lanka, Bhutan and East Timor sent their expert teams to Gujarat to study disaster management. Many Indian states have sent their top officials to study the same. Besides that, a number of national and international study teams have visited the State to understand the way the government tackled the post earthquake Gujarat.

Coming back to the story of Kutch, the government made sure that even students in schools were taught those few important steps that go a long way in saving people in situations of disaster. The syllabus of Gujarat schools has been revised to include lessons on disaster management. NGOs are actively involved in giving training and conducting mock drills, and all schools now keep fire safety equipment.

***

History of Riots in Gujarat
Godhra Contextualised

The limitation of riots, moral questions aside, is that they cannot win and their participants know it. Hence, rioting is not revolutionary but reactionary because it invites defeat. It involves an emotional catharsis, but it must be followed by a sense of futility.
—**Martin Luther King, Jr.**

Minor local incidents involving personal issues have often snowballed into large-scale riots in Gujarat. Justice P Reddy Commission that looked into the 1969 riots had recommended that the youth should be educated in such a way that they develop a broader outlook and become more tolerant. Even after so many years, the situation has not changed much, showing that the society has not moved forward, at least in communal understanding.

Lack of a broader outlook and tolerance have percolated down to those in administration, particularly the police. No wonder, most commissions set up to look into the reasons of conflict in India have found the police to be either inactive or not doing enough. The case of Gujarat in 2002 was no different.

Most of us commit the mistake of trying to understand the post-Godhra riots in isolation. Hence, we end up seeing things from the wrong end of the telescope. The answer to most questions would emerge after a better understanding of the context in which riots have been taking place in Gujarat. The social context of the state must first be understood properly.

While blaming the administrative head for any riot is fine in the context of accountability; taking it a step further and blaming a single person or organisation as solely responsible will be a travesty of justice. A peek into the history of riots in Gujarat will help analyse the situation and put things in the right context. Though communal riots have taken place in the Sindh-Gujarat region since the 7th Century, here is a study of instances that are closer in time. That way our understanding of the situation will be more contemporary.

1893 Riots

Hindus and Muslims clashed in the temple town of Somnath (Junagadh) when a group of Muslims took out a *Tazia* procession and decided to end that at a place considered sacred by Hindus. The ruler, who was a Muslim, had passed an order prohibiting the procession route, but a group of Muslim youth paid no heed. It led to violence that resulted in the deaths of many innocents. The issue remained alive for almost three years and drove a lasting wedge between the two communities.

1927-28 Unrest

After the withdrawal of the Non-Cooperation Movement, the Hindu-Muslim unity achieved by Mahatma Gandhi crumbled. The period 1927-28 was marked by riots particularly in Surat and Godhra. Morarji Desai, who was the deputy collector of Godhra at that time, was accused of helping Hindu communalists. He resigned in protest over the allegations.

No riots took place in Gujarat during the Partition. There was tension when efforts were being made to rebuild the Somnath temple. For the renovators, it symbolised restoration of the past glory. Mahatma Gandhi diffused the situation by urging that the restoration be carried out by private funds only.

1937 Separate Electorate for Muslims

On the line of separate electorate, the British rulers introduced separate Hindu and Muslim constituencies in Gujarat in 1937. Candidates belonging to both the communities addressed their respective parochial issues to win their seats. No one actually needed to appeal to the larger section of the society. This helped intensify the 'us versus them' feeling. Later, it also manifested in Hindu revivalism that stressed on glories of the past.

1969 Riots

The worst Hindu-Muslim riots since Independence took place in September-October 1969 in Gujarat. The violence injured 1,074 and claimed the lives of as many as 660 people. More than 48,000 people lost their property. Of the 512 deaths reported by the police, 430 were Muslims. Dalit Hindu workers, mostly from outside the state, had attacked the *chawls* of their Muslim neighbours. Unconfirmed reports said that the casualties were higher than the official figure.

On 3 March 1969, a Hindu police officer moved a handcart to clear the traffic in Kalupur district. While doing so, a copy of the Qur'an that was placed on the handcart fell on the ground. A small Muslim crowd gathered around the spot and demanded an apology. It led to violent protests in which 12 policemen were injured.

On 4 September, a Muslim sub-inspector, while dispersing a Ramlila festive crowd, hit a table. As a result, a copy of *the Ramayana* and an *aarti thali* (plate containing things used for worship) fell down. The Hindus alleged that the police officer had also kicked the book. This led to formation of the Hindu Dharma Raksha Samiti (Hindu Religion Protection Committee) that organised protests in which anti-Muslim slogans were raised. Bharatiya Jana Sangh leader Balraj Madhok visited the city and delivered fiery speeches on 14 and 15 September. Another incident included an alleged assault on some Muslim *maulvis* (clerics), who were trying to construct a mosque in the Odhav village near Ahmedabad.[1]

On 18 September 1969, a Muslim crowd gathered in the Jamalpur area of Ahmedabad to celebrate local *urs* (festival to mark the birth of a saint) at the tomb of Sufi Saint Bukhari Saheb. At the same time, *sadhus* of the nearby Jagannath temple were shepherding their cows back to the temple compound as a part of their routine. When the cows moved through the crowded streets, some Muslims got injured. In retaliation, some young Muslim men attacked the *sadhus* and damaged the temple windows. The head priest of the temple sat on a fast in protest. When a delegation of local Muslim leaders met him and apologised, he gave up the fast.

However, the matter did not end there. Later, some Hindus damaged a *dargah* (mausoleum) near the temple. A crowd of around 2,500-3,000

Muslims gathered in the area in the afternoon and attacked the temple on 19 September. On 20 September, a Muslim youth, upset about the destruction of his property, announced that he would seek revenge. Some Hindus beat him up and asked him to shout "*Jai Jagannath*" (Hail Lord Jagannath). The Muslim youth said he would rather die. The Hindu crowd poured petrol on him and burnt him to death.

This led to large-scale violence, death and destruction. It began from Ahmedabad but spread to other areas like Vadodara, Mehsana, Nadiad, Anand, Kheda, Gondal, Sabarkantha, Banaskantha, Surat, Rajkot and Jamnagar. The riots continued for three days.

"For full three days, the state government could not control the situation... In 1969, I remember Atal Bihari Vajpayee, who was then in the Opposition, asked in Parliament, 'Who started the riots in Gujarat?' I asked... how do you decide who started the Gujarat riots?"[2]

The Justice PJ Reddy Commission that was set up to inquire into the incident questioned the role of the police during the riots. The commission held that shops of Muslims were identified in advance and then systematically destroyed.

The riots had taken place during the tenure of Chief Minister Hitendra Desai of the Congress. There were reports of a conspiracy theory that held that the violence was 'deliberately engineered' to discredit the chief minister who was not loyal to then Prime Minister Indira Gandhi.[3]

Congress (O) leader Morarji Desai said after the riots, "We were caught unawares." The chief minister got away by blaming Hindu fundamentalists.

The Reddy Commission said in its report, "The situation got out of control at the very commencement of the riots.... The police were overwhelmed by the situation which confronted them."

Although 1969 was marked by the frequency and intensity of the riots, the entire decade witnessed many smaller incidents of communal violence. Between 1961 and 1971, there were 685 instances of communal violence in the urban areas of Gujarat. Another 114 cases were witnessed in rural areas.[4] Out of the 685 incidents, 578 happened in 1969 alone.[5]

Back in 1969, as seven large mills in Ahmedabad were shut down, and around 17,000 workers lost their jobs, the labour issue was seen through the communal lens wherein the Dalits among Hindus—over-represented among these workers when compared with the Muslims—felt a greater sense of insecurity, as the local Muslim workers were perceived to be more skilled in skills such as weaving.[6]

1980-1982: Riots revisited

Small-scale riots had taken place in Godhra in October 1980 over clashes between Sindhi and Ghanchi Muslims hawkers. Members of the two communities gathered and clashed, setting houses and shops on fire. Five Sindhis were burnt alive. Between March and September 1981, more riots took place that claimed the lives of 10 people.

In 1982, communal clashes occurred when Dussehra and Muharram coincided. Liquor traders from both the communities clashed with each other and looted each other's property. The news of the transfer of a Hindu police commissioner due to pressure from the Muslim community spread like wildfire, and the situation worsened. Hindu leaders used the opportunity to criticise Muslims for opening an Islamic study centre in Vadodara. As many as 19 riots occurred in the city in a short span of 10 months.[7]

1985: Reservation and Riots

The first half of 1985 witnessed communal clashes again. The state witnessed caste conflicts among the Hindus on the issue of enhanced reservations for the Other Backward Castes (OBCs). This later got overshadowed due to communal clashes between Hindus and Muslims. Riots began in Ahmedabad in February and continued till July.

Upper caste Hindus had declared a *bandh* on 18 March to oppose the government's enhanced reservation policy for OBCs. Violence spread to other parts of the state and the army was called to control the situation on 16 April 1985. Hundreds of people lost their lives. The state was under curfew for more than six months.

Between 1987 and 1991, close to 106 communal incidents took place in Gujarat. Political rivalry and conflicts during elections were responsible for triggering around 40 per cent of these riots. Tensions related to 'religious processions' were responsible for another 22 per cent of these clashes.[8]

The Dave Commission that inquired into the 1985 riots held the police responsible for not acting swiftly to stop violence. It also held that the police were totally unaware of the preparations for the agitation.

Some Muslim boys eloping with Hindu girls or vice versa have often become a reason for rioting.

The Black 1990s

Between April and December 1990, Gujarat witnessed nearly 1,400 incidents of communal violence that left 224 dead and 775 injured. Between January and April 1991, there were 120 cases of riots claiming 38 lives and injuring 170. The state witnessed riots after LK Advani's Ram Rath Yatra that started from Somnath in 1990. Violence continued for days and months.[9]

In September 1990, on the occasion of Ganesh *visarjan* (ceremony for immersion of the deity's idol), the walled city of Vadodara witnessed the worst-ever riots. First, the procession was attacked by some local Muslims. In retaliation, shops owned by Muslims in the walled city and Raopura were opened using gas cutters and then looted and burnt. The riots took place in full view of the police.[10]

Incidents of communal tension took place after the demolition of the controversial Babri Masjid on 6 December 1992. The riots that followed all across India were the worst seen in the country since the Partition. Close to 325 people were killed.[11]

Surat witnessed unprecedented violence after the Babri demolition. Though the official death toll in the city stood at 152, many went missing, and property worth crores was damaged. But nobody has been held accountable for the mayhem. The Chimanbhai Patel government set up a commission to inquire into the Surat riots under Justice IC Bhatt. Later, when Bhatt was appointed as Lokayukta in 1995-96, he was replaced by Justice PM Chauhan. The commission sought several extensions.

Shankersinh Vaghela, who was the chief minister then, ordered termination of the inquiry commission ruling out all objections by human rights groups. While giving justification for the termination, Vaghela said, "I am strongly against giving extensions to the inquiry commissions as they become an instrument of getting various allowances only." Whatever findings the commission may have got were buried in the process. The truth of the Surat riots is still being debated.

The only candid admission came from BJP MLA Atmaram Parmar, who defended those accused in the riot cases: "To the best of my knowledge, not a single person had been convicted in any case of 1992 riots."[12]

Godhra Riots (2002)

Fifty Nine *Ramsewaks* were burnt to death in the Sabarmati Express train at Godhra on 27 February. Large scale riots followed in various parts of the State, showing unprecedented barbarism. A detailed report on this follows in the next chapter. Official figures put the number of deaths at 790 Muslims, 254 Hindus and 223 missing.[13] Unofficial estimates by human rights groups put this figure between 1500 and 2000.

Reasons for Riots

Perusal of the history of riots mentioned above demonstrates that riots can be triggered by frivolous reasons and can last for months. Rather than blaming one group or the other, it is essential to understand the reasons for these riots. A brilliant analysis of riot triggers is given by Saba Naqvi and Smruti Koppikar.[14]

- **Social:** The feeling of being left out of the discourse. This is especially prevalent among minorities who are excluded, deliberately or otherwise, from mainstream events and activities, leading to ghettoisation.
- **Economic:** The feeling of being left behind. Poor education and unemployment lead to marginalisation of the have-nots. This feeling is heightened by a sense of deprivation and sight of conspicuous consumption.
- **Political:** Parties and politicians play on the emotions of vote banks, often to expand it, by mobilising mobs and whipping up passions and fears over illegal immigration and demographic change.

- **Administrative:** The feeling of being targetted and/or ignored by the immediate touch-points of government— the police and civic administration. Denial of rights and harassment spawn a sense of injustice.
- **Religious:** Perceived slights to sentiments. Can be sparked by a procession in a 'sensitive' area; a loud prayer, a road blocked for prayers, or an animal's carcass thrown into a place of worship.
- **Commercial:** Rivalries sparked off by encroachment of traditional areas of business and economic activity.
- **Verbal:** Provocative speeches that stereotype and instigate the intended target on the basis of language, religion and sexual habits. Rabble-rousing about 'appeasement'. Sporting events as a test of patriotism and nationalism.
- **Global:** Rumours and whispers that travel across the wired world about defacement or denigration of Holy Scriptures and holy figures in books, movies, newspaper articles, posters, cartoons.

The Dark Days
Godhra and Post-Godhra Riots

Things fall apart; the centre cannot hold;
Mere anarchy is loosed upon the world,
The blood-dimmed tide is loosed, and everywhere
The ceremony of innocence is drowned;
The best lack all conviction, while the worst
Are full of passionate intensity.

— WB Yeats in "The Second Coming"

27 February 2002, Godhra

One of the most ghastly tragedies witnessed by the people of Gujarat took place in Godhra on 27 February 2002 when 59 innocent *Ramsewaks* returning from Ayodhya were charred to death. The plot of this tragedy was laid on the night of 26 February 2002 at the now infamous Aman Guest House in Godhra. The riots that ensued after the burning of the express train were inhuman to say the least, and they still invoke a feeling of outrage towards the barbaric behaviour of a human being towards another. The riots will be etched in the memory of all for a very long time.

Night of 26 February 2002

Salim Panwala, Salim Jarda, Irfan Patiala, Jabir Behra, Imran Bhatuk, Kasim Biryani, Hasan Charkha, Shaukat Lalu and a few others—all Ghanchi Muslims—took a green coloured 'tempy rickshaw'(small delivery van) and went to the petrol pump of Kalabhai at 9:30 pm. They were soon joined by Razak Kurkur, who had obtained petrol from the same pump. They had got hold of seven to eight carboys of 20 litres each. They then stored the filled carboys at the Aman Guest House owned by Kurkur.

The same night when they were standing at a *paan* shop of Razak

Kurkur, two leaders of their community Haji Bilal and Faruk Bhana came there and told them that they had met *Maulvi* Husain Haji Ibrahim Umarji and that the *maulvi* had asked them to set S6 coach of the Sabarmati Express on fire. Since the train was running late from its scheduled time, they decided to meet again at 6 am the next morning.

Salim Jarda, who did not want to associate with such an evil act, was slapped and threatened that if he told anything about the plan to anyone, he would be killed. Razak Kurkur then asked him to go inside a room and sleep.

On the morning of 27 February 2002, at about 7:30 am, Razak Kurkur told Jabir Behera, Irfan Patiala, Irfan Bhodha and Shaukat Lalu to take out the carboys from the room and put them in the tempy and go near the 'A' cabin.

Jabir's brother Ramzani drove the tempy. Mahebub Latiko and Shaukat Lalu sat with him. At the rear of the tempy, there were Jabir Behra, Irfan Patiala, Irfan Bhodha, Rafik Bhatuk and a Hindu boy. Salim Panwala followed them on his vehicle. Razak Kurkur, who was going with Salim, was carrying a petrol-filled carboy with him.

III-Fated Sabarmati Express

The ill-fated 9166 UP Sabarmati Express had started from Muzaffarpur in Bihar on 25 February 2002 for Ahmedabad. At Ayodhya, the train was boarded by *Ramsevaks* who had gone there to perform *yajna* as part of the programme organised by the VHP. The train was heavily crowded and about 2,200 *Ramsevaks* were travelling in it, most of them without reservation. The train had a trouble-free journey from Ayodhya to Godhra.

On 27 February 2002, the train that was scheduled to arrive at Godhra at 2:55 am was running late by about five hours. It reached the station at 7:43 am and left the Godhra station at 7:48 am. In those five minutes of halt, some minor skirmishes happened between some *Ramsevaks* and Muslim vendors on platform no. 1 where the train had stopped. Salim Panwala, who had gone to collect petrol the previous night with the others, spread a rumour that *Ramsevaks* had attempted to abduct a Muslim girl Sofiabanu. This agitated some people who were standing outside the station on the front side of the train. They started pelting stones, aimed at the passengers. Some passengers standing on the platform also threw stones back at them. Two police constables intervened and asked the passengers to sit in the train.

Soon after, the train started chugging forward. But suddenly, the chain was pulled simultaneously from four different coaches Nos. 83101, 5343, 9273 and 88238 at 7:49 am; the train stopped after moving about 60-70 metres. All these coaches were at the rear end of the train. The guard at the rear end of the train set the chains right in two coaches. Assistant driver Mukesh Pachori, who came from the engine side of the train, set right the vacuum in the other two coaches. After the chain pulling was set right, the train resumed its journey at 7:55 am.

When the train was beginning to pick up speed, a mob standing on the left hand or the Singal Falia side—"singal" is how "signal" is known colloquially in Gujarat—started throwing stones at the train. Someone pulled the chain again. The driver noticed that the brakes applied automatically due to the vacuum thus generated. At about 8 am, the train gradually stopped at the 'A' Cabin, which was about three-fourths of a kilometre from the Godhra railway station.

A mob of about 400-500 persons were standing there on the left side; they were pelting stones at the train. The guard disembarked on the right hand side and informed the station master of Godhra and requested for police help. The guard had also seen a mob towards the front side of the train with weapons in their hands. The passengers in the coaches closed the shutters of the windows.

The driver of the ill-fated train, Rajendrarao, spotted a big mob near the 'A' Cabin from the Masjid side on the right side of the train. Some persons in the mob got closer to the engine and threatened Rajendrarao and his assistant Mukesh Pachori that if they got down from the train, they would be cut into pieces. They closed the windows and doors of the engine and locked themselves from inside.

The mob continued to throw stones at the train while moving towards the rear side. Some persons in the mob were shouting *"Maar daalo, kaat daalo"*. At 8:05 am, the station superintendent informed the city police, collector and deputy superintendent of police of Godhra about the continuous stone-pelting at the train. The guard and the driver had already reported the matter to the station superintendent on phone.

At about 8:15 am, smoke was seen coming out of the S6 coach. The fire brigade was informed at 8:20 am, and they reached the site at around 8:30 am. By then, the coach was burning intensely. Two Muslim leaders, Haji Bilal and Faruk Bhana, who were leading the mob, prevented fire tenders from reaching the 'A' Cabin where the train was stopped and attacked.

Coach S6 of the Sabarmati Express was overcrowded. There were more than 200 persons therein, most of whom were Ramsevaks. Many passengers sat on the floor of the coach. They sat between the seats and in the passage right up to the lavatories on either side of the two ends of the coach. The coach was jam-packed and there was hardly any space to walk.

At about 8:25 am, the guard of the train informed the station superintendent of Godhra that the fire brigade should be summoned because some coaches were on fire. Stone pelting on the S6 coach continued for another 10-15 minutes. Some of the passengers were so frightened that they took shelter on the upper berths or under the lower berths. The conspirators arrived near coach S6 with the carboys. Mohmed Latika cut open the canvass of the adjoining coach S7, and through that opening, he and Jabir climbed on with two carboys. The connecting door of S6 was then forcibly opened.

After entering the coach, someone opened the door of S6 on the 'A' Cabin side. From that door, Irfan and other persons carrying carboys entered the coach. All of them stood near the lavatories and threw the carboys in the coach. The guard observed that the window panes of quite a few coaches were broken and there was fire in one of the coaches.

About 60 litres of inflammable liquid was used to burn the entire coach that further led to a big fire and killed 59 passengers (one person succumbed to his burn injuries). Among the dead, there were 27 women and 10 children. Forty eight passengers were seriously injured.

Passengers inside coach S6 had seen the mob outside. Some members from the mob threw stones, burning rags and other inflammable materials inside the coaches through the broken glass windows. Smoke blinded everyone inside the coaches. It was later found that 13 of the 19 windows of the S6 coach on the Singal Falia side were damaged or broken. These openings were used to throw burning rags and bottles filled with inflammable material inside the train. The action and conduct of the mob was frightening.

Another attack by the mob took place sometime between 11 am and 11:45 am when the train was being shunted. Two large Muslim mobs of about 700 were seen coming towards the train, where the passengers and other railway staff were waiting. This mob also started pelting stones. They were repeatedly ordered to go away, but they did not pay any heed. Apprehending serious consequences, the police resorted to baton-charge and firing. Two persons died and one got injured. Around six or seven policemen were injured in the stone-pelting by the miscreant mob.

The events described above are as per the findings of the Nanavati-Shah Commission that looked into the incident and concluded that the Godhra train carnage was a "pre-planned conspiracy". The GT Nanavati-Akshya Mehta Judicial Inquiry Commission, during its six-year probe examined more than 40,000 applications and testimonies of more than 1,000 witnesses to reach its conclusion. There are other versions as well, but this judicial commission is considered the most authentic and impartial.

Shah Commission

On 6 March 2002, the state government set up a commission under Justice KJ Shah, retired judge of the Gujarat High Court, to inquire into the "incident of 27 February 2002 and subsequent incidences of violence in the state". The commission was to give its report in three months.

Nanavati-Shah Commission

There was a hue and cry across the country after the appointment of the commission since a one-member commission could be questioned on the ground of impartiality. Justice Shah was a government pleader. The appointment came under criticism from riot victims' organisations, social activists and political parties. Most of them wanted that the commission should be headed by a Supreme Court judge; some even said that the presiding officer should be a non-Gujarati. On 21 May 2002, the commission was reconstituted into a two-member commission. Retired Judge of the Supreme Court of India, Justice GT Nanavati was appointed as the chairperson of the commission. Nanavati had held the position of Chief Justice of the High Courts of Karnataka and Orissa before his elevation to the apex court.

On 3 June 2002, the government extended the term of the commission to 5 December 2002. It also redefined the scope by saying that the inquiry should cover "events and incidences between 27 February 2002 and 30 March 2002".

Through an Extraordinary Notification on 20 July 2004, the state government widened the scope of the commission. First, it widened the period that was to be covered. Now all the incidences between 27 February 2002 and 31 May 2002 had to be covered. Second, it sought to take care of the widespread criticism that the role of the chief minister, ministers, officials of the state government, other individuals and organisations were not being inquired into. The notification brought all these within the mandate of the commission.

Now the commission also had to inquire into the dealings of these organisational heads with political or non-political organisations that may have been involved in the incidents, and how these people may have acted while providing protection, relief and rehabilitation to the victims of communal riots. As per this new notification, the report was to be submitted on or before 5 December 2005.

Nanavati-Mehta Commission

Justice Shah died on 22 March 2008. The vacancy caused by his death was filled up by the government through a notification on 5 April 2008. It appointed retired judge Akshay Kumar Mehta (of the Gujarat High Court). The commission, henceforth, came to be known as Nanavati-Mehta Commission. The commission submitted the first part of its reports related to the Godhra incident on 18 September 2008.

The commission received 46,494 statements or affidavits, of which 2019 were from government officers. In respect of Godhra and post-Godhra incidences, the commission examined and recorded (till 22 October 2005) evidence of 1016 witnesses. The hearing continued till 26 June 2007. Asked for his opinion on the reconstitution of the commission, former Chief Justice of Gujarat High Court, Justice TU Mehta said: "It is a bit strange. It is something new. But appointing a retired Supreme Court judge leaves no scope for any controversy now."

In January 2014, the term of the commission was extended to 30

June 2014. This was the 21st extension given to the commission. The commission's findings on the post-Godhra riots have yet not come. Some political commentators had contentions challenging the theory of Justice Nanavati. The commission rejected those arguments. On the various theories that were doing the rounds, the commission gave its own opinion.

Possibility of attack from outside

The commission disagreed with the contentions of the Justice UC Banerjee Committee* and the Jan Sangharsha Manch, which represented the riot victims before the commission, that alarm chains could not be operated from outside under the modified system introduced by the Railways in 1995. Quoting a railway officer of the carriage and wagon department, Ahmedabad, it said the alarm chain could still be pulled from outside. Quoting a number of surviving passengers, the commission said that they had seen the mob outside the coach throwing stones and also some "burning rags" and some "inflammable liquid materials" through the windows. "The passengers had informed DSP Raju Bhargava at about 8.30 am that the train was attacked by a mob and many passengers were injured and killed. Where was the time or reason for the passengers to concoct a false story," it asked.

"Considering the situation prevailing then, it is highly unlikely that the passengers had any discussion amongst themselves and they had decided to give a false version about the attack on the train," it said. The report said, the passengers immediately after getting down from the coach, gave the same version of the mob attack and throwing of inflammable materials inside the coach to the district collector.

---

*　On 17 May 2004, Lalu Prasad Yadav became the Union Minister of Railways. In September 2004, Yadav appointed former retired Supreme Court Judge, Justice Umesh Chandra Banerjee to investigate the incident. In January 2005, two days before election in Lalu Prasad's native state of Bihar, Banerjee concluded that the fire was accidental.

Banerjee's findings were challenged by Neelkanth Tulsidas Bhatia who was injured in the incident. On 13 October 2006, the Gujarat High Court termed the setting up of the panel as illegal and quashed the conclusions of Justice Banerjee. It ruled that the investigation was "unconstitutional, illegal and null and void", and declared its formation as a "colourable exercise of power with mala fide intentions", and its argument of accidental fire "opposed to the prima facie accepted facts on record". On 3 July 2006, the Supreme Court refused to stay the order of the Gujarat High Court that termed the panel as "illegal".

The commission cited the second instance of attack when the coach was being shunted and concluded that this refuted the theory that the fire was accidental.

No evidence of abduction or attempt thereof

The commission said that there was no evidence to justify the contention that the *Ramsevaks* had been fighting with Muslim vendors at stations before Godhra as alleged earlier, though there were some minor scuffles with three Muslim vendors on the Godhra platform. Although there was no reliable evidence to show that any attempt was made by the *Ramsevaks* to abduct Sofiabanu, Salim Panwala spread a "false rumour" to that effect to collect a mob that started pelting stones at the passengers.

No possibility of "accidental fire"

The Nanavati commission rejected the "accidental fire" theory stating that the reasoning that a fire was caused by the overturning of a burning stove used for cooking by some *Ramsevaks* in the compartment—or that it was set off by an electric short circuit—were baseless. There was no space for anyone to light a stove in the overcrowded coach carrying more than 200 passengers, and any spill over of kerosene from the stove, though out of the question, could not have caused such heavy fire and damage.

Short circuit theory dismissed

The commission said, in such an event, the passengers would not have climbed up to the upper berths to protect themselves, as electric lines were going through the top of the coaches; rather, they would have climbed down to the floor. In such an event, the windows on the platform side of the coach would not have been closed or broken by stone throwing.

"The smoke before fire" did not necessarily mean electric short circuit as propounded by the Manch, the commission opined, explaining that the fire was caused by some inflammable materials thrown on the floor of the coaches from outside.

The commission said the Centre or the Railways had not appeared before it to claim that the fire was accidental. On the contrary, the railway officials and the Government Railway Protection Force personnel present on the spot had stated that the attack was by Muslim mobs and that the coach was set ablaze by petrol.

Conviction

In March 2011, Additional Sessions Judge PR Patel held 31 persons guilty of a "pre-planned conspiracy" and setting fire to coach S6.[1] In the incident, 59 people, mostly *Ramsevaks* of the VHP, were killed. Of the 31 found guilty, the court sentenced 11 convicts to death, particularly those it believed were present at a meeting held the previous night at the Aman Guest House. The other 20 convicts were sentenced to life imprisonment. The Government of Gujarat challenged the trial court's decision to acquit 61 persons in the Godhra train burning case before the Gujarat High Court and sought death sentences for 20 convicts who had been awarded life imprisonment in the case.[2] The trial is now on at the said high court.

Post-Godhra riots

The media reported extensively on post-Godhra events. A Special Investigation Team (SIT) was appointed on 26 March 2008 by the Supreme Court to probe into the nine reported riot cases in Gujarat in 2002. The five-member SIT was headed by former CBI director RK Raghavan. Other members were CB Satpathy (ex DGP), Geeta Johri (then IGP now Additional DGP), Shivanand Jha (then IGP now additional DGP) and Ashish Bhatia (IGP). The following details are based on media reports and findings of the SIT.

On 27 April 2009, the court asked the SIT to look into the complaints of Zakia Jafri, wife of former Congress MP Ehsan Jafri who was killed in the riot at Gulbarg society. The SIT was asked to particularly look into her charge that the chief minister had wilfully allowed the 2002 riots and that the whole State machinery including the police was complicit.

The SIT submitted its first interim report on 12 May 2010 and the second on 17 November 2011. Because of certain issues raised by the *amicus curiae*, senior advocate Raju Ramachandran, about findings of the SIT's interim report, the Supreme Court on 5 May 2011 asked him to assess the SIT report and look into the lapses, if any, and examine witnesses.

The *amicus curiae* has questioned the SIT report particularly about the role of the chief minister on the night of 27 February 2002 and the presence of two ministers at two police control rooms the next day.

The SIT submitted its closure report to the Supreme Court in February 2012 that was made public on 8 May 2012. It disagreed with the *amicus curiae*'s contention and said that Mr Ramachandran had based his findings on only one witness.

"This recommendation of *amicus curiae* is based on the sole testimony of Sanjiv Bhatt, then DCI (Security) who has claimed to have attended a meeting called by the Chief Minister on 27.02.2002 night (day of Godhra train carnage) at his residence," the report said.

"It may be mentioned here that seven other participants of the said meeting, who are senior officers, have categorically stated that Shri Sanjiv Bhatt did not attend the said meeting."[3]

The Supreme Court did not take any position on the two reports, but disagreed that the riots cases cannot get justice in Gujarat courts. It sent both the reports—of the SIT and the *amicus curiae*—to the court trying the Gulberg society case. The trial court rejected Zakia Jafri's protest petition in December 2013.

One may differ from the findings of the SIT, since this is part of democracy, but an average person has no other credible basis to frame his opinion than this report which is exhaustive, comprehensive and answers most questions. The voluminous SIT report runs into 541 pages; the team has done detailed investigation into the cases assigned. It also cross examined the chief minister of Gujarat.

Senior BJP leader and distinguished lawyer Arun Jaitley has rejected the opinion of the *amicus curiae*: "There is no provision under the code of criminal procedure of the Evidence Act for the opinion of a lawyer or an *amicus curiae*. Investigation is exclusively a police function and not a lawyer's function. Police is trained for investigations but a lawyer is not."[4]

Also, the SIT investigations in other cases of riots helped bring the cases to a logical conclusion. Its investigations were considered by and large fair.

Riot Chronology
27 February 2002

As the news of burning of the Sabarmati Express train spread (27 February 2002), an infuriated VHP called for a state-wide *bandh* (strike).

Tight security was put in place as the VHP declared a *bandh*. Criticising this measure in the town, the VHP Joint Secretary RS Pankaj said they (the government) had created hurdles in the movement of vehicles carrying food for *karsewaks* (*Ramsewaks*). "The unnecessary curbs should be withdrawn and our religious functions should be allowed to be performed in peace," he said.[5]

"Indefinite curfew was clamped and the shoot-at-sight order issued in Godhra town immediately after the incident as large-scale violence erupted."[6] By the end of the day on 28 February, curfew was declared in 27 towns and cities.[7]

Early in the morning at 9 am, the chief minister came to know through a top government official what had happened in Godhra. He immediately held discussions with Minister of State for Home, Gordhan Zadaphia, ACS Narayan and other officials of home and police departments. He asked them to collect facts so that he could inform the assembly that was in session. He underlined the sensitivity of Godhra and directed the officials to take all necessary steps such as imposing curfew and rushing more forces to Godhra.

The chief minister had to attend the assembly because the state budget had to be declared the same day. After the assembly proceedings were over, Modi left for Vadodara by a government chartered plane. From there, he took an ONGC helicopter to rush to Godhra. Only two officials, his secretary Anil Mukim and PRO Jagdish Thakkar, were with him. He reached Godhra at 5 pm. He was received by Jayanti Ravi who was the district magistrate. They all drove to Godhra railway station.

After seeing the dead bodies, the two burnt coaches and interacting with the agitated crowd, Modi left for the civil hospital to meet the injured. Before leaving, he told the crowd that they should maintain peace. From the civil hospital, he went to the collectorate and held a meeting with government and police officials. By this time, two other ministers—Ashok Bhatt, then health minister, and Zadaphia—had also reached there and attended the meeting.

In the meeting, it was decided that all the bodies would be taken to Ahmedabad. The chief minister instructed that the dead bodies be kept at the Sola civil Hospital on the outskirts of Ahmedabad to avoid the situation from becoming tense. It was concluded that the relatives of the victims need not come to Godhra for identification and claiming of the bodies as the town was under curfew. The modalities for carrying out the operation were left to the administration.

In his interaction with the media at Godhra, Modi asserted that "the culprits would not be spared". The chief minister stated that the incident appeared to be "serious and pre-planned conspiracy". And he also announced that a compensation of Rs 2 lakh would be given to the families of all the deceased. He clarified that his assessment was based on the facts narrated to him by persons who were present on the spot as well as the injured people in the hospital.

At 7:30 pm, the chief minister, along with Mukim and Thakkar, left for Vadodara from where they took a chartered flight to Ahmedabad. Modi reached his Gandhinagar residence at 10:30 pm and summoned top officials for an emergency meeting. This meeting, which took place at about 11 pm at his residence, was attended by Swarna Kanta Varma, Acting Chief Secretary (ACS), Ashok Narayan (ACS Home), K Chakarvarthy (DGP), PC Pande (Commissioner of Police, Ahmedabad), K Nityanandam (Home Secretary), PK Mishra (PS) and Anil Mukim.

Modi briefed the officials about his visit and they too informed him about the precautionary measures taken. He instructed them to take all possible steps to maintain peace. He asked ACS (Home) Narayan to inquire from the local army headquarters about their availability. He also asked them to seek additional forces from neighbouring states. Since he had come to know of the VHP *bandh* call for the next day, he asked them to take all measures to prevent any untoward incident. He categorically told them "to maintain peace and communal harmony".[8]

28 February 2002

The news of the Godhra train incident flashed across all newspapers. The English dailies referred to the attackers at Godhra as belonging to "a certain community", both in their headlines and the reports. *The*

Times of India reported, "… some unidentified persons attacked the train…" PTI called them "miscreants", and so did *rediff.com*. The report in The *Financial Express* used the PTI wire and called the attackers "an angry mob".

Gujarat Samachar and *Sandesh*, the two Gujarati language newspapers, described the attackers as "*jhanoni tatva*" (mad elements) and "*rakshasi todu*" (devilish band) respectively. *Sandesh* kept harping on one fact throughout its reports that Hindus were the victims in the train burning incident.[9]

A ministry official held that although the circumstances were tense in Vadodara and Ahmedabad, the situation was under control. He was also confident that the police deployed were enough to prevent any violence. In Vadodara, the administration also imposed curfew in seven areas. The deputy superintendent of police stated that the Rapid Action Force (RAF) had been deployed in sensitive areas in Godhra. Gordhan Zadaphia, the state home minister, believed there would be no retaliation from the Hindu community.[10]

The Gujarat legislative assembly was in its morning session. It lasted for only 10 minutes. After paying homage to the victims, the assembly adjourned at 8:40 am. The chief minister gave a statement in the assembly where he ordered a judicial inquiry. He rushed for a cabinet meeting after which he took a review meeting of the law and order situation. The officials informed him that the army was not available in the Ahmedabad cantonment. Modi spoke to Union Home Minister LK Advani and requested him for immediate army help.

The SIT has stated that the requests for additional security forces were made to the then Congress-ruled states of Madhya Pradesh, Rajasthan and Maharashtra by the Gujarat government on 28 February but were refused. Seeing the situation go out of control on 28 February, a fax to that effect was sent to the defence ministry at 2:30 pm.[11]

Modi interacted with the media in the afternoon. He informed them about the decision to set up an inquiry commission. He issued an appeal through the media asking the general public to maintain peace and communal harmony. He got the same message recorded and it was continuously broadcast on Doordarshan.

Modi's request for army help was immediately responded to by the

Nationa Democratic Alliance (NDA) government that was in power at the Centre. The army started arriving from the night of 28 February and continued to pour in the next day. Modi had instructed the administration to immediately requisition the army and deploy them.[12]

On 28 February, an indefinite curfew was clamped in Ahmedabad as violence erupted in the city during the VHP-sponsored Gujarat *bandh*. Curfew was imposed also on the Rajkot town.[13]

Troops were airlifted in 40 aircraft from the border. They started landing in Ahmedabad by midnight. In addition, shoot-at-sight orders were also issued by the Gujarat government.[14] Modi requested then Defence Minister George Fernandes to visit Ahmedabad. Fernandes reached the city in the night of Thursday and had a detailed discussion with Modi on the prevaling situation.[15] The Union government despatched around 1,000 paramilitary personnel to Gujarat and asked the army to be on standby to maintain law and order in the state. Eleven companies of paramilitary forces were dispatched to Gujarat and were supposed to reach there by Thursday night.[16]

The reports from Vadodara in two major newspapers, *The Times of India* and *The Indian Express*, were unnerving. The Islamic Study Centre on Ajwa Road was destroyed. Human rights activist Prof JS Bandukwala's cars were burnt in his house compound. *The Times of India* office in Vadodara was stormed by a mob demanding more pro-Hindu news. Mobs attacked shops, *laaris* (hand-pulled carts of vegetable and fruit vendors) and cabins across the city. Stabbings took place at various places. Curfew was imposed on Karelibag, Wadi, Navapura, Raopura, Panigate and city police station areas.

There were no signs of violence abating in Ahmedabad, where nine columns of the army were deployed just before noon. The size of some rioting mobs was as large as 5,000.[17] Various newspapers and magazines reported that the strength of people in the crowd varied from 5000-15,000.[18]

Naroda Patiya

The same day a mob of about 5,000 attacked and attempted to burn alive all the residents of Naroda Patiya, a suburban town in Ahmedabad. The rioting began at 9 am when the nearby Noorani Mosque was destroyed by exploding LPG cylinders.

The rioters hacked, looted and stabbed the victims, sexually assaulted the women and burnt alive as many people as they could. Many people were burnt alive individually. Some groups were set on fire after chasing them into huge pits and setting fire to them using LPG cylinders. A number of buildings in the residential and working areas were also destroyed by the use of LPG cylinders. The burnt bodies were then thrown in a dry well.[19]

The massacre lasted for over 10 hours, and claimed lives of around 125 people. After the riots were over, 94 bodies were recovered; three people were reported missing and were later declared dead. More than 30 people were found injured. The dead comprised 36 women, 35 children and 26 men.

The SIT's findings added 24 names to the 46 people arrested by the police making the number 70. Before the trial began, six of the accused died. In 2009, the trial started, during which three of the accused died. Thus, the final report covered 61 people.

Maya Kodnani, Babu Bajrangi and a few others instigated the mobs and supplied weapons to them while Suresh Chara and others raped and killed women, the SIT report said.

Special Trial Court Judge Jyotsna Yagnik delivered the first verdict on 29 August 2012. It convicted Maya Kodnani, sitting MLA from Naroda and former Minister for Women and Child Development of Gujarat, and Bajrang Dal's Babu Bajrangi, for criminal conspiracy and murder. It also convicted 30 other people for murder, criminal conspiracy and other criminal charges, and acquitted 29, giving them the benefit of the doubt.

The sentencing that came on 31 August gave Kodnani a 28-years prison term. Bajrangi received life imprisonment. Of the rest, 22 were sentenced to a minimum of 14 years and 7 to a minimum of 21 years in prison. One of the convicted, Suresh alias Shahjad Nekalkar, absconded and his sentencing was deferred.

Gulbarg Society

On 28 February 2002, at about 12:20 pm, the control room received a message from Police Inspector of Meghaninagar police station that

Gulbarg society, a Muslim society in the area, had been surrounded by a mob of 10,000. They were pelting stones and also setting fire to nearby shops and rickshaws. The police inspector requested the control room for additional forces.

On receipt of this message, three officers—GD Solanki (Dy SP group VIII), Ajit Kumar Gupta (Dy SP group XII) and AB Qureshi (PI CID crime)—were deputed to go to the spot to assist the police inspector at Meghaninagar. At about 1:45 pm, some troops of CISF were also sent. At 2:05 pm, MK Tandon (Joint CP sector II) sent a message to the control room that the people and Ehsan Jafri (Ex MP) had been surrounded by the mob in Gulbarg society and extra force and PI Sardarnagar be sent there to shift them.

At 2:14 pm, another message was received from senior PI KG Erda, Meghaninagar PS, that a mob of about 10,000 person had gathered at Gulbarg society (Kalapinagar) and were about to set fire to the entire society and as such ACP, DCP along with additional force be sent immediately. At 2:45 pm, Erda sent a message to the control room that Muslims in Gulbarg society had been surrounded by a mob of 10,000 from all sides and even the police force was surrounded by the mob.

When MK Tandon (JCP) reached Gulbarg society at 4 pm, he found that many houses had been set ablaze and many people were killed including Ehsan Jafri and his family. The mob was still there pelting stones and throwing acid bombs and burning rags to prevent the police from rescuing the surviving inmates. He ordered firing by the CISF, which led to casualties.[20] As many as 69 people were killed in the riot.

On 8 June 2006, Zakia Jafri, widow of late Ehsan Jafri, wrote to the DGP seeking registration of an FIR against Narendra Modi and 62 others. After getting a negative response, she moved the Gujarat High Court on 1 May 2007. On 2 November 2007, the Gujarat High Court rejected her plea for registration of FIR against the chief minister.

On 3 March 2008, the Supreme Court issued notices to the Union Government and Gujarat government on Zakia Jafri's plea. It also appointed an *amicus curiae* to assist the Court. On 26 March, the apex court appointed a Special Investigation Team (SIT) under former CBI Director RK Raghavan, to investigate the riot cases. On 27 April 2009, the Supreme Court asked the SIT to look into her complaint as well.

The SIT has given its closure report that has exonerated Chief Minister Narendra Modi of any blame for the riots. *Amicus Curiae* Raju Ramchandran disagreed with the SIT report on this part. The Supreme Court asked the Ahmedabad Metropolitan Court to study both the reports and arrive at its own conclusions. After studying the SIT report, Zakia Jafri submitted her final argument before the magistrate in September 2013, challenging the contention of the SIT. On 26 December 2013, the court rejected her protest petition and asked her to approach the higher court to seek relief in the matter.[21]

1 March 2002

The officials of the government of Gujarat met George Fernandes at 8:30 am and requested that paramilitary forces and BSF be deployed in Gujarat. Five companies of paramilitary forces were subsequently deployed. Thereafter, the chief minister met the governor and issued instructions for safe passage of Haj pilgrims. He even met a delegation of Congress leaders whom he assured of the best possible help in the situation. Later, Modi convened meetings, announced compensation for victims, discussed relief packages for camps being run by NGOs and gave directions for essential medical and other services to be provided to people in the riot-affected areas. By the evening, the army was fully deployed, "within 24 hours of the riots starting".[22]

In the morning, Fernandes toured the city along with Minister of State for Defence Harin Pathak and later told reporters that a brigade of the army was already in Ahmedabad and that another would be coming shortly.[23] The army began flag marches in the worst affected areas of Ahmedabad, Rajkot, Vadodara and Godhra cities and shoot-at-sight order was extended to all 34 curfew-bound cities and towns in Gujarat. The chief minister said that the flag marches had a salutary effect. He pointed out that one army brigade had already begun the flag marches, while another brigade was expected to arrive in the night.[24] Modi asked the police to "strictly deal" with arsonists.[25]

The chief minister said that 136 people had died and 1,137 were arrested in the two days of violence since 27 February. Of these, 119 persons had died in Ahmedabad. Police fired 311 rounds all over the state that killed 17 people. Curfew was imposed in 14 districts and

Ahmedabad and Vadodara witnessed maximum casualties.[26]

The state-wide figure included victims of an incident where members of a funeral procession burnt 33 people alive at Bakor-Pandarwada village, 70 km from Godhra. The funeral procession turned into a rampaging mob, apparently to avenge the death of three people earlier in the day.[27] Roshan Nagar in the Navy Yard in Vadodara was attacked twice; here two people died in police firing. Muslim families living in tense areas moved towards Wadi, Binanagar and Tandalja. Three men were burnt alive in a mosque; four died in police firing in Navayard, Gayatrinagar and Kisanwadi. Factories in Sardar Estate were burnt down.[28]

On 1 March, Vadodara again witnessed attacks by an angry mob. Factories in GIDC were attacked. Three people were burnt to death in a warehouse. Halol Trucks, Lucky Studios and factories were burnt on the Halol-Kalol highway. One person was killed in police firing in Savli. By the turn of the day, the toll of violence in all of Gujarat had risen to 252.[29]

Sardarpura Riots

A strong mob attacked a Muslim locality in Sardarpura village of the Vijapur *taluka* in the Mehsana district. They surrounded a lane called 'Sheikh Vaas', the habitation of the minority community, on the intervening night of 28 February and 1 March 2002. Members of the community took shelter in a house owned by one Ibrahim Sheikh. The mob torched the house after throwing petrol on it. This killed 33 people including 22 women.

In all, 76 accused were arrested in the Sardarpura case by the police. The court framed charges against 73 in June 2009 and initiated a trial. The trial court acquitted 42 accused but convicted 31 for murder and other charges. Two of the accused died during the trial, while one accused, who was a juvenile, is being tried in a juvenile court.

It was a historic verdict since it was the first case in which such a large number of people were convicted for mob violence. The maximum record was for conviction of 14 people in the Bhagalpur riot case.

This was the first case, probed by the Supreme Court-appointed SIT, on which the verdict has been pronounced.[30]

The Best Bakery Case (Tulsi Bakery Case)

A small bakery outlet in the Hanuman Tekri area of Vadodara was attacked by a mob on 1 March 2002. A family of Sheikh ran the bakery. The mob set fire to the bakery killing 14 people who were present inside. This included the entire family of the Sheikh and three Hindu employees.

The trial court let off all the accused due to lack of sufficient evidence. The judgement of the Additional Sessions Judge, HU Mahida, of the Vadodara fast track court that came on 27 July 2003 said: "It was proved beyond doubt that a violent mob had attacked the bakery and killed 14 persons. However, there was no legally acceptable evidence to prove that any of the accused presented before the court had committed the crime." The judgement was critical of the police for delay in registering an FIR and for not investigating the incident properly and harassing innocent people. It let off all the 21 accused.

The State government challenged the fast track court's acquittal but the Gujarat High Court dismissed the appeal in 2003. The Supreme Court admitted Gujarat government's appeal against the acquittal in March 2004. Later, the apex court ordered a retrial and shifted the case to Mumbai.

Sessions Judge Abhay Thipsay in 2006 convicted 9 of the 17 accused, who were retried since four others were absconding.

Prime witness and complainant Zaheera Sheikh repeatedly changed her stance. In 2006, the Supreme Court sentenced her to one year of imprisonment for contempt of court after a high-powered committee indicted her as a "self-condemned liar". She served her jail term in Nasik jail and came out in June 2007.

In July 2012, the Mumbai High Court, however, acquitted five of the nine accused. It upheld life term for four.

2 March 2002

Curfew was clamped in five police station areas in Surat and cable operators were told to shut down operations following overnight violence.

A British national Mohammad Aswat Nallabhai visiting Gujarat was killed and two of his family members went missing. The family was assaulted in Himmatnagar, 160 km from Ahmedabad, when Nallabhai was on his way from New Delhi to Lajpur village in Gujarat for a social visit, along with three of his relatives. That day about 250 people were killed in the violence.[31]

On the political front, the Congress accused the chief minister of making provocative statements. The chief minister immediately issued a rebuttal. "This charge is totally baseless. I am the chief minister of Gujarat and I am committed to maintain law and order in the state. Neither I nor any of my colleagues has made any statement, which helped in spreading violence in the state," he stressed. He was responding to Congress president Sonia Gandhi's charge that some statements of his had encouraged hooligans to go on rampage in the state.[32] However, he accused news channels of deliberately playing up the pictures of violence.

3 March 2002

The communal violence that flared up in parts of Gujarat in the last four days had so far claimed 427 lives. The death toll in Ahmedabad alone mounted to 213 as more and more bodies were recovered from the debris of burnt houses in Naroda, Bapunagar and the outskirts of the city.[33] Of the 427 deaths, 73 were killed in police firing at different places.

The most tragic incident on this date, however, was the Bilkis Bano case in Dahod district.

Bilkis Bano

On 3 March 2002, Bilkis Bano, a 19-year-old pregnant Muslim woman, along with some members of her family and neighbourhood, left Radhikpur village (Dahod district) in search of safety and refuge. After taking refuge at various places, they were moving towards village Pannivel when she saw 25-30 people carrying deadly weapons and shouting "kill Muslims". The crowd killed 14 people of her group and gang-raped her. When she became unconscious, they left her believing her to be dead. When she regained consciousness, she found herself lying naked with dead bodies around her. Till the morning of 4 March, she kept hiding at a hillock. On seeing a man in uniform near a vehicle, she approached him and was taken to the Limkhera Police Station.[34]

On 25 March 2003, the trial court closed the case for lack of evidence. The Supreme Court ordered a CBI probe. In January 2004, the CBI arrested all the accused named in the complaint. In August 2004, the apex court shifted the trial to Mumbai. In January 2008, the Mumbai trial court convicted 13 accused of criminal conspiracy, murder and rape and 11 were given life imprisonment.[35]

This is the first case in independent India, where a case of rape during communal riot got established through a judicial process.

March–April 2002

On 4 March in Surat, a mob burnt down Mamata Cinema along with 10 shops. The school examinations were postponed to 18 March.

The first positive attempt to bring peace was witnessed when people from various religious groups took out a silent peace march amidst heavy police escort. Around 1,000 people took part in the six-km long march, from Kochrab Ashram to Sabarmati Ashram; both set up by Mahatma Gandhi.[36]

On 7 March, over 25,000 victims took shelter at various relief camps in Gujarat. More dead bodies continued to be recovered from various parts of the state. The toll in Ahmedabad had gone up to 275.

On 10 March, the chief minister countered allegations that the state administration had not acted promptly to control the riots and pointed out that over 100 people were killed in police firing and over 4,000 were arrested. He asserted that riots were controlled within 72 hours. "The fact is that I had given orders to the home and police departments on the night of the Godhra incident to make arrangements to control any flare up," he told a television channel.[37]

On 25 March, Muslims of Gujarat cancelled activities commemorating Muharram. The Hindu festival of Holi on 30 March passed off peacefully.

Sporadic incidents of violence would flare up suddenly when one would think that peace was being restored. Some of these incidents included police firing on a mob on 14 March, or the stabbing of Nitish Kumar Parmar, nephew of sitting Congress MP Pravin Rashtrapal, in the sensitive Shahpur area of Ahmedadad.

Modi met then Prime Minister Atal Bihari Vajpayee in Delhi on

27 March for two hours and explained the steps taken to contain riots and order relief and rehabilitation. The state government also submitted a 400-page report to National Human Rights Commission (NHRC).

A report on 2 April said that some gamblers were keeping Gujarat's cycle of violence going, "A resident of Cambay squarely laid the blame for riots in his ancient city on gambling syndicates... He told rediff.com, 'Some businessmen in my circle had offered us a bet before Holi (29 March) on the possibility of riots in Cambay. These *satodias* (betting syndicates) were offering us odds of 1:1.5.' Thus, if you bet Rs 10 on riots breaking out on a stipulated day, you stood to get back Rs 15. A source said, 'Gamblers in our city, both Hindus and Muslims, had already pledged around Rs 40 lakh by Friday. I am told that the local police were also aware of this betting.'"[38]

On 3 April, a day before the arrival of Prime Minister Vajpayee, the state again witnessed violence and at least nine people were killed, six of whom were burnt alive, and over 11 injured. Preventive arrests were made in Godhra on 4 April. During his visit, Vajpayee told Muslims of Gujarat that they were not alone in this time of crisis and that the entire country was with them.[39]

While addressing the media, Vajpayee's famous *rajdharma* statement came about. But he also said, "I am sure Narenbhai is doing it." Media reported the first part—and has been harping on it ever since—and conveniently ignored the second.[40]

On 6 April, the National Commission for Minorities (NCM) slammed the government of Gujarat. At the end of a three-hour meeting with the five-member team from Gujarat headed by the state chief secretary, G Subarao, NCM head Justice (retd) Shamim said that the commission was satisfied with the presentation made by the team, but dissatisfied with the steps taken by the State government.

Panchayat election on 7 April was a landmark. It witnessed 65 per cent polling for 1059 gram panchayats for the posts of sarpanchas and ward members. No major incidents were reported.[41]

There was a brief relief from the incessant violence from 9-11 April, but this lull was short-lived as violence resumed on 12 April. The army was deployed in Ahmedabad in the night as members of the two communities clashed again, leaving 40 people wounded. Twenty-five shops and houses were also set on fire in Danilimda locality.

A demand for the resignation of Modi from within the BJP and also from allies of the BJP-led NDA started circulating and people thought that Modi's days were numbered.

Towards the end of April and beginning of May, sporadic riots were witnessed in the state, with Ahmedabad being the most affected. This took the form of stone pelting and attack on residences in curfew-bound areas. Police firing also killed people in such incidents. On 23 April, six people were killed in police firing in Shahpur and Behrampur areas.

A BJP worker was injured in a shooting on 3 May. Three incidents of stabbing were reported in Ahmedabad. A BJP worker, who owned a provision store near Piraman Naka, was shot from point-blank range on 2 May, but was later out of danger.

Chief Minister Narendra Modi led a peace march in Vadodara on 2 May 2002.[42]

On 8 May, mobs of both communities clashed again in Ahmedabad, leaving 16 dead. The Army was called in again after the police failed to disperse the crowd. KPS Gill, security adviser to the chief minister, requested for the deployment of 1,000 extra specially-trained riot police from the Punjab state to combat the violence.[43] On 10 May, many fresh incidents of rioting and arson were reported across Ahmedabad. A police constable Mahendra Singh was severely beaten up and his motorcycle and rifle was snatched from him in the Khwaja Darwaza area of the city. The mob burnt the motorcycle and the police could not recover the rifle.[44]

It is clear that while the first few days of the riots were devastating in terms of damage to life and property and also in terms of shaming humanity, the latter part followed a pattern similar to other major riots of the past.

***

Dispelling Myths
'Hang Me If I Am Guilty'—Modi

Have patience awhile; slanders are not long-lived. Truth is the child of time; erelong she shall appear to vindicate thee.

— **Immanuel Kant**

When the Supreme Court judgement came on 2 September 2011 asking the Ahmedabad trial court to look into the SIT report that had given a clean chit to Modi, and the report of Amicus Curiae Raju Ramachandran that held otherwise, the Chief Minister tweeted, "God is Great," and launched a *sadbhavna* fast to invoke peace and harmony. On 26 December 2013, when the trial court held him not guilty in the Gulbarg society case and rejected Zakia Jafri's petition, he tweeted, "*Satyamev Jayate.*" (Truth Alone Triumphs).

The Metropolitan Trial court of Ahmedabad upheld the conclusion of the SIT report that gave a clean chit to Modi. (Refer to the earlier chapter where this case has been given in detail). The SIT argued before the court that no direct or circumstantial evidence had been found during the probe which could *prima facie* link Modi and others to the conspiracy behind the riots.

The next day, Modi expressed his inner feelings on the riots, something he had rarely done in public for fear of being charged with attempting to garner sympathy. There was also the apprehension that the spin doctors among his rivals would misconstrue an expression of grief as an admission of guilt. But after being vilified for so long without evidence, he could not suppress his emotions when the judgement came forth.

"I was shaken to the core. 'Grief', 'sadness', 'misery', 'pain', 'anguish', 'agony' — mere words could not capture the absolute emptiness one felt on witnessing such inhumanity'" he said. "Can you imagine the inner turmoil and shock of being blamed for the very events that have shattered you!" he asked in the blog.[1]

Critics found fault with the expression of remorse, saying the sentiments were not genuine or that they were intended at an image makeover in view of Modi's projection as the BJP's prime ministerial candidate. Why now, asked the Congress while describing this as "a belated reaction aimed at electoral gains".[2] They forgot that exoneration of Modi by the court was Modi's moment of triumph after being vilified for so long. He did not boast or take his detractors to task but expressed remorse in the most sober way.

One of Modi's bitterest critics, film maker Mahesh Bhatt, sounded positive. He said he was not surprised by the sentiments expressed by Modi. "He had told the same thing to me in 2003. Today he has merely stated the same in public." Bhatt wanted that all those claiming to represent the minority community should come forward and reciprocate the gesture rather than be guided by political considerations: "The injured party must recognise this and see for a moment without the prism of cynicism and see it as a positive step and also reciprocate. That this is a makeover for political objective is something that the political parties can say and should say for their own survival. But we are civil society members."[3]

One would be tempted to ask: Is it right to continue to blame Narendra Modi for the riots when a sizeable population came out on the streets and took part in the orgy of violence that engulfed Gujarat for more than four months? The issue is whether we will judge him with the standards adopted for fairness and justice, or create a different standard because he belongs to the Sangh Parivar? Or, just because some people do not like him winning all the time, as Salim Khan, noted film script writer, said.

"The same media — I won't mention names — which is raising questions (about Modi) like 'What right do you have to rule?' ... or finding artificial, dummy props to challenge him, never raised these questions with Narasimha Rao. Narasimha Rao *ke yahaan to teen ghante ke riots nahin hue thay, teen din ke riots nahin hue thay; teen mahine ke riots hue thay* (In Narasimha Rao's era, riots did not last for three hours or days, but three months). I have covered riots all my life. There has never been such astonishing psychological plus physical assault on any minority community as happened in Bombay between December 1992 and February 1993," said veteran journalist MJ Akbar.[4]

A Judicial Commission — the Nanavati-Mehta Commission — and a Supreme Court-appointed Special Investigation Team (SIT) have separately exonerated Modi of any personal wrongdoing. Yet, there are certain vested interests keen to keep the blame-game going. An inquiry by a Judicial Commission and an investigation by a high-powered committee do carry some weight. Should a person be condemned merely because of perceptions of some people?

This chapter relies on the Nanavati-Shah Commission report and the SIT report. First, no parallel authority has examined thousands of witnesses unlike the said commission and the investigation team. Second, on close scrutiny, the works of the political detractors of Modi turned out to be relying more on hearsay rather than evidence. Articles slamming Modi in newspapers rely on three or four interviews, books damning him for the riots or unverified reports.

UK parliamentarian Barry Gardiner questioned the reason for not accepting the clean chit given by the Supreme Court-appointed SIT. While justifying his invitation to Modi to visit the UK, he fumed at the television presenter who wouldn't settle for anything less than a cancellation of the invitation to Modi by Britain, "It seems that you have absolutely no respect for your own Supreme Court. The Supreme Court of India has looked into these allegations, I believe, on a number of occasions and has always absolved Narendra Modi completely of those allegations. For you to be bringing them up on Indian Television I find it extraordinarily strange."[5]

Nanavati Commission said: "There is absolutely no evidence to show that either the chief minister or any other ministers in his council of ministers or police had played any role in the Godhra incident or that there was any lapse on their part in the matter of providing protection, relief and rehabilitation to the victims of communal riots,"

"Law and order review meetings were held by Modi and all the things were done to control the situation... the army was called on time to contain the communal violence...Modi was busy with steps to control the situation, establishment of relief camps for riot victims and also with efforts to restore peace and normalcy.... In view of the detailed inquiry and satisfactory explanation of the person involved, no criminal case is made out against Narendra Modi," the SIT said.[6]

While the chief minister must be held accountable as the head of the State administration for any lapse in law and order, one must find out whether or not Modi took the steps he should have taken as the chief minister. He has said a number of times, "I have done no wrong," and that he tried to do the best that was possible. It is in this context that instead of apologising for a sin he has not committed, he has said, "Hang me if I am guilty."

A right analysis would be to compare him with other chief ministers of Gujarat under whose regime riots took place. Or, better still compare him with chief ministers of any other Indian state. Why are people not asking uncomfortable questions to Uttar Pradesh Chief Minister Akhilesh Yadav, for example?

Trivial incidents of eve-teasing and vengeance killing were allowed to degenerate into large-scale riots in Muzaffarnagar. If an all powerful chief minister with guidance from a former, experienced chief minister, his father, Mulayam Singh Yadav, and another experienced minister, Azam Khan, could not do anything in the riots that happened in one district, is it right to blame one man for not able to control riots that took place in many areas of Gujarat?

One can now theorise ex-post facto that the administration could have acted in some hypothetical manner, but if we take the version of the Gujarat police, the situation could have been worse if they had not taken action.

Then Police Commissioner PC Pande lauded his force for containing the violence. "I would like to compliment my officers and men who have done a commendable work in containing violence in Ahmedabad," he said.

When asked about his earlier "I hang my head in shame" statement, he clarified that he was misquoted. "I was referring to the Godhra incident and the retaliatory violence that followed." He said that the police had anticipated trouble in the old city following the 27 February incident. "We were successful in curbing violence there, but then the trouble spread to other areas and strained our resources. We have six thousand policemen for a population of five million (Ahmedabad). Despite the odds, we managed to do a good job." Five hundred persons were arrested in connection with arson and rioting, he pointed out and said, "We did not make any distinction of religion or party affiliation while making the arrests."[7]

He elaborated further: "It's not possible to man such a big area. In a normal course you are not even visiting those areas. At the best at every point one can provide three or four policemen. And when there is a crowd of 10,000 at one place, I can visualise what must be the position of my policemen."

In some cases, the strength of the mob of rioters went up to 5,000 or even 15,000. A media report of 28 February said:

"That the police was ineffective is clear. But was this intentional? Ahmedabad has a police force of 6,000, including 1,500 armed personnel. In addition, the entire State has just four companies (530 *jawans*) of the Rapid Action Force (RAF) of which only one company could be spared for Ahmedabad. Considering that the mobs that simultaneously surfaced at nearly half a dozen places numbered from 2,000 to 10,000, the forces proved woefully inadequate. At one point on February 28 there were at least 25,000 people targeting the Muslim localities in Ahmedabad alone."[8]

Gujarat has one of the worst police-to-people ratio. While the national average is 1 policeman for every 761 persons, the average in Gujarat is 1:1,021. In some other States, too, it is not good. For example, in Bihar the ratio is 1:1,456.[9] The police ratio shows whether the State is prepared to handle such a situation of rioting. In a localised riot scenario, additional police would be rushed from a peace area to riot areas. But this option was not available to the Gujarat police.

What would a state government do in such a situation? Ask for police help from neighbouring states and requisition the army. Modi did exactly that. At the emergency meeting he held with his top officials on 27 February night at his residence he asked them to get police help from the adjoining states and also check out about availability of the army. The next day he was told in a review meeting that help from other states was not coming.

The officials also told the chief minister that the army was not available in the Ahmedabad cantonment. He immediately spoke to then Home Minister LK Advani and got a fax sent to the Defence Ministry about army help. It was 2:30 pm of 28 February when the government sent the fax.[10] The army was airlifted to Ahmedabad on the same night and also in the morning of 1 March 2002. The army was deployed on 1 March. Union Defence Minister George Fernandes was in Ahmedabad on 28 February night and had taken a round of the city in the morning the next day.

Various newspapers reported deployment of the army and the flag March on 1 March. A newspaper said:

"So, it was only after 11 am on Friday that the army could stage its first flag-march in Ahmedabad, as also fan out to Vadodara, Rajkot and Godhra. As of now, say officials, two army brigades, with a 'bayonet strength of around 2,000 soldiers each', will be placed at the disposal of the civil administration. While one brigade is already positioned in the strife-torn State, the second is expected to begin deploying by Friday night. At present, nine columns (70-100 soldiers each) of the army have been deployed in Ahmedabad, while another three columns are present in Vadodara, Rajkot and Godhra."[11]

Gujarat in 2002 saw one of the fastest deployments of army in the history of riots in India. One does not remember any State or Union Government tacking the issue with so much of urgency.

In Delhi, anti-Sikh riots began in the evening of 31 October 1984. The army was not deployed till 2 November 1984. The army took a day further to become effective in some areas.[12] In 1993 Bombay riots, Police commissioner SK Bapat asked for permission for calling 40 army columns on the day when violence broke out (6 January 1993). But the government delayed it for four days.[13] Violence in Assam broke out on 20 July 2012. Army was deployed after 5 days.[14] The violence involving Bodo and Muslim settlers rendered more than 5 lakh people homeless and killed more than 90 people.[15] Muzaffarnagar riots were a classic example of State's lethargy. Incidents of violence started from 28 August 2013 and the army was deployed only on 8 September 2013.[16] In Muzaffarnagar riots 62 persons were killed and more than 50,000 families displaced.[17]

But as events unfolded, it turned out that even the army was no antidote to the mayhem that was unleashed in Gujarat. It was as if the civil society had collapsed? Although the presence of the army brought in a salutary effect, it did not stop violence altogether. Many reports of that time held that neither the army nor the shoot-at-sight orders given to the Gujarat police could stop the riots on 1 March.

Detractors of the Modi government often mislead by saying that three crucial days were lost in taking the decision to deploy the army. False! If the train was burnt on the 27th and the riots broke out on the 28th in the month of February that has 28 days only, how is the army action on the very next day late by three days?

The SIT report concluded that there was no delay in calling the army: "So it can be said that there was no delay whatsoever in requisitioning of army and its deployment in the state as and when they realised on 28/02/2002 that situation was out of control. More significantly Union Defence Minister arrived on 28th night so that army could take positions before any delay."[18]

Shoot at sight orders were issued to the police and the army was deployed when they were available. What more could the State have done? The problem was that the combined strength of the police and the army deployed proved insufficient.[19]

The meeting at the chief minister's residence on 27 February has been put under the lens. The SIT has given a clean chit to Modi saying that he never said anything objectionable and had merely asked the officials to do their duty. But *Amicus Curiae* Raju Ramachandran did not concurr with the SIT report and arrived at a different conclusion, demanding prosecution of the chief minister.

While commenting on *amicus curiae's* view, renowned lawyer Ram Jethmalani told the author that that was merely an opinion. "I can also hold an opinion. It does not count."[20] The SIT closure report has disagreed with the *amicus curiae's* conclusions saying that he had erred by relying solely on the statements given by suspended IPS officer Sanjiv Bhatt:

"This recommendation of amicus curiae is based on the sole testimony of Sanjiv Bhatt, the then DCI (Security) who has claimed to have attended a meeting called by the Chief Minister on 27.02.2002 night (day of Godhra train carnage) at his residence...It may be mentioned here that seven other participants of the said meeting, who are senior officers, have categorically stated that Shri Sanjiv Bhatt did not attend the said meeting."[21]

As per the evidence recorded by the SIT, Bhatt was not present at the meeting. Even officials who were present denied that Bhatt had attended it. In his deposition to the SIT, Modi *suo moto* clarified that, "As far as I recollect, GS Raiger (then ADG Intelligence) and Sanjiv Bhatt (then DC Intelligence) did not attend as this was a high level meeting. None of my cabinet colleagues were present..." How can then Bhatt's claim, based on his attendance at the meeting, that the chief minister said something objectionable be taken as true?

The SIT has concluded that Bhatt fabricated witnesses to corroborate his version that he had attended a meeting at the chief minister's residence.[22] Also not explained is Bhatt's silence for nine years![23]

But, why were the dead bodies transported to a communally sensitive Ahmedabad rather than asking the relatives of the dead to go to Godhra and collect the bodies? Modi told the SIT that the decision was taken unanimously during the evening meeting at the collectorate in Godhra on 27 February. None of the officials at the meeting on 27 February at the chief minister's residence opposed the decision to bring the bodies to Ahmedabad. They all discussed ways to facilitate the process, the SIT has said. The bodies were to be kept at the Sola Civil Hospital on the outskirts of Ahmedabad. Relatives of those dead would have found it difficult to go to Godhra for identification and claim the bodies because the town was under curfew. More importantly, the small, ill-equipped town of Godhra had no facility to conduct autopsy on so many bodies.

While in retrospect one can say that the bodies could have been handed over to relatives at Godhra, the relatives might have asked the administration to transport the bodies to Ahmedabad since most belonged to that city.

Modi's alleged 'action reaction theory' has been widely talked about saying that he justified killings by making those remarks. This was a massive case of misreporting. *The Times of India* had published a news item on 3 March 2002 purportedly as if Modi had given an interview to them, whereas the truth is that nobody from the newspaper met him, indicating that his so-called action-reaction theory justifying the violence was not true.

Modi told the SIT, "*The Times of India* had published a news item purportedly as though I had given an interview to them. The truth is that nobody from *(The) Times of India* had met me. The falsehood of the so called justification 'Action- Reaction Theory' is evident from this fact. The State government issued a denial with regard to my not having given any interview and the same was belatedly published in a remote corner of the newspaper...It has been my constant opinion that violence cannot be a reply to violence and I had appealed for peace. I had not and would never justify any action or reaction by a mob against innocents. Hence I deny all allegations in this regards."[24]

The SIT notes: "It was brought to the notice of the editor twice in writing before the CM's clarification was published on 23rd March—a good 20 days after the original story was published on 3rd March 2002. What is worse, while the inflammatory misquote attributed to Modi was published on the front page of TOI in both the national edition as well as in the Ahmedabad edition, the clarification by the CM's office was published on 23rd March in a remote corner in the inside pages of the Ahmedabad edition while the Delhi edition did not carry it at all."[25]

What had actually happened was, Modi gave an interview to a private Hindi television news channel in which he said in Hindi: "*Kriya pratikriya ki chain chal rahi hai. Hum chahte hain ke na kriya ho, aur na pratikriya* (A chain of action and reaction is going on. We neither want action nor reaction)." This was said in response to a query about the massacre at Gulbarg society in which former Congress MP Ehsan Jafri was killed. Modi referred to a report that Jafri had first fired at the violent mob, which provoked mob and thereafter, it stormed the housing society and set it on fire.[26]

When the reporter asked the chief minister about widespread violence in Gujarat post-Godhra, he replied: "*Godhra mein jo parson hua, jahaan par 40 mahilaon aur bachchon ko zinda jala diya, is mein desh mein aur videsh mein sadma pahunchna swabhavik tha. Godhra ke is ilaqe ke logon ki criminal tendencies rahi hain, in logon ne pehle mahila teacher ka khoon kiya and ab ye jaghanya apradh kiya hai jiski pratikriya ho rahi hai."* (Given what happened in Godhra the day before yesterday, where 40 women and children were burnt alive, this country and even foreign countries are shocked. People of that area of Godhra have criminal tendencies; they had earlier killed a lady teacher and now have committed this heinous crime, reactions to which are coming forth).

The SIT held that the alleged utterances by Chief Minister Narendra Modi were not sufficient to make out a case against him. It gave a clean chit to Modi and said that the statement was quoted out of context. The SIT also held that Ehsan Jafri's action provoked the mob.[27]

Modi kept on denying that he ever justified riots. "After the riots began, I was quoted as saying that every action has an opposite reaction. The fact is I never said anything of that kind but one newspaper had a headline that said I had. I later wrote to the editor of the newspaper asserting that I had never said it. The electronic media was there at that press conference of mine. You can check the tapes."[28]

Did Modi refuse to take a call from Ehsan Jafri or he took the call and did not take action? There was only one telephone connection in Gulbarg society, the SIT has noted. Besides, there was no mobile. Modi has clearly denied having received any phone call from Ehsan Jafri. He has even stated that he was informed about the attack on Gulbarg society at the law and order review meeting at night.[29]

The call details of Pande (CP) shows that 302 incoming/outgoing calls had been received/made to/from his mobile phone on 28 February 2002 between 00:35 hours and 24:00 hours. A close scrutiny of the call details show that Pande received or made calls to or from his mobile phone almost every minute or every two minutes. His phone was never switched off. However, no calls had been received either from late Ehsan Jafri, ex-MP or any other resident of Gulbarg society.[30] Ehsan Jafri is reported to have called Pande. But the record of Pande does not show any call made by Jafri to Pande or from Pande to Jafri.

The other major allegation against Modi is that either he did not take enough steps for relief and rehabilitation of riot victims or he discriminated when the inhabitants in the relief camps were Muslims. One may recollect that Vajpayee's famous *rajdharma* (statesmanship) statement came after he had visited the Shah Alam refugee camp in

Ahmedabad. That time media had come out with various reports saying that the relief work was tardy and it served as immediate provocation to the prime minister.

The SIT report said, "The chief minister said that relief and rehabilitation measures were initiated immediately and compensation packages were announced and implemented... Modi said that perhaps for the first time in the country, a committee was constituted under the chairmanship of the governor to review rehabilitation efforts. This high-level committee included leader of the opposition, members from the chamber of commerce, members from prominent NGOs and others."

Modi had rubbished the charge of discrimination when the SIT confronted him with this question: "Relief camps were opened in the affected areas and they were served by the NGOs and local social leaders. The government contributed funds as per policy and the relief operations were supervised by the *Samiti*. The necessary arrangement for food, drinking water, medicines, and cash doles etc., were made in these camps. Arrangements were also made in the camps for the education of children."[31]

One may recollect that the State government had on 25 March 2002 constituted a 13-member committee, to be headed by then Governor Sunder Singh Bhandari, to oversee and review the working of relief camps for the violence-affected people in the State. This was a follow up of an announcement Vajpayee had made in Lok Sabha on 16 March.[32]

When Modi was in power in Gujarat, there was a BJP-led NDA coalition in power at the Centre. Some people often say it was a conspiracy by the RSS family (Sangh Parivar) to kill Muslims in a pogrom. A closer analysis would show that is far from the truth. It was not that the Muslims were silent spectators, though it is equally true that they became the target of mob fury at more places. The figures of death show that about one third of those who died were Hindus and more than 200 people were killed in police firing.[33]

SIT lawyer RS Jamur rubbished the complaint of a larger conspiracy hatched by Modi. "Modi came to Gujarat in 2001 and this all happened within almost three months after he became Chief Minister. How can he hatch a larger conspiracy within that short time?"[34]

What people tend to forget, Modi's ascendancy was not easy. His predecessor Keshubhai Patel had not taken his replacement lightly. Modi wore a crown of thorns. He had no control over either the Vishwa Hindu Parishad, other wings of the RSS or even the BJP. He was struggling to understand administration and governance and was keen to implement his vision of development.

The VHP, the Bharatiya Kisan Sangh and some RSS leaders were the first he confronted during his reign while trying to push reforms. One can say that these came later when he started asserting himself. But one must not forget that Modi did not have a free hand to do whatever he liked. Prime Minister Atal Bihari Vajpayee, known for his secular image, would not allow any communal agenda to takeover. The BJP depended on allies and the allies could walk out.

The Prime Minister was not liked by the RSS because of the policy of further liberalisation. The RSS had clearly termed the NDA's economic policy as 'not in the interest of the country.'[35] Modi was a step ahead in economic liberalisation. He had learnt the development mantra from the Vajpayee government. There was no question of his becoming a part of any grand conspiracy or hatching one himself.

Back then, Modi was quite junior in the party hierarchy. At any national level BJP meeting, chief ministers would not sit on the dais. He knew that if he did anything that would spoil the image of the NDA government, Vajpayee would ask him to quit.

As subsequent developments showed, Vajpayee had actually explored the possibility of Modi's resignation. It was only after a bitter realisation that such a resignation would aggravate rather than calm the situation that Vajpayee changed his mind. The BJP national executive meeting in Goa in 2002 asked Modi to seek a fresh mandate.

The latter years of Modi demonstrated he has not been wedded to *Hindutva* as people have been trying to paint him. In an interview to an international news agency, he said he was a Hindu nationalist but this was a different Hindu nationalist: "I'm nationalist. I'm patriotic. Nothing is wrong. I'm a born Hindu. Nothing is wrong. So, I'm a Hindu nationalist. So yes, you can say I'm a Hindu nationalist because I'm a born Hindu. I'm patriotic so nothing is wrong in it. As far as progressive, development-oriented, workaholic, whatever they say, this is what they are saying. So there's no contradiction between the two. It's one and the same image."[36]

Modi, the development man, has put in place several examples where religious affiliations have not come in the way of administrative actions. Mosques or temples are secondary to the need for providing better amenities to citizens. More than 80 temples or their encroaching boundaries were razed to the ground in Gandhinagar in the drive against encroachment in one month. (33) This angered the VHP and Ashok Singhal had to intervene when local VHP leaders spoke against Modi. (34) Praveen Togadia also got upset.

At the peak of communal tension in 2002 when bureaucrats advised Modi to move the transport junction from the Muslim-dominated Juhapura area to some other place, Modi put his foot down. He insisted that the hub would not only stay right there but would also be developed further with world-class facilities.

Modi's 'sin' was that he was the chief minister and, therefore, the buck should stop at his desk. But it is also true that ex-post facto virtues were not available with him. Even prominent Muslim leaders have started realising this: "This was his misfortune that he was presiding over as the chief minister that time," said Mufti Aijaz Arshad Qasmi, a member of All India Muslim Personal Law Board.[37]

The right thing will be to assess whether he did enough. And there is nothing to suggest he did not. If riots become the reason for sacking chief ministers, the country would witness unprecedented political chaos. There are enough vested interests to convert smaller incidents into riots. Should a chief minister be held accountability for inaction of the in-charge of a police station? Can a chief minister have so much of administrative control?

The larger issue is: Is he being sinned against by vested interests even when he has not sinned? He has asserted he did nothing wrong and he did everything that was possible at that time. Those who tried to paint a different image — and now realise that they committed a mistake somewhere — insist that he should apologise. He has questioned why he should apologise when he has not done anything wrong. If he has done something wrong he should be punished; apology would not be enough. He has maintained this stand consistently.

A reconciliatory note came from his one-time bitterest critic, film director and social activist Mahesh Bhatt: "Modi needs to publicly demonstrate remorse. Not just by means of an apology with empty words, which will add to nothing, but at least an attempt made to take India to that zone which Nelson Mandela had taken post his release from Northern Island after 27 years of imprisonment. He fought against White domination and against Black domination with vigour, and refused to become a prophet. He said, 'Don't make me a prophet. I am one of you. But I will fight both White and Black domination with my might.' Then he went about creating situations where there was reconciliation between the communities which had moved far away."[38]

This suggestion of Bhatt came before Narendra Modi's blog on 2002 riots on 27 December 2013. After the blog, Bhatt appeared a transformed man and held civil society must reciprocate.

While few can have objections to Bhatt's prescription, Modi's critics may not be aware of the fact that the positive energy released by the Modi government has persuaded many Muslims to come forward and support the BJP. Modi has already taken development to the homes of the minority community without saying so. Muslims of Gujarat have started reaping the fruits of development discussed elsewhere in this book.

Many Muslim parents in Gujarat are happy that the youth of the community no longer idolise goons like Lateef who once roamed the streets of Ahmedabad. For lack of opportunity of upward mobility, they wanted to become like him. An anti-social element had a halo around him for the Muslim youth because they were not educated enough to apply for jobs or launch respectable businesses. Now, they are all caught up in the development wave and they want to go in for higher education and jobs, said Asifa Khan who moved to the BJP from the Congress some years ago after she realised her older party was using Muslim faces merely as tokens.

Some sections are clearly unhappy with this change in perception. Mahesh Bhatt would not like to count himself in such a group; he calls himself a conscientious citizen. "I do not depend on this to earn my money. I make my living through entertainment."[39]

Another noted film personality Salim Khan was all praise for

Modi. He disagreed with those who singled out the Gujarat chief minister for criticism. "Do we remember any other chief minister since independence under whose regime riots took place? Why? There have been many riots in India before 2002; there have been several after it. Why don't the politicians talk of the Gujarat riots of 1969? Or, why are they not talking of the Muzaffarnagar riots that happened in 2013?"

When asked to explain, he said, "This is because he has won elections thrice in Gujarat and is within striking distance of being the country's prime minister. If he had lost the assembly elections of 2012, rival politicians would have stopped targeting him any further.... The allegation that Modi is communal does not hold. Do the people who allege so mean that the people who are continuously voting for him are communal, too?"[40]

He narrated the story of a blind man who boarded a train with a revolver that was loaded with six bullets. The train was crowded and someone slapped him. The blind man took out his gun and fired six rounds. He killed six people but not the one who had slapped him. This is what happens in a riot, he pointed out.

Salim Khan, the famous screenplay writer of the Salim-Javed duo and father of actor Salman Khan, has emerged as an ardent advocate of Hindu-Muslim unity, forgetting the wounds of 2002 Gujarat riots. He said "Modi is the leader who would make the difference."

Or, as former Deputy Prime Minister of India LK Advani asked, 'has Narendra Modi become a part of a vilification campaign?' The BJP patriarch in his book *My Country My life* said, "I consider the outcome of Gujarat polls (2007) significant for another reason. It showed how a leader with integrity, courage and competence could count on people's support to beat back a personalised campaign of vilification. I cannot think of any other leader in Indian politics in the past 60 years who was as viciously, consistently and persistently maligned both nationally and internationally, as Modi had been since 2002."[41]

***

Modi's Resignation had no Takers

One does not attain freedom from the bondage of Karma by mere resignation. No one attains perfection by merely giving up work.

— 3:4 *Bhagvad Gita*

Vajpayee has always been sensitive to public opinion. When Uttar Pradesh's notorious politician DP Yadav was inducted into the BJP in 2004 to strengthen the party in western Uttar Pradesh, the BJP faced a barrage of criticism from the media for his controversial image. By evening, Yadav was forced to resign. Such had been Vajpayee's sensitivity.

Naturally, the the prime minister was not going to be unaffected by the criticisms in the media about Modi not handling the Gujarat riots in the best possible manner. He contemplated removing Narendra Modi from the post of the chief minister. Everyone knew, if Vajpayee wanted Modi removed, no one could change his mind. Modi also knew it well and was unhappy that some of his own partymen were baying for his blood before the prime minister. He was ready with his resignation, which he offered before the BJP's national executive meeting in Goa in 2002. The entire executive rose in one voice to turn down the resignation. Vajpayee, the democrat, sensed the mood and did not insist on Modi's ouster. Later, addressing a rally after the executive meeting, he chided those who were critical of the BJP in handling the Gujarat riots.

Vajpayee's initial thoughts were shaped by his visit to relief camps in Gujarat where he issued the famous *rajdharma* statement.

Vajpayee could not visit Gujarat immediately after the riots due to the elaborate security arrangements that accompany the prime minister. His visit happened in the first week of April. On 4 April 2002, when the prime minister inspected the burnt coaches in Godhra, he was accompanied by Modi and Arun Jaitley. Vajpayee appeared to be apologetic about his late visit; he said that he wanted to visit the affected areas earlier but could not do so because of security considerations.[1]

He got emotional during the visit and said he had come with a "broken heart" and what happened in Gujarat was "shameful". The prime minister, however, ruled out the possibility of removing Modi or a snap poll in the State.

He told riot victims at the Shah Alam relief camp in Ahmedabad that they were not alone in their hour of crisis. "We all are with you. The entire country is with you. *Apne desh mein refugee ho jana, yeh dil ko cheerne wali baat hai*" (becoming a refugee in one's own country is heart-wrenching). What happened in Godhra was condemnable and what followed in other parts of the state must also be deplored, he stressed. "*Yeh pagalpan band hona chahiye*" (This madness must stop). India's standing in the comity of nations for its pluralistic character "has been badly affected by the violence in Gujarat", he said while adding "with what face, I do not know, I will go abroad after what all has happened here."[2]

What made the visit controversial was his *rajdharma* remark when he addressed mediapersons in Ahmedabad. When asked what was his message for the chief minister, he said: "Chief minister *ke liye mera ek hi sandesh hai ki vo rajdharm ka palan karen... Rajdharm. Ye shabd kafi sarthak hai... Main usi ka palan kar raha hun... Palan karne ka prayas kar raha hun... Raja ke liye, Shashak ke liye praja praja mein bhed nahi ho sakta... na janm ke aadhar par, na jaati ke aadhar par, na sampraday ke aadhar par...*"

(I have only one message for the chief minister that he should follow the duty of the ruler, that is statesmanship. The word is worthwhile. I am following that. I am trying to follow that. For the king, the one who is heading the state, there cannot be any difference between those ruled, the citizens, on the basis of birth, caste or religion.)

Modi, who was sitting on Vajpayee's left, said: "*hum bhi vahi kar rahen hain saheb.*" (I am also doing the same).

At this point, Vajpayee said without looking at Modi: "*Mujhe vishvas hai ki Narendrabhai yehi kar rahen hain...*" (I'm sure that Narendrabhai is also doing the same).[3]

The prime minister was disturbed by reports of discrimination by the State government in distributing relief to riot victims and its failure to control riots. The statement came essentially in that context. He had already ruled out the possibility of the removal of the chief minister or the possibility of an early poll.

***

Goa National Executive Meeting, 2002

On the morning of 12 April 2002, Prime Minister Atal Bihari Vajpayee and his three senior ministers, LK Advani, Jaswant Singh and Arun Shourie, were travelling by the same flight to Goa. Vajpayee had asked Shourie to join him. Jaswant Singh and Shourie sat facing each other. Vajpayee and Advani sat on the other side. For quite some time, Advani and Vajpayee did not speak to each other. Vajpayee picked up a newspaper and started reading it. Advani did the same. After a while, Shourie gently pulled the paper away from Vajpayee's hand and said, looking at both Vajpayee and Advani, that they both had to address the Modi issue.[4]

Vajpayee asked, "*Gujarat ka kya karna hai?* (what should be done about Gujarat?)... *Gujarat ke bare mein sochna chahiye* (we must think something about Gujarat)". Advani got up from his seat and went to the bathroom. Vajpayee looked towards Jaswant Singh and said, "*Poochhiye kya karna hai* (ask him what should be done?)" It was a 737 aircraft. Jaswant Singh moved towards Advani and asked. Advani said only one thing, "*bawaal khada ho jayega party mein* (there will be commotion in the party)."[5]

A consensus was achieved during the journey that the party should explore Modi's resignation and that the onus of doing that would be on Advani. India's Home Minister had sensed the mood of Vajpayee and had already deputed Union Law Minister Arun Jaitley in advance to talk to Modi and find out what were his views.

Advani accepted that there was pressure on the prime minister from allies and other quarters to ask Modi to quit. But it was Advani who resisted this move. He expressed the reason for this in the Rajya Sabha on 6 May 2002 as quoted in his book *My Country My Life*: "We should look for a real solution to the situation in the state, and removing Chief

Minister Modi is not a solution. There has been a sustained campaign against him, which is not correct. It is also not correct or proper to allege, as Leader of the Opposition Dr Manmohan Singh has done, that there is gross communalisation of Gujarat police. I plead with everyone not to make such sweeping charges against the police force. There are some shortcomings and I am aware of them, but let us not forget that, in Modi's government, the police force saved a large number of Muslims during the riots.[6]

"I also resisted proposals for Modi's resignation made inside party forums. I am happy that my confidence in him has been fully vindicated by subsequent developments. His chief ministership, between 2002-2007, was characterised by the fact that there was not a single communal riot in Gujarat; not a single incident of terrorism, and not a single hour of curfew imposed anywhere in the state in those five years."

Party President defends Modi

The Goa national executive meeting began on a tense note. Contrary to the party's tradition of starting the meeting at 11 am, it started late. This was done to let all important leaders reach Goa first. The meeting began at Hotel Marriott at 4:30 pm. The original plan was to end the first day of the meeting with the party president's inaugural speech and allow members to go to the Campal grounds to attend the public rally. But a chain of events forced the national executive to start its first formal session post dinner.[7]

BJP president Jana Krishnamurthy in his speech gave a spirited defence of Gujarat and the way Narendra Modi had handled the situation. He said: "I strongly condemn the hue and cry of those who demanded the head of chief minister of Gujarat. The nation needs to be saved from these forces whose only aim seems to be to destabilise the BJP government even when the situation demanded the cooperation of everyone to restore normalcy in a riot-torn state."

Krishnamurthy's assertion had a context. On 10 April, two days before the national executive meeting, the Telugu Desam Party (TDP) had demanded Modi's ouster. While returning from his tour of Singapore and Cambodia, Vajpayee was asked this question when he was still in the aircraft. The prime minister replied that he would consult his colleagues before taking a call on the matter. On 11 April, Krishnamurthy in the flight from Delhi to Goa told some journalists that there was no question of Modi's resignation.[8]

Modi offers to resign

The moment Krishnamurthy finished his speech, the Gujarat chief minister, who was sitting with Union Law Minister Arun Jaitley, rose from his chair and raised his hand. Jaitley had rushed to Gandhinagar on the night of 11 April to have a one-on-one talk with Modi on his views. They both had come together from Gandhinagar. Modi sought the president's permission to speak on Gujarat. He said he wanted the executive to have a free and frank discussion because this was a grave issue for the party. He then offered to resign in order to facilitate this discussion. But before sitting in his chair, he dwelt upon the situation in the state and how he had worked to contain the riots. But he still owned the moral responsibility for whatever had happened.

Modi's resignation offer set the cat among the pigeons. After Krishnamurthy's strong defence, the resignation had become superfluous. The national executive was fully charged-up. Venkaiah Naidu, who was general secretary of the party, rose up from his seat and rejected the resignation then and there. How could Modi resign? Arun Jaitley also stood up and said the same thing. Pramod Mahajan, who was close to the prime minister, stood up and opposed the resignation move and sided with his younger colleagues. The fourth person to stand up was Ananth Kumar. After this, the mood of the executive completely changed.

Keshubhai Patel, who was supposed to be upset with Modi ever since the latter became the chief minister, rose up and spoke in Modi's defence. "Modi cannot be removed. This was not possible now", he told the executive.[9]

Two people who were in favour of resignation – TN Chaturvedi and Shanta Kumar— were silent. Shanta Kumar who was food minister had criticized Modi a day before: "Modi's continuation in office was beyond human norms".[10] The RSS clearly did not like it. Later, Jana Krishnamurthy even spoke about taking action against Shanta Kumar. The entire executive knew that they were the prime movers for Modi's resignation move. Everyone clapped in support of Modi.

There were two sets of people: One who thought that removing Modi would send a wrong signal and this was not correct. Riots had happened in other places as well but those had not led to resignations of chief ministers. The other set of people were those who concluded that removing Modi would complicate the situation. This would lead to more riots. Then Rajasthan chief minister, Bhairon Singh Shekhawat, also supported Modi saying it was not correct to blame the chief minister for the riots.

Modi had apparently sensed the mood of the BJP leadership. He also knew that if Vajpayee had wanted him to resign nobody would be able to save him. But he also knew that Vajpayee was a democrat. It was the same Vajpayee who had asked him to go to Gujarat as chief minister. He told a media portal after the executive meeting that he had decided to resign five days before the national executive meeting.[11]

The meeting had to end without reaching any conclusion due to the rally in the evening. The BJP president announced that the executive would hold its first session after dinner. Krishnamurthy later clarified to the media, before the start of the public rally, that the meeting would discuss threadbare the issue of Modi's resignation and take a decision.[12]

Vajpayee addresses a rally in Goa

When the BJP leadership assembled at the public rally ground, they saw a new prime minister—one who was no longer apologetic. He was rather combative. He appeared to be rebutting those who had criticised the BJP and him on the issue of Gujarat. This is what he said: "The wheel of victory and defeat rolled on. But during their centuries long history there isn't a single instance of a Hindu king destroying temples or breaking idols when he attacked another Hindu king. The kings who were victorious used to build a new temple. If Vishnu was being worshipped there earlier, later Shiva began to be worshipped. If Shiva was being worshipped at one time, then other deities began to be worshipped later. Nevertheless, no king destroyed a temple or damaged the deities' idols at the time of attacking another king.

Vajpayee then spoke these lines which almost everyone in the BJP was saying: "What happened in Gujarat? If a conspiracy had not been hatched to burn the innocent passengers of the Sabarmati

Express alive, then the subsequent tragedy in Gujarat could have been averted. But this did not happen. People were torched alive. Who were those culprits? The Government is investigating into this. Intelligence agencies are collecting all the information. But we should not forget how the tragedy of Gujarat started. The subsequent developments were no doubt condemnable, but who lit the fire? How did the fire spread? Ours is a multi-religious country, a multi-lingual country, we have many different modes of worship. We believe in peaceful and harmonious co-existence. We believe in equal respect for all faiths."

Vajpayee came down heavily against terrorism and 'such' Muslims, who were working against peace: "Today the threat to our nation comes from terrorism. Wherever I went around the world, the heads of state or of elected governments complained to me that militant Islam is sowing thorns along their paths. Islam has two facets. One is that which tolerates others, which teaches its adherents to follow the path of truth, which preaches compassion and sensitivity. But these days, militancy in the name of Islam leaves no room for tolerance. It has raised the slogan of jihad. It is dreaming of recasting the entire world in its mould."

"You will be surprised to hear this — indeed, I too was surprised — that some terrorists belonging to Al-Qaeda were arrested in Singapore. The rulers of Singapore couldn't even have imagined that Al-Qaeda would be active in their country, too; that Al-Qaeda would hatch a conspiracy in Singapore too. Some 15 or 16 persons were arrested; an investigation is underway, which will reveal the truth. The same is happening in Indonesia. The same is happening in Malaysia. Wherever such Muslims live, they tend not to live in co-existence with others, not to mingle with others; and instead of propagating their ideas in a peaceful manner, they want to spread their faith by resorting to terror and threats. The world has become alert to this danger."[13] Vajpayee was no longer apolegetic about Gujarat riots.

Take Fresh Mandate, Tells BJP

Later, senior leaders re-assembled after dinner to discuss Modi's resignation. The first formal session of the national executive meeting (post inaugural session) began at about 9-9:30 pm and continued till 11-11:30 pm.

The overall mood was to reject the proposal of resignation. Accepting the demand for Modi's resignation was like succumbing to the propaganda of those opposed to the Sangh Parivar, many leaders who spoke at the meeting said. Many also contended that the chief minister could not be blamed for failure of the administrative machinery in the context of provocation of the highest order.

Meanwhile Vajpayee had mellowed down on the resignation decision taken in the aircraft. He seemed to have softened his original stand on exploring Modi's resignation. His fiery speech at the public rally had charged up the executive. Backroom management by Pramod Mahajan, Arun Jaitley and Venkaiah Naidu achieved a compromise which was agreeable to both Advani and Vajpayee. The consensus was to ask Modi to seek a fresh mandate. The national executive, that very night, adopted a resolution that advised Modi to seek a fresh mandate in Gujarat: "Instead of accepting his resignation, the national executive advises him to seek dissolution of the Assembly, go to the people and seek their verdict."

The resolution that was titled, "Godhra and its aftermath," said: "In a democracy there is only one way to put the issue and the calumny to rest. The people are the one who can and must decide." It described the Godhra incident as a pre-meditated attack and gave full credit to the State administration and police for bringing incidents of massive rioting under control. The resolution said "Modi called the Army to assist the civil administration within 16 hours and by contrast the earlier Congress governments faced with a similar situation took 5 days to call up the Army".

It asked, "… in which communal riot in the history of India have so many arrests been made and such firm action taken by the police that 139 persons got killed in police firing alone?"

Gujarat Assembly Dissolved

On the night of 19 July 2002, the State government led by Modi recommended dissolution of the assembly and fresh polls. Two hours after this, the Governor issued a notification dissolving the house and asked Modi to continue as the caretaker chief minister. Giving reasons for early polls, Modi told newspersons, "I wanted to remove the uncertainty regarding early polls. Certain forces tried to take political advantage of the Godhra incident and what followed it. The attempt continues even today. To bring an end to this, I decided to go to the people, who are the final decision makers."[14]

This decision came in the context of a few preceding developments. First was the appointment of KPS Gill as the security adviser to the chief minister on 2 May 2002; second, the Congress had challenged Modi, saying he was scared of facing elections; third, the Election Commission had said publicly that the situation in the State was not conducive to hold free and fair polls.

A no-nonsense man, one of India's top cops recognised for dismantling terrorism in Punjab in late 1980s and early 1990s, Gill was to help the State government check communal violence. The suggestion for the appointment had come from the central government. Two days after the appointment, Modi said that the move was aimed at bringing more professionalism in the police force of the hyper-sensitive State. "This is what even the National Human Rights Commission has suggested", he told mediapersons in Ahmedabad.[15]

When Modi did not recommend dissolution of the state legislative assembly immediately after the Goa executive meeting, it was largely understood by the opponents that he was scared of facing the polls. "*Wo dar gaya hai* (he has got scared)," president of Gujarat unit of the Congress, Amarsinh Chaudhary, said. He charged that the decision to defer the dissolution 'exposed' Modi's lack of guts in facing the electorate even when he claimed their overwhelming support.

After Modi recommended dissolution of the assembly, the Election Commission in general and Chief Election Commissioner James Michael Lyngdoh, in particular, stood as the major stumbling block. Lyngdoh had already ruled out elections in October saying that the law and order situation was far from normal and the wound of communal violence had not yet healed.[16]

Vapayee explains his stand in Parliament

Those who think that Modi or Advani outclassed Vajpayee are grossly unaware of the fact that Vajpayee always had his way whenever he wanted. It was only because he too thought that the decision to remove was not correct that he did not insist.

Intervening in a debate on Opposition-sponsored censure motion in the Lok Sabha on 6 May 2002, Vajpayee said that the demand for removal of Modi was considered but it was decided that the change of leadership in Gujarat "was not appropriate". Terming the decision not to remove Modi as "right", he said that any change in leadership could have further worsened the situation.

Talking about his *rajdharma* statement before the Goa executive meeting, the Prime Minister said the media only highlighted his statement but did not pay attention to the fact that Modi had responded saying that he was doing the same. He sought to know whether there was no other way to follow *rajdharma* other than seeking the resignation of Modi.[17]

***

Three Victories in a Row

Great spirits have always encountered
violent opposition from mediocre minds.

— **Albert Einstein**

When the BJP asked Modi to seek a fresh mandate, his detractors thought that he would lose the elections. This produced glee in the Opposition camp. Advancing polls could have been suicidal since the party needed time to consolidate governance. There was fear; there were doubts and there were controversies. Modi was written off. But fate had willed otherwise. Modi won not just the 2002 assembly elections but also the ones in 2007 and 2012. In 2012, Modi gave an open challenge to the Opposition Congress to walk on his turf and debate development. During the debates that were witnessed across the country, he left his opponents miles behind. These victories made Narendra Modi a cult figure in Gujarat as well as the country.

With the three campaigns, Modi transformed his image step by step.

2002: In the Shadow of Godhra

The BJP's campaign in 2002 began in the form of opposition to the Election Commission. The party challenged the commission's decision not to hold the elections by October. Then Union Law Minister Arun Jaitely launched the tirade against the Commission: "Those whose orders tie up constitutional knots must have the statesmanship to untie them." He argued that the reasons for not holding the polls in Gujarat were not valid, more so because the central government was endeavouring to hold an election in Jammu & Kashmir.[1]

The last session of the Gujarat assembly in 2002 had taken place on 6 April. The assembly was dissolved on 19 July. Since there could not be a gap of more than six months between two sittings of the assembly, the new assembly had to be reconstituted before 6 October. This was the common understanding till the Supreme Court ruled otherwise.

The Election Commission, which was in a combative mood, made 'adverse law and order situation' and 'absence of revised electoral rolls' to be major reasons for postponing the elections. The situation got further aggravated as Chief Election Commissioner (CEC) James Michael Lyngdoh suggested imposition of President's rule in the state.

This provoked the BJP-led NDA government at the Centre. LK Advani, who had become the Deputy Prime Minister by then, strongly objected to the Election Commission's recommendation and referred the issue to the Supreme Court through a presidential reference.[2] Jaitley countered Lyngdoh saying that the electoral roll was not an issue since names of individuals missing from the rolls could easily be included through the normal process. He also argued that the Election Commission's decision to not hold elections by October was unconstitutional.

The Supreme Court judgement on the presidential reference was a win-win situation for all. The apex court held that the provision of not more than six months gap between two sittings of the assembly was applicable to 'live' and not to 'dissolved' Assemblies. The court upheld the supremacy of the Election Commission but put a limit on its discretionary power. It decreed that the election must be held within six months of dissolution of the assembly and held that public disturbance should not be the occasion to postpone elections.[3] The suggestion for imposition of President's rule became redundant as the Supreme Court refused to pass an interim order in the first week of October while entertaining a PIL that questioned Modi's continuation as the caretaker chief minister.

It had become evidently clear from the deposition of the Election Commission before the Supreme Court that elections would take place in the month of November-December.

The conflict between the BJP and the Election Commission, and the fact that most parties joined the issue, generated a lot of debate and helped further consolidate the BJP's core support base. Lyngdoh later announced that the state would witness one day polling on 12 December.

Modi had decided to launch the Gujarat Gaurav Yatra (Pride of Gujarat procession) from 4 July but it had to be shelved as Prime Minister

Vajpayee intervened, thinking that this could lead to communal tension. The National Human Rights Commission had held that the *yatra* should not be organised during that time in view of the possibility of a distinct "potential for disturbing communal peace".[4]

The Prime Minister had come to learn that the state's riot victims in relief camps were scared of returning to their homes since they feared trouble during the Gaurav Yatra.[5] Added to this was a letter which the leader of the Opposition Ms Sonia Gandhi wrote to Vajpayee. She apprehended that the *yatra* would damage the "already sensitive and communal situation in the State. I hope you will take the constructive step of dissuading the Gujarat chief minister from undertaking the Gaurav Yatra," she said.[6]

While many thought that the *yatra* was called off, the BJP was determined to merely postpone it. The Congress, which had planned a similar *yatra* a week later in July postponed theirs. The Congress's official position was that it wanted to counter the influence of Modi's *yatra*. It had announced the same route as that of the Gaurav Yatra.

The BJP later announced that the Gaurav Yatra would begin on 3 September from Kheda district, one of the worst affected by riots. The BJP state unit chief Rajendrasinh Rana and Narendra Modi were to lead. The place from where the *yatra* was to be launched was significant. Some 200 years ago, Bhatiji Maharaj was killed during a campaign against cow slaughter at Phagvel in Kheda district. (BJP announced the *yatra* on 20 August 2002, as reported by the media). Sonia Gandhi wrote to Vajpayee again in the month of August, urging him to stop the *yatra*. This time the prime minister was in no mood to relent.

The Congress under Vaghela was determined to create problems for Modi. He announced a parallel programme from the same Bhatiji Maharaj temple. Modi avoided a clash and postponed his *yatra* to 7 September. The party justified the decision saying that a large number of *sadhus*, some eminent citizens and others had expressed concerns over the worsening situation in Phagvel.[7]

The *yatra* was postponed again by a day since 7 September was *Shravani Amavasya* when people would be busy with religious ceremonies. Incidentally, 8 is Modi's birth number; the Gaurav Yatra launched on this day proved a great success for Modi.

In a letter addressed to Vaghela, Modi pointed out that despite knowing too well about the BJP's programme, which was announced much in advance, the Congress had come out with a similar programme on the same day at the same place. The Congress had also not taken permission from any authority. Modi's letter wished Vaghela well, although it asserted that the BJP was on the side of the truth.[8]

In a war of wits, Arun Jaitley, who was the party's in-charge for Gujarat, claimed in Delhi, "By launching this *yatra*, the Congress has come around to what we have been saying—that the situation is normal. The party, by its action, has conclusively re-emphasised it."[9]

The Gaurav Yatra was a way to take the battle of Gujarat to the opposition camp. This was best explained in Modi's own words: "I am determined to take out the *yatra* and tell the world the *gaurav gatha* (story of pride) of five crore people of the State. It is not the story of Godhra, Naroda Patia or Gulberg. Gujarat is not a State of murderers and rapists as the pseudo-secularists and power-hungry Congress leaders are attempting to project."[10]

The *yatra* was to criss-cross the State and cover all the 182 assembly constituencies in 45 days. Modi wanted to contact at least 1 lakh people every day. The *yatra* was to happen mostly between Friday and Monday so as to cause least trouble to people. It took the shape of a full-fledged political campaign when election dates were announced. The *yatra* covered 4,200 km during which Modi addressed 400 rallies in 146 constituencies. "This tour instantly met with great popular success."[11]

Talking about the popularity of the *yatra*, Jafferlot said, "On 9 September in Himmatnagar, for instance, a huge crowd gathered along the roadside and at the place where Modi was to hold his rally, which he did not even reach until 2 am."[12]

When the chief minister launched his Gaurav Yatra on 8 September, his target was not Vagehla but Congress President Sonia Gandhi. He referred to Mrs Gandhi as "daughter of Italy" and said, "the Congress cannot return to power by wearing Italian spectacles." BJP's then general secretary Rajnath Singh, who had flagged off the *yatra*, added to Modi's comment saying that he could not conceive of a person "not born of an Indian mother's womb ruling the country".

Modi attacked the Nehru family by saying that it had insulted

Gujarat by sidelining Sardar Vallabhbhai Patel and Morarji Desai: "She did not know that Mahatma Gandhi was born in Porbandar, else she would not have talked of Godse's Gujarat."[13] He was referring to her statement where she had said some people were bent upon turning Gandhi's Gujarat into Godse's Gujarat. He questioned the role of Congress in the Godhra carnage.

His speech at Becharji, Mehsana, became controversial because of media reports that said he had attacked Muslims on the issue of fast population growth. The report quoted him as saying: "What brother, should we run relief camps? Should I start children-producing centres there? We want to achieve progress by pursuing the policy of family planning with determination. *Ame paanch, Amara pachhees* (We are 5 and our 25)... Can't Gujarat implement family planning? Whose inhibitions are coming in our way? Which religious sect is coming in the way?"[14]

Modi denied having said this. In his deposition before inquiry officer AK Malhotra of the Supreme Court supervised SIT in 2010, Modi said, "This speech does not refer to any particular community or religion. This was a political speech in which I tried to point out the increasing population of India... My speech had been distorted by some interested elements who had misinterpreted it to suit their designs. It may be mentioned here that no riots or tension took place after my election speech."[15] The SIT in its final report said that "no criminality has come in respect of this allegation".

At his public meeting at the Chikhli leg of the *yatra* (Third Phase), he clarified that his statement was not directed at any community and that it was merely highlighting the issue of population explosion. He said, "*Paanch na pachhees ane pachees na 625*" (from five to 25 and from 25 to 625).

The chief minister clarified that his remark wasn't directed at Muslims, but at those who did not believe in family planning. He pointed out to the hue and cry over his statement at Becharji and said, "The BJP is not ruling in China but the country has introduced family planning. My utterances about family planning have been given a communal colour. If something is wrong, it is wrong. I don't know why the Congress is interested in increasing population. Probably to increase slums!"[16]

In total, the *yatra* had 11 phases. After the seventh phase, the *yatra* was renamed campaign *yatra*. The Election Commission on 28 October announced the date for polling as 12 December and the BJP was quick to rename the *yatra* the next day.

Modi tried to keep his focus on development issues such as linking of Sabarmati River with Narmada, commencement of work on Sardar Sarovar Project and creation of thousands of check-dams. Added to that was an attack on the Congress for "failing to fight terrorism". The theme kept changing depending on the context.

If it was a direct attack on Sonia during the first phase of the *yatra*, during the second phase, Modi articulated issues related to Dalits. The second phase was also named as Dalit Yatra.[17] He quoted statistics to assert that the BJP had the largest representation of Dalits either at the level of parliament or at the level of the State legislative assembly.

Critics had said the *yatra* would divide the society. Modi countered this by pointing out that Hindus and Muslims together fought against the British in 1857. But by 1947, the society and the country got divided. The BJP was not even there and the Congress committed the sin of dividing the country, he said.

The fourth phase of the *yatra* was launched on 5 October after the terrorist attack on the state's Akshardham temple. Modi's anti-Pakistan, anti-Musharraf focus became more pronounced. He would refer to Musharraf as "*Miyan* Musharraf" and talk of chopping off his hands.[18] Here, he appeared to be expressing his anger at the outcome of the Agra summit where General Pervez Musharraf had tried to outsmart Vajpayee.

The immediate provocation was General Musharraf's speech at the United Nations 57th General assembly on 12 September in New York where he had referred to 2002 Gujarat riots and questioned India's secular credentials.

"*Miyan* Musharraf has defamed Gujarat from the pedestal of peace… We will not accept this. What amazes me, however, is that there is no difference between the speech of Musharraf and that of the Congress. Both speak the same language. Even the drafting of speeches is the same.[19]

"Musharraf should remember there are more Muslims in India than in Pakistan," he said while repeating what Vajpayee had told the UN as a retort to Musharraf. In all the rallies, he spoke of Hindu-Muslim unity in the country and referred to the first war of India's Independence in 1857.[20]

He dismissed the impression created in certain sections of the media that the terrorist attack was due to his speeches during the Gaurav Yatra. Terrorists had launched the attack to stop elections in Jammu & Kashmir and demand release of 10 jailed terrorists, he stressed.[21] But the shape of things to come had already become clear on the Anti-Terrorism Day on 1 October. He said at a function in Ahmedabad, "I will continue to refer to him as *"Miyan* Musharraf"*. If the pseudo-secularists don't like it, they can go and lick Musharraf's boots. I dare him to send more terrorists to Gujarat, we are prepared this time. *"Arey miyan, taari goli khuti jashe"* (*Miyan*, your bullets will get exhausted).[22]

Prime Minister Vajpayee sensed that the situation had become very tense and appealed to everyone to exercise restraint on the Gujarat riot issue. The Congress, however, was determined to hold the State government as responsible. LK Advani got enraged. While replying to a debate in the Rajya Sabha on Gujarat, Advani held that the Gujarat riots were unfortunate and shameful, but he maintained that these were not instigated by the State government or the police. He warned the Congress in the following words, "I will like to tell you that looking at several speeches that have been made... against the Gujarat government, against Modi... then do you think we will not raise questions about what happened in Godhra...We will surely raise this issue."[23]

This found a more combative note in the statement of BJP president M Venkaiah Naidu, who said, "if opposition is violent, we will not be silent."[24]

When Sonia Gandhi launched her campaign in Gujarat, she attacked Modi's Gaurav Yatra for "spreading terror and fear among people through communal divide. Hate, destruction and backwardness are not the *gaurav* of Gujarat," she said.[25] Sonia performed *puja* at the Ambaji temple at Banaskantha district before launching her campaign even when the Congress had attacked Modi for visiting temples during Gaurav Yatra.

Modi gave a resounding reply as if he was waiting for such an occasion. While addressing a rally at Bhuj the next day, he charged the Congress as "being a mother of terrorism" and "responsible for all problems faced by the country". On the charge of dividing the society, he countered saying, "The sin of dividing the country can be attributed to the Congress". He took a dig at Sonia: "Her speech had surprised everybody. It is *ulta chor kotwal ko daante* (the thief blaming the cop).[26]

On the poll day, Modi predicted a landslide for the BJP in Gujarat. "I see an emotional frenzy in the BJP's favour." On the fate of the Congress, he said that he did not see any battle and "we remain unchallenged". On the issue of fighting terrorism, he clarified that he was merely raising the issue of people's security. "I am not talking about terrorism. Last night in Asarva constituency, I told the voters that if you have the best of the luxuries of life, but if your sons do not return home safely in the evening, what's the use? People do understand my point."[27]

Modi's campaign mesmerised people. At some of the election meetings, one could witness people's eyes riveted in the direction of Modi's face and hands. The meetings were marked by a large presence of women; they waited for hours till late in the night to listen to him. A BJP leader had said then that Modi had emerged as the only saviour who could guarantee peace and security. His plank succeeded. People discovered a leader who was genuinely concerned with their fears and issues.[28] Women, in particular, started looking at him as someone who would protect their children.

The ultimate testimonial of Modi came from his mother Hiraba. Modi has given strict instructions to his family and kin not to interfere in his political life. But a mother is a mother after all. Seeing her son attacked from all sides, she could not restrain herself. Defending him, she says, "My son is not against anybody. For him, *desh prem* (love of the nation) is more important than anything else in life." When a reporter told her that Muslims dislike him, she said, "Ask the Muslims of Vadnagar. They will never say anything against my son. He is not against Muslims. He always used to tell me that if there is one person who is ready to die for the country, it is him."[29]

In the results for the assembly elections that came out on 20 December 2002, the BJP swept Gujarat, winning 127 out of 182 seats. The Congress won only 51 of the 180 it contested. In terms of votes polled the BJP polled 49.85 per cent against 44.81 per cent it had polled in 1998. The Congress this time polled 39.28 percent as against 34.85 per cent last time.[30]

Campaign Trail 2007: Modi Wins Despite All Odds

When the State started gearing up for the next assembly polls, Modi became the longest serving chief minister of Gujarat. He completed 2,063 days in office on 1 June. The earlier record was held by Hitendra Desai who had completed 2,062 days in 1970s. Modi had come as a night watchman but continued on the crease uninterrupted with no one knowing how to bowl him out.

He set out to make development the main theme of his campaign in 2007. But, the Congress had calculated that personal attacks on Modi and raising the riot issue would pay rich dividends electorally. Rebellion within the BJP, perhaps, made the Congress sense victory even before the elections.

The intensely polarised election campaign of 2002 had not allowed any rebellion within the BJP. Some leaders loyal to Keshubhai Patel, such as Haren Pandya, did maintain some semblance of rebellion, but finally quit the Modi cabinet in August 2002. Soon BJP leaders realised that Modi was there to stay and was becoming immensely popular with the electorate due to his no-nonsense approach.

Gradually, Keshubhai became the fulcrum of all dissident activities. But Modi never attacked him. The chief minister maintained the decorum befitting the seniority of Keshubhai. He always touched Keshubhai's feet, something taken very positively in the traditional Gujarati society.

Dissidence got translated into rebellion as elections approached near. When Keshubhai Patel returned from the United States in August 2005 after treatment of his ailing wife, at least 39 legislators, six members of Parliament and hundreds of party workers gathered at his residence seeking a change of leadership in the state.

Legislator Bechar Badhani even told the media that they wanted a change in the political leadership. Vadodara legislator Yogesh Patel, who had written a letter to Modi expressing concern with the condition of Gujarat, said the same.

Senior leader Kashiram Rana said, "MLAs have expressed their feelings. Discussions on the issue will be held in the coming days. About 60 MLAs have come in support of Keshubhai, and this number will increase."[31]

The anti-Modi camp in the BJP had started working to a strategy.

The Koli conference organised by the Gujarat Koli Seva Samaj witnessed participation by dissident BJP MLAs who took pot-shots at Modi and questioned the government on the issue of law and order. Gordhan Zadaphia (general secretary of the BJP state unit) was also present at the meeting.[32]

Zadaphia was leading dissident activities under the banner of 'Sardar Patel Utkarsh Samiti' run by a Patel businessman. He could thus lead the dissidents and also claim his meeting to be apolitical. He organised many such meetings to reach out to Patel farmers before holding a Patel farmer *mahasammelan* (big meeting) in Rajkot. He would tell them how their problems remained unsolved in the last five years, how the crime rate had zoomed, and how rural development had taken a backseat.

At the *mahasammelan* in Rajkot on 14 September, nearly two lakh people were present. A resolution adopted at the meeting urged people to defeat the chief minister at the polls. In a no-holds barred campaign, the dissidents criticised both Modi and his mentor Advani. A call was given to defeat any BJP candidate projected by the chief minister and the only way to do this was 'voting for the Congress united'. BJP MP from Surendranagar, Somabhai Patel declared before the gathering: "Even if my son is contesting on a BJP ticket, defeat him."[33]

In October, the Election Commission announced two-phase polling for the assembly, on 11 and 16 December, and brought momentum in the campaign. Modi's campaign, this time too, began with a confrontation with the Election Commission since the latter was unhappy with the transfer of officials that was carried out in the first week of October. Well before the announcement of the election dates, the government of Gujarat had carried out a major reshuffle in the bureaucracy and transferred 41 IPS officers. Of these, 19 were transferred with promotions. These were transfers as per the guidelines of the Election Commission as the chief electoral officer of the state had attested.[34]

The Congress and others complained to the Election Commission. After the model code came into effect, the Commission transferred eight top officials in the name of free and fair polls. The BJP strongly objected to the transfers and sought to know the reason while alleging that the Commission was merely acting on the basis of complaints of the Congress.

In October, three things happened that went against Modi and gave reason for celebration to the Opposition camp. These were in the form of open display of fratricidal war in the Sangh Parivar. This happened on three successive dates: 21-23 October 2007. On 21 October, Keshubhai Patel attended a function in Ahmedabad to honour Gordhan Zadaphia where he said, "Unless Ravan is destroyed, Ram *rajya* can't be ushered in". On 22 October, *sadhus* convened a Hindu Dharma Raksha Sant Sammelan in Amreli and announced the formation of a 'Hindu Suraksha Manch'. They took a pledge to remove Modi. On 23 October, *Sah Prant Prachak* of RSS, Mukund Deovankar, said, "The Sangh would not support any party in Gujarat." He expressed his unhappiness with the infighting in the BJP. This was like two grown-up sons in a family fighting, he explained while pointing out the reason for not casting support with one or the other.

The same day Praful Sanjaliya, president of the Bhartiya Kisan Sangh, a frontal organisation of the RSS said, "If necessary, the BKS will coordinate with the Congress to remove Modi."[35]

Senior BJP leader Suresh Mehta, the brain behind the rebel strategy, rubbed salt into the wound: "The BJP in Gujarat was built by thousands of workers. But Modi has turned everything on its head, and the high command remains a powerless mute spectator before this one man."[36]

A few days before that when Modi was addressing a rally at Surat, some miscreants set fire to vehicles parked near the venue. This prompted Modi to challenge those who were fomenting trouble. "I challenge them to set me on fire." He later described the incident as the handiwork of "either the opposition party (Congress) or rebels... Their intention was to reach the stage and cause harm to people but adequate security prevented them from doing so. As a final resort, they set the vehicles ablaze."[37]

The rebels' strategy was to attack Modi both from inside and outside the party. According to the strategy, "Keshubhai and former Union textile minister Kashiram Rana won't leave the BJP. Suresh Mehta and suspended rebel Zadaphia will resign from the party but will neither join the Congress nor contest elections. They'll run the Sardar Patel Utkarsh Samiti which will coordinate the effort to defeat the BJP in Gujarat. However, a few rebel legislators will be ensured Congress tickets."[38]

All these campaigns were overtaken by the BJP's carpet bombing campaign on 27 November. About 80 BJP leaders addressed public rallies in various parts of the state. Among those who participated included party president Rajnath Singh, former president Venkaiah Naidu, general secretary in-charge of Gujarat elections Arun Jaitley, former Union Ministers Sushma Swaraj and Ravishankar Prasad; and Gopinath Munde, Sushil Kumar Modi, Arjun Munda, Vinay Katiyar, Kalraj Mishra, Navjyot Singh Sidhu and Smriti Irani.

Two themes dominated the campaign: 'development' and 'attack on the Congress'. Modi, who launched the campaign from Botad (Bhavnagar), highlighted the achievements of his government, such as bringing Narmada water to parched lands of Saurashtra, making the state electricity board profitable, giving uninterrupted power supply for 24 hours, controlling crime and making the administration work. He spoke about his own personal integrity and his commitment to make the state more developed.

His attack on the Congress included discrimination against Gujarat—"overnight theft of 200 MW from Gujarat's quota of power", backing off from its promise of giving a power project at Pipavav, excluding Saurashtra region from employment guarantee scheme and for failing to develop the state in the last 45 years.

He condemned the Congress for the UPA Government's affidavit in the Supreme Court that stated that there was no scientific evidence to prove the existence of Lord Ram* and raised the issue of engraving a "Cross" on a two-rupee coin in place of the map of India.**

---

*   The UPA Government had on 12 September 2007 filed an affidavit in the Supreme Court on the issue of Sethusamudram Shipping Canal Project. In this, the government had said among other things that there was no proof of the existence of Lord Ram or other characters in *The Ramayana*. The affidavit was filed by the Archaeological Survey of India. The government was trying to build a case for approval of the project even if it meant damage to the mythological *Ram Setu* (Adam's Bridge). Later, after opposition from many quarters including LK Advani's demand for an apology from Prime Minister Manmohan Singh and UPA Chairperson Sonia Gandhi, the government withdrew the controversial affidavit on 14 September

** The RBI issued a two-rupee coin in 2006. The coin did not have map of India but it had an equal armed cross with the beams dividing into two rays with dots between adjacent beams. The RBI explained that "four heads sharing the common body" represented "unity and diversity". The RSS demanded immediate withdrawal saying that the design resembled "Jerusalem Cross". It held that using a religious symbol on a coin is against the country's secular tradition.

Modi attacked Prime Minister Manmohan Singh's statement that Muslims must have the first claim on resources* and sought to know the reason for not granting asylum to Taslima Nasreen while allowing "Bangladeshis to live in lanes and by-lanes of the country."[39] He offered to give asylum to Taslima.

But things were going to change soon since the Congress was determined to put Modi on the mat on the 'communal' issue. The state congress unit came out with a charge-sheet against Modi on 1 December and attacked the BJP for harbouring "contempt and hatred against Muslims of Gujarat". It said, "Riot-affected Muslims are still living in miserable conditions. The State government has offered them less than a pittance." The chargesheet was released simultaneously at Surat, Rajkot, Vadodara and Ahmedabad.

The chargesheet spat venom. It read: "It is very sad state of affairs that a constitutionally bound state government has grossly failed in protecting the lives and property of Muslim citizens. It believes that its only duty is fulfilled by passing on the central government assistance to the riot-affected people."[40]

The same day, while addressing a rally at Jamanpada village in Chikli reserved assembly constituency, Sonia Gandhi stunned everyone by calling Modi "*maut ka saudagar*" (merchant of death): "During the rule of people who claim a '*bhaya-mukt samaj*,' nobody is safe. So many of my sisters, children and brothers have been exploited and are being exploited even now. Only criminals are safe; those who are getting protection from the government. The truth is that… today, those running the Gujarat government are liars, betrayers and merchants of fear and death."[41] Senior Congress leader Digvijaya Singh spoke of "existence of Hindu terrorism in Gujarat". The BJP condemned his remark and demanded an apology. The Election Commission asked for an explanation from him.[42]

The Congress chargesheet, Sonia's aggressive statement and Digvijaya Singh's unprovoked attack showed that the Congress had realised it must

---

*   Manmohan Singh said this at a meeting of the National Development Council in Delhi on 9 December 2006. BJP chief ministers including Narendra Modi who was present at the meeting had challenged the Prime Minister's assertion. Modi had contended that every citizen had equal rights over the country's resources. "Such a statement does not behove a senior leader like the PM. It is unfortunate," he had said

polarise voters and prevent Modi from walking away with a trophy for winning the debate on development. It also became obvious that even if Modi won, the Congress did not want him to acquire a secular image that could propel him to stake claims at the Centre.

Many reports quoted Modi as having justified the killing of gangster Sohrabuddin in a police encounter in 2005. The chief minister, however, rejected this charge and proved himself right in his reply to the Election Commission.

He was quoted as saying different things in different reports on the same issue. One such report which became controversial came from a rally at Mangrol (south Gujarat) on 4 December. A report that appeared in *The Times of India* on 5 December quoted Modi as having said, "You tell what should be done to Sohrabuddin?" People at the rally shouted, as reported by the newspaper, "Kill him, kill him." Modi replied, "Well, that is what I did. And I did what was necessary."[43]

Another newspaper apparently either did not have the original report or they published the report a day late. *The Statesman's* report of 6 December quoted Modi as saying, "He (Sohrabuddin) has got what he deserved". *The Hindustan Times* wrote on 6 December: "Well then, that's it." (from the elaborate reply Gujarat CM filed before the Election Commission)

After scrutinising the CD provided by the Commission on 7 December, Modi gave his reply: "I find none of the above statements are contained in my speech as recorded in the CD. The EC notice is issued on the basis of unverified and false media reports. I have gone through my speech on the CD supplied. It is merely a response to Mrs Sonia Gandhi calling me '*Maut-ka-Saudagar*'. This part of my speech was entirely against terrorism. I responded that the '*Maut-ka-Saudagar*' are all those who attacked parliament. At no point of time I have either justified the specific encounter of Sohrabuddin's case, nor have I used the specific inculpatory sentences used in *The Times of India* report... The CD clearly indicates that this sentence was an invention of the author and not the orator... Nowhere in my speech have I explicitly referred to the religion of any person. I have spoken against terrorism. It is not my speech but the complaint which assumes terrorism is linked to a religion."[44]

Modi had become a victim of false reporting once again. Clearly, there could not have been so many versions of the same speech. Modi definitely did not utter the last sentence which could be construed as justification.

The Election Commission held Sonia Gandhi's statement as violation of the code, whereas it warned Modi to be more cautious in future in adhering to the model code of conduct.

The assembly elections of 2007, therefore, became a Modi-centric election with the Congress trying to defame him and Modi trying to brave all odds. In that context, Advani showered praise on Modi for his performance saying, "Such an economic miracle would not have been possible in any other state." Former Union Disinvestment Minister Arun Shourie showered unqualified praise for Modi and hailed him to be the "prime ministerial candidate". He said that Gujarat and Modi had become synonymous with performance and for getting things done.[45]

The Congress was jubilant watching the war within the Sangh Parivar. Overconfidence was evident when the party rejected the exit poll of 18 December that predicted a win for Modi. Spokesperson Abhishek Singhvi asserted the Congress would win a clear majority. The party was confident of its unified but decentralised election strategy that took support from everyone who could affect Modi.[46]

When the results came out on 23 December, the BJP had won 117 out of 182 seats, polling 49.12 per cent of votes. The Congress won just 59 seats and polled 39.63 per cent votes on the seats it contested. Congress contested 173 seats, leaving the rest for its allies.

On 25 December, Modi was sworn in as chief minister for the third time. On the election result day, Keshubhai congratulated Modi for the victory and said that both the ruling and opposition party should work together. The first thing which Modi did after his swearing-in was to visit Keshubhai Patel's residence and touch his feet to seek his blessings.

Modi was humbled by his decisive victory. At a meeting of the BJP legislative party, Modi, choked with emotions, had this to say: "Those who say that Modi is bigger than the party don't know the history of the BJP and the Jana Sangh. A son cannot be bigger than his mother."[47]

2012 Polls: Underwriting the Future

Having learnt its lessons from two successive defeats, the Congress tried to build up on the organisational support base and worked to neutralise the advantages Modi had. About a year before polls, the Congress launched mass contact programmes to achieve a better connect with people. It took the *yatra* route with four theme-based *yatras*. It systematically focussed on different sections of the population. It also organised caste rallies aimed at specific communities such as the OBCs or Dalits.

The fortnight-long *'hisab do, jawab do'* (give account, give reply) from 6 February 2012 tried to punch holes in the government's claim that it was honest. It was first launched in Ahmedabad and then extended to other places. In reply, Modi, who was on a one-day *sadbhavna* fast at Bardoli, asked Prime Minister Singh to give a reply to what happened to Rs 1,76,000 crore in the 2G scam. He said "either you answer or leave the government."[48]

The 12-day *Sardar Sandesh Yatra* in the first fortnight of January 2012 was to witness six mini-yatras from different parts of the state but converging at Anand, five km from Karamsad, where Sardar Vallabhbhai Patel spent his childhood.

The Jansampark Parivartan Yatra of the Congress was initiated to seek explanation from the state government. It was launched on 10 April 2012 and concluded on 25 April 2012. It focussed mainly on development and governance issues. Narhari Amin said, "We will be highlighting the failure of the BJP government in the state on all the fronts, which is pinching the middle class and urban citizens.

The Congress organised *Kshatriya Asmita Sammelan* at Patan on 6 May 2012 in a clear attempt to woo the Thakur voters, which form a major chunk of the Kshatriya bulk vote. During the conclave, Vaghela asked Kshatriyas not to vote for Kshatriya candidates of the BJP. He said, "When there is a Kshatriya candidate from BJP contesting an assembly poll, you should stay away from voting in his favour. If situation arises, vote for a Rabari candidate of Congress, but not a Kshatriya of the BJP."[49]

The party also tried to woo the Patidar (Patel) community. A Congress stalwart explained, "From the total population of 6.03 crore in the state, 1.5 crore are from the Patidar community. The present State government has divided these people using Machiavellian practices. But now these people stand united and will express their solidarity with the Congress in the forthcoming sammelan."[50]

After a good response from the two caste conferences, the Congress launched *Kinara Bachao Yatra* for people in the coastal areas and *Adivasi Adhikar Yatra* for tribals.

The Congress promised free electricity to the tribal people and poor consuming 50-100 units per month.[51]

The Congress was helped a lot by Keshubhai who resigned from the BJP (4 August)—his party of 60 years—and formed a separate political party, the Gujarat Parivartan Party, within two days of his resignation. He claimed this to be "the real BJP" and termed the Modi-rule as "total misrule". Senior BJP leader Kashiram Rana also left the BJP along with him. Keshubhai asserted that his new outfit would provide a viable third front in the face of polarised politics between the BJP and the Congress. The Mahagujarat Janata Party, founded by Gordhan Zadaphia in 2007, merged with the GPP on 8 August. In September, Patel announced he would undertake an election campaign *yatra* by the name Parivartan Yatra (march for change).

These developments emboldened poll pundits to predict doom for Modi since Keshubhai was a powerful caste leader who could easily damage the BJP's Patel votes. Also, this time the Congress was much better prepared and had launched its campaign much in advance. The Congress had attacked the plank of development and made tall poll promises that could woo anyone shaped in the old order, where the government was a provider of freebies in exchange for votes every five years. The battle was tough indeed.

About a year before election, Modi started a movement of 'Sadbhavna Mission' under which he sat on fast for three days from 17 September. "I deeply believe that this fast will further strengthen Gujarat's environment of peace, unity and harmony. 'Sadbhavana Mission' is completely dedicated to the society and the nation," he said in his appeal.

This came after the Supreme Court judgement on 12 September 2011 by which it asked the trial court to look into the two reports—the SIT report and the report of Amicus Curie Raju Ramachandran—and then decide on the course of the case filed by Zakia Jafri in the Gulberg Society riot case. This was interpreted as a big relief for Narendra Modi and the BJP. Most BJP leaders were jubilant. Modi tweeted: "God is Great".

Leader of the Opposition in the Rajya Sabha, Arun Jaitley, said that the Supreme Court verdict had vindicated the BJP's consistent stand that allegations against Narendra Modi were totally false and there was no shred of evidence to connect him with the unfortunate riots.

Leader of the Opposition in the Lok Sabha, Sushma Swaraj, said through her tweet: "Narendrabhai has passed *agnipareeksha* (test by fire) today. My heartiest congratulations to him. *Satyamev Jayate. Varshon baad aaj satya ki vijay hui hai* (truth has triumphed after many years)."

BJP patriarch and Modi's mentor LK Advani welcomed the verdict and described this as a big relief to the BJP. He said this in Mumbai: "Never in the history of India has there been misinformation propaganda against any political leader as it has been against Mr Modi."[52]

Modi, while launching the *sadbhavna* fast, said, "One thing is apparent from the Supreme Court's judgement. The unhealthy environment created by the unfounded and false allegations made against me and Government of Gujarat, after 2002 riots, has come to an end. For the past 10 years, it has become fashionable to defame me and the State of Gujarat. These elements who could not tolerate any positive development of Gujarat have not left any stone unturned to defame Gujarat. It is difficult to say whether this campaign of defamation will stop even after the judgement of the Supreme Court. But one thing is certain that the credibility of those who have been spreading lies and defaming Gujarat has come to its lowest ebb. The people of this country will not trust such elements anymore."

He spoke about the vilification campaign against him: "After 2002, Gujarat has not spared any effort to march towards peace, harmony and progress even amidst false propaganda, lies, conspiracies and allegations."

His appeal had a more humbling tone and an unequivocal assertion on unity and diversity. He was keen to overcome the bitterness of the past and make a new beginning: "The Indian history is a witness that casteism and communalism have never done any good to society. This is also my own firm conviction. Gujarat has understood this and having overcome these evils, it has adopted the path of Inclusive Development. We are committed to work for a developed Gujarat for a developed India."[53]

Good wishes came from other corners as well. LK Advani said that "there are many misunderstandings about Narendra Modi and with the objective of overcoming these misunderstandings he has started this *sadbhavna* fast. I, as a senior to Mr Modi, give him my blessings for this mission." Both Advani and Arun Jaitley were present when the fast began.

While ending the fast on 19 September, Modi declared that he would undertake *Sadbhavna* fast in every district of the State where he would spend one day from morning till evening. "Above *Rajneeti* (politics) is something called *Rashtraniti* (politics for nation); this fast and mission is *Rashtraniti* not *Rajneeti*."

After observing 36 fasts cross the states, Modi concluded the Sadbhavna Mission on 16 February 2012 at the Ambaji temple town. He described the task undertaken as "*Ashwamedha Yajna* for peace and unity."* The three themes of these meetings were "stop spreading lies about Gujarat", development mantra is "medicine for all problems" and "the State government rules with sensitivity and care".

The mission was one of the massive public contact programmes undertaken by Modi outside the election time. More than 50 lakh people from about 18,000 villages of the state participated. Modi encouraged community participation to spread the message of goodwill. Youth and newlyweds denounced social evils such as dowry and child infanticide and pledged to adopt *anganwadis*. Drawing, elocution and essay competitions were held on *sadbhavna* theme in which about 10 lakh children participated.[54]

The hallmark of Sadbhavna Mission was also to explain the government's stand towards the minorities so that there were no misgivings. While concluding the three-day *sadbhavna* fast at Ahmedabad on 19 September, Modi clarified that his government did not work for either majority or minority. An interesting read from his speech: "Let me narrate a previous experience of mine to you. A few years ago, the Government of India had set up a commission, the Justice Sachar Committee to look into the socio-economic conditions of the minority communities in India. When Justice Sachar and his team visited Gujarat, they undertook their study surveying every department after which their meeting with the chief minister was fixed. During the meeting, they asked me what I do for the minorities in my state. Brothers and sisters,

---

*   *Ashwamedha Yajna* used to be organised by Kings in ancient India by which they would allow the yagna horse to go wherever it liked. Allowing the horse to pass through one's territory was taken as accepting the authority of the King, whereas stopping the horse was challenging the authority and hence an invitation to fight.

let me tell you the answer I gave them—I said my government does not work for minorities. They were stunned. How could one speak in such a fashion? I made it very clear that my government does not work for minorities. Then I told them to add another line—that neither does my government work for majority! My government works for six crore Gujaratis. Well-being of all and development of all, this is the motto of my government. For me, such differences, this compartmentalisation, weighing everything as majority and minority and vote bank politics are not acceptable. In my State, all my citizens are my own. Their sadness is my sadness, their pleasures my pleasures and their dreams my dreams."[55]

When elections came close, Narendra Modi embarked on a month-long Swami Vivekananda Yuva Vikas Yatra beginning 11 September (2012); a day when Swami Vivekananda delivered his famous Chicago speech about 120 years back. This was launched from Becharaji in Mehsana district and concluded at Pavagadh on 11 October in Panchmahal district. The *yatra* was carried on in a motorized rath.

During the launch of the *yatra*, he clarified that the comparison was between the achievements of the Gujarat government under him and the achievements of the central government under Prime Minister Manmohan Singh. He compared the Congress to a "cancer-causing *gutkha* (tobacco mix)" and gave a call for a "*gutkha*-free Gujarat, Congress-free Gujarat". He attacked the Congress and the Prime Minister on the issue of corruption such as 2G case and asked them to set-up a SIT team under the Supreme Court if they were so confident of themselves. He charged the Congress with using the CBI to fight elections.[56]

The *yatra* concluded on the birth anniversary of Loknayak Jayaprakash Narayan who had inspired Modi during the anti-Emergency struggle in the 1970s. Also, the day was being celebrated as International Day of Girl Child. Modi dwelt at length on detailing his government's efforts at reducing female foeticide. He recalled how he got tears in his eyes when the 2001 census showed Gujarat as a state with adverse sex ratio.

Modi was not shy of mentioning his adoration of Swami Vivekananda. He recalled how Narendra Nath (Swami Vivekananda) had visited Maha Kali Maa but sought nothing. He said, "Narendra was divine soul, but this Narendra is an ordinary person who has sought prosperity, good monsoons, protection against natural calamity, harmony, peace, unity, education, health and dignity of women."

The *yatra* covered 3,500 kilometres during which Modi announced formation of 7 districts and 45 new *talukas*. He delivered 32 speeches over 16 days. His theme was development and criticism of the Congress for not doing enough.

The Vivekananda Yuva Vikas Yatra was in progress when the Election Commission announced (3 October) that the State would witness elections on 13 and 17 December with counting of votes on December 20. The *yatra* speeches, therefore, became election speeches as well.

The Congress was very confident and had decided to fight Modi on the issue of development. When Sonia launched her first public rally at Rajkot, she focussed on puncturing the development claims of Modi. She did not even refer to the issue of her foreign trips raised by Modi.

The very next day, when Modi addressed a public meeting at Dahod, he described Ms Gandhi's speech as "lacklustre". He took a dig at her and said she was scared of speaking in Gujarat for fear of a backlash. He charged the Congress with "cheating" the people by not fulfilling the promise it made in 2009 LokSabha Elections that it would curb price rise within 100 days of coming to power.

The heat of statements and the failure to put Modi on the mat made Congress leaders bitter. Local Congress leaders heaped abuses on Modi. State Congress President Arjun Modhwadia described Modi as a "monkey". This is what he said while comparing Modi's perpetual attack on Dr Manmohan Singh:

"He is like a monkey who is challenging the king of jungle to a duel from the top of a tree. He should know where he stands. The king of jungle will not climb the tree but the monkey will have to come down to the land some time… Modi doesn't have anything to say about what he had done for Gujarat in the past so many years, but every now and then he will blame Soniaji and Manmohan Singh and even challenge the PM to fight elections against him from Gujarat."[57]

While senior Congress leader Mani Shankar Aiyar compared Modi with Ravana and called him a '*lahu purush*' (blood man), Congress parliamentarian Hussain Dalvi compared him with a 'rat'. Shankersinh Vaghela in his speech held Modi Government directly responsible for the Godhra riots for which the Election Commission issued a notice saying that Vaghela's speech was inflammatory.

At his first address using 3D technology from Gandhinagar, Modi lashed out at the Congress for using such language. However, he accepted the terms they used for him saying these creatures were "messengers of God".

"Had Congress leaders studied the *Ramayana*, they would have got a fair idea of *vanar shakti*. I accept the title given by them to me... Devotion and services of Lord Hanuman are known globally... I have got the chance to serve Gujarat, so the six crore Gujaratis are like Ram to me. I am their Hanuman."

Replying to the 'rat' comparison, he said that the Congress leader was unaware of the significance of rats in Hindu mythology. "A rat is considered to be the vehicle of '*vighnaharta*' Ganesh... I feel proud that with Lord Ganesh on my back, Gujarat faces no problems."[58]

When Manmohan Singh addressed his first election rally in tribal Vansda district (9 December), he charged that the state government had worked for a handful of corporates and called upon the electorate for "liberating" the state from divisive politics. He also spoke about insecurities of the minorities; an issue which the Congress had not spoken about till then.[59]

Modi launched a sharp attack on both Sonia Gandhi and Dr Manmohan Singh and charged them with playing vote bank politics. Referring to Sonia Gandhi's claim that the Congress was a party that believed in service to the people, Modi said it was not service but "*mewa-bhawik*" (benefits) that motivated the Congress. He punched holes into the allegations that the State was not developed and reeled out statistics to prove his points.

While referring to the prime minister's comments about 'divisive politics', he said, "I thought being the prime minister of the country he would treat all the states equally. But hearing him speak a language of minority and majority would hurt any Gujarati."[60]

His address was beamed simultaneously at 53 places, making the Congress uncomfortable because of the huge impact it could create.

Rahul Gandhi was not going to take the back seat in attacking Modi. In his first election rally in the state at Sanand (11 December), he termed Modi a "marketeer": "The marketeer says Gujarat is shining. But tell me for how many hours do people get water? People get water for 25 minutes in every three days. But marketeer says Gujarat is shining. There are 10 lakh unemployed youth in Gujarat. But marketeer says Gujarat is shining."[61]

Modi retorted: "I am the only person who says my Gujarat is shining due to 6 crore Gujaratis. But how individualistic are you? Five thousand schemes have been named only after your father, your grandmother and your great grandfather. You are *parivarvadi* (dynastic); you are individualistic and have crippled democracy... Rahul *baba zaban sambhal ke bolna* (Rahul Gandhi speak carefully). Your language does not suit democracy."[62]

Modi asked him to realise Gandhiji's wish and disband the Congress. Rahul Gandhi had quoted Mahatma Gandhi in his speech. Modi said, "He said I am walking on Gandhiji's path, but if he is actually walking on Gandhiji's path, then one wish of Mahatma Gandhi would not be left incomplete—to disband the Congress after Independence." He continued to address Rahul Gandhi as "Rahul Baba".[63]

Modi further said on Twitter, "Mr Rahul Gandhi talks of respect for Vidhan Sabha but his own attendance in Lok Sabha between May 2011-May 2012 was 24 out of 85 sittings!"

Results

The result left the Congress dumbstruck. Modi won Gujarat again. This time the BJP won 115 of the 182. The Congress won 61 and Keshubhai Patel's party won 2 seats. In terms of vote share, the BJP polled 48.3 per cent, whereas the Congress polled 40.59 per cent. Patel's party had contested from 167 seats and it lost deposits from 159 constituencies. However, it polled 3.99 per cent votes in the seats contested and seriously dented the prospects of the BJP on many seats.

Keshubhai claimed credit for denting Modi: "We did not win as many seats as we expected, but we succeeded in reducing Modi's majority by two seats compared to 2007... We damaged the BJP's chances in at least 15, especially in Saurashtra. Can you imagine Modi's overall tally had we not been in the race? He would easily have pocketed 130 to 135 seats."[64]

Yet, Modi tried to forget the bitterness of the past and went to seek the blessings of Keshubhai Patel on the victory day. But one thing was not missed by anyone. This was an election in which the people of Gujarat defeated caste politics and supported the development agenda. People voted against the vilification campaign against Modi. The state witnessed a record turnout of 71.30 per cent rating. It was 59 per cent in 2007. Going by conventional wisdom, it should have helped the opposition. What prompted people to come out and vote in such large numbers? It was a positive vote for governance.

Modi had his work to speak for himself. No one believed development could be a clincher. A large number of young voters turned out to vote. What many analysts ignored was the fruits of development the people of Gujarat had begun to reap. Modi had transformed Gujarat and they were witness to this phenomenon.

3D-Campaign

On 18 November 2012, Gujarat created history of a different kind. The tech savvy chief minister used holographic projection technology and satellite link-ups to produce 3D images and flashed his televised address across four cities of the State. Audiences at Ahmedabad, Vadodara, Rajkot and Surat could see the virtual Modi who was sitting in a studio in Gandhinagar delivering his address.

The virtual images looked real and people could get a feel of having interacted with their leader, though he was present in a studio. The audiences did not need the special glasses to get the 3D experience. "You are witnessing a unique and first-ever incident," he said while highlighting the importance of the address.

In doing so, Modi revolutionised electioneering and became the first Indian to use this technology that has been used in the West by singers Madonna and Mariah Carey, Prince Charles of the United Kingdom, King Abdullah of Saudi Arabia and former US Vice President Al Gore.

However, this revolutionary address paled in comparison to the technology used on 10 December; a technology used never before and which subsequently entered into *The Guinness Book of World Record.*

Modi's speech was broadcast simultaneously at 53 locations in the state's 26 cities. The speech was 55-minute long. Raj Kasu Reddy and Mani Shankar, who head the Hyderabad-based Nchant 3D (India), were the men who made it possible. In March 2013, this was recognised by the Guinness Book as the most simultaneous broadcast of the "Pepper's Ghost Illusion".

The chief minister tweeted 14 March 2013: "Gujarat election campaign-2012 becomes even more memorable with 3D interaction, creating Guinness World Record."[65]

On 4 December, Modi was at Nizar (Tapi district) to address a rally at 9 am and Mandvi (South Gujarat) at 10:30 am, Chiukhli (Navsari district) at 11:45 am and in the evening address simultaneously at 52 places using 3D technology and go for another meeting at Sanand in the night.

In all, he made five addresses linking with people at 188 places. His first was on 18 November when he addressed people in four cities. He did the same at 26 places on 29 November, 52 places on 4 December, and 53 each respectively on 10 and 14 December.

Modi's website has described this as a "game changer".[66]

In his thanksgiving speech, he dwelt at length on how the people of Gujarat had voted for development. But the way he thanked them, it seemed he was almost bidding farewell. His entire speech was in Hindi. And he sought forgiveness of the people of Gujarat if he had done anything wrong in the last 11 years of his being in power, "*Ek insaan ke naate kahin koi meri kami reh gayi ho... kahin koi meri galti reh gayi ho to main, mere 6 karod Gujarati bhaiyon aur behnon....uske liye main aap sab ki kshama mangta hun...*" (If, as a human being, I have committed any mistake... any mistake anywhere... I seek apology from you, six crore brothers and sisters of Gujarat).

He continued and outlined his future role: "*Bhaiyon behnon, kaun jeeta kaun hara wo kaam pura ho chuka hai... ab yug shuru hota hai ek nayi zimmedari ka... log sochte the jab main pehli baar chun kar ke aaya... logon ko lagta tha ab Modiji aram karengey... wo unki soch galat nikli... 2007 mein main ne teesri baar shapath li to phir logon ne kaha ki ab itni vijay aa gayi hai... to mauj karengey... par phir galat nikle... main 2012 men saamne se kehta hun mere sambandh mein aisaa mat sochna... aane wale 5 saal har pal ye janta janardan ko samarpit hain... meri taraf se parishram mein koi kami nahin rahegi.*"

(Brothers and sisters, who has lost who has won, this work is over... Now starts a new era of responsibility and accountability... When I got elected for the first time, people thought now Modi will rest... their thinking was proved to be incorrect... In 2007, I took oath for the third time and people said again, now that he has been getting victories, he would sit and enjoy... They were proved wrong again... I am telling you before, don't think such things about me... In the coming five years, each moment of my life is devoted to the cause of people... There will be no dearth of hard work from my side.)

He pooh-poohed those who thought that government employees did not wish to work and held that they would not vote for the BJP since he had made them work very hard. But when ballots of government employees were opened, about 75 per cent of them had voted for Modi.

An emotional Modi said, "*Log mujhe patthar marte rehte hain per main un pattharon se seedhee bana leta hun.*" (People keep throwing stones at me but I convert these stones into a ladder). "I have got many medals (positive) and stones (negative) but the biggest medal for me is the one which my people have given me today."[67]

***

Development Challenges

I'm a greater believer in luck, and I find
the harder I work the more I have of it

— **Thomas Jefferson**

The Gujarat growth story is, "freeing up space for private sector expenditure in capital formation", increasing the efficiency of public expenditure, "more bangs for the bucks, so to speak" and "governance innovations" such as use of IT (information technology) to make government transparent and more accountable.[1]

In an interview to the author in 2004, when asked why he was not divesting the state-controlled PSUs on the pattern of the NDA coalition at the Centre. Modi said: "I am a Gujarati and I know business. If I sell these loss making PSUs now, the state may not get the real value of the efforts that have gone into this. I want that first these should be made profit-making PSUs. After that we can think of divesting."

He was talking about two loss-making PSUs—Gujarat Alkalies and Chemicals Ltd (GACL) and the Gujarat State Fertiliser Chemicals Ltd (GSFC). The GSFC was in dire straits with huge losses of Rs 392 crore in 2003. The government would have earned Rs 91 crore by selling 43 per cent of its shares. The GACL, one of the largest caustic soda producers in India, was running in losses and it had already achieved a turnaround in 2003. The government would have got Rs 81 crore by selling its stake, which was 36 per cent.[2]

Instead of selling these industries and making some quick money for the government, Modi decided to give them time and make them profitable. The units achieved the turnaround. Modi's solution was simple: 'Put the right man on the right job.'

He focussed on transparency and accountability and promised to create an environment conducive to growth of the private sector. He was confident that Gujarat would be able to achieve more than 10 per cent growth only if the state was able to forge a symbiotic partnership with the private sector. He gave the motto of '*Sauno Saath, Sauno Vikas*' (let everybody come along; let everybody progress).

Ordering development and weaving growth stories were something that Modi had always dreamt of doing. He had great faith in the famed entrepreneurial capacity of Gujaratis who had gone to distant lands to make money. During the Emergency, he had seen the power this community wielded influencing policies of other countries and in mobilisation of funds. In that sense, he had a legacy, but he had to translate that skill into action.

When the NDA came to power, he got a feel of what a government could do in terms of development. Atal Bihari Vajpayee had emerged as the icon of development and, being stationed in Delhi, Modi got a first-hand experience of the vibrancy it had produced. Also, he accompanied Vajpayee during some of his foreign visits as a member of the PM's delegation. Vajpayee had revolutionised the country through strengthening of the national highways, and everyone who drove on the roads appreciated his vision and leadership. Modi learnt that users would pay if they were given the facilities.

When he became the chief minister, the state was faced with power crisis, water crisis and governance deficit. Everything needed to be tackled simultaneously. Modi found this to be a challenge as well as an opportunity. These were infrastructural needs and, if these could be tackled, he could think of development in a big way. People were paying taxes but were not getting the facilities. This was the time to deliver on governance. The biggest stumbling block was the state bureaucracy. In fact, the most difficult task for any political leader is to make the bureaucracy function efficiently. The bureaucracy of Gujarat made news for all the wrong reasons—corruption and inefficiency. Modi produced a miracle within a short time. In the chapter on governance we will know how he made changes and turned the same bureaucrats efficient.

His next big challenge was to bring government closer to the people. In this, he was guided by the old Arabic adage phrased by Francis Bacon, in *Essays*, 1625:

"Mahomet called the Hill to come to him. And when the Hill stood still, he was never a bit abashed, but said; If the Hill will not come to Mahomet, Mahomet will go to the Hill." Swami Vivekananda had used this expression to talk about education and Modi, being an admirer of Vivekananda, was greatly impressed.

Ergo, "if the poor cannot reach educational institutions, the institutions must reach them—at the plough, in the factory, everywhere." Modi made it happen. It was a great spectacle to witness the chief minister, all the ministers, government officials and MLAs visit various municipal and panchayat schools across the state to encourage enrolment, improve standards and bringing in more accountability in the education system.

The revenue-deficit state could not do much without private investment. Since 1993-94, Gujarat's fiscal deficit had been increasing sharply, ranging between 3 to 5 per cent of the Gross State Domestic Product (GSDP). The situation further deteriorated in the year 2001, when the state reached a fiscal deficit of more than 5 per cent of GSDP.[3]

Gujarat in FY12, moved from a revenue deficit position (Rs 5,076 crore in FY11) to a revenue surplus of Rs 3,215 crore, in line with the 13th Finance Commission roadmap for fiscal consolidation for state governments. Revenue surplus of the state has consistently risen and is budgeted at Rs 4,602 crore in FY14. This has been achieved with a combination of tax rationalisation measures and expenditure prudence.[4]

The investors would come only when they would be assured of returns on their money. They also wanted proper infrastructure and security of investment. Modi rolled out a red carpet for them; the retinue of officials followed the instructions with rapt attention. The same businessmen, who had to wait for months for appointment with these bureaucrats, were happy to find them all under one roof.

There are not one but many stories that narrate how Gujarat has embraced development. They will be known as other chapters unfold. But before that, let us know where Gujarat stands today in terms of numbers.

Gujarat Today

People across India are discussing the Gujarat growth story. There are many positives such as a sustained higher economic growth contributing to the overall growth of the Indian economy and an infrastructure that can be described as one of the best in the world.

Those who deny the growth story want to talk in terms of social indicators. Social indices in the state have either improved or are improving. Most importantly, people in the state have started getting benefits of development and have recognised Modi's efforts by voting for him again and again. There are no more queues in front of government offices since most services are available online. Land records are computerised and education has become a mission.

While social and governance thinkers are still trying to stress the significance of introducing technology to bring in transparency and accountability, Gujarat has already adopted these measures and is reaping the benefits. The more one comes to know about Gujarat, the more one comes to realise that one state of India has already implemented transparency and accountability—the major demands of any anti-corruption movements.

The growth is also seen in terms of successes in sectors such as manufacturing and processing facilities. It has already emerged as India's leading automobile hub after Tamil Nadu. Name any auto manufacturer and it has either set up its unit there or is planning to set up one.

It is not without reason that Ratan Tata said, "One is always struck by the pragmatism and the charisma and the capability that have been displayed in the leadership that Mr Narendra Modi has brought to the state. What I would like to say is that, as we move forward, (the) Tata Group will look at Gujarat as it should in the area of implementing schemes in information technology, in tourism, in other forms of manufacturing because, in course of time, I think (the) chief minister will find that he will not have to attract people to Gujarat but (the) question will be, 'You are stupid if you are not here'."[5]

The period from 2004-05 to 2011-12 saw Gujarat's GSDP grow by over 10 per cent, which is a remarkable feat.[*] In terms of constant prices, the per capita net state domestic product was Rs 17,227 in 2000-01. It became Rs 32,021 in 2004-05 and Rs 52,708 in 2010-11. The all India average was Rs 35,993 in 2010-11.[6] There were other bigger states as

---

[*] GSDP is the total value of goods and services produced in the state in one year.

well that did remarkably well, such as Tamil Nadu and Maharashtra. The Gujarat growth story is significant since it happened despite the state facing a volley of crisis.

While comparing Gujarat with States like Tamil Nadu and Karnataka, one must not forget that these were the first states to witness the IT sector boom. Moreover, both these States have one big metropolis each that drives the economy. Maharashtra's capital Mumbai is the country's financial capital. None of the cities in Gujarat can match the economic activities handled in Chennai, Mumbai or Bengaluru. The Gujarat growth story is driven by all three sectors of the economy namely manufacturing, agriculture and services.[7]

Critics often compare the progress of Haryana with Gujarat. But it is an unfair comparison. Haryana is a small State where most of the growth is driven by Gurgaon.[8] Therefore, it would be difficult for Haryana to keep the growth momentum and also to achieve a spiralling effect all across the state.

The Numbers

In terms of numbers, Gujarat is one of the better States. People often criticise growth and per capita figures, saying that the average cannot be the rule, and that despite growth, the society has witnessed a big gap between the rich and the poor. The real argument should be whether an average citizen of the state is better or worse off compared to 2001. Does he have better or worse access to the various initiatives taken by the government or schemes launched by the government for their benefits? These questions will be easier to answer after a better understanding of governance and other issues.

Another argument that has been forwarded against Gujarat is that other states have also witnessed similar or better growth, but while saying so, one must understand that a State which has not done well in earlier years may, with a little effort, witness 100 per cent growth. For this, we need to first understand the quantum of GSDP and also whether the growth is coming from sectors that can sustain it for a longer period of time. Also, the measure of success has to be based on whether the growth happened because of government spending or because of private initiatives.

Bibek Debroy says, "There has been high growth since 2002. That growth has resulted in a sharp drop in poverty, particularly in rural Gujarat. There is no evidence of any increase in inequality in the distribution of consumption expenditure. Those are objective statistical facts that cannot, and should not, be disputed."[9] The fact remains that agriculture witnessed consistent rapid growth, contributing to the increase in rural income.

"The Gujarat story is reflected in high GSDP growth since 2002, decline in poverty and no significant increase in inequality."[10] And this has been achieved by a government determined to work tirelessly to bring governance to the common man.

The state had nearly 21,280 factories with a fixed capital investment of Rs 2,71,965 crores (Annual Survey of Industries, 2010-11). This makes it around 16 per cent of the total fixed capital investment in the country, highest in the country, with other leading states such as Maharashtra and Andhra Pradesh, accounting for around 14 per cent and 10 per cent respectively.

The success story of Gujarat must be seen in the context of the devastating earthquake in 2001 and various other natural disasters such as cyclone and floods respectively in 1999 and 2006, and drought in certain areas in 2009. Braving all odds, Gujarat demonstrated resilience, overcame adversity and translated them into opportunities. The impact of drought was minimal because better irrigation facilities in other areas compensated for the loss of production. Farmers who suffered because of drought were adequately compensated. Bandish Patel in Himmatnagar, a North Gujarat district, had suffered due to untimely and excessive rains in 2012. Farmers in the area were compensated within a month for destruction of their cotton crops, he said.

'Build Back Better' was the theme of earthquake relief and rehabilitation. The epicentre of the earthquake, Bhuj, and other *talukas* such as Bhachau, Anjar and Rapar have bounced back and emerged as major investment destinations. Bhuj, which has an airport, has already attracted investment of more than Rs 25,000 crores since 2001. Mundra has emerged as a major privately run port and also a port-based industrial and thermal power hub.[11] One just needs to visit any of the earlier devastated towns and talk to residents there to understand the appreciation the government gets for changing the entire look of the town. People have more economic activities. Mukund, a mobile shop owner in Bhachau, said that almost every person in the town had two mobile phones, a clear sign of prosperity and economic activities.[12]

Gujarat is the world's largest producer of castor and cumin, has the largest gas-based single location sponge iron plant; it is also the largest producer of processed diamonds and the third largest producer of denim. Besides, it also has Asia's largest grassroots petroleum refinery at Jamnagar and the country's only LNG import terminals at Hazira and Dahej.

In terms of its presence across sectors, Gujarat contributes significantly to the country's soda ash production (98 per cent), salt production (78 per cent), diamond processing (80 per cent), plastic industry (65 per cent), petrochemical production (62 per cent), onshore crude oil (53 per cent), onshore natural gas (31 per cent), mineral production (10 per cent), chemicals (51 per cent), groundnut (37 per cent), pharmaceuticals (35 per cent), cotton (31 per cent) and textiles (31 per cent)[13]

The State surpassed the target of Rs 1,11,111 crore in the 11th Five Year Plan and attained the plan size of Rs 1,28,500 crore. It has already promised to double this figure to Rs 2,83,623 crore in the 12th Five Year Plan (2012-17). "By 2020, the state would have a per capita income of more than US $ 4036 if the state grows at an average 8 per cent."[14]

Gujarat has the highest share (11.06 per cent) in 2011 in outstanding project investments by states in India. It was followed by Maharashtra (10.07 per cent), Orissa (9.1 per cent) and Andhra Pradesh (8.28 per cent) as on 2011.[15]

When one talks about the Gujarat model, one essentially talks about better governance that has encouraged people to invest in the State and participate in the growth story. The model is also about decentralised planning and empowerment of people at the grassroots. At the level of bureaucracy, it translates into preparing specific schemes and allocating matching expenditure for targeted beneficiaries. It also ensures implementation of these schemes without pilferage. Better monitoring ensures efficiency and time-bound implementation. It entails making bureaucracy powerful but at the same time making it more accountable and transparent in their actions. Existence of already developed entrepreneurship in Gujarat helped the growth story.

Success of Gujarat is the success of leadership. Modi provided a decisive leadership and launched a war against corruption using information technology to the hilt. This helped enforce decentralised planning and quicker delivery of goods and services to people.

Development Challenges

All these may look easy and a natural process of empowerment. But things were not as easy as they seemed. Bringing the state to the growth trajectory without compromising on basic values is the Gujarat growth story. If industrialists are falling over one another to be in the state, it is not because of their love for Modi. The State promises business with dignity, less corruption, better governance and a responsive administration. The huge infrastructure that has been created works as an added benefit.

But this was not the scenario when Modi had come in as the chief minister. Those who say that Gujarat was good even before Modi forget the state's history. Moving across the state and interacting with various sections demonstrates that the new government has brought new dynamism. Most significantly, if everything had been good, he would not have been sent there. Media reports of that time painted a grim scenario about the state in general and the BJP in particular. There were adverse reports about Keshubhai that had led to his fall. Modi was the BJP's last hope.

Water

Gujarat had faced terrible drought (1998-2001) in the recent years. Some said this was the worst drought of the century.[16] While about 80 per cent of the state was adversely affected, regions such as Rajkot, Surendranagar and Jamnagar were the worst hit. More than 12,000 villages in 22 districts were caught in the drought cauldron, impacting 2.9 crore human population and about 1 crore cattle population.[17] The main concerns were low rainfall, a depleted water table (underground water), and lack of institutional mechanism for conservation of water.

People in the State had got used to a normal drought situation but not a drought of this intensity. This was unprecedented. Millions of farmers either sold their cattle or left them on the streets to die. The Kutch region known for its vast stretch of sands was the worst affected. It had more cattle-to-man ratio; hence it was the worst affected. It was a torturing sight for farmers to see their livestock die this way. Traditionally, the relationship with cattle has been the mainstay of rural life in Gujarat, more so in Kutch where these cattle are taken as life providers.

The State had witnessed 'water riots'. Police had to open fire in Phalla village in Saurashtra when a group of farmers objected to water being taken to Jamnagar city. They thought that city people were being taken care of at their cost. Women in Junagadh attacked the Mayor for failure to arrange water. Residents at Rajkot city attacked workers of municipal corporation. In Porbander, a man reportedly killed his father in a dispute over irrigation water. Riots broke out in Surendranagar, Rajkot, Bhavnagar and Jamnagar since people did not get water for as long as five days.[18]

Water scarcity in the state sought to destroy social life. When faced with a crisis, the first instinct is survival. There were some instances when people refused to give their daughters in marriage into villages with acute water shortages.[19] Examples like Dedhaan, a remote village in Saurashtra, one of the driest regions in Gujarat, are now few and far between.[20] There was a time when women walked miles under the scorching sun to get a bucket full of water. In many areas, farmers had to walk for an entire day in search of water. Their lives revolved so much around water that thinking of education or work became impossible.

When Advani went to campaign in Gandhinagar for the Lok sabha elections in 1999, he was often greeted by the slogan *"Pehle Paani, Phir Advani"*[21]

Water Scenario in General

Gujarat is a water-scarce state, with wide regional variation. While some regions have adequate water supply, most fall in the water-stressed category of less than 1200 cu m (United Nations criteria). The State's total water availability is 50 BCM (billion cubic metres). In 2010, the demand was 35 BCM and is likely to rise to 46 BCM in 2025 and 57 BCM in 2050. Rapid industrialisation, irrigation need for agriculture and domestic usage together fuel this increase in the demand.[22] Since the primary sector, that is, agriculture and allied sector contributes up to 20 per cent of the state's GDP, any shortfall in water requirement may affect the state's growth in the coming years. Water requirement for industry is about 7 per cent hence its non-availability would impact industrialisation.

The state's average water availability is 1137 cu m per person per year compared to the national average of 1820 cu m. The per capita availability of water is 1932 cu m in south and central Gujarat, whereas in north Gujarat it is only 342 cu m. South Gujarat is flood prone whereas other regions are drought prone.[23] In Saurashtra and Kutch, the per capita water availability is only 540 cu m and 730 cu m respectively.[24]

The biggest challenge the state faces is water management. Related to that is the people's health in areas where the water table has depleted. Excessive drawing of water from the ground over the years has led to qualitative deterioration, thereby fuelling health problems due to excessive fluoride, nitrate and saline.

Power

Adequate and regular supply of affordable power is needed by any state for planned development. When Modi became the chief minister of Gujarat, power cuts were more a norm than an exception. It was a power-deficit state in 2001 with a shortfall of 2000 MW.[25]

The State Electricity Board was plagued with corruption and the people by and large had got used to power cuts and subsidised power. It was a situation that justified the notion that good economics was bad politics. No one dared to touch power subsidy in the agriculture sector for the fear of alienating farmers, a huge voting population.

"As a result, there existed a considerable gap between politician's reform-rhetoric at the political level and their willingness to implement (it) at the ground level."[26] Some reform initiatives were taken earlier, but they could not be implemented due to lack of strong political leadership and bureaucratic lethargy.

The Transmission and Distribution (T&D) losses was 35.9 per cent in 2002-03. Incidents of theft were also alarmingly high. It was difficult for the Gujarat Electricity Board (GEB) to recover the production cost and the losses mounted up every month. As on 31 March 2002, the GEB was the top loss-making company in India with a deficit of Rs 2208.58 crore followed by Madhya Pradesh (1371.30 crore), Bihar (992.04 crore), Delhi (833.93 crore) and Assam (695.07 crore).[27] The loss as per the government was primarily due to unchanged tariff structure since 1993.[28] There was no way the situation could improve unless reforms were strictly implemented.

Bureaucracy

It is useless to blame the bureaucrats when a government fails. They reflect the determination of the political leadership. Ex-IAS KJ Alphons said that they were selected from amongst the best brains in the country.[29] Why would they not perform? The underlying theme is that bureaucracy performs only when the babus know that the person sitting at the top is a no-nonsense man. Another IAS while refusing to be quoted told the author that political instability is good for bureaucrats since it is an opportunity for them to wield more power.

Bureaucracy thus tests a new person who comes to the job, judges his approach and then decides whether to work or not. While an underperforming leader may be tolerated, a hyperactive one would definitely be shunned. When Keshubhai came to power, he was seen as a no-nonsense man and hence the officials began to respect him. But he apparently did not have the desire to learn and deliver. Worse, vested interests drew close to him. "Over the years, the man who started out as a relentless crusader against sloth and corruption has re-invented himself as a leader constantly willing to make compromises."[30]

The inefficiency of Gujarat bureaucracy was highlighted by the international media during the post-earthquake relief and rehabilitation. In a startling admission, the government of Gujarat admitted to widespread corruption in the building department. While conceding to the "practice of collective corruption", a government resolution of August 2001 said: "... In the process of constructing buildings under instructions from engineers of the roads and buildings (R&B) department... consciously and with intention, wrong bills are prepared, and everyone from small officers right up to the departmental engineers resort to serious irregularities." It further added: "Often, with evil intention, work is shown as having been completed on paper and huge sums are paid against them. Some jobs are not even carried out. Some work is qualitatively extremely weak and of poor standard."[31]

The nexus between the building mafia and politicians had become an issue of discussion when many substandard buildings had collapsed during the Bhuj earthquake. A few ministers were close to the building mafia. The story was no different than the ones often heard in other states known for their higher rank in the corruption index.

The state bureaucracy was so maligned that the image came in the way of relief and rehabilitation. Donors were apprehensive of misuse of funds.[32] So much so that the Gujarat High Court had asked District Judges to act as Lokayuktas on relief and rehabilitation works. This was to bring some confidence among people.[33]

Right after Modi's ascension to the post of Gujarat's Chief Minister, *India Today* carried a story that spoke about the state of affairs then: "Cases are being filed by the dozen and builders and officials who have had anything to do with the fallen buildings are being charged with culpable homicide and criminal conspiracy. If convicted, they could get jail terms of 10 years each. Nearly all the builders who have been charged have fled the city."[34]

A builder in Ahmedabad said that the patronage by State—whether ministers or officials—had brought in elements of crime in construction industry. "File would move only if money was paid to the right people. Only people with such nexus could survive. Now it is no longer the case. Files move and we know about the movement. Everything is time bound. We do not have to pay anything to anyone."[35]

***

Surmounting Challenges
Infrastructural Development

Men make history and not the other way around. In periods where there is no leadership, society stands still. Progress occurs when courageous, skillful leaders seize the opportunity to change things for the better.

—Harry S. Truman

At the *India Today* conclave on 18 February 2011, Modi redefined development. He said that he was making rapid progress in all sectors represented by the three colours of the National Flag. One could understand the new thrust on enhanced milk production through the white revolution and an agriculture boom through the green revolution. What about saffron? He said that saffron stood for energy revolution. He gave an interesting turn to the meaning of the colour saffron. His paper presented at the conclave was titled, "How can India develop in the next decade?"

Economic growth or social development cannot happen unless infrastructural issues are resolved. When Modi came to power, bureaucracy, power and water were the three issues that needed immediate attention if any long term development plan was to succeed in Gujarat. Other components of infrastructure such as roads, ports, etc., were also somehow linked to these. The State's biggest challenge was to create space for private sector participation in growth so that the government could take care of the social sectors in a focussed way.

If someone is asked to pick up any one issue for which Modi should be voted to power, he or she would say—for bringing unprecedented water consciousness in the state, for building international standard roads and linking all villages with *pucca* roads, and for ensuring 24-hour power supply to all the villages.

At the heart of every success lies a philosophy that drives it.

Modi gave the development vision in the integrated philosophy of *Panchamrut*. It seeks to achieve a synergy of *Jal Shakti* (water), *Urja Shakti* (Power), *Gyan Shakti* (Education), *Raksha Shakti* (Defence) and *Jan Shakti* (People). Through the mantra of 'Sauno Saath, Sauno Vikas' (cooperation of all, growth for all) and the *Panchamrut* philosophy, Gujarat witnessed a significant increase in income and employment of its citizens.

To achieve this, the chief minister needed a system that would deliver, which meant taming the bureaucracy.

Tackling Bureaucracy

That government is the best which governs the least. This famous quote from third US President Thomas Jefferson guided the BJP when it was struggling to come to power at the Centre. All its manifestos spoke of a government that would least interfere in the lives of citizens. The BJP came to power at the Centre in 1998 promising *suraj*, which means better governance. The party, however, did not succeed since it did not know how to tackle the bureaucracy and corruption by its own people.

Modi's biggest challenge was to bring the government closer to people by making it citizen-centric, transparent and more accountable. This is considered tough for any politician, more so, if he has no experience of being in government. The mammoth task of building infrastructure to sustain growth was not possible without a bureaucracy committed to the vision of the chief minister to make Gujarat a model state, not only in terms of growth but also in terms of governance.

He was a newcomer but he had one asset few politicians have; he could sit for hours listening to others, process the information and ask intelligent and meaningful questions.

Most people in Gujarat bureaucracy and the media talk of the first meeting Modi had with his top officials. A top-ranking *babu* turned up chewing masala (a mix of tobacco and betel nuts). Modi was disturbed by the discourtesy. He asked the bureaucrat to immediately go to the washroom and come back after cleaning his mouth.

That very first encounter with Modi, said a senior journalist, was enough to send the message across to the entire bureaucracy that the chief minister was a strict disciplinarian and would not tolerate any nonsense.[1] His *pracharak* image helped further this cause.

Some of the bureaucrats who interacted with him during the initial months say that Modi would rarely open his mouth but ask everyone else to speak. "Each department's anatomy, agenda, problems and tactics had to be presented. It was as if his mind and ears were tuning in, listening to notes of discord and making them bend to his will."[2]

Some of these bureaucrats used to laugh at the greenhorn Modi and they would be gloating in their presentations or notes of dissent. "We were as proud of them as if they were Supreme Court judgements, discuss them, and describe how we brought a minister's unreal proposal to heel with dissent notes till it sounded the way we wanted."[3]

Modi changed the rules of the game. He would either return the memo or subject it to silent dismissal till it was written the way he wanted.

A senior IPS officer with about 20 years of experience said, "Bureaucrats are always used to leading the way and showing direction to the politicians. This is a rare occasion that the political leadership is leading us. Modi is actually making bureaucrats dance to his tunes. Even after 20 years of knowing Gujarat, we look like students before him. He will always come out with some question to which we will not have any answer."[4]

Earlier, the bureaucrats were keen to please him; they tried to find out what he wanted. Most of the times, he would sit silently and not reveal his thoughts until he had reached some conclusion. Before that, he would allow others to freely give contrary opinions. In such meetings, everything would be everyone's business and, by the end of the meeting, everyone would have a general sense of what was going on. He would hold a series of what his bureaucrats referred to as "4 pm meetings". These meetings lasted 4-6 hours with senior officials of each department. Such meetings went on for four to six weeks. The purpose was to give a sense of how the department was working and prepare the future roadmap.[5]

It was as if he was holding a party meeting as organisation secretary where he was supposed to listen and not speak. A senior official recalled: "He was a sponge. He sat, listened and absorbed for a year. It is not as if he was assimilated or diluted by us. It is as if he domesticated and colonised us. He remained a *pracharak* but the secretariat became a magnified *pracharak's* world. We became a cadre of clerks, a *shakha* of bureaucrats."[6] Later, Modi was to organise bigger *shakhas* of all bureaucrats in a more formal way.

The Supreme Court held (October 2013) that that there should be "a minimum assured tenure" for top bureaucrats to check arbitrary transfers of non-pliant bureaucrats. The court also asked bureaucrats to record oral orders from politicians even if these were not given in writing. The order was hailed as landmark since it gave protection to honest bureaucrats.[7] Modi has already implemented security of tenure to bureaucrats in Gujarat bureaucracy. His logic has been that this would make them more accountable and allow them time to work free of stress.

In Gujarat, politicians do not decide whether an FIR is to be registered or not. Political interference happens only when there is a complaint that someone is not doing his duty or is trying to do something he should not do. The system of citizen charter and grievance mechanism works at the level of police too, insulating it from political influence of any kind.

Modi realised that the bureaucrats were demotivated and shunned taking decisions either for fear of going wrong, or to avoid doing extra work. Moreover, most officials were unsure of the security of their respective tenures. Dr KP Shah from Houston Texas, who participated in *Pravasi Divas*, summed it nicely when he told the chief minister during an interaction that, "the most important thing is that we need one or two responsible people in the government who are not going to have transfer within six months so that we can deal with them on a regular basis".[8]

Postings and transfers used to happen for factors other than performance. "The chief minister erased the role of middlemen in postings of bureaucrats. The bureaucrat now knows that merit alone will matter in postings," said senior IAS officer Ravi Saxena.[9] Modi assured a minimum tenure of two-three years to most bureaucrats. He gave them targets and evolved systems to monitor their work. The bureaucrats came to realise that merit alone would be the criteria for a posting.[10] He asked them to take decisions without fear but on the condition that the intention was good.[11]

"Modi has given a rare professional touch to the bureaucracy through an imaginative mix of firmness, accountability and freedom to work and precise goal-setting. In a way, he has de-bureaucratised the bureaucracy," IIM (Indian Institute of Management) professor TV Rao said.[12]

A bureaucrat commented: "Modi grew in front of us. What we welcomed with contempt, we now treated with awe. The 'bumbler' was more than a trickster; he was, to use TV terminology, the mastermind. There is a vulnerability of bureaucrats that one must confront. Few dissent. Most who do, seek a transfer, a different comfort zone, a move to Delhi. He, who treats them with contempt, commands their awe, their allegiance. We want to please him, to share his power, his manliness, and his assertiveness. Power commands its own sacrament. There is a Masonic conviviality to closeness. Everyone knows the signs of power."[13]

Modi's simple solution to the problems of governance was that "politicians should learn to say no and bureaucrats should learn to say yes". He said he was quoting a Congress leader who said so. Modi suggested that the government should come out of ornamental activities and concentrate on providing basic services to people. "This would reduce red tape and win back people's faith which has completely eroded over the last few years."[14]

Some of Modi's critics in Gujarat say that bureaucrats have become more powerful and politicians have lost their ealier clout. One BJP leader complained that it was difficult to reach Modi and hence nobody is bothered about meeting party leaders to get their work done. On closer analysis, it appeared that politicians have lost the power to act as power brokers since the bureaucrats also know who is doing what. A businessman setting up a factory now does not need a political power broker. He can straightaway approach the department and in case of a complaint, the CMO. No official refuses a minister or an MLA trying to implement a people-oriented programme. In case someone does, the CMO looks after that as well.

It is interesting to see how Modi converted bureaucrats into thinking human beings and performers. He brought innovative ideas, discussed them threadbare in a group, applied correctives and implemented them with missionary zeal. Since the officials too were party to the decision making, none could refuse implementation and accountability.

One such unique concept was the *chintan shibir* or brainstorming sessions, to find solutions to larger issues facing governance with the overall focus on "*Main nahin, hum*" (Not I, but we). This annual three-day retreat has proved its worth in team building based on the credo of one vision, one mission and one team. Senior officers climb down from their high pedestals and try to understand what the young and enthusiastic officers have to say. Initiatives by young officers in delivering goods have started getting recognised. The chief minister, officiating as the team leader, interacts with everyone and tries to understand their difficulties. This helps build an element of trust between political part of the government and the bureaucracy. They are together referred to as 'Team Gujarat'.

While speaking at the *Mehsana Chintan Shibir* in 2011 on the importance of the camp as an instrument, Modi said, "The main reason for the success of *chintan shibir* is that we decide our own goal and course of action as a group... When we all decide together, our conscience will ask whether we have accomplished the task or not... When we get attached, there is never dearth of sacrifice, hard work and austerity."[15]

The *chintan shibir* has enabled top policy makers and those implementing decisions to understand the gap and apply correctives. On the one hand, there are ministers, secretaries and the chief minister who participate largely in the planning and taking decisions; on the other hand, there are key executives who implement the decisions— the district collectors, district development officers and municipal commissioners.

That making mistakes with good intentions would be condoned was the outcome of the first such *shibir* held in 2003 in Kevadia. Some of the major governance practices such as *Swantah Sukhaya* (benefit of all) that create space or ingeniousness of officials; *Gunotsav* (celebrating quality) for assessing quality of education in government schools; *Krishi Mahotsav* (agriculture festival) to improve agriculture and rural life; Mission *Mangalam* (welfare) an integrated poverty alleviation approach; *Aapno Taluko Vibrant Taluko* (ATVT) to decentralise governance from district to the taluka level, emerged from these brainstorming sessions. The powerful slogan, "*Chalo jalayen deep wahan, jahan abhi tak andhera hai*" (let us light the lamp where there is still darkness) also came from the first *shibir*.

The sixth *chintan shibir* in 2009 was significant since it was held in the Dhordo Tent city of the Rann of Kutch. About 250 officials and ministers attended it and former President of India Dr APJ Abdul Kalam addressed the meeting. He praised the state for development-centric environment, for announcing solar power mission and use of green energy technology.[16] "Gujarat has tremendous scope of development and the administration too has great capability to achieve it, which needs to be tapped," Kalam said at the meeting.

The *shibir* also became a platform to encourage performers to do better. And what better way to do it than to give recognition to the performers before the entire bureaucracy. One such example was the best collector's award given to Vijay Nehra. Nehra had played a pro-active role in bringing about 12,000 senior citizens under the Indira Gandhi National Old Age Pension Scheme (2008-09). Vadodara became the first place in the country to implement the scheme.

The concept of *chintan shibir* for increasing efficiency of the government has been adopted by other state governments also such as Rajasthan and Madhya Pradesh.[17]

The other major initiative was to encourage government officials to become *karmayogis*. What do you do when government employees do not perform and just want to limit themselves to the official timing? You can either motivate them through rewards or force them by inducing in them the fear of punishment. Modi's approach towards bureaucracy will help policy makers understand this class better and, thereby, extract the kind of performance desired from the institution. He did not go by the hackneyed concept that an average bureaucrat does not want to work. He began with the assumption that these officials must be given an opportunity to make their life more creative and hence more meaningful.

The chief minister came out with a novel Karmayogi Scheme to make these officials turn into dedicated workers. Who is a *karmayogi*? A *karmayogi* is one who performs the role assigned to him or her with full concentration, skill and finesse. Sri Krishna instructs his disciple Arjuna (in fact, all of mankind) "to do their work most sincerely & with expertise and skill they have mastered, and without any attachment or expectation of rewards".[18]

Skill development and orientation training was to be imparted to about five lakh employees of the State government on skill enhancement, *pranayam* (breathing exercises) and yoga. It gave them relief from their routine life and helped them learn new technology and methods to become more meaningful in their jobs and ultimately appreciate their role in the development of the state.

The scheme was formally introduced in 2004, and in less than a year, the state government made the *karmayogi* course compulsory for all Class I and II non-IAS officers. All these employees were to compulsorily finish the course by December 2005. This was going to be a minimum three-day affair after which a certificate was to be issued. In 2005, about 2.25 lakh employees were already trained.

Many analysts concluded that all these steps that made employees work extra hours would drive them to take revenge and vote against Modi in 2012. But their assumption was proved completely wrong. Most government employees voted for Modi for respecting their self-pride and for making their work more meaningful. While acknowledging their support, Modi said:

"I specially thank all the five lakh government employees. I know you have to work even on holidays. Earlier you used to go home by 5 pm, but now you don't go back till 10 pm. By voting for me, you have proved that you are ready to work for the people... It was being said that government employees were angry and unhappy under the Modi rule... Today when the postal ballots were opened, everyone was surprised. 70-75 per cent votes of the government employees went with the BJP."[19]

Swantah Sukhaya initiative was another innovation by Modi to motivate higher bureaucracy. It means "joy for the self". Here a person derives happiness by performing an action of his choice. He does it for inner satisfaction. In the context of Gujarat bureaucracy, the person is invited to take initiative to perform a public service of his choice and derive contentment from the creativity that his efforts unfold.

Most bureaucrats don't get the time or opportunity to do something creative outside the structured work since they are busy implementing various government schemes. Some who try are shunned by their colleagues for trying to be 'too smart', rather than fitting into the steel frame of bureaucracy. Still there are some who refuse to become a part of the system and keep on trying to do one ingenious thing or the other. They are the innovators and factors for change.

Swantah Sukhaya encouraged tremendous innovation, creativity and fulfilment at work places besides giving an immense sense of achievement and motivation to individuals who implemented these ideas.[20] Some innovative schemes become eligible for cash prize of Rs 25,000 from the government.

An example of such initiative was provided by a *taluka* development officer in Sabarkantha district. He discovered that there were no fans in the primary schools. Poor children studied in these schools and had to bear the heat. There were 88 primary schools and a total of 284 rooms. The officer calculated that Rs 2,10,000 would be needed to provide fans in all the schools. He pro-actively reached out to the community for help and arranged funding of the project through donations.

One of Modi's biggest achievements has been to make bureaucrats realise that they too needed to go to the field rather than plan and monitor sitting in their air-conditioned rooms. Curbing the ego of top bureaucrats was necessary to make other officials work. Former Bihar Chief Minister Lalu Prasad Yadav did that by making senior IAS officers make *khaini* (chewable tobacco) for him in full public view and transferring them at will to seek compliance.[21] But his approach was humiliating, undignified, personalised and not intended for public good. Modi gained the confidence of his officials by making them feel important but telling them at the same time that the aim of bureaucracy was to bring good governance to people.

Being a workaholic himself, Modi demanded hard work from others too. As he became more experienced, bureaucrats learnt to come to him fully prepared. He had access to all information and, within minutes, could call anyone's bluff. The best thing was his punctuality. Proverbially, the importance of an Indian politician is directly proportional to the delay in the time of his arrival at a particular meeting. In the case of

Modi, he never made his guests wait.

Former Additional DG Gujarat Police AI Saiyed said that Modi never interfered in the functioning of bureaucracy. "I have seen least interference from the office of the chief minister. I have never seen him ordering you do this, you do that. He always said it is your responsibility, you know better how to do it the best way. He always treated officials with respect. And this is the reason today bureaucracy is with him."[22]

One of the surest and most effective ways to make bureaucracy more accountable and governance come to the doorsteps of people was introduction of information technology in all government departments. This ensured transparency and reduced the interface between officials and public. It would suffice to say that Modi used IT to increase people's trust in government and administration. If there were grievances, he had SWAGAT (State-Wide Attention on Grievances by Application of Technology) to tackle them; if there were manipulations in government contracts, his solution was e-procurement and e-tendering to keep the process transparent.

Water issues

Bringing Water to Parched Lands

In the mythological land of Bharat, Bhagirath prayed to Lord Brahma to release the waters of river Ganga, and then to Lord Shiva to control the flow and get salvation for the people of his clan. The Ganga has been flowing ever since, providing peace, prosperity and life to the people along the banks.

In real life, something similar happened in Gujarat. Modi literally brought water to all the rivers of the state that had dried up due to absence of perennial water supply. This happened due to inter-basin transfer of waters from Narmada to other rivers. This changed the landscape of Gujarat and filled nearby aquifers. These rivers suffer when the water level in Narmada goes down. However, once the height of Sardar Sarovar Dam will be fully raised, the state will witness unprecedented prosperity.

Since most works on the project were completed by the Modi government, the biggest achievement was to involve people in the massive drive of recharging ground water and involving women in decentralised decision making through water committees (pani samitis). They took all the decisions about water availability, problems and solutions and tax collections. The tax collection rate has been 98-99 per cent.

The issue of uneven distribution of water posed a problem. While about 30 per cent of the area had 71 per cent water, the rest 70 per cent of land had mere 29 per cent. This imbalance needed to be corrected. This was achieved by the Sujalam Suphalam Yojana, and by drawing water from the Narmada Main Canal through pipelines.

A major issue now is how to prevent wastage of water in cities like Ahmedabad. A city dweller in Gandhinagar consumes about 310 litre of water per day, which is the highest among 20 major cities in the country.[23] Citizens of Ahmedabad waste around 39 crore litre of water every day; this is equivalent to water requirement of 22 lakh people.[24] Water discipline is also a key issue.

The city is fast developing water consciousness. In most houses, people do not offer you full glasses of water, as in the case of the Nanabhai family that lives on the prestigious Race Course Road in Rajkot. They offer only half a glass of potable water to visitors. More water is given only when requested. The hotels ask clients to use the same towel at least for another day. In the washroom of the state secretariat, there is a chart on top of the basin that tells the amount of pressure one should exert on the tap so as to get the required quantity of water for use.

Sardar Sarovar Dam on river Narmada came as a boon to the water-starved Gujarat, but its people had to wait for long to enjoy the fruits. This dam stores the water of the river at Kevadia and gives enough for irrigation and other needs. It has helped bring more land under agriculture. The Narmada Valley River Development Project is the single largest river development project in India.

With its height at 121.92 metres today, the dam has started giving benefits to the state in terms of drinking water supply, water for irrigation and hydro-power generation. In 2001, only 705 million cubic metre (mcm) of water flowed in Narmada canal network, which is the largest irrigation canal network in the world. Later in 2003, it was increased to 5,195 mcm and further to 6,194 mcm in 2004. Using the canal network of Sardar Sarovar Dam, inter-basin transfer to other rivers was achieved.

The waters were released in the dry beds of Heran, Orsanf, Karad, Dhadhar, Mahi, Saidak, Mohar, Shedhi, Watrak, Mesho, Khari, Sabarmati and Saraswati rivers.[25] This helped cover a command area of 500,000 ha. In addition to this, the Narmada water was used to fill about 700 village tanks which substantially improved irrigation.

When fully complete, the dam height will be 146.5 metre with a water level of 138.68 metre. This will generate 1450 MW of power, 57 per cent of which would go to Madhya Pradesh, 27 per cent to Maharashtra and only 16 per cent to Gujarat. It is expected to irrigate 1.84 million ha of land across 15 districts and 73 suburbs, including the drought-prone regions in Gujarat, as well as two districts of Rajasthan. It is also expected to supply drinking water to 29 million inhabitants across 131 towns and 9,633 villages in the state.[26]

The waters from the Narmada would be taken to North Gujarat and Kutch through a network of a 532-km long main canal (of which 458 falls in Gujarat and the rest 74 km in Rajasthan), 40 branch canals, and sub canals that emerge out of these canals. Total length of canal network would come to about 85,000 km when fully complete. Work on most of the canal network is complete but this will reap benefits only if the dam height is fully raised to store enough water.

The controversy now surrounds installation of 30 gates to take the height to the final level. The state government has been asking for permission of the central government to install these gates so that when the permission to increase the height is given by the Supreme Court, the state does not lose time to reap the benefits. The state wants to be ready since installation of these gates will take more than a year by an average estimate.

The state came up with a unique Sujalam Suphalam Yojana (SSY) for taking fresh water to Panchmahal and North Gujarat to bring water-based prosperity. Sujalam in this context means 'fresh water' and suphalam means 'good results (for society)'. The scheme was launched in February 2004.

Narmada waters from the SSD were already taken to River Mahi through inter-basin transfer of water. This filled the Kadana dam with enough water that was, in turn, meant to feed the Sujalam Suphalam spreading canal of 332 km. This canal passing through seven districts is ready. Some additional structures as per local requirements are being constructed. The surplus water of Kadana dam and the Narmada Main Canal has been flown into this canal already.[27]

Another vertical of the yojana (plan) includes taking waters from Narmada Main Canal to different water bodies such as lakes and smaller dams. Water is being pumped through huge pipes. Nine pipelines will fill nine reservoirs of North Gujarat regions. Eight are already completed.

The Kutch region faced salinity of water due to its proximity to the sea. This made life difficult and people had even started migrating to other places. The government undertook various measures such as changing the crop pattern, providing fresh water, recharging wells, construction of check dams, afforestation and constructing tidal regulators. Narmada water is supplied through a thick pipeline to Kutch region to meet its irrigation needs.

The state has constructed the world's largest pumping station (by volume) in Surendranagar district (at Dhaki). When Modi inaugurated it in 2007, the pump was lifting 230 cubic metre of water per second to a height of 71 metre and then allowing it to fall so that enough pressure was generated to push the water to areas of Saurashtra region. This has produced a cascading effect on irrigation and drinking water availability in the region. This is also an engineering marvel and every student of engineering in Gujarat is mandated to visit the site and study the feat. The chief minister told the author that every engineering student from all over the country should see this to appreciate the marvel of human effort.

Narendra Modi had brought a revolution by constructing water bodies, check dams, village ponds and boribands. Water harvesting became a social movement by involving larger community participation.[28] Farmers faced water crisis due to absence of proper storage structures. During the rainy seasons, rain water would flow out without recharging the depleting water table. Before Modi became the chief minister, the concept of check dams was already there. The Sardar Patel Participatory Water Conservation Scheme (SPPWCS) for conservation of water through public participation was already implemented in January 2000 under Keshubhai Patel. What made Modi different was the speed and determination with which he launched this. For him it was a mission.

Check dam was one solution to prevent rain water from draining out during monsoon. This involved constructing suitable concrete structures of 1.5 metre and 2 metre on the course of rivers and preventing water from running off. This helped store water and recharge the wells and underground water bodies, thereby, bring the water table up in the adjoining areas.

The first phase of SPPWCS that continued till February 2001 helped construct 10,257 check dams. Later, the scheme saw three more phases with some modifications. As per the data collected by various departments in every district, 158,000 check dams were constructed as on 31 March 2013. The Planning Commission congratulated Gujarat for its check dams.[29]

The state has 17 river basins in mainland Gujarat, 71 in Saurashtra region and 97 in Kutch.

A mechanism to retain rainwater in farm land was constructing village ponds or *khet talavadi* using public participation. The existing village ponds were further deepened. The state acted with a missionary zeal and in 2004-05 launched a 100-day campaign for construction of village ponds. About 1.3 lakh ponds were constructed in a record time.[30]

The scheme was implemented mostly in north and central Gujarat where building check dams was not possible due to the topography of the place. More than 5,000 existing ponds were further deepened to increase water retention quantity.[31]

When monsoon got delayed in 2009, Modi launched a 20-day campaign to create lakhs of *boribunds* (sandbag dams). About 2.65 lakh *boribunds* were constructed in 14,826 villages. These helped conserve water and proved very good for agriculture. By December 2008, the state had only 55,917 *boribunds*.[32]

A *boribund* is a seasonal small structure built using empty cement bags. These bags are filled with sand, clay and small pebbles and then the mouths are closed. These are then placed one upon the other as barriers in the channel of the streams which are not more than five metre in width. These water bodies created thus can be described as tiny dams on rivulets and *nullahs*. The cost of a *boribund* was Rs 1,500-3,000.

Over the years, Gujarat has developed an effective water supply grid to supply drinking water all across the state. This network of water system draws Narmada waters to feed the grid. In September 2013, the government asserted that Gujarat had become a water-surplus state in terms of supplying drinking water to its citizens. Each citizen is getting more than the prescribed per capita of quantum of water.

"We have turned into a water-surplus state. According to central government norms, each village should get 50 litre per capita per day (lpcd) of water, while each city should get 140 lpcd. In Gujarat, we are now providing 100 lpcd of water to every village and 150 lpcd to every town," Mahesh Singh, member secretary of Gujarat Water Supply & Sewerage Board (GWSSB) said.[33] Even during the summers when Saurashtra and Kutch faced severe water crisis, the government said it provided about 88 lpcd to the villages and 140 lpcd to the towns and cities.

This grid as of 2013 connects 8,700 villages and 131 towns in Gujarat through bulk water pipelines. The government says it is confident to connect the remaining villages in the grid in the next two years.[34] About 76 per cent of the houses in Gujarat have tap-water connections, while the national average is only about 34 per cent.

Scarcity of water over the years has been considerably reduced. For example, in Kutch region in 2001, a large area of the state needed water supply through tankers. In Kutch alone, 350 villages demanded this service. In 2013, even in scarcity of natural water supply, only 56 villages needed the state's assistance in form of water tankers. This shows achievement in direct terms as well as in terms of revenue the state would save for not sending water tankers.

To encourage public participation in management of water and sanitation, WASMO (Water and Sanitation Management Organisation) was set up in 2002. This was to empower people in management of scarce resources and relegate the government to being a facilitator rather than a provider.

Special attention was given to encourage women's participation in decentralised decisions and their implementation. The logic was that women, who used to walk miles for a pitcher full of drinking water, would be better equipped to understand the importance of water and, hence, they would use it optimally.

The WASMO was instrumental in formation of *pani samitis* in each village. These are democratically elected teams of 10-12 members from the gram sabha (village assembly) with full responsibility to plan, implement, manage, own, operate and maintain village water supply system. Majority of the members are women. *Pani samitis* also collect water taxes, and the success rate of these women in collecting taxes is 97 per cent.

The unique vision of WASMO was awarded by the Prime Minister of India for Excellence in Public Administration for the year 2006-07.

An important feat in water management was to make the Panam High Level Canal Project more useful. The Panam Dam across the river Panam (Panchamahal district in Central Gujarat) irrigated a command area of 130 villages and provided drinking water to more than three lakh people. However, the 100-km-long canal served the command area on its right side only. Farmers on the left side could not get the irrigation facility due to inconvenient topography.

The government had the option to dig an open canal or lift water from the reservoir through pumping—the two traditional methods normally used. Both were costly and less environment friendly. Modi, after consultations with experts, decided to get an irrigation tunnel constructed at a much lower cost and without displacement of people. The tunnel is 3.4 km long, 6.6 m wide and 6.6 m high. It has made life easier for people.

The development of the Sabarmati River Front has transformed city life in Ahmedabad. It is a major tourist attraction now. The river that looked like a drain with no water a few years back is now brimming with clean water. This vision was shaped by the transition Modi witnessed about Sabarmati: "One day while passing through one of the bridges of River Sabarmati that connects eastern Ahmedabad with its ever-expanding western side, I saw a few children playing cricket on the dry riverbed. A thought struck my mind with lightening speed. 'Oh! this generation, if asked about river Sabarmati, will only term it as large playground, completely unaware of the rich ecology and bustling water resources that it once possessed. No! We should not deprive our children of the eternal happiness they would derive from flowing water and the adult denizens of the city, of pleasure of living by the river side, I said to myself.'"[35]

The river bed had slums located on it. Contaminated sewage and dumping of industrial waste into the river basin posed major health hazards. There was no way to recharge it other than to bring the Narmada waters into the river basin. The Narmada Main Canal had an escape structure that envisaged safe release of canal water into the river basin, in case of excess water that could pose a threat to the canal's safety. However, the concept of inter-river basin transfer of water was not thought of. This was possible once the height of the Sardar Sarovar Dam was raised. This enhanced the available storage of water and the escape structure became a perennial source of water for Sabarmati. Regulated gates now release water into River Sabarmati and bring in all its associated benefits. The released water gets stored in a stretch of 10.6 km, right from Subhash Bridge to Vasna barrage.

The chief minister had to directly intervene to ensure transfer of 202.79 ha land to Ahmedabad Municipal Corporation. The Sabarmati River Front Development Corporation Ltd (SRFDCL) then took up the task of riverfront development. The project involved creating embankments on both sides of Sabarmati's 10.6 km stretch. This also helped in controlling floods in low lying areas during excess monsoon.

The riverfront development includes major interceptor sewer lines on both banks of the river, capturing more than 38 sewage discharge points and routing sewage to newly-commissioned treatment plants south of Vasna barrage. The river has been channelised to a constant width without altering the flood carrying capacity of the river.

A key feature of this project is a two-level, continuous promenade on both sides of the river. It is built just above the water level to serve only pedestrians and cyclists and to provide access to the water. The upper promenade intends to host a variety of public features: cultural and educational institutions, leisure activities, large public parks and plazas and a few areas for commercial and retail development.

What can become a never before kind of development in the country is constructing a 30 km dam across the Gulf of Khambhat connecting Bhavnagar with Dahej and creating the world's largest fresh water reservoirs. It would be a gulf closure dam that would store about 10,000 million cubic metre (mcm) water from the nine rivers that drain into the gulf—Narmada, Dhadhar, Mahi, Sabarmati, Limdi Bhogavo, Sukhbhadar, Utavali, Keri and Vagad. These rivers together account for about 25 per cent of total surface water resource of the state. This will be the world's largest fresh water reservoir.

The Gulf of Khambhat extends from north to south about 200 km and the width varies from 25 km at the inner end to 150 km at the outer mouth, covering an area of about 17000 sq km. The Kalpasar Dam will enclose 2000 sq km. This will cost between Rs 50,000 to Rs 60,000 crore over a period of 5-7 years.

It would generate 5,880 MW of power using tidal waves. The top of the dam will be 100 m wide, which would enable a 12-lane coastal highway and a railway line, reducing the distance between the two places by more than 200 km.

Some other benefits of the project include an irrigation facility to about 10.54 ha land in six districts of the Saurashtra region, reclamation of land that gets frequently submerged in the Gulf of Khambhat, and direct employment to about one lakh people in fishery and allied activities.

Various feasibility studies have been conducted on every aspect of the project. The National Institute of Ocean Technology, Chennai, is conducting the final feasibility study, which was likely to be completed by the end of 2013. The project is expected to commence in 2014.

Power

All 18,000 plus villages in Gujarat have 24-hour electricity and farmers in Gujarat are paying for the power they consume. Even Modi's bitterest critic concedes this to be one of the biggest achievements in Gujarat. But giving power to every home was a mammoth task. This involved reform in the power sector to make the state electricity board self-sustaining, insulate power from populism and increase power generation capacity.

Like any other State Electricity Board, the Gujarat Electricity Board (GEB) was also running in losses. It had incurred a massive loss of Rs 2,246 crore for the year 2000-2001 on a revenue base of Rs 6,280 crore.

The interest burden on the borrowing alone amounted to Rs 1,227 crore. Transmission and distribution (T&D) losses were pegged at 35.27 per cent. While load-shedding was normal, the state had no funds to invest in power generation. The private sector operations would have further added to the losses since the Power Purchase Agreement these private players had signed with the state government entailed buying power costly but selling it cheap to the consumers.

Modi has a knack of picking up the right person for the job, and vesting in that person full authority and accountability. In this case, he chose Manjula Subramaniam, a Gujarat cadre officer, who had served as joint secretary in the Prime Minister's office from 1993 to 1998. She had played a key role in the first phase of liberalisation the country witnessed in the early 1990s. She was appointed as chairperson of the GEB and principal secretary of power. She became the first woman to head the GEB when she took charge of the office on 13 December 2001.

The GEB board could not raise further money since it had already raised a sum of Rs 2000 crore through bonds. The Power Reforms Bill was pending in the legislative assembly amidst stiff opposition by about 50,000 GEB employees. The situation needed to be handled with great care, or this could bring the entire state to a halt. Farmers were opposed to introduction of meter-based tariff that the Gujarat Electricity Regulatory Commission (GERC) had proposed.

Subramaniam spoke about involving private players in the realisation of pending electricity bills, reducing T&D losses by taking out a drive against pilferage, curbing expenditure and introducing computerisation.[36]

She found out that the GEB was too large a structure to be managed efficiently. While she made plans to resolve the issue, her immediate priority shifted to building the employee's morale and restructuring some of the loans that the GEB had taken on a very high rate of interest. Imagine these loans invited an interest of 18 per cent! As a part of debt restructuring, she smartly renegotiated the loans with the banks and brought the interest rate to a lower level. This led to a saving of Rs 500 crore in 2002-03.[37]

Manjula discovered that the power purchase agreements (PPAs) the board had entered into were highly inflated. Such rates were predetermined rates at which the government had committed to buy power from these private companies. The private players actually might have decided to invest in power generation because of these PPAs. Touching this issue was extremely sensitive.

The new GEB chief, however, decided to renegotiate the PPAs. This produced stiff resistance. To deal with the issue, the government constituted a committee and stood firm on its stand. For the GEB, it was a matter of survival since every unit of power bought would mean adding to the loss. After more than 18 months of intense bargaining, the private players agreed to lower the rate. This led to a saving of Rs 675 crore in 2002-03 and of Rs 1,000 crore in 2003-04.[38] The power purchase cost declined gradually from Rs 2.59 per unit in 2001-02 to Rs 1.99 in 2005-06.[39]

In 2003, the government came out with a new law that transformed the GEB into a holding company called the Gujarat Urja Vikas Nigam Ltd (GUVNL). The GUVNL was to look after the activities of six separate companies, one each for generation and transmission and four for distribution in various regions. All these companies became fully operational in 2005.

The restructuring programme was carried out after taking employees into confidence, sensitising them to the need to be efficient and assuring them that their jobs would not be lost. About 43,000 of the 50,000 employees were given a special training to understand the importance of staying relevant and competitive.[40]

The task of plugging the leakages in distribution and controlling power thefts were taken up simultaneously. While in urban areas power theft was in the range of 20 per cent, it was as high as 70 per cent in rural areas. Most governments ignored the issue due to the likely high political cost this could incur.

The Modi Government brought out a 'prevention of power theft bill' to tackle power theft. The state was losing Rs 1,800 crore due to this, energy minister Saurabh Patel said in 2003.[41] The government set up special courts and police stations at five places—Rajkot, Surat, Vadodara, Bhavnagar and Mehsana—to detect power theft. Added to that was the decision to recruit ex-servicemen to tackle theft and collect pending power bills. Justifying this decision, Modi asserted at an ex-servicemen rally in Rewari (Haryana) in 2013, that "appointing thousands of ex-servicemen had a moral impact on people and power theft stopped".[42]

Power theft was made a criminal offence and special checking squads were instituted. Sealed and tamper-proof meters were installed and electronic billing was introduced. A drive was undertaken for replacement of joints in service cables and meters. As a result of these efforts, the number of cases of theft came down considerably from 107,985 in 2003-04 to 77,068 in 2006-07. Losses from transmission and distribution came down from 35.9 per cent in 2002-03 to 21.5 per cent in 2006-07.[43] They came further down to 21.1 per cent in 2008-09 and 20.13 in 2010-11.

Gujarat became the first state in the country to implement a full-fledged Enterprise Resource Planning (ERP) solution in the power sector using end-to-end IT solutions. This was named *e-urja* (e-energy). To collect cash, innovative ways were devised such as use of post offices, tie-up with banks, mobile collection vans and increasing duration of office time for cash collection counters.

These changes brought improved efficiency. The financial turnaround that the state achieved in the power sector was made possible without any significant increase in power tariffs.[44] The state electricity board posted its first profit of Rs 203 crore (after tax) in 2005-06. The net profit jumped to Rs 533 crore in 2010-11. The tariff collection efficiency is now at 100 per cent.[45]

Gujarat's power distribution companies (discoms) scored the highest credit ratings out of 39 utilities taken up for financial evaluation at the behest of the Union Ministry of Power. These discoms—Dakshin Gujarat Vij, Uttar Gujarat Vij, Madhya Gujarat Vij and Paschim Gujarat Vij—got A-plus rating which meant very high operational and financial performance.[46]

Power generation was a major issue. But in the last 10 years Gujarat has witnessed a transition from being a power deficit to a power-surplus state.[47] Also the per capita electricity consumption of Gujarat at 1615.24 kW (2009-10) was almost double the then national average of 778.71 kW. This can be considered most definite evidence of development and prosperity of the state.[48]

The state's installed capacity of power in 2000-01 was 8,588 MW. In 2010-11 the installed capacity through conventional source was 13,134 MW. Of this, 2116 MW was from wind energy. By 2012 March, the installed capacity increased to 15,306 MW. The Central Electricity Authority gives a figure of 23,927 MW for Gujarat. In this, 6286 MW is from state utilities, 14,249 MW from private sector and 3392 MW from central utilities. The Sardar Sarovar Project has also led to an additional generation of 15,070 million kW of electricity till March 2010.

As one drove along the national highways from Halvad to Malia towards Bhachau, one could see huge windmills on both sides of the road. The same was the scenario when one drove along the coastal areas. They were in thousands and each was connected to transformers to transmit the energy.

Some farmers in Kutch region are using these windmills to run their tube wells and this has come as a boon to the salt farmers. They earlier used diesel pump sets to pump out seawater for making salt. They have also reduced their expenses by about 40 per cent.[49]

Gujarat has adopted the latest technology to make solar power generation efficient and cost-effective. The process is costly, but mass production of equipments may make it competitive and cheap.

Gandhinagar is fast turning into the country's first solar capital. It already has solar rooftop systems with power generation capacity of between 1 kW and 150 kW installed at more than 150 locations, aggregating a capacity of 1.39 MW. The new building of the Gujarat Pollution Control Board (GPCB) is completely powered by solar energy.[50] The government has evolved a rooftop solar plant policy to encourage people to produce their own power and encash it by selling the surplus to the grid.

The state accounts for about 66 per cent of India's total solar power generation.[51] Of the total of 979 MW of solar power plant set up, Gujarat has 654.8 MW followed by Rajasthan (197.5 MW) and Maharashtra (20 MW). Gujarat is already attracting investment in solar energy and soon it will set new records.[52]

In April 2013, the state became the first in the world to have a canal top solar power project. The project of 1 MW on the Sanand branch canal of the Sardar Sarovar Project was commissioned. Located at Chandrasan village near Mehsana, 45 km from Ahmedabad, it will generate 1.6 million units of clean electricity per year. It is being set up by the US-based Sun Edison and is developed by the Gujarat State Electricity Corporation Limited (GSECL).

There already is another solar park in Patan, which generates 214 MW of electricity every day. Film actor Ajay Devgn is an investor in the project. "The thought behind our entry is that we believe that solar power is the future of industry. We are aiming to reach 500 MW within three-five years with a total investment of Rs 5,000 crore," he said while recognising the importance of solar power for people.[53]

Building solar panels over canals has extra benefits. While it reduces the need for extra land to set up such projects, it helps prevent evaporation of water. It also keeps the lower part of the installed system cool, thus increasing efficiency. The Mehsana project will save 9 million litres of water by preventing evaporation. It has been set up at a cost of 17.50 crore.

Considering that the entire length of Sardar Sarovar Project canal network in Gujarat is around 19,000 km, "even if 10 per cent of it is used for this type of projects, it could generate 2,400 MW of clean energy annually," the chief minister said.[54]

The project will eliminate the need of 11,000 acres of land required for a solar project of this magnitude and save 2 billion litres of water annually. The state's solar power initiatives would help save Rs 6,500 crore over the next 25 years, besides reducing carbon emissions to the tune of 8 lakh tonnes. "This initiative of Gujarat on Narmada branch canal network has the potential to bring down per unit cost of clean energy from solar panels to between Rs 8 to Rs 8.50 in future," Modi said.[55]

The government has given incentives to promote solar power, but these are available only to those companies that install solar power generators by 31 March 2014, of capacity between 5 MW to 500 MW. They can then avail the incentives for 25 years. The government has fixed a purchase price of Rs 15 per kW for solar photovoltaic and Rs 11 per kW for solar thermal.

Solar panels are being used to light streetlights in Gandhinagar and to operate traffic signals in towns. One should not be surprised to find the narrow lanes of a village being provided solar panel power streetlight. In some of the coastal villages, the state is already using solar energy to light homes, streets and provide community drinking water.

Power saved is power generated. Creating water recharging structures and providing surface water for irrigation through canals have already saved a lot of power that was used to draw water from tube wells. Now farmers use less powerful motors and save on power bills.

The government adopted power-saving measures in all its departments at the secretariat. It now uses energy efficient lights, optimises use of lifts in offices and efficiently uses air conditioners. These measures helped reduce government power bills substantially. Similarly, street lights of Gandhinagar that used to have 100 W of bulbs (7500 in numbers) were replaced with energy efficient 14 watt T/5 tubes. This led to massive saving of power and money.[56]

Bandish Patel in Himmatnagar was busy making automated switches operated on SIM-based services. A person can control the power device by using a mobile phone from anywhere in the state. He demonstrated the efficacy of his local innovation and said this could be used to control street lights, water pumps in fields, or even a system running at home. "This automated switching off will also help in saving power," he said.[57]

The state government had promised 24-hour continuous three-phase quality power supply to every village under Jyotigram Yojana (lighting every village) scheme. But this needed infrastructural changes. A unique scheme was evolved to separate the feeder line that supplied power to the rural areas into two—one to supply power for agricultural needs and the other for household and other needs.

Earlier, villages used to be supplied electricity through the same feeder that catered to both agriculture and domestic use. The power supply was irregular. Voltage fluctuations, that led to frequent tripping of power pumps, forced farmers to spend a lot of money on repairs. There was no proper accounting since subsidised power for agriculture was used for household chores as well. This added to the loss incurred by the government.

Separation of feeders helped assess the need of farmers and supply power accordingly. Now a dedicated feeder supplies uninterrupted three-phase power for eight hours each day for agriculture purposes. The remaining rural load—domestic, commercial and industrial—was also supplied three phase power for 24 hours.[58] For domestic use of farmers residing on farms, specially designed transformers on agricultural feeders was installed.[59]

The state had saved capital expenditure of around Rs 23,000 crore, or about 5,000 MW of power according to an estimate by the Indian Institute of Management.[60]

More than 18,065 villages were provided 24-hour electricity as promised. The remaining 132 villages were electrified through solar energy. The scheme was launched in 2003, and in 2006, then President APJ Abdul Kalam dedicated the 'Jyotigram Yojana' to the nation.

The Jyotigram Yojana involved erection of 1.6 million electric poles, installation of 15,500 transformers and laying down of 75,000 km of electric lines. This was implemented in two and a half years from October 2004 to March 2006.

Roads

Gujarat roads are some of the best in the country. The Bombay High Court had observed in 2009 that the roads in Gujarat are in better condition than those in Maharahstra. Hearing a PIL, Justice JN Patel said, "People say that Gujarat has got best of the roads... as long as you have not crossed the border (into Maharashtra). It's a shame for our government that we cannot build good roads."[61]

Three World Bank Reports in three successive years from 2010 praised Gujarat for different indicators of road development. The first report (2010) that studied implementation of World Bank-funded Gujarat State Highway Project (GSHP) during the period 2001-07 said other Indian states should replicate the example of Gujarat.[62] In 2011, the World Bank said that Gujarat offers an example of international best practice in roads management. The report that compared the roads of South Africa, Argentina, Brazil, Indonesia, Karnataka and Gujarat said that reforms in Gujarat in the roads sector have come close to international standards.[63] In 2012, the World Bank report on quality of roads said that 13 of the 16 Gujarat state highways were better than international standards. The study that was undertaken in 2012 was based on roughness index of the roads. It commended the state for managing the roads in a professional manner.

The state has 77,265 km of planned roads, of which it has national highways stretching up to 3,262 km, state highways of 18,421 km, major district roads of 20,503 km, other district roads of 10,227 km and village roads of 24,852 km.[64] About 92 per cent of Gujarat roads are paved ones as against the national average of 58 per cent.[65]

Of these 98.46 per cent of state highways and 97.11 per cent of major district roads, 91.93 per cent of ordinary district roads and 88.43 per cent of village roads have asphalt surface often called black topped roads. In addition to these, there are panchayat roads or rural roads of 30,019 km.[66]

The World Bank study of 2011 gave full credit to the political leadership of the state: "Gujarat is one of India's industrially advanced states and a leader in pursuing economic reforms. Its track record in implementing modern road management systems is not as long as that of South Africa or Argentina, but it has demonstrated political will to sustain the quality of road assets... Its political leadership has sought and secured the active participation of private stakeholders in planning, financing, and managing road development and operations."[67]

Ports

The state that prospers is the one that understands its natural advantages and works accordingly. Gujarat is blessed with a 1600-km long coastline along the Arabian Sea and this is 21.28 per cent of India's total coastline of 7,517 km. Gujarat ports act as the nearest sea route point to other states of northern and central India, if goods are to be traded to and from countries of Middle East, Africa and Europe.

Outlining the vision on port development, the chief minister said, "Our progress and development is not just limited to ports. Our vision is for port led development with port based Special Economic Zones, warehouses, cold storage networks, railroad connectivity and related infrastructure facilities being established."[68]

And indeed, as one drove towards Dahej port, one could find GIDC developed SEZs around the port region. For miles one could see various industries dotting the four lane international standard roads that connected the ports. The strategy seemed clear. The industries in the area should either act as feeder for export or use imported raw material to manufacture goods and export them. Being located in SEZ would provide various concessions in taxes.

The state has 42 ports of which one, the Kandla Port, is under the Union Government. Rest 41 ports are under Gujarat Maritime Board (GMB). While Kandla handled 82.5 million tons of cargo in 2011-12, the state ports (non-major ports) handled 259 million tons, which was almost double from 135 million tons in 2001, when Modi came to power. The non-major ports accounted for 28 per cent of the total cargo handled by all ports of India. The cargo handled by the state's non-major ports increased by 12 per cent. It is envisaged that by 2015-16, ports in Gujarat will have traffic handling capacity of more than 500 million tons, and of more than 1,000 million tons by 2020.

Gujarat has taken to port development in a big way. Some of these all-weather, direct-birthing, deep-sea ports represent the country's first Greenfield ports developed in the joint sector on BOOT (Built, Own, Operate and Transfer) basis. The state has identified 10 Greenfield sites under this. Road and rail linkages play a major role in development of port and port-led industries. Pipavav, Mundra, Navlakhi, Bhavnagar and Okha ports are connected with broad gauge rail network.

The Mundra Port developed jointly by the Gujarat government and Adani group is world class commercial port. Gujarat Pipavav Port limited, the first private port developed by the state, got connected with broad gauge rail connection with commissioning of double stack container train. The chemical port at Dahej, that handles liquid and gaseous chemicals and petroleum products, is the most modern port terminal with services matching international standards.

In January 2012, the state laid the foundation for beginning Ro-Ro ferry service between Dahej and Ghogha. The distance between Dahej and Ghogha by seaway is just 31 km as against 360 km by road.

***

Governance

The basis of effective government is public confidence.
— **John F. Kennedy**

Good governance does not come by wishful thinking or banal promises. It comes by logical thinking, simplification of procedure, putting up systems of checks and balances and preparing the mindset of the implementing agency to accept changes. With bureaucracy ready to do his bidding, Modi introduced some major changes without disturbing their equilibrium.

Those who do not want change are primarily those who benefit from the system. If a minister asks for money in taking government decision, he cannot bring transparency. Why will he or his officials reduce the sphere of discretion if they stand to gain maximum from enormous discretionary powers that come from obfuscation or delay? To make a government accountable, one needs to create institutions and processes that are easily understood by the common man.

Only that government will be transparent that has nothing to hide. One of the key demands of anti-corruption crusader Anna Hazare was that every government department must have a Citizen Charter whereby a citizen can know what he has to do if he has to get work done from that particular department in a time-bound manner. The Gujarat government has implemented Citizen Charter in all 23 government departments having any dealing with the public. This charter system has been decentralised up to the district level and efforts were being made to implement the same at the *taluka* level. Making citizens aware of their rights is a part of the Citizen Charter.

A World Bank Report on road sector in Gujarat had the following comment to make on the state's good governance: "Gujarat has been a pioneer in strengthening governmental policies, institutions and procedure for better governance…"[1] Though this comment came while analysing the road sector reforms, the same was true for most areas of government.

India's known crusader against corruption, Kiran Bedi, tweeted on 5 December 2013: "When Narendra Modi speaks on governance and development, it appears others need to go to school!" A few minutes before that she had tweeted: "Hearing NaMo! Extent of his hands on experience in governance is unmatched! Country needs this experience desperately to recover lost times."[2]

Ankita, born in Gujarat, lives in Delhi. In her passport, her mother's incorrect name was entered by mistake. She wanted to get the entry corrected and for doing this she was asked to come to the passport office and meet the concerned official. She had to visit the office twice once to know what to do and how to do it, and at the second time to submit documents. Why could the process not be simpler with someone answering specific questions on e-mail and allowing her to fill the form and submit scanned copies of her documents online rather than making visits to the concerned office twice? Even if a fee was needed, the same could have been done online.

Introduction of IT to achieve e-governance has been experimented earlier too. When IT had yet not become a buzzword way back in 1998 then Andhra Pradesh Chief Minister, N Chandrababu Naidu, made use of IT. He had started a project called 'electronic government' project He used to call himself the "CEO of Andhra Pradesh Inc" and used to interact with his bureaucrats at the district level using IT. In 2002, he had said that the benefits of e-governance would start coming in two to three years. He made great contributions to the IT industry of Andhra Pradesh but his failure to produce quick results for people cost him the job. He lost the assembly elections in 2004.

Where Naidu failed, Modi succeeded. Modi knew that nothing could be imposed unless the ground work was done. Once the officials were ready to play by his rule, he started implementing his vision of good governance. The ultimate compliment to Modi came when Chandrababu Naidu heaped lavish praise on him and the Gujarat model of governance in October 2013. "The Gujarat CM's model of governance was ideal for the country… After Modi became CM, the nation has started looking at Gujarat as an ideal state. The whole country needs to learn from Modi's model of good governance," he said.[3]

The Governance Knowledge Centre of the central government came out with the following explanation on why e-governance failed in most states but succeeded in Gujarat. It said: "An incomplete e-governance would create mafias of corruption, layers of hazy government rules and obligations, divided responsibilities and a rule of vendors over citizens. This is a dangerous application and most states where e-governance has failed show these symptoms. However, Gujarat has overcome most of them and aspires to look forward and evolve."[4]

We have seen how Modi used to encourage BJP workers to become IT savvy when he was in Delhi. Use of technology was something that came easily to him. He had high-end mobiles when people had not even heard of them. Some RSS people used to laugh at his fetish for technology. The same people are now viewing him as the man who is capable of giving a modern vision to the country's youth. Introducing e-governance was the natural outcome of a man who was so trustful of the new technology.

This was an effective way to reduce the possibility of interface between public and government officials and remove opportunities of corruption. People come to a government department for utility needs such as licenses, ration cards, caste certificates, etc., Modi decided to make the entire process online. Unlike many Indians, he had a penchant for detail. He would conceptualise implementation at the field level and ensure monitoring of a pilot scheme to understand the bottlenecks. In many cases, his interaction with secretaries would prove embarrassing to them since they had developed the habit of leaving the details to their junior officers.

He broke government works into various sectors and gave new and catchy names to various schemes for easy identification. Discussing some of them makes an interesting read. His approach was that of a layman and he always began with the basics.

In a normal life situation, a common man may not have understanding about which department to approach for his work and which documents to provide. This often leads to corruption and harassment. So, the person ends up contacting a middleman to get things done. A normal government office appears intimidating to him. Modi launched the Jan Seva Kendra

(JSK) or Centre of Public Service to provide a one-stop solution to all citizen centric services mentioned in the Citizen Charter. An individual can go to the official website and file an online application for 156 types of public services such as land, civil supplies, driving license, other certificates, affidavit, etc. Those who are not tech-savvy can submit the application at a specified counter.

These services have been categorised as *tatkal* (prompt), 'one day governance' and 'non-one day governance'. In *tatkal*, it takes a maximum time of two hours to process the application and deliver the work. Important services such as affidavits, alteration in ration card and land revenue payment fall in this category. According to the state government data, about 20 per cent of all the applications fall under this category.

In 'one day governance' scheme, it takes 12 hours to process the applications. The documents get delivered the same day if the application is submitted before 1 pm, or next day if submitted after that. Caste, income, birth and death certificates fall under this category. About 40 per cent of applications come under this category. In 'non-one day governance', it takes 3-90 days to process the application. Issues such as land allotment, change of land use and arms licenses fall in this category.

All clearances from various departments are taken by Jan Seva Kendras and people are protected from the harassment of running from one government department to the other. Other than in *tatkal*, intimation to an applicant is sent through Short Messaging System (SMS) once the application is processed. JSKs have provided queue-free operations and brought the government closer to people in the district and at *taluka* levels.

JSKs also organise mobile weekend camps in remote villages for taking applications and delivering these services at the doorstep. In 2007, Government of India's Department of Information Technology assessed the project as "a model project in the country for district level e-governance".

The success of JSKs was replicated at the city level with the name e-City. With the state increasing its expenditure on making better urban centres, IT was used to deliver municipal services making expenditure more transparent. Ahmedabad opened 50 e-City centres to take requests for any municipal service. Grievance complaints are also taken by these e-City centres.

Wherever one goes in the district administration, one can meet scores of satisfied people who say that they had no problems with the government. One just needs to make an application. The rest is done by the government.

It is not that everything is hunky-dory. It is not that *Ram Rajya* has been established and there is no corruption. It would not be difficult to spot a traffic policeman taking money to not issue a *challan* (an official receipt for payment or delivery) to a two-wheeler driver for violation of some traffic rule. But a common man can live with honesty if he wants. And action is surely going to be taken if a corruption incident is reported. The Chief Minister's Office (CMO) works at zero level of corruption. Everyone we spoke to said that there was no corruption in the upper echelons of bureaucracy.

Modi's leadership has inspired officials to put a check on corruption. Truckers crossing NH-8 at Acchad (Maharashtra) border to Gujarat were surprised that those posted at the Bhilad check post (near Valsad) late in the night refused to take bribe and allow entry to the truck that was overloaded. The junior officer posted at the check post said: "*Abey yeh Narendra Modi saheb ka RTO post hai. Yahan rishwat dene wale ke haath tod diye jaate hain. Yahan per rishwat nahin, imandari chalti hai.*" (This is RTO of Narendra Modi. Anyone offering a bribe gets his hands broken. Here honesty works, not bribes). The truck owner had to finally pay the money and get the truck released. Bribe did not work.[5]

The check post on the Maharashtra side earns less than half of the profit earned by the check post on the Gujarat side. The number of truckers who pass through the two check posts is the same. This has been the trend for a decade.[6]

A system has been put in place whereby a person need not pay bribe to get his or her work done. The young director of Neptune Reality Group and also Atlanta Electricals, Niral Patel, who recently ventured into real estate business, said that it used to take a lot of time to get land converted from agriculture to non-agriculture use. Also, there were multiple authorities to give permission for developing an area. The situation has changed now, remarkably more so in the last five years.

"We need to make out an application for change of land use. Within specified period of time, the administration would get back to us saying whether it is possible or not. It has often happened that the administration would call all interested parties such as buyer, seller, others remotely connected with land and take a decision," he said. When asked whether he needed to pay any bribe, he said that he had not paid any bribe to anyone. "Since the decision would come in a time-bound manner, we can take faster decision", he added.[7]

Ravindrabhai Vepari, who is a chartered accountant in Surat, narrated an incident where the city mayor complained to the chief minister about the corrupt act of a bureaucrat and the official was immediately transferred. An official may still indulge in corruption but he always has the fear of getting caught.[8]

An official narrated an incident where villagers complained of extortion by a local officer. Following the complaint, the officer was caught red-handed accepting a bribe. The chief minister could have sacked him but chose not to since the officer had children studying in school. He called him to his office, reprimanded him and merely transferred him to a different place with a warning that there should be no repetition of the act. The officer is a completely transformed person today.

And if a bureaucrat is not being helpful or if someone is being harassed, one has the option to directly approach the chief minister. The CMO has a unique concept of grievance redress mechanism under State-Wide Attention on Grievances by Application of Technology (SWAGAT). The chief minister and other functionaries of the government interact directly with the affected persons and use video conferencing to talk to officials located in districts.

The fourth Thursday of every month at the CMO is earmarked as the SWAGAT day. Only policy matters and long pending cases that have remained unresolved for at least six months are taken up for action by the CMO. The applications come from anyone. The scheme was launched on 4 April 2003.

SWAGAT uses the Gujarat State Wide Area Network (commissioned in 2001) to connect the state secretariat with all ministries and departments and all government officers at the district and *taluka* levels. The system connects to over 12,000 nodes of more than 2,300 government offices across the state. Most governance issues are resolved using SWAGAT at the level of district and *taluka*. SWAGAT initiative won second place in the United Nations Public Service Award for improving transparency, accountability and responsiveness in public service in 2010.

On a typical SWAGAT day, grievance applications are registered online at *Jansampark* (public relations) office of the chief minister between 9 am to 12 noon. Applicants reach the office directly. The applicants do not need to inform anyone. Details are immediately made available online to concerned officials of different departments. Between 12 noon to 3 pm, officers enter their information and responses. By 3 pm when the chief minister sits to discuss the issue with the applicant and senior officers, they must be ready with a response. District and sub-district officers attend the programme through video conferencing. Cases are redressed the same day or in a time-bound manner. All directions given by the chief minister are formally recorded. Once a case has been discussed and instructions given for solution, the next applicant is called.

Imagine how much fear it must be creating in officialdom to ensure that a complaint against their non-delivery should not reach the highest level. No one knows who will complain and about what. This has definitely made officials more responsive at the local level. During one such SWAGAT hearing the chief minister ordered legal action against the land mafia and any government officer involved in such illegal activities.[9]

The SWAGAT online programme has empowered the common man because of such quick response and effective orders by the chief minister. About 99 per cent cases are resolved.

Most high-level corruption cases are detected at the level of tendering. The government is the biggest buyer of goods and services from the market. Lack of transparency and discretion without checks and balances often leads to corruption. Those allotting the tenders become powerful and manipulate discretion to favour vested interests. This often results in exchange of illegal gratifications by the dispenser of the contract. Modi has tried to resolve this problem by introducing e-procurement for purchases in all the government offices, state PSUs and in institutions funded by government. E-procurement is a system of bidding online. Since physical contact with authorities is avoided, the role of middlemen is removed. Those filling the tenders can know the result of each step in the tendering process online. Pre-bidding and bidding is done online. Negotiations also go online.

Niral Patel deals with selling transformers to the government. He explained how he bid through e-tendering or e-procurement. Atlanta Electricals has tough competition from a dozen other companies but it still survives and does good business because of transparency of operation, said the management graduate from the United States. Atlanta has 18 per cent of the market share in transformer business and it plans to challenge bigger multinational corporations.

"When a tender is floated, it is advertised and made available online. The first bidding is done online and whatever has been bid once cannot be changed. Thereafter, once a company qualifies in preliminary bidding, it is called for detailed technical and financial bidding which have to be done together in sealed copies. Information about processes is available online. There is no renegotiation. The lowest bidder is given the tender but if there are more bidders ready to match the lowest price, some work is given to them as well. Politicians stay out of it and no correction is allowed once the tendering process is over."

"The best thing is that the supplier does not have to run pillar to post to get the payment for the goods delivered. Most payments come in 60 days", he said.[10]

The World Bank Report on road reforms noted the comment of the Gujarat Vigilance Commission that held that procurement-related complaints have decreased significantly with the advent of e-procurement.[11]

This was true for other cases too. This system has saved time and money. The number of tenders passed during the year 2011-12, through this process, was 23,502. Recognition came by way of prestigious awards including the Government Technology Award.

Thanks to the innovative thinking of the Gujarat chief minister, NRI Gujaratis can log in to the internet to know the situation of their land in Gujarat. This has been made possible due to computerisation of all village land records under the e-Dhara scheme and then making them available to citizens online in an easy and transparent manner. Within six months of launch of the scheme, about 1.5 million records in all 225* *talukas* were computerised. The aim of computerisation of the records

---

* When this was undertaken the state had 225 talukas. Now the number of talukas is 248

was to enable automatic update. For this, *e-Dhara Kendras* (e-DKs) have been set up. A nominal user fee is charged.

Now, a farmer can easily access copies of Record of Rights at the level of village panchayat. The Village Computer Entrepreneur (VCE) gets the request from the farmer on the government portal after which the Deputy Mamlatdar at e-DK processes the ROR and uploads it on to the central server. After this, the VCE takes a printout and gives it to the applicant.

The *e-Dhara* scheme has been successfully implemented in all the 33 districts and 248 *talukas*. Earlier the state had 26 districts and 225 *talukas*. In 2013, seven more districts and 23 more *talukas* were created from the existing ones for better administration.[12] Over 4 crore copies of RoR have been issued from e-DKs since its inception.

Linked to that is the initiative of *e-Jamin*. Under this, all stakeholders will be integrated with land records. Registration of land has already been linked with *e-Dhara*. Immediately after registration of agricultural land, a notice for mutation is generated by *e-Dhara*.

The e-Gram scheme is another IT innovation that seeks to bridge the digital rural-urban divide. It was launched in October 2008. It sought to establish *e-Gram* Common Service Centres (CSC). E-Gram Vishwagram Society has been established as a special purpose vehicle for e-governance at the panchayat level. Village Computer Entrepreneurs (VCE) had been appointed under PPP to deliver services to rural citizens through *e-Gram* centres. Under this scheme, 13,685 e-Gram Common Service Centres were established.

A Technical Support and Training Service Provider Team (TSTSP) is deployed at village, *taluka*, district and state levels to provide hardware and software support. This team also trains VCEs to increase their skills to make them more effective in discharging services. The VCEs are crucial since villagers approach the administration through them. Some of the services provided by the government to the people include issuance of certificates such as birth, death and character; RoR certificates; collection of electricity bills, cyber teaching classes, etc. Farmers can also access other services such as e-ticketing for railways and airlines, utility bill payments, APMC rates, online education, etc.

Most of the administrative needs are addressed at the *taluka* level and most government schemes are dependent on the effectiveness of *taluka* administration. *Apno Taluko, Vibrant Taluko* (ATVT) was conceptualised to completely decentralise administration in conformity with the citizen-centric approach. It was conceptualised as a new growth model based on grass root planning and people's participation. ATVT scheme was visualised at the seventh *chintan shibir* at Mehsana.

This scheme aims to provide basic amenities like internet, village roads, sewage disposal system, drinking water, solid waste disposal system, etc. Each *taluka* was given the independence to adopt its own model of development based on the context in which it operated. SWAGAT scheme of deliverance and other e-governance schemes were implemented. This was launched on 28 April 2011.

Even Modi's worst critics do not level charges of corruption against him. The court at the highest level has rejected any wrongdoing on the part of the leadership or the government in allocation of resources. Gujarat has been a frequent winner of *India Today's* State of the States Awards in the last 10 years. A US embassy cable to the American Administration quoted senior Congress leader Digvijaya Singh as saying that "Modi is incorruptible". "Modi's reputation for being completely incorruptible is accurate, and if he were to become a national leader he would crack down on corruption throughout the BJP," the US cable by Consul General Michael S Owen said.[13]

The United States, which is so fussy about issuing Modi a visa, ended up formally lauding Gujarat's governance model. A congressional report of 2011 showered praise on Chief Minister Narendra Modi, saying the state, under him, had become a key driver of national economic growth.[14] "Perhaps India's best example of effective governance and impressive development is found in Gujarat, where controversial Chief Minister Narendra Modi has streamlined economic processes, removing red tape and curtailing corruption in ways that have made the state a key driver of the national economic growth," said the report.

"Politics is all about muscle and money power. All political leaders pretend to fight corruption. But they exercise political will only when there is a vote factor or there is no alternative for a difficult situation," former Chief Vigilance Commissioner (1998-2002) N Vittal said. Vittal said Gujarat was fortunate, as compared to other states, to have a chief minister like Modi who had the political will to take some unpopular decisions. "He (Modi) was the one to say that we will give electricity in all villages, but people will have to pay (the bill), whereas in some states it is promised for free," he said.[15]

One parameter to rate good governance is any state's law and order situation. The last decade has been the most peaceful decade in the history of Gujarat ever since its creation. There has been not a shred of violence and nobody remembers curfew, *dharna* (sit-in demonstration) or police *lathi* charge. In 2008, there were a series of 21 bomb blasts in 70 minutes in Ahmedabad, killing 56 and injuring about 200.[16] Some of the blasts took place in communally sensitive areas. However, no untoward incident happened in reaction to these blasts. People demonstrated solidarity and the city came back to normal. Despite blasts and world economic recession, Gujarat bagged the ambitious Tata Nano project in October 2008 and the 2009 Vibrant Gujarat brought in record investments.[17]

There is no political interference to force the police to act one way or the other. The mandate given to the police chief is 'do your best'. Because there is no patronage to any caste group or religion, administration is able to act as per its understanding. But the CM office is watching. Lethargy on the part of the police or failure to crack a case could land the police commissioner into trouble. And this accountability has percolated down to the lowest level.

A Rajasthani businessman in Surat said, "Unlike Maharashtra, there is no one to raise anti-non-Gujarati passion. No one comes and collects extortion money. If there is a problem, we go to the police and we do not need to pay anything. When we go to Rajasthan, we know how backward we are. Now many people from Rajasthan and Bihar are migrating to Gujarat."

When Rakesh Asthana was posted as Surat's Police commissioner, Modi had just one brief for him: go and do something exemplary that will make the city safe. The city was known for incidents such as pick-pocketing, petty thefts, chain snatching, car theft etc. With more and more people coming to the city for jobs and homes, Surat became as heterogeneous and complex as any other modern growing city. The Traffic Education Trust, in association with the police, came out with the concept of 'Safe Surat City' and got installed high resolution camera surveillance. Hiren Diwan, a chartered accountant and a trustee, said that the cameras are remarkable for their high resolution images. The city planned to have 1,500 cameras.

He narrated his own experience when he was caught driving without a seat belt. He got a notice for payment of fine. This proved the efficacy of the system although he was caught unawares. If anyone is doing mischief, he will be caught. If a person on a two-wheeler is driving without a helmet, he is bound to get a fine notice, he said. This has brought better traffic discipline in people. Also it has helped to put a check on crime. Petty crimes like snatching have got drastically reduced, he said.

The same trust model is being copied in Ahmedabad, Vadodara and other cities. In a recent incident of hit and run in Ahmedabad (2013), the police used CCTV images to nab the culprit. Everyone in the city is aware that they are being watched. This has prevented the crime rate from shooting up.

The city is experimenting with another important mechanism in crime prevention—the Setu scheme, which acts as bridge between the public and the police. A person was travelling in a train but had a liquor bottle with him. A co-passenger clicked his photograph and uploaded it on Setu application (Setu apps) on his mobile. By the time the train reached Udhna railway station near Surat, the police came and arrested him. This proved the efficacy of the system developed. Anybody can do live online interaction with the police under the Setu scheme. In Surat a DCP has been assigned the task to look after this. The same scheme is being replicated in other cities as well.

Now people can see women driving two-wheelers late in the night without any fear. This is the case even during the time of festivals. Earlier, parents were scared whether their children returning home late would be safe. The situation has completely changed now, Asma Khan Pathan, a resident of Nadiad, said.

***

Profitable Agriculture &
Prosperous Villages

*Man's survival, from the time of Adam and Eve until the invention
of agriculture, must have been precarious because of his inability
to ensure his food supply*

—Norman Ernest Borlaug

Praveen Makwana, a farmer in Mespur, was not ready to believe that his village and 4,000 other villages of the region were declared drought-hit in 2012. For him, "drought is a thing of the past". Also, for many other farmers of Saurashtra, drought is something which they no longer dreaded. They were confident of a good harvest and a consequent good profit.

Girdhar Satasia, a farmer in Boria village of Rajkot, said that the groundwater level had gone down to 182 metres in 2001, but now it was only six metres below the ground due to the aquifers getting recharged. Now farmers grow three crops a year. Ever since they built check dams in their area, the profit has gone up by 300 per cent![1]

Such stories are there in plenty in every village that was water-starved and used to fear a bad monsoon. This turnaround in mood has been made possible due to the community based water structures that have come up in large numbers. A bad monsoon now is rather a test of the water conservation mechanism that has been put in place over the last few years. While the water table has come up in many areas, a regular supply of power has ensured that farmers can plan irrigation in a much better way.

The main reason for Modi's victory in 2007 and 2012 assembly elections could be that the rural voters felt empowered and had high stakes in keeping him in the saddle. While writing about 2007, a commentator said, "...An excellent new study suggests that the secret of

Modi's success lay in agriculture, an area completely neglected by political analysts." He further said, "Since the bulk of Gujarat's population is still rural, this mega-boom in agriculture must have created millions of satisfied voters. Hence it must have played a major role in Modi's victory. Yet, I did not see a single media analyst mention it."[2]

If this was a discernible factor in 2007, the story in 2012 was doubly so. Modi's attempt at increasing agriculture productivity and honouring young farmers for their excellent performance multiplied his support base. Those who talk of Modi as a friend only of business need to take a walk in the rural areas. They will then realise that he has performed almost a miracle in the agricultural field as well.

It is no wonder that Gujarat clocked close to 10 per cent growth in agriculture in the decade 2002-12, when the average growth projected by the Planning Commission for the entire country was about four per cent. "Between 2001-2012, the agricultural component in Gujarat's GSDP has grown at a real average rate of annual growth of 10.5 per cent, nothing short of remarkable."[3] Total agriculture income increased from Rs 14,000 crore in 2001 to Rs 80,000 crore in 2011.[4]

Gujarat is the largest producer of castor, cumin, fennel seeds and psyllium husk in the world.[5] The state ranks first in India in terms of groundnut and cotton production with groundnut accounting for 36 per cent share, whereas cotton accounts for 32 per cent of the total production.

High productivity of non-food crops is remarkable. Oilseed productivity was 1,600 kg per hectare in 2011-12, nearly 470 kg more than the all-India average, and higher than the yield recorded for Madhya Pradesh and Rajasthan—the two states which produce more oilseed than Gujarat.[6]

To add to the sector's performance is the strong growth in foodgrain production since 2000. Substantial growth has been observed in case of wheat, with production increasing from 1.1 million tonnes in 2001-02 to 4.2 million tonnes in 2010-11.[7]

Gujarat's 1,600-km long coastline has ensured availability of commercial varieties of marine fish such as Pomfret and Shrimp and they constitute 88 per cent of state's fish production. The state earned foreign exchange worth Rs 2,534 crore in 2011-12 through the export of 1,98,650 tonnes of fish and fish products.[8]

High-value horticulture products have been another source of growth, thanks to strong crop productivity. Gujarat contributes nearly a tenth to India's fruit output (by volume) and ranks amongst the top five vegetable producers (by volume) in the country. Major fruits grown in Gujarat are banana, mango, citrus and sapota.[9]

It is true that the growth was primarily driven by cotton and livestock, and fruits and vegetables. If better rainfall, good pricing of cotton by the central government or factors other than government has driven the growth, which is argued quite often, one would need to think why other states failed to deliver the same. In Gujarat, farmers are paying for the water and power they consume and this is a big achievement for the government.

Better irrigation facilities even in water-scarce areas has enabled farmers to grow multiple crops. Instead of a meagre one or two crops a year, they are now cultivating three-four crops. The state government is bubbling with enthusiasm that their hard work coupled with community participation has brought the state on the cusp of a new Green revolution—something that the chief minister speaks quite proudly of.

Total area that has come under agriculture has increased every year. A comparison of 2001 with 2012 will elucidate that it has increased from 108 lakh hectares to 135 lakh hectares. Amidst fears from certain quarters that allotment of land to industries may reduce farm lands and create an agrarian crisis, Modi has asserted that he would not let the agriculture land get reduced.[10]

Area under cultivation of cotton and tobacco has also witnessed substantial increase. There was a fall in foodgrain production largely due to decrease in the cultivation area since people adopted cash crops in a big way.[11] In 2001, the state produced 23 lakh bales of cotton compared to 1.23 crore bales in 2011-12.[12]

Even as the share of agriculture to GSDP has declined because of higher growth in industries and services, the fact remains that agriculture provides employment to more than 50 per cent of the state's population.

To keep the agriculture momentum going, the Gujarat Agro Vision

2010, which is a 10-year plan to conclude in 2020, has envisaged an annual growth rate of 6.8 per cent in agriculture (including animal husbandry). It has recognised the importance of agriculture for removing rural poverty. It made specific provisions for providing resources to poor farmers and agricultural labourers, particularly in tribal areas. The two vehicles identified to achieve this were horticulture and animal husbandry. By the end of the vision period, per capita income of population dependent on agriculture is expected to be Rs 13,534; almost twice the figure of Rs 7,155 per year in the beginning of the vision period.

Agriculture Scientist MS Swaminathan has stressed time and again that agrarian distress can be addressed by bringing down cost of agriculture production and increasing the income of farmers. He suggested that all states should tackle five issues — namely soil, water, credit and insurance, post-harvest and technology to address farm sector issues.[13]

Modi has tried to tackle the issues at all these five levels. Improving agriculture performance has become a movement as more and more farmers have started calculating their produce in terms of market values. Better road connectivity and easy access to APMC rates (Agriculture Produce Market Committee) on mobile phones has made it possible for farmers to know the existing price in different markets. This has brought down the importance of middlemen.

In 2004-05, the government took the bold step of allowing private companies to buy crops from farmers a year in advance, better known as contract farming. While a minimum price was guaranteed, the farmer was protected against any likely price increase. On the one hand, it reduced market risks for the farmer; on the other hand, it encouraged companies to invest in farming indirectly.[14]

The government has also allowed private players to set up their own *mandis* (local wholesale markets) bypassing the APMC mechanism. By 2007, eight corporate houses were allowed to set up these *mandis* and buy directly from farmers. These were to run under government guidelines and could not be set up within a five km radius of an existing APMC.[15] The private *mandis* were to be equipped with food-processing units, grading, cleaning, washing and packaging facilities, adding to the value chain of the produce. In that way, we can say that this intended to enlarge the reach of farmers to a more modern market.

But these statistics or efforts would have no meaning unless these have helped farmers to get empowered. The water table is down in the Nana Borsara village in Mangrol *taluka* near Surat. The village cannot take water from the canal that gets water from the Ukai Dam because the land is 30 feet higher than the canal level. The government has sanctioned Rs 48 lakh to make a special pipeline to pump water from the canal to the village pond. For irrigation, the villagers depended on rain water and the village pond with a good retaining capacity that sustained them for more than eight months. Farmers drew water from this pond through motors and pipe. At other times, they depended on underground water. They had to ration water. After the new water system is put in place, they would like to experiment with more crops such as sugarcane that takes more water and has a cycle of one year.

Kalidas Prajapati, who is a Dalit and has only five bigha (1 bigha—1/3 of an acre) of land, does not worry much that he does not have an independent water drawing system. The rich farmer in the adjoining land, Dilipsinh Mohansinh Chauhan, helps him and charges money for the water used. The rate is fixed by the Nana Borsara Peet Sahkari Mandari Trust. So there cannot be any exploitation due to dependence. Prajapati said that he made an annual profit of more than Rupees one lakh with one cotton crop. And he now grows three crops—one of cotton and two others of mixed vegetables.

Once the water system is fully in place, they can even grow two cotton crops or have a longer cotton cycle for better productivity. The farmers knew the nutrients of the soil, the use of fertilisers and the schemes of the government. Dilipsinh said that a government loan was easily available and at a subsidised rate of three per cent and there had been no case of default.

To test the prosperity brought by agriculture, one just needed to visit the house of Natwarbhai Kilabhai Vasava, a tribal. The family was staying in the *pucca* accommodation given by the government and the household had a big refrigerator, a colour television and two table fans. One could see how agriculture productivity was fuelling demand for industrial goods.

The problem farmers are facing is lack of land, preventing expansion. Also, the land prices have gone up many times, thereby making fresh buying almost impossible.

Ravindrabhai Vepari, a chartered accountant with a thriving practice in Surat, said that water and power have created wonders in Saurashtra. Most farmers from Saurashtra came to Surat for working in diamond industries. The influx stopped once agriculture became lucrative. "I have heard so many people from Saurashtra talking about the new agriculture boom there," he said. Modi has almost performed a miracle, he added.[16]

The new water arrangement system has changed the face of Gujarat agriculture. The salinity of water had increased by the steadily declining underground water table over the last 15-20 years in north Gujarat. At some places, it had already reached about 600 ft below ground level, "risking irreversible salination of aquifers". This led to increased dependence on high-power pumps and increased expenditure on electricity. In 1967, a farmer used 5 HP pump to draw water from beneath the ground, which gradually went to 72 HP pump. The new water system has changed the situation.[17] Since 75 per cent of people now depend on surface water instead of drawing water from the wells, dependence on power to run pumps has decreased. Earlier, the state had 85 per cent dependence on ground water. Now, 75 per cent of the supply comes from surface water. Now agriculture is flourishing in the region and groundwater table has come up almost everywhere.

Animal Husbandry: Rural Lifeline

Every rural family tries to keep a cow that not only gives it extra income but also takes care of basic needs such as milk, *ghee* and butter for good health; dung cakes for fire; and a feeling of harmony with nature. No wonder the state's cattle population is a part of the State's economic and social life. One sure way the government has adopted to eradicate rural poverty is to provide a bovine to every poor rural family.

There are many success stories. The one which is being discussed almost by everyone is the story of Ramilaben Govindhbhai Patel from Sabarkantha's Pentarpura village. She is not educationally qualified but, at the age of 43, she earns Rs 1.10 crore per year by milking cows. Her dairy farm has an output of 5.55 lakh litres per annum. Having started this in 2000 as a backyard business, she has now emerged as a symbol of success in the land of white revolution. About 12 years ago, she had registered herself as a primary milk producer with a village level milk society and hired five cross-bred cows on a bank loan.

Now she has 280 cattle on a five-acre farm, giving employment to 40 workers. Her dairy farm has four automatic milking machines. She visited Israel with her husband to find out the right technology for modernisation even when it was costly. She has become an inspiration to many other women who are actively involved in the dairy business.[18]

When Modi says, "The Delhi government won't get tea unless Gujarat provides milk to it," it is an indication of the confidence the state has gained under his leadership. Gujarat began the White Revolution, and now it has witnessed 68 per cent increase in milk production in the last decade.

The state has 17 cooperative dairy plants with a handling capacity of 125 lakh litres of milk per day (2012-13). There are also 25 private dairy plants and 16,044 cooperative societies. Gujarat Co-operative Milk Marketing Federation (GCMMF), the country's largest milk cooperative that markets brand Amul, procured 164 lakh kilogram milk per day (2013) breaking its own record of 2012.

Banaskantha based Banas Dairy in north Gujarat became the largest milk producing dairy in the country with production of 35 lakh kilo litres per day. Water-starved Saurashtra has also witnessed tremendous growth in milk production.

While a good price for milk offered by the cooperatives definitely contributed to better milk collection, the increase in milk productivity has been due to successive measures the government took in the last many years. The special care the government has been taking of the cattle population includes organising 25,000 health camps for bettering animal health in the last 10 years. The government claims to have eradicated 112 diseases affecting cattle. The state has 185 new veterinary clinics to facilitate animal healthcare at the doorstep.

The state organised special cataract camps for treatment of cattle. Modi's vision in this was evident when he wrote: "Our work does not stop at preventing killing of the mother cow; we also ensure their well being. This inspired us to organise cataract operations for cows."[19]

The state is proud to have India's first animal hostel at Akodara village in the Himmatnagar *taluka* of north Gujarat's Sabarkantha district. This hostel provides shelter to animals in villages and is based on a PPP model. It is based on the concept that the cow as a mother and giver of health must be taken better care of. This has helped reduce the burden on women to take care of the cattle the whole day. This hostel has helped even those people who would otherwise not have kept cows due to lack of space or manpower. The space is allotted as per '*khunta*' and the payment is per '*khunta*' ('*khunta*' is the place which is reserved for a cow). Doctors come on visits to these hostels. Earlier the village used to produce about 700 litres of milk daily but after the animal hostel came up, the production shot up to about 2200 litres, said Palak Patel, a graduate farmer who has come full time into dairy business.

Residents of Akodara village talk of Ameechandbhai Prajapati, who has witnessed unprecedented prosperity by entering into the dairy business. Earlier, he used to run a paan shop in the village and had kept one buffalo since he did not have any space. In 2013, he kept five cows and four buffalos at the animal hostel. He made a two-storey *pucca* house in the village showing his new empowerment. Easier loans from banks for buying cattle and their links with milk cooperatives, which buy the milk in advance and pay the instalments, have transformed dairy into a lucrative business. There has been no case of any default said Kirit K Patel of the district cooperative bank.[20]

Water harvesting and micro irrigation under the slogan of 'per drop more crop' is revolutionising agriculture in the state that falls in the semi-arid zone. The focus has been to make agriculture more effective through drip irrigation—a scientific method that carries water and nutrients to the plant's root area drop by drop. Drip irrigation and sprinkler irrigation have become the main technologies to carry forward the message of "per drop more crop".

Ganesh Patel, a farmer of Kumbhalmer in Banaskantha district had very little to do with pomegranates. But the 60-year-old produced 20 tonnes of pomegranates in 2011 worth Rs 15 lakh on 35 acre land. Shankar Mansa, a tribal farmer of Virampur village in the same district, increased his farm income many-fold on the same seven acre land he had. His earlier income of Rs 11,000 in 2008 increased to Rs 92,000 in 2011. What did the trick for him was adopting high-yielding crops and switching over to drip irrigation. He also produced more fodder for his two cows and a buffalo that helped him increase his dairy income from Rs 18,000 to Rs 41,000.[21]

The arid and rocky soil of the region had made Banaskantha one of the most backward districts of western India. The place has now witnessed a unique agricultural revolution based on drip and sprinkler irrigation. More than 70,000 acres of land has been using this technique.[22] The district has witnessed a four-fold increase in the production of potato and is rated as one of the largest producers of potato in the country.

The state set up the Gujarat Green Revolution Company (GGRC) in 2003 to push drip and sprinkler irrigation by providing technological know-how and offering a massive subsidy for setting up the micro-irrigation structures. The subsidy is more for tribal and poor farmers.

It was a major success story when 10 villages in the state adopted 100 per cent micro irrigation by 2009. All these villages had doubled their agricultural production after adopting drip and sprinkler irrigation. The GGRC said that more than 93,000 farmers in the state had adopted drip irrigation over 1.51 lakh ha land.[23]

Mahendrabhai, a rich farmer from Khoraj village in Sanand near Ahmedabad, owned a greenhouse farm on four-acre land that gave him very handsome returns. He got subsidy for installing the drip irrigation structures and had no problems in getting quick reimbursement from the government. The idea to set up such a massive structure came to him when the government took more than 100 farmers from the area to the agriculture colleges in Anand during one Krishi Mahotsav and demonstrated maximising agriculture through drip irrigation. He said that he has been making a handsome profit every year. "Agriculture has become very lucrative and I have no incentive to sell the land."[24]

The state sent a group of 600 farmers to Israel in 2012 to participate in the 18th International Agricultural Exhibition in Tel Aviv. From a desert, Israel has transformed into a green country and the chief minister wanted the young farmers to know and learn from the experiments there.[25]

One major instrument to popularise new technology in agriculture is the Krishi Mahotsav (Grand Agriculture Festival) organised by the government on a regular basis since 2005. It is an annual exercise in education of farmers. More than one lakh government employees, from the chief minister to the *taluka* level staff, spend a month during April-May in rural areas to spread awareness about good agriculture practices.

The *mahotsav* is marked with lectures and demonstrations by subject experts on issues such as use of fertilisers, insecticides, crop suitability, government schemes, crop insurance, soil testing, cattle vaccination and distribution of agriculture kits to poor farmers. Expert teams of scientists that accompany the decorated tractors conduct on-the-spot soil testing and issue soil health cards to farmers. In 2012, the government used 232 *krishi raths*.

Other states are also borrowing this concept from Gujarat. Union Agriculture Minister Sharad Pawar was so impressed that he asked Gujarat Minister Dilip Sanghani to make a presentation on the project in 2008.[26]

The Krishi Mahotsav of 2012 initiated cluster-based approach under which farmers of 4-5 villages gathered at one place for interaction with experts and government officials. The concept of video conferencing was also introduced. The chief minister, while concluding the *mahotsav*, had called upon people to use drip irrigation in a massive way and produce a record foodgrain production.[27] The main theme of the *mahotsav* in 2013 was micro irrigation/drip irrigation and animal husbandry.

A novel concept to increase productivity has been the introduction of soil health cards in 2003-04. Since Gujarat is divided into eight agro-climatic zones, it becomes necessary to know the health of the soil. Each soil has its own crop. This was necessary to make farmers aware of the composition of the soil so that they could achieve maximum productivity. The soil health cards (SHCs) are distributed to farmers free of cost.

These cards contain information such as mineral composition, water retaining capacity, productivity, etc. The cards also suggest the use of best inputs like fertilisers, seeds, pesticides and quantity of water or irrigation. These cards contain recommendations on the use of NPK (nitrogen, phosphorous and potassium), helping a farmer judge what to use to get the best results.

The government has set up 103 soil testing laboratories to update the health of soils. All panchayats have been asked to show government websites to farmers in the local language to know about various issues affecting agriculture. Under *e-Gram*, it is now possible to understand government help through the internet. Already 742 agriculture scientists have been deputed to work at *taluka* level.

Modi has often been heard saying that every state should have its own export policy. Gujarat has taken steps to encourage export of agricultural products. On the pattern of the central government, the state government is mulling a proposal to have Agriculture Export Zones for groundnut, sesame seed, castor, isabgol (psyllium seed husks), banana, potatoes, cumin and fennel seeds. The main objective of an AEZ is to provide higher returns to the farmers by enhancing their accessibility to export and extending their capacity to produce export specific quality products. This is an extension of the chief minister's argument that every Indian state should have its own export policy.

Gujarat is experimenting with making fertilisers from solid waste management in 50 towns. The chief minister sent suggestions to Prime Minister Manmohan Singh years ago to improve the state of agriculture and introduce solid waste management in 500 Indian towns so that fertilisers thus produced could be given to farmers in the nearby regions.[28]

Some of the other programmes intended to promote agriculture are e-Krishi Kiran and Kisan Cedit Cards (KCC). Anand Agriculture University (AAU) has been given the task to implement the *e-Kiran* scheme. Earlier, this was known as soil health card programme.

AAU has developed the web-based application software which generates and provides the fertiliser recommendations for each soil and the nutrient requirement for each crop. The main objective is to advise individual farmers in the field and suggest alternate cropping pattern for better productivity.[29] The Planning Commission report of 2012-13 mentions *e-Kiran* as a successful state initiative.

A total of 11,268 Kisan Credit Cards were issued till 31 March 2000. This scheme was launched by the NDA government in 1998-99. By the end of December 2000, about one crore KCCs were issued across the country but the figure of Gujarat was poor. The figure improved in 2012 when the number of KCCs issued went up to 35,63,064.[30] Considering that there are about 42.39 lakh farmers in the state, the coverage shows that farmers in Gujarat have better access to loan facilities.

Gujarat has done what the Union government should be doing. It organised a two-day convention of farmers at the Global Agriculture Summit in the state's capital in September 2013. More than 5,000 farmers from across the country attended it. This was the first time that any state government had taken initiative to take agriculture consciousness to this level. Farmers from as far as Nagaland and Assam were present at the summit. These farmers were identified for excellence they had achieved in agriculture and the summit rewarded them for their extraordinary achievements.

More than 200 companies from 15 countries were there to showcase their machinery and other equipments.[31]

Imagine this coming from a farmer from Assam, Shadul Islam: "*Hum to un men doob gaye. Bahut achcha kaam karte hain* (We are quite impressed by him/Modi. He is doing very good work)." Another farmer from Assam, Mrinal Das, said: "I had never stepped outside my district. In fact, I boarded a train for the first time to come here. I got Rs 51,000 cash reward for my progressive work and attended international seminars. For the first time in my life, I stayed in an air-conditioned hotel room."[32]

"*Shauchalaya* more important than *Devalaya*" is a concept of Nirmal Gujarat that means clean village. One of the biggest achievements of the Modi government has been to create awareness about toilet use and incentives given to set up toilets. Recently, the chief minister said at a function, "*Pehle shauchalaya, phir devalaya* (first toilets, then temples)"—a statement that came under attack from the Vishwa Hindu Parishad, but clearly showed Modi's vision.[33]

In February 2013, the state launched a training programme for rural officials on how to generate awareness about toilet use. This came after the realisation that people at many places were not using toilets built by the government. They preferred open defecation as a traditional practice and due to lack of awareness about hygiene.

The State has helped build about 46 lakh toilets for individual households, schools, Anganwadi centres and more than 1,700 community toilets between 2004 and 2012. And Gujarat needs about seven lakh more. However, at most places these toilets have been converted into storerooms. Above all, toilets are not seen as a priority item.[34]

Although Gujarat has an impressive figure in toilet use compared with other states, it has still to catch up with the better states. In 2001, only 44.6 per cent households in Gujarat had access to toilets. This figure rose to 57.3 per cent in 2011. Only about 23 per cent people in Bihar had access to toilets. Kerala had 95.2 per cent people with access to toilets as per the last Census.

The Nirmal Gujarat campaign seeks to make village life cleaner and more hygienic. While it discourages open defecating, it also encourages updating and cleaning of office records. The programme also includes imposition of scavenging tax, shifting of dung hills to places outside the dwelling places and door-to-door collection of garbage. The idea is to make village life healthier and more meaningful. About 4,000 villages have become nirmal villages, demonstrating improvement in village life.

In order to make village life peaceful and socially more integrated, the State has come up with Samras Gram Yojana (promoting harmony through consensus in villages). Panchayat elections across the country become divisive and violent. This has happened more so after devolution of development funds directly to panchayats. Since panchayat elections are not contested on party symbols; this creates more groups and resulting frictions. Factitious politics makes development decisions more difficult. Under the Samras Gram Yojana, villagers elect their candidates to the panchayat and also the sarpanch through a consensus.

Virdi, a small village in Dholka Taluka, made news as the government gave Rs 3 lakh as incentive for achieving complete harmony. The village got Rs 2 lakh for electing all members of its gram panchayat unanimously. It was given an additional sum of Rs one lakh for making the panchayat an all women representative body.[35] It qualified as a Mahila Samras Gram.

To ensure continuity, the government gives 25 per cent extra grant to second and third time Samras Grams. A village becoming Samras Gram can also avail funds for cement-concreting of roads. If the same village becomes Samras Gram for a third time, it becomes entitled for additional grant for solar lighting. This encourages villages to compete for development. Examples multiply through examples.

A level above a Samras Gram is a Teerth Gram (holy village). It was implemented in 2004 to promote brotherhood, social goodwill, peace and overall development. The village declared a *teerth* village gets Rs one lakh as incentive to keep the momentum going.

Villages with no crime for the preceding five years get selected for classification as *teerth* villages. There should be no production, sale or intake of any intoxicating substance in such a village. Besides being a clean village, there should be a high level of development for women and low dropout rate. There should be no communal dispute, and if there is one, the same should be resolved through discussion.

Deprived sections such as the Scheduled Castes (SCs) and the Scheduled Tribes (STs) should have access to the same level of primary facilities as others in the villages. The concept has been modelled on the Gandhian concept of an ideal village.

Gardens with trees, benches and tracking paths are provided in villages under Panchavati Yojana. Provision for a water fountain and swings, etc., has been made to make entertainment wholesome. The scheme notes that children no longer have these facilities near their homes and are missing something crucial in their growing years. This would recreate faith in traditional villages and take care of the environment as well. Coastal areas are being secured by constructing protection walls. The western coast of Gujarat is brushed by the waves of the Arabian Sea. Coastal erosion has been witnessed in the western and eastern boundaries of coastal districts by which the sea has been entering into land. The communities that live in these areas are not ready to leave the area and shift to safer places because their nearness to the sea allows them to go on fishing as and when they want.

Coastal erosion leads to heavy damage to their houses, fertile land and other properties. Sea facing areas of some villages of these districts face this problem—Valsad, Navsari, Surat, Bharuch and Jamnagar, Bhavnagar, Amreli and Junagadh.

***

Unleashing Entrepreneurial Energy
Favoured Destination for Industries

*Leadership is lifting a person's vision to high sights, the raising
of a person's performance to a higher standard, the building of a
personality beyond its normal limitations.*

—Peter Drucker

Nano is the biggest story everyone talks about in Gujarat. West
Bengal's loss became Gujarat's gain. That one-word SMS
from Narendra Modi to Ratan Tata, "*Swagatam*" (welcome), when
many other chief ministers were speculating what Tata would do,
demonstrates the Gujarat chief minister's farsightedness. Unlike other
chief ministers, Modi did not write any letter to Tata.

He knew that after the fiasco in West Bengal, Tata would take a very
calculative decision. The Tatas were looking for "trust and confidence",
and from all points of view, Gujarat had everything that an entrepreneur
would look out for. Pushing Tata would not yield anything. But he
knew that Nano would do to Gujarat what nothing else had done before
in rewriting the state's industrial history. He waited patiently. "Other
states may have written letters to him but I never did that," Modi said.[1]

On the morning of 7 October 2008, Modi was ecstatic. Ratan Tata
called him over the phone and informed him about the decision to move
Nano, his dream project to Gujarat. The Tatas were negotiating with
other state governments like Karnataka, Andhra Pradesh, Uttarakhand
and Maharashtra. Modi had earlier rolled out a red carpet for the Tata
officials to understand the state but was unsure what decision they
would take. Tata described the decision as "a homecoming" and the
State government handed over 1,100 acres of land to them almost
overnight. But preparation for this was already made by the confident
chief minister much in advance.

"*Aapde ahiya na chiye ane aapde ahiya paachaa aavya* (We belong here and so we have come back here)" is how Tata described his feeling. "There is a good 'M' and a bad 'M' and we have made the transition".[2] The reference here is to the chief ministers of West Bengal and Gujarat—Mamata and Modi; initials of both being 'M'.

Nano was not just Tata but India's future since it had opened up a strong possibility of exporting a fully indigenous car to the outside world. Tata was keen to rewrite India's auto history. Sanand, about 30 km from Ahmedabad, was sure to come on the world map. Modi said without mincing words that he was not looking at Nano as a project for Gujarat but as a project that would drive the country. Even when Tata was in Singur, Modi had wished that the project would take off, demonstrating his national vision.[3]

Ratan Tata gave a full-scale testimony to Gujarat in order to justify his decision: "We chose Gujarat because of the conducive and industry-friendly environment as well as infrastructure. Also, the location of the land that was being offered was very attractive... We promise to become good corporate citizens of Gujarat and stand for all that Gujarat stands for."[4]

He lauded the pace with which the Gujarat government facilitated the project, terming this to be "unbelievable". Not many governments do that since those sitting in power imagine themselves to be real rulers rather than servants of the people. Modi too acknowledged that his government moved faster than the Tatas. And there were reasons for that. Nano was not an ordinary project. The Tatas needed to catch up on the time lost due to problems in Singur (West Bengal).

Modi's thought process was clear: "I can tell you that in the last three days, after signing the MoU, our government has moved faster than the Tatas to sort out all the small details before they move in... If we had gone into the process of land acquisition, it would have taken time. For the Tatas, urgency was critical and it was important for me to address that. But the situation is that I am a step ahead of Tata in terms of speed. I have told him that we want the smallest car in the shortest time. I am going to make this a model case study of how fast a government can work."[5]

Nano signalled Gujarat's arrival as a big auto landmark. "The Tata Motors plant at Sanand is a reminder of the incredible speed at which the Nano project made its journey from Singur. It is here that Gujarat signalled that it could be a viable automotive destination. The government pulled out all stops so operations could kick off in less than 18 months from the time the Tatas dropped Singur. There is no doubt that it is the Nano project that spurred others to take a serious look at the state."[6]

Sanand has now transformed into a hub for other auto giants as well. Tamil Nadu had faced a lot of embarrassment when PSA Peugeot Citroen announced in September 2011 that it would set up its car manufacturing unit in Gujarat. The government of Tamil Nadu had announced in June that the car maker was setting up the unit in the state. Peugeot later backed out from Gujarat as well due to economic slowdown in Europe.

Not that Sanand could replace Chennai, a city that accounts for 40 per cent of the country's car production and about 60 per cent of the automobile exports. But Sanand, backed by excellent infrastructure and many other advantages, was going to give it a tough fight. The large area developed by GIDC gives enough room for ancillary industries to come up and reap rich dividends.

Ford India decided to invest Rs 4,000 crore in Sanand for their second unit in July 2011. Its entry in Chennai in the 1990s had heralded an auto era. A second unit in Gujarat must have forced people to take notice. An analyst marked this development:

"Gujarat does not have a strong auto component base (back in 2011). Its pool of skilled manpower is still suspect. But what it has is adequate and quality power and good governance... Tamil Nadu has in the past lost car makers such as Volkswagen to other states. That did not hurt much. But when a car maker who, till recently was your poster boy, decides to expand in another state, alarm bells should start ringing. It is a wake-up call indeed."[7]

Kel Kearns, Ford's Director of Manufacturing for the Sanand plant, gave his own justification for selecting Sanand: "We wanted to buy government land to start with. This was the first sort of call we made about the sites that were available." The choice was because of more crucial factors such as the cost of labour, good industrial relations, adequate power, road connectivity, and overall governmental support.[8]

Maruti Suzuki India Limited decided to set up its Rs 4,000 crore manufacturing unit 100 km north of Ahmedabad. This is the seventh unit of Maruti and the first outside Haryana. The plant is to be commissioned in 2015-16. A buoyant Modi said that the auto companies choosing Gujarat for their facilities will change the identity of the state. His government was quick to allot hassle-free land to Maruti. Its initial capacity is 250,000 units per year.[9]

In 2013, Maruti bought additional 500 acres land, 18 km away from its present site to set up a purely manufacturing unit. This would take Maruti's total manufacturing capacity to two million by 2015-16.

The auto industry is not the only one to thrive. The story of the auto industry's prosperity helps understand the positive mood of investors about Gujarat. A bureaucracy sensitive to business, adequate infrastructure in terms of power, water and transport and an ambience for growth are attracting all kinds of industries from small to medium to large. The state holds promise of a handsome return on investment.

Gone are the days when businessmen used to open industries in areas that had natural resources. Natural resource is only one of the key factors today. Security and protection offered by the state, a less garrulous society and other basic infrastructure are more important. Nearness to a port and easy import policy has more than offset this distance from natural resources.

The incident involving Tata employees in Singur highlighted the significance of a good law and order situation for industrial development. When the Tatas were still trying to find a solution to the stalemate in Singur, two of its security personnel at the plant's paint shop were beaten up by unidentified armed men with iron rods.[10] Days after that, the Tatas announced their decision to leave Bengal for Gujarat.

One reason that most industries move out from a state or hesitate to set up industries at a particular place is adverse law and order situation. The investor, who is coming to put in his hard earned money, also wants security of his life and property. And, he also wants to be seen as contributing to the society's growth. After all, his investment is creating job opportunities and creating wealth.

The traditional approach has been to treat a businessman with contempt. Babus rejoice in making a businessman wait for hours for a scheduled meeting and then treat them casually. And they revel in doling out favours in exchange for some considerations. The business situation has changed the world over. Honest businessmen want to do business with honour and are looking for opportunities to grow. So, if you treat them with contempt, they are ready to walk away and take their business elsewhere.

Name any international brand and it is most likely to have its unit or headquarters in Gujarat. Bombardier Transportation, one of the largest companies in the world for rail equipment manufacturing and servicing, is situated in Savli (Vadodara). The coaches manufactured for Delhi metro came from its plant at Savli that became operational in 2009.

Himalaya International Limited has set-up a mega processing facility in Vadnagar (Mehsana) for natural mushrooms, frozen appetisers and dairy products. It is the single largest frozen food facility in India.

Modi has unleashed this huge entrepreneurial energy. If he finds any merit in a proposal, he encourages the person to implement it. And the chief minister is accessible. What more can one ask for? In extending support to the project, he does not discriminate between a Gujarati and a non-Gujarati.

The classic case is that of Nirmal Kumar, founder of G-Auto. Nirmal Kumar, an IIM Ahmedabad graduate of 2008, approached Bihar Chief Minister Nitish Kumar with his idea of organising auto rickshaw drivers. Nitish had given an encouraging response during his visit to IIM but did not meet Nirmal in Patna. He then met the chief secretary of Bihar but was aghast at the cold response. "Everyone seemed to be creating hurdles rather than facilitating the project," he said. His first choice was Bihar since he comes from the state's Sivan district.

It is then that Nirmal thought of contacting Narendra Modi. He wrote a mail to the chief minister detailing the plan and was given an appointment for 15 minutes. Modi found a lot of worth in the proposal and the meeting continued for two hours. After a few days, Modi appointed an IAS officer to ensure that the scheme did not suffer due to lack of adequate response or a follow-up.

"The access was easy, and Modi was keen too. I requested his presence at the inauguration and he obliged. He allotted funds and designated a senior bureaucrat to ensure we got the money and other government help in the quickest possible time," he said. Even after the inauguration, Modi deputed an officer to ensure that Nirmal did not face any setback due to lack of governmental support.

His trust, Nirmal Foundation, runs the campaign. The trust pays for his salary as well as the salary of 21 more people employed to keep G-Auto running. This is a major success story in Gujarat. Now most of the money comes from advertisements carried on the autos. Any auto driver violating the norm loses the membership of G-Auto and if cops harass them, G-Auto management comes to the rescue. About 10,000 auto-rickshaws are members of G-Auto.[11]

The University of Michigan gave it the SMART Mobility Award. The Union Urban Development ministry wrote to all states to emulate the model. Nirmal wants to expand his G-Auto to other states as well.

It is significant that Gujarat's manufacturing sector contributes 13 per cent of the output of manufacturing sector at an all India level. The state is the largest producer of processed diamonds and denim in the world and accounts for a significant proportion of the production of soda ash, salt, petrochemicals, plastics, pharmaceuticals, crude oil and chemical production of the country.

The GSDP grew at 8.5 per cent in 2011-12 at a constant price of 2004-05 but at the current price the growth was 15.3 per cent. The share of secondary sector to the GSDP was 36.1 per cent.

Total number of factories in the state increased from 15,576 in 2009-10 to 21,282 in 2010-11 indicating rapid industrialisation. Production value from factories increased from Rs 643,000 crore in 2009-10 to Rs 807,000 crore in 2010-11 at current prices. This was an increase of more than 25 per cent.

This led to an increase in employment opportunities. Total employment in the factories sector increased from 11.59 lakh in 2009-10 to 12.90 lakh in 2010-11, an increase of 1.3 lakh jobs. The state has the lowest rate of unemployment in the country.

The national manufacturing policy 2011 aims to increase the share of manufacturing in the GDP from 18 per cent to 25 per cent by 2025. In Gujarat, manufacturing sector already contributes to 27.6 per cent of GSDP. The State government plans to take this to 32 per cent by

2017. The identified areas to achieve this target are textiles, food and agro industries, auto ancillaries, solar and wind equipments etc.[12]

Gujarat's textile policy of 2012 sought to enhance the growth of cotton produce through better price realisation, strengthening of the value chain and facilitation of the State to become a leader in manufacturing of yarn, fabric and garments. The focus was five F's—Farm, Fibre, Fabric, Fashion (Garment) and Foreign (Export). It envisages creation of spinning capacity of 25 lakh spindles in next five years which means more fibre. This explains that cotton production driven agricultural growth is going to stay.

Gujarat has 10.05 per cent share in the total number of industries in the country. Its share in providing employment is 10.14 per cent whereas the share in output is pegged at 17.22 per cent. The net value added is 12.55 per cent.

Industrial activity has expanded geographically as well. Earlier, it was limited to Ahmedabad, Baroda, Surat and Rajkot and also in isolated locations of Mithapur and Valsad. Now, almost all districts have witnessed industrialisation. While the Gujarat Industrial Development Corporation (GIDC) established industrial estates, provided developed plots and built-up sheds for setting up industries, new institutions were set up to provide term finance and assistance for purchase of raw materials, plant and equipment, and marketing of products.

To expedite setting up of industry, the government has effectively implemented the single window system. It has become such an effective tool of governance that the administration is experimenting with it in other areas as well, such as in giving clearance for shooting of Bollywood films. The chief minister has announced a single window clearance policy for setting up of studios.[13]

District Industries Centre (DIC) has been set up in each district to act as single window for all requirements of small and village industries. The functioning of DICs is monitored by the industries commissioner.

The biggest single window is the CM office. For any project worth more than Rs 100 core, an industrialist can directly approach the chief minister. Principal secretary (Industry) has been assigned the responsibility of providing hassle-free clearance if a proposal is worth Rs 50-100 crore.

Hiteshbhai Sanghvi, who runs a hotel business in Ahmedabad, narrated an incident of Balaji Wafers who planned to set up another unit in Telegaon in Pune (Maharashtra). They already had a unit in Rajkot. Hitesh suggested that he should set up the new unit in Valsad rather than risking an uncertain future in Maharashtra. But Balaji Wafers faced problems when they tried to get land conversion done. They represented the case to Modi. He called for the files in his office and permission was given the next day. "There is no political corruption in Gujarat," Hitesh stressed.[14]

Hiteshbhai was upbeat about hotel business in Gujarat. Earlier, there were no international names in the state. Bigger brands such as Marriott and Radisson have come into the city indicating the vibrancy.

The instrument which has facilitated rapid industrialisation is Special Economic Zone. Modi wanted to have islands of growth on the pattern of China. Industries set up in these areas would use the best infrastructure and hence become globally competitive. Nearness or symbiotic linkages to ports made these SEZs more attractive to investors.

A giant leap was taken when the Government of India notified the Gujarat Special Economic Zone Act 2004. Gujarat became the first Indian state to make this law.[15] The purpose stated in the act was: "To achieve rapid economic growth and to attract investment and to ensure systematic and integrated development of industry".

Any person could now apply for a SEZ to the state government, which—after studying various issues such as environmental clearance and feasibility of the proposal—can send the same to the central government for approval. The authority set up under the act would provide necessary infrastructural facilities and create a single window clearance for licenses and all no-objections. The state gives various concessions such as exemption from payment of taxes, duties, fees and other facilities to make investment attractive. Various tax concessions from the central government are also available.

The state has identified 57 SEZs covering an area of 36869.29 hectares approximately. Out of these, 15 are in Ahmedabad, 16 in Kutch, 8 in Bharuch and 6 in Gandhinagar, 3 in Vadodra, 3 in Surat and 2 each in Amreli and Valsad, and 1 each in Jamnagar and Mehsana.

These SEZs are involved in several sectors such as IT, engineering, textiles and apparels, chemical, pharmaceuticals, port based, etc.

The SEZs also intended to do away with the 'inspector raj' of the state to make operations hassle-free and allowed easier labour norms.

One of the most successful sectors in Gujarat is the pharmaceutical industry. Gujarat accounts for more than 40 per cent of medicines manufactured in India. It is home to global pharmaceutical giants such as the Sun Pharma and hosts major players including India's second oldest drug-maker such as Alembic, Cadila Healthcare Ltd (Zydus Cadila), Intas and Torrent Pharmaceuticals.

India's first pharmacy college, LM Pharmacy College, was established in the state in 1947. Now, the state has as many as 90 pharmacy colleges.

India's domestic pharmaceutical market size was about Rs 60,000 crore in 2012, with a growing rate of 15 per cent. The country exports medicines worth about Rs 42,000 crore; of this, Gujarat has a share of medicines worth Rs 17,000 crore. India's pharmaceutical market size is over Rs 1 lakh crore per annum.[16]

The state has also emerged a leader in patent applications in India. Various SMEs, research organisations and academic institutions have filed nearly 1,000 patents over the last five years. Gujarat also accounts for 40 per cent of India's contract research and manufacturing (CRAM) companies and pharma machinery production, and 28 per cent of India's exports in this sector.

Biotechnology has emerged as a major developing sector. The landscape of Gujarat's biotech industry features more than 50 biotechnology companies (14 per cent of India's) and 66 support organisations The thrust areas of the biotech industry in the state include healthcare, pharmaceuticals, agriculture biotechnology and industrial enzymes.

One of the major growth areas in coming years is likely to be the Delhi-Mumbai Industrial Corridor (DMIC). It is a mega road corridor infrastructure project of the central government to be implemented in collaboration with the Japanese government. This world class corridor will be 1483 km long and pass through six states—Delhi, Haryana, Uttar Pradesh, Rajasthan, Gujarat and Maharashtra. Gujarat has 38 per cent of the total length of the corridor and Rajasthan has 39. Haryana and Maharashtra will have 10 per cent each whereas Delhi NCR and Uttar Pradesh 1.5 per cent each.

The corridor, that would run parallel to the national highway, is expected to have a spiralling economic effect in the states it would cross through. At present, most states are involved in the process of land acquisition. The cost of the project is estimated between USD 90-100 billion. The states would also contribute in constructing this corridor. The central government has already allotted USD 3.24 billion (Rs 17,500 crore). The corridor's planned vision for Gujarat falls in the Ahmedabad-Dholera investment region.

To make the best utilisation of opportunity given by the DMIC corridor, Gujarat has decided to set up six mega industrial nodes—four industrial areas and two investment regions. It came up with the proposal to set up Special Investment Regions (SIRs) and promulgated an ordinance by the name Gujarat Special Investment Regional Ordinance 2009.

The SIR Act empowered the state government to declare Investment Regions (IRs) or Industrial Areas and to designate them as SIR. While an investment region will be developed in an area of more than 100 sq km, an industrial area will be developed in an area of more than 50 sq km.

This provided for single window clearance for projects set up in the region. The Gujarat Infrastructure Development Board (GIDB) was declared the apex authority for establishing economic activities, infrastructure or amenities in the SIRs. The aim was to set up world-class economic hubs on the pattern of fast growing economies.

Gujarat had its share of controversies that came in the way of its industrial growth. In order to undermine the overall growth story, people try to project the government as a complete sell out to the corporate sector and more particularly for favouring certain industrial houses.

This is far from the truth. If we want smaller ancillary industries to compete with big brands of MNCs, we have to encourage big industrial houses to build such a brand. If Nano is a big brand that can take on anyone in the world, it is supported by many ancillary auto units that work in tandem. Big industries in the state have not come at the cost of the smaller ones. Maximum investment proposals in terms of units have come for small scale industries.

And if the state does not have the resources to invest, it will have to take the help of big private companies. The growth story of Gujarat must be understood in this context. Modi has been championing small industrial houses to become brand conscious and packaging conscious. They must make brands such as 'made in Gujarat' or 'made in India' on the pattern of 'made in China'.[17]

The main opposition, the Congress, had come up with 15 charges against the Modi government saying that it had favoured certain business houses by giving land at throwaway prices and in awarding contracts. Congress leaders had taken a representation to the President of India in June 2010 listing the charges.

These included allegations that land was given to industries near Gandhinagar at very low prices; Rs 33,000 crore concessions to Tata's Nano project, land allotment to Adani Industries at Mundra port, illegal allotment of coastal regulation zone and forest land to Essar group, prime land given to L & T company at throwaway prices at Hazira-Surat, etc.[18]

Since the charges were serious, the state government set up a judicial commission in August 2011 to probe them. Retired Supreme Court Judge, Justice MB Shah was asked to head the commission. This was set up under the Commission of Inquiry Act, 1952. The commission was also asked to look into whether any previous governments of Gujarat after 1980 also gave any special relaxations to industrial houses in the above mentioned criteria.

Such judicial commissions are normally not set up by a state government to probe charges against itself. It is only when one has nothing to hide that you present yourself to such scrutiny. A PIL challenging the validity of the appointment of the commission was dismissed by the Gujarat High Court.

The Shah Commission in its interim report in September 2012 gave a clean chit to Modi Government of any wrong doing. All the decisions were in accordance with the prescribed policies of the present and past state governments and the central government, the report said.

***

Showcasing Gujarat to Investors

A state government cannot woo investors with mere slogans or promises. We are a policy-driven government. We put things in black and white, with a minimum of grey areas.

— Narendra Modi

Gujarat was a revenue deficit state till 2007. When Modi came to power, the problems were first to tide over the financial crisis and then to arrange investment for the state's development needs. This way the state could take care of other needs such as poverty alleviation, malnutrition, etc.

With the government adopting the role of a facilitator, investors could be attracted. Gujarati Non-Resident Indians, better known as NRGs, were the first to be approached. They could be tapped since they had the financial muscle and were still linked to their roots. There are an estimated six million Gujaratis settled abroad in different parts of the world. "We want this vast Diaspora to get involved in Gujarat's development," Narendra Modi said while talking about his vision of Vibrant Gujarat summit.

Investment would not come easily unless potential investors were persuaded to believe that the situation had changed for the better and the state promised good returns on their investment. This meant showcasing Gujarat with a completely new instrument. The state had established an investment promotion agency in the form of Industrial Extension Bureau (iNDEXTb) for hassle free experience to prospective investors. It has been playing a pioneer role in organising Vibrant Gujarat summit since 2003.

Investors abroad wanted a guarantee and security of returns. The government used lack of proper infrastructure such as rough roads and stagnating cities as oppurtunities to attract investment. The state's big market with its huge cosmopolitan middle class population offered an extra attraction.[1]

Industries minister Anil Patel, who had taken a delegation to the United States and Canada, was clear that the first target was Gujarati NRIs. "Non-resident Indians control nearly $500 billion worth of business abroad. Of this, 40 per cent is controlled by Gujarati NRIs. It would be a great achievement even if we are able to tap just 10 per cent of them."[2]

The chief minister played a dynamic role in promoting Gujarat among the community leaders settled outside India. Those who say that Gujarat was already developed—and attribute the present development to the famed Gujarati entrepreneurship—need to appreciate the fact that the chief minister faced an uphill task in courting investors. The image of Gujarat had taken a beating after 2002 riots. Wherever he went, Modi was faced with a barrage of embarrassing questions. Any person in that situation would have thrown his hands up in despair and given up.

But not Modi! He was not scared. This came from single-minded determination that he had done no wrong and that he needed to catch the nation's attention through development. He knew that he would face difficult times and hostile public opinion. In that way, he got an opportunity to explain his stand as well as and prevent the world community from ganging up against him. His experience from the anti-Emergency days had taught him that international opinion could not be brushed aside. He even deputed his ministers to do the same.

Among the countries he visited included the US and the UK (before his Visa denial in 2005), Australia, China, Singapore, Israel, Japan, Uganda, Kenya, Astrakhan and Russia. He also visited Hong Kong. While the main purpose was to showcase Gujarat and invite businessmen to invest in Gujarat, his visits also tried to convince the world community that Gujarat was not what it was painted out to be after the riots. It was one of the safest investment destinations in the world, secular and peaceful.

And to buttress his claims, he took a retinue of officials and eminent businessmen on these trips. They talked about their experiences in Gujarat and they also got a chance to explore trade opportunities with the countries they visited.

When he visited London, there were protests with placards heaping abuses on him. Yet, he was undaunted and, with single-minded focus, he attracted investment. During his address at the Wembley convention, he said: "You are all the real friends of Gujarat and I have come to reciprocate that loyalty... We have slept in the street of death and today I have come to repay a debt of friendship to those who helped us in our hour of need." He described Gujarat as India's most progressive and dynamic state and predicted annual growth of 10.2 per cent. He said this would be the wonder of the world that was witnessing slow growth.[3]

There was thunderous applause and shouting of "*Chhote Sardar*" when he said that IT was not Information Technology but 'India Today'. BT is not bio-technology but 'Bharat Today'. He also said "IT and IT equals IT. That means Information Technology and Indian Talent is India Tomorrow."[4] The visit helped boost the confidence of Gujarati investors.

Scouting for investors took him to Switzerland. Here, he made the visit memorable by bringing back the ashes of Shyamji Krishna Varma, a freedom fighter from Gujarat. He got a memorial erected for the great revolutionary and dedicated the same to the country in 2010. Varma had died in 1930 and had wished that his mortal remains be taken to his motherland when it would achieve independence.

During his private talks with close aides or while speaking at public forums, he was clear that he was not competing against any Indian state. His competition was with China. "I want Gujarat to compete with China," he asserted in an interview before his visit to China in 2006. During interaction with a select group of people in Ahmedabad before his departure, he said, "Gujarat is not competing with other states like Maharashtra, Karnataka, and Andhra Pradesh. We may surpass them. I want Gujarat to compete with China, Germany and Japan."[5]

He was accompanied by a high-level delegation of 35 Gujarat-based industrialists and top state bureaucrats. His agenda was to study the functioning of the SEZs in China and, if possible, invite them to help Gujarat build China-style SEZs. He also wanted to attract Chinese investment in Gujarat in the power sector. Among the top industrialists who accompanied him were Essar Group Chairman Shashi Ruia, Torrent Pharma Chairman Sudhir Mehta, Adani Group Chairman

Gautam Adani, and Nirma Chairman Karsanbhai Patel.

Modi was acutely aware of the importance of China for Gujarat cotton. The country imported about 75 per cent of cotton produced in Gujarat. He wanted Chinese help for value addition to the cotton chain.

Every country Modi visited, he tried to learn new things and figure out if the same could be implemented in Gujarat. If he was impressed with zero tolerance against corruption in the country of Lee Kuan Yew (Singapore), he was also impressed by the tall buildings that housed business offices. The plan to have tall towers in Gandhinagar was drawn up after his visit to Hongkong in 2004.[6] He wanted to create an international financial hub on the same pattern, said the managing director of Gujarat International Finance Tech (GIFT) City, Ramakant Jha.[7]

Modi visited the Three Gorges Dam to understand how this worked for China. This is the world's largest Dam at 181 metres on Yangtze River and produces 20,000 MW of electricity through 32 units of 700 MW each. Three Gorges Dam President Gwang Giang explained to Modi that the construction of the dam took 10 years and involved resettlement of 13 lakh people. The dam provides inland waterways for ships of 10,000 tonnes and the site has become a tourist attraction with about 4 lakh people visiting annually.[8]

He tried to translate this while developing the Narmada canal system. The site of Sardar Sarovar Dam today is a great tourist attraction.

Modi's visit to the East African countries of Uganda and Kenya were of no less significance. A number of Gujaratis reside there, some of whom are among the richest people in the world. Modi visited the famous Maasai Mara Wildlife Sanctuary in Kenya. While he interacted with nature, he also tried to learn and observe things that could be implemented in Gujarat's Gir forests. He was a man completely focussed on development of Gujarat, said Subha Ranjan Tampi who had accompanied Modi on behalf of the Confederation of Indian Industries.[9] She also said that she was deeply impressed by the respect with which he interacted with members of the delegation.

Modi knew that he could not win investors by phoney rhetoric. "A state government cannot woo investors with mere slogans or promises," he said while interacting with media persons in Chennai after the Vibrant Gujarat summit of 2007. "We are a policy-driven government.

We put things in black and white, with a minimum of grey areas."[10]

The Vibrant Gujarat summit of 2013 was the best ever since inception and surpassed all parameters of success. The exhibition, that goes along with the summit on a regular basis, was spread over 1,04,000 sq m and gave opportunity to 1,195 exhibitors to display their achievements. About 1.6 million people visited the six-day fair. About 200 leaders of business, politics and diplomats shared the dais.

It had an awe-inspiring international dimension. About 2,100 delegates from 121 countries participated in the summit. As many as 58,000 domestic delegates also participated. It attracted 17,719 business proposals with investment worth Rs 40 lakh crore.

Shashi Ruia of the Essar Group announced an investment of Rs 15,000 crore and held that Modi had proved that 'good economics and good politics can stay together'. He said that under the leadership of Narendra Modi, Gujarat remains the torch bearer of the country's economic growth. He described Modi as a man with a mission and conviction.[11]

Tata chairman emeritus Ratan Tata was the last to speak at the inaugural. He said: "Today when an investor looks for location to make an investment, they of course look for industry friendly and investment friendly, but they also look forward to locations that in fact execute promises, where infrastructure is adequate and good, and where labour environment is friendly and conducive to productivity."[12]

While talking about his famous quote where he had said, one was stupid if not in Gujarat, he said:

"The first time I came to this function, I believe I said that one would be considered stupid if not investing in Gujarat. The second time I came, it became clear that I was amongst the stupid because, barring large investments in Tata Chemicals many years ago, we had no new investments in Gujarat. That time I had vowed that we would make a difference. Today, the Tata Group has invested or committed to invest Rs 34,000 crore in the state of Gujarat."[13]

The biggest challenge was holding the first summit in 2003 which was actually testing the waters. Since it was in the process of evolution, it became an integrated platform for cultural exchanges, trade, commerce and enterprise. Modi stressed that he would continue to focus on his slogan "Develop Gujarat to Develop India".[14]

The event was a success since 76 MOUs worth Rs 66,068 crore were signed. Power projects had the major share with Rs 14,270 crore followed by chemical and petroleum sector at Rs 12,720 crore. There was an additional investment commitment of Rs 6450 in power through wind energy.[15]

The summit was inaugurated by the Deputy Prime Minister LK Advani. Among others who attended were Union Ministers Arun Shourie and Ram Naik, Mukesh Ambani of Reliance Industries, ex-US senator Larry Pressler, Michael Clarke from British Gas and about 700 business delegates, including 125 from 45 foreign countries.

The summit in 2005 was larger and drew on the experiences of the previous one. More than 6000 people from across the world attended the inaugural function. The summit was designed to coincide with the Kite festival, *uttarayan* (movement of the Sun into the northern hemisphere) that marks the change of season.

The state had sent delegations to foreign countries to tell industrialists about the investment climate in the state and persuade them to come and participate in the development of Gujarat. Modi strongly defended showcasing Gujarat abroad, saying that two funds— the NRI/NRG fund and the NRG Charity Fund—were made known to thousands of Gujaratis staying outside. He felt that only if they would know the mechanism, they would be able to participate in the development process or help in times of need such as in a natural calamity.

He recalled his own experiences and those of his officials where NRGs walked up to them and told them that they had never met any government official from Gujarat before. To invite participation from across the world, five delegations led by senior ministers from Gujarat visited different parts of the world to hold discussions with NRIs, NRGs and other foreign investors.

Vice President of India Bhairon Singh Shekhwat inaugurated the summit. Mukesh Ambani of Reliance, Gautam Adani of the Adani Group, Shashi Ruia of Essar and Nigel Shaw of British Gas participated along with other prominent names.

Close to 200 exhibitors participated. There was a quantum jump in the number of MOUs signed. Compared to the previous summit, it was almost three times (226 while only 76 MOUs were signed in the previous summit), with investment worth Rs 1,06,160 crore. The highest Rs 38,003 crore was in power sector followed by Rs 16,451 core in engineering and automobile, Rs 15,585 in port and Rs 13,137 in oil and gas.

'Sow a Rupee and reap a Dollar' was the message of the summit of 2007. It was buttressed with another slogan, 'In Gujarat, there is only Red Carpet and no Red Tape'.

Detailed investment opportunities in 12 priority sectors were prepared by the government. The four-day event in January also had a multimedia presentation on strengths and weaknesses of various industries by the name "Gujarat Discovered". The International Kite festival at the Sabarmati Riverfront Development site was opened. There was also a Global Investors' summit at Science City, Ahmedabad. Other events such as urban summit and IT summit were also held alongside.

This marked the emergence of Gujarat as a global investment destination and the role played by the state as a driver of the Indian economy. Around 200 representatives from abroad participated in the sector seminars and around 20 world renowned industry experts delivered their lectures. Delegates came from the United States of America, China, Japan, Singapore, Australia, South Korea, Italy and Israel.

The summit reached a new peak with investment worth Rs 4,65,310 crore. The number of MOUs went up to 343 for 454 projects. Of these, the highest Rs 1,70,889 crore was signed for investment in SEZs, followed by Rs 1,33,429 crore in power and Rs 46,370 crore in oil and gas.

The rush of MOUs had surprised even the state government as it had to shut the doors on many proposals. Modi was exuberant. He said: "It is an expression of faith of India's business community in Gujarat's growth potential and the systems it has developed. Those who are late in coming to the state will not only miss a bus but a luxury bus."[16]

It is at this summit that Ratan Tata issued his famous statement "One is stupid if one is not in Gujarat today." All industry leaders heaped praise on Modi for leading the state so effectively. Mukesh Ambani announced investment worth Rs 67,000 crore and said, "Modi has shown amazing clarity of purpose and determination. He has given Gujarat a newfound confidence." Anil Ambani's words summed up everyone's sentiments: "Gujarat's is a great story and all great stories need a good actor. Gujarat's story has largely revolved around Narendra Modi's dynamic leadership."

Modi was back in the saddle and investors' confidence was upbeat. The overall theme of the summit of 2009 was 'Gujarat Going Global'. It brought business leaders, investors, corporations, thought leaders, policy and opinion makers from across the globe on the same platform. The spectrum was very wide.

Japan was a partner country; the first time ever that a foreign country became a partner of a province or a state of another country. The world seems to have realised that if one wanted to do business with an Indian state, one had to get in direct contact with that state. Over 600 foreign delegates from 45 countries participated in the summit.

The exhibition was organised on a space of about 19,200 square metres, catering to 232 stalls from various companies including those from 16 countries. This summit showed a quantum jump and 3346 MOUs for 3574 projects were signed worth Rs 12,34,898 crore. This included Rs 2,11,895 crore in power, close to Rs 1,01,443 crore in urban development, Rs 100,000 crore in Special Investment Regions (SIRs) and Rs 85,720 crore in port. Hallmark of the summit was also Rs 9540 crore in MSME projects.

Former Deputy Prime Minister of India LK Advani quoted a newspaper report to justify his endorsement of Vibrant Gujarat efforts: "This is how *The Hindu* newspaper reported it: 'The Chief Minister's announcement was greeted with resounding noise of clapping with even foreign delegations and prominent industrialists from the country and abroad giving Mr Narendra Modi a standing ovation for the achievement by a state in attracting industrial investments at a time when the global economy was facing recession.'"

The activities as a result of investment promised in the 2009 summit were expected to generate 25 lakh jobs, mostly benefitting the skilled manpower. This came amidst a bad economic situation: "My heart is swelling with glory that despite the recessionary trends and pessimistic economic climate, Gujarat has replaced crisis, meltdown, recession and slowdowns with confidence, opportunity, vibrancy and stability. The message of confidence and hope has gone in to the world from the summit. The Investors' Summit is established as the World Economic Conference of Davos. Gujarat is playing a decisive role in making India an economic Super Power."[17]

The Summit of 2011 sought to convert the meet into a Global Business Hub. Will the momentum continue to rise or will the institution start losing its shine? There were hopes and fears. Hopes that the summit would scale new heights were interspersed with fears that it may lose its shine.

Due to the new focus, the summit events witnessed participation from many countries, Indian states and companies. More than 13 country and state seminars were organised with enthusiastic participation from investors. Over 350 speakers had participated in more than 30 seminars.

Even from the investment point of view, this summit successfully broke all previous record. MOUs worth Rs 20,83,182 crore were signed through 8380 MOUs. Around 100 tie-ups with leading institutions from across the globe for knowledge exchanges were forged. There was participation of 1400 delegates from 101 foreign countries. More than 35,000 participants were Indians.

Power topped the investment chart with commitment of Rs 3,73,310.03 crore, followed by Rs 2,54,467.47 crore in urban development, Rs 1,83,000 in financial services and Rs 1,36,841.74 crore in SIRs and Rs 1,02,889.28 crore in ports or port based activities. Significantly, MSME investments were to the tune of Rs 19,036.85 crore. According to government estimate articulated by the chief minister, the investment pledge was expected to provide employment to 52 lakh people.[18]

A very big task now is to convert the summit of 2015 into a 'Vibrant Gujarat Global Trade Show'. The registration dates have been opened and the event dates and venue have already been announced in advance. The focus is to perform better than 2013.

What began as a platform to attract investment is now maturing into a platform for global and national players to share information and look out for ways to improve performance. The state is ending up doing what the central government should do and on a much bigger scale. But for the centre to do this, at least some states must be ready with a system that is in place in Gujarat. Unless one can match the speed and efficiency of Gujarat, one cannot challenge the concept.

Gujarat will continue to attract investment because of the vast opportunities opened up by the DMIC. The Special Investment Regions along the DMIC have already started attracting huge investment. Because of its pro-active policy, Gujarat is better prepared than other states to take the benefits from DMIC.

The state government is trying to bring in other states as well so that they too can get some investors here. At least Rajasthan will be a big beneficiary if it plans in a similar way for the DMIC. Those who find Gujarat attractive may be willing to invest in Rajasthan as well.

The world is driven by ideas and every business opportunity first starts as an idea. The success of Gujarat is likely to encourage some other chief ministers to think of creating similar situations. It is not just about achieving better figures. It is about achieving better governance since without a responsive administration, business cannot thrive.

With more than 20,000 products on display, this event seeks to have 20 per cent international participation from more than 100 countries. Twenty five commercial sectors will be on display. More than one crore people are expected to visit the exhibition.

***

Urbanisation: Changing Gujarat's Landscape

'Aatma Gaanv Ki, Suvidha Sheher Ki'

We will neglect our cities at our own peril for in
neglecting them we neglect the nation.
—John F. Kennedy

Gujarat is among India's most urbanised states after Delhi. The urban population has increased from 37 per cent in 2001 to 43 per cent in 2011 (As per the 2011 Census). And the state is likely to witness unparalleled urban growth since it has announced that it would spend Rs 75,000 crore on urban development between 2012 and 2017.[1] This remarkable increase of about six per cent is the highest in the country and much ahead of Tamil Nadu (4.41 per cent), Maharashtra (2.80 per cent) and even the national average of 3.35 per cent.

Urban population in the state increased by about 36 per cent whereas rural population increased by less than 10 per cent in 10 years (2001-2011). The increase in urban population was a result mainly of rural to urban migration. Urban infrastructure development is, therefore, a major challenge. The budgetary allocation for urban development increased from Rs 127 crore in 2000 to Rs 5, 600 crore in 2013.[2]

Modi said he wondered why urbanisation was seen as a challenge in our nation. "It's better that we see it as an opportunity. If we do this, then the whole approach will change, and in Gujarat, we have accepted it as an opportunity," he said.[3] Elaborating further, he said, "Rurbanisation is a well-thought initiative. Our quest is *'Aatma Gaanv Ki, Suvidha Sheher Ki'* (to retain the soul of villages but facilities of a city)...Why can't we do this?"

The increase in the state's urban population owes not only to migration from small towns to large cities but also because villages are getting urbanised. The point to ponder for most policy makers is—will the villagers migrate to cities if they get 24x7 electric supply, a good road network, essential health services, communication etc., in their villages. Almost all villages are on broadband connectivity and they can access information through computers. Their markets have come closer due to cluster markets by private players and better road connectivity has made travel easier. Even in rural areas, one can find one family keeping more than one two-wheeler.

Former President of India APJ Abdul Kalam's (Provision of Urban Amenities for Rural Areas) PURA concept got fully implemented in some Gujarat villages which are on way to become model villages. Union Minister Jairam Ramesh criticised Kalam's PURA concept, instead he should have seen how this can be implemented for everyone's benefit.[4] The PURA concept basically intended to check migration to cities. One needs to visit Punsari village in Himmatnagar to understand how it can work—a modern village with 24 hour power and broadband connectivity.

None of the villages or cities in Gujarat have problems of water or power. As per the norms of the central government, every city should get 140 litres per capita water per day, but in Gujarat the government is providing 150 litres.[5] Wastage of water is an issue in top cities.

A phenomenal increase in urban population has been registered in the tribal districts of Valsad, Sabarkantha, Banaskantha and Kutch. This proves that urbanisation in Gujarat is significantly and equitably spread out. It also indicates that the momentum of urban growth in Gujarat is fuelled by the tier-2 and 3 level towns rather than the established cities such as Ahmedabad. Ahmedabad has already got the distinction of being the best Indian city. Forbes has ranked it as the third fastest growing city in the world after Chengdu and Chongqing.[6]

Urban policy initiatives of the State government have put the thrust on developing rurban areas (semi-urban areas in vicinities of cities), and this strategy has become quite successful. While urbanisation level varies from 8.99 per cent in Dahod to 84.05 per cent in Ahmedabad, there are at least 12 districts that have witnessed higher percentage of urban population than the national average of 31.16. Some of the more urbanised cities are Surat (79.68 per cent), Rajkot (58.12 per cent), Vadodara (49.54 per cent), and Porbandar (48.77 per cent).

The concept of twin-city growth has really caught up such as

Ahmedabad-Gandhinagar and Surat-Navsari. Surendra Nagar-Wadhawan, Vadodara-Halol, Bharuch-Ankleshwar, and Morbi-Wankaner are also being developed as twin cities. This is leading to a cascading effect in all surrounding areas leading to 'rurbanisation' where even rural areas get an urban look.[7]

Waste management is one of the biggest problems facing urbanisation. If the cities do not have the mechanism to dispose of the garbage, they will collapse. Rural areas may refuse to take the garbage and this can create a situation of conflict. Already there is a feeling in rural people that cities are more pampered while their villages are being treated as junkyards.

Gujarat is trying to tackle the problem by generating energy from waste in 50 cities. Pilot projects in all these cities have been planned under which solid waste management plants are to be set up to generate power, fertiliser and reusable water. All these would be provided to rural areas for use in agriculture. The plants are to be erected under People-Public-Private Partnership (PPPP) using cutting-edge technology from Japan.

"This is a part of a two-way strategy in which both urban as well as rural areas gain," Modi told the Vibrant Gujarat's national summit on Inclusive Urban Development. This will also check rural to urban migration due to large-scale development of rural areas. This would help to reduce dependence on chemical fertilisers and encourage organic farming.[8]

In Delhi, the government has erected iron grill barricades to prevent people from throwing flowers, etc., in river Yamuna. In Ahmedabad, the government has placed a number of special golden coloured pots on the bridge to prevent people from throwing dry flowers and other leftovers from religious rituals in the river. The government has also created awareness that people should use these containers rather than throw things directly into the water.

The Ahmedabad Municipal Corporation employed 175 workers for cleaning of the Sabarmati riverbed and these people removed about 200 tonnes of solid wastes within a month. Cameras are being installed at these bridges to keep tabs on offenders who throw plastics and other items into the river.[9]

A city's development is also tested by how commuter friendly it is. This is a factor of transport infrastructure. One wonders why did the Bus Rapid Transit System (BRTS) not succeed in Delhi, whereas it has excelled in Ahmedbad? Ever since its introduction in 2009, Ahmedabad BRTS has been winning awards for almost all parameters of urban transport.

Along with CEPT (Centre for Environmental Planning and Technology), the Janmarg Limited (AJL) that runs the BRTS received two awards—the UITP Indian Political Commitment Award, and Design Award. Both the awards were given by the International Association of Public Transport at the 60th UITP World Congress Geneva in 2013.[10] The United Nations awarded BRTS the Momentum for Change Award in 2012. The UITP Germany gave it Sustainable Transport Award and Outstanding Innovation in Public Transportation Award in 2010. A technical team comprising world-renowned experts has given it a silver rating.[11]

Even the Government of India has given so many awards to this urban success: Best Mass Transit Rapid System Project Award in 2009, Best ITS Project Award in 2011, and Best Innovation Project towards improvement in urban mobility through new technological innovations in Janmarg BRTS, 2010.

The BRTS has smart cards, designer stops, AC buses, dedicated fast lanes with barricades and public address systems that announce the coming of the bus stops much in advance, both in English and Gujarati language. The BRTS has provided alternative smart public transport and commuters prefer these over private transport. The once congested city is much better to negotiate. The frequency is good like the metro in Delhi—every two minutes during peak hours and about 10 minutes generally. And each station has security personnel.

After the grand success of BRTS in Ahmedabad, it is now being introduced in cities such as Surat, Rajkot and Vadodara. Rajkot BRTS rolled out in October 2012 with free rides for the first three months. Now the constructed stretch is about 10 km, but when finally constructed, it would be 29-km long.[12]

In Surat, which is the eighth most congested and the fourth largest growing city of India, everything was firmly in place for the BRTS to become functional. Special narrow buses and narrow lanes have been designed for the congested city.[13] Two stretches of BRTS were planned of which one that ran on either side of the canal was ready. People were excited that BRTS would reduce dependence on private transport.

Many flyovers have come up in the city clearing traffic bottlenecks. The roads have been widened and sky rise structures have come up in the diamond city. Even Modi's bitterest critic Vasant Gajera, owner of Laxmi Diamond that runs 'Cygnus' brand of diamonds, could not deny that development had taken place. He is one of the biggest beneficiaries of urban expansion. His multi-storey commercial complex is expected to give him handsome returns.

Modi's development of the Sabarmti River Front is story of vision and determination. One is forced to ask why Delhi or other Indian cities are not able to develop river fronts. The Sabarmati River Front Development Project (SRFDP) has made city life better in Ahmedabad.

During his election campaign for the Delhi assembly elections in 2013, Modi asked the reason behind Delhi's failure in cleaning and developing river Yamuna, despite spending so much money: "I could not study in big institutes like them (elite class), but while they could not clean Yamuna even by spending Rs 3400 crore, our government could fix Sabarmati river with an expenditure of just Rs 900 crore." He invited them to Gujarat to see the development of the Sabarmati river front.[14]

And if you take a walk along the Sabarmati, the stark contrast between the filth of the Yamuna and the beauty of the Sabarmati becomes apparent. You do feel that Delhi has failed to develop river Yamuna into a landmark tourist spot. While Sabarmati has not become as vibrant or as cultural as the river front on river Thames, on which London is located, it has given a boost to the cultural life of Ahmedabad. The river used to look like a drain since all the filth of the city used to get discharged in it. Now, there is a drainage system on both sides to prevent pollutant discharge into the river that is recharged by the waters from Narmada.

The SRFDP bagged a national award for its innovative infrastructure development in April 2011. Only about 14 per cent of the space is sold for commercial establishments, leaving the remaining 86 per cent for public utility. There are walkways, public spaces, roads, community centres, informal market and cultural centres. There is also an urban forest in an area of 25 acres and gardens which are spread over 15 acres. Earlier, the SRFDP bagged the prime minister's award for the best concept and design of a public project.[15]

An old picture in the science journal *Down to Earth* shows children playing with the onions rotting on the embankments, which doubled as a wholesale market for vegetables in the evenings.

Slums are a major challenge to city life. Most urban poor live in slums that increase in numbers as more and more people migrate in search of non-skilled jobs. Gujarat is the only state that saw reduction in the number of slums. This achievement is commendable since reduction has happened despite people moving to the state due to increased economic activities.

The 13 major states of the country—Andhra Pradesh, Karnataka, Kerala, Bihar, UP, MP, Maharashtra, Rajasthan, Punjab, Haryana, J&K, Odisha and Tamil Nadu—witnessed marginal to manyfold increase in the shanties of their urban areas. While there is a 17.50 per cent increase in slums in Bihar, slums have quadrupled in Kerala since 2001.[16]

One of the main highlights of Gujarat's slum rehabilitation policy (of 2010) is the rule that slums that exist on any government land, semi-government or even private land, before or on 1 December 2010, would be rehabilitated at the same spot where they existed—that too in multi-storey blocks.

The policy offered free flats to slum dwellers residing at their existing sites. Private builders were encouraged by giving them increased floor space index (FSI). These private developers were permitted to persuade slum dwellers to agree to construction of apartments on the land they were squatting on, in exchange for a free of cost flat.

"As for example, if a slum has 100 residential units on a land of about 10,000 square feet, the developer could construct 100 flats on the ground plus three storey apartments on half of this land, and buy and develop the remaining area for his own housing project."[17]

The developer is allowed to construct a wall separating the two areas. The land will be bought by the developer as per the prevalent market rate. But the developer would get the go ahead only if 75 per cent of the bona fide slum-dwellers agree to the plan. The construction will be time bound. The ownership rights would be given to slum dwellers after they stayed in the flats for 15 years.

The party's manifesto for the assembly elections had promised about 30 lakh new jobs for the youth and about 50 lakh houses for the poor over the next five years. Modi termed it an all inclusive commitment document that enlisted the vision for the coming years. The Congress had built about 10 lakh houses in the last 40 years whereas the BJP government had built 22 lakh houses in the last 10 years. Now the commitment was to build 22 lakh houses for urban poor and 28 lakh for rural poor at the cost of Rs 33,000 crore, he said.[18]

The resolve to fulfil the commitment was seen in July 2013 when the government cleared various government schemes that fall under the Mukhya Mantri Aawas Samruddhi Yojna (MMASY). The four parts of the schemes were the slum rehabilitation scheme, affordable houses for neo-middle class (income up to one lakh rupees), affordable houses for lower middle income group, and housing schemes on private land where slums have come up. The last scheme would be executed in Public Private Partnership (PPP) mode.[19]

As per the state urban development department 1,13,488 dwelling units have been approved in five cities under the Basic Services for Urban Poor (BSUP) plan as on 30 April 2013. These cities are Ahmedabad, Surat, Vadodara, Rajkot and Porbandar. About 90,000 houses were allotted to slum dwellers of Vadodara alone in two years.[20]

Everyone in the state is now talking of the GIFT city (Gujarat International Finance Tec-City) that is sure to change the skyline of Gandhinagar with 110 high-rise towers of 29 storeys each. Gift 1 building was inaugurated by the chief minister in January 2013. The second building Gift 2 is also ready. Gujarat government and Infrastructure Leasing and Financial Services Limited (IL&FS) are together developing the city on 50:50 partnership basis.

Located on the bank of river Sabarmati and about 12 km from Ahmedabad airport, the project will be accessible by 4-6 lanes from all directions. The government has earmarked Rs 78,000 crore to build this city, designed as a grand new financial city. The city will generate about a million jobs, half of which would be indirect.

This will be a modern commercial city spread over 886 acres of land that would also house hotels, community centres, entertainment centres, schools and other services needed for modern living. There is land earmarked for Special Economic Zone for financial and IT services. In the Centre of the Gift city would be an 87-floor 400 metre high Diamond Tower for commercial activities of diamond merchants. The plan is to take this height to 110 storeys. The city would have 20,000 residential units available only to those who would be working there.

With financial services available in the same GIFT complex, this Diamond hub may make Mumbai less attractive to diamond merchants. However, managing director of GIFT Ramakant Jha said that GIFT city would compete only with Dubai and Antwerp (Belgium)—the two places from where international diamond trading is done. Jha was instrumental in urban town planning of Navi Mumbai and Bandra-Worli sea link. When he retired from there, Gujarat invited him to Gandhinagar with the new responsibility. Jha narrated that Narendra Modi visited Hong Kong financial centre in 2006-07 and was impressed with the high rises and the kind of financial support the centre was giving to the country's economy. He decided to have a similar centre in Gujarat. Sudhir Mankad, the then chief secretary, also accompanied him. He asked Mankad to prepare the concept and do the groundwork. When Mankad retired, he was asked to head the project. He is now the chairman of GIFT project.

Even since then, the chief minister has been taking personal interest in the project. The big problem came during transfer of land. Jha said: "There was a meeting at the chief minister's office on 29 December 2002. Almost everyone in the bureaucracy was against free transfer of land. I argued that to make the position attractive, something needed to be done. It was then that the chief minister took the principled stand that the government was not in the business of selling land. We will have to provide jobs to people and create international competitiveness. And the land was given for development almost free of cost."[21]

Non-Resident Gujaratis (NRGs) are getting attracted to the state like never before. Jay Patel, who is in hotel business in the United States, was in Gandhinagar with his father to explore investment opportunities in the GIFT city. "We are businessmen. We go anywhere we see a business opportunity. Now, we see our state progressing. I think Gujarat is going to be more and more developed and 100 per cent credit goes to Modi since without the right leader there can be no development. Gujarat is competing at international level."[22]

A PIL was filed in the High Court of Gujarat in 2013 based on the CAG report that questioned the allotment. The court rejected the PIL and refused to interfere. The petitioner appealed to the Supreme Court which also rejected the PIL.[23] The Supreme Court held that the decision taken by the government was "transparent" and that "non-floating of tenders or absence of public auction or invitation alone is not sufficient reason to characterise the auction of a public authority as either arbitrary or unreasonable or amounted to mala fide (sic) or improper exercise of power."

Environment consciousness is seen in every action of the government including rapid urbanisation. Gandhinagar is developing fast as India's first solar city in the sense that most of its power needs will soon be met by solar energy. To achieve this, the government has come out with a rooftop solar project under PPP route. It has potential to reduce 6,000 tonnes of CO_2 equivalents. The same model is being replicated in five other cities—Mehsana, Vadodara, Surat, Rajkot and Bhavnagar. Each city will have a capacity of 5 MW. These will be pilot projects.

Private buildings will be identified by developers to participate in the project. Of these, 80 per cent will be government buildings and 20 per cent private houses. These will be connected to the grid of the private developer. The energy generated will be first used to meet the power requirement of these buildings/homes and only additional power generated would be passed on to the grid. This project is slated to get a big boost since surplus power generated would be bought at market rate.

Sun Edison and Azure Power, independent power producers, are each installing 2.5 MW of solar plants on the roofs of houses or office complexes of Gandhinagar that are willing to rent their roof for the purpose. These companies will get Rs 11 per unit from the government but will have to pay Rs 3 to owners of the building. These producers will be responsible for setting up equipment on the rooftops at their own cost. The agreement with owners of the buildings shall be valid for 25 years. Implemented by Gujarat Energy Research Management Institute (GERMI), this rent-a-roof programme is the first-of-its-kind in India.[24]

The success of the experiment is capable of creating a revolution that may be replicated in cities similarly placed. Gujarat has already shown the way. Other states such as Kerala, Andhra Pradeh, Karnataka and Tamil Nadu are also picking up fast.[25] This will probably lead to India's success in finding alternative source of energy through non-conventional means at an affordable price.

***

Raising Green Consciousness

A nation that destroys its soils destroys itself. Forests are the lungs of our land, purifying the air and giving fresh strength to our people.
— **Franklin D Roosevelt**

*A*n *Inconvenient Truth* is an Academy Award winning documentary film that shows former United States' Vice President Al Gore's vigorous campaign to create awareness about global warming and climate change. A book by the same name was also brought out. The inconvenient truth that Al Gore talks about is that the reality of climate crisis is being ignored by most leaders because this would mean they would have to act to correct the situation.

Narendra Modi accepted this as a challenge and documented the steps he had taken after coming to power. His book was interestingly titled *Convenient Action: Gujarat's Response to Challenges of Climate Change* and was published in 2011. Here is one leader who has not only recognised the challenge but has gone a step ahead and shown the ways to tackle the crisis. Coming from the chief minister of one of the most industrialised states of India, the book could be a blueprint for action for most leaders in the developing economies.

Modi's critics have left no stone unturned to belittle his achievements in this sector. They often say that development is being undertaken at the cost of damaging the environment. This is far from the truth. However, they need to learn to be patient as efforts undertaken in the last few years have started bearing fruits. The Tree Census of 2013 indicated that there were 30.14 crore Trees outside Forest (ToF) in Gujarat, witnessing a growth of 19.2 per cent in the last decade (2003-13).

In 2003, there were 25.1 crore trees but Dang was not included in the first census. The second census in 2008 showed that there were

26.87 crore trees (including Dang). This means that even if one forgets the percentage, there has been an increase of 3.27 crore in the last five years over 2008. This is a commendable achievement.

"ToF contributes about Rs 5,000 crore in tangible benefits to the state economy. It stores over 56 million tonnes of carbon in its growing stock, with a decadal growth of about 20 per cent in carbon sequestration (removing carbon from the atmosphere)."[1]

When we talk of environment consciousness, we essentially try to find out if the state and its citizens are aware of the harm they cause to the environment by their day-to-day activities. This can be seen in the practice of throwing garbage into the rivers, allowing industries to discharge waste into the rivers without proper treatment, use of polluting vehicles, depletion of forest covers, felling of trees and many more such activities. Basically, some activities boost production of greenhouse gases leading to global warming, while others pollute water, earth and air, making life inhospitable.

Modi said that he read the *Prithvi Sukta* of *Atharvaveda* during his college days and this helped shape his outlook towards living creatures and nature. "The 63 *suktas* (couplets) composed thousands of years ago, contain a whole spectrum of knowledge which is now being propounded under various scientific, academic, and analytical banners during discussions on global warming, damage to earth's environment and the resultant climate change."[2] The underlying theme is that there is a mother-son relation between man and earth, whereas rain clouds have been likened with father since these bring life-sustaining water.

Modi's vision on climate change is further elaborated when he says that climate change is definitely affecting the future generation which has no voice in the actions of the present generation. He quotes the UN term of "unsustainable ecological debt" which the present generation is incurring for future generations to inherit. "Then let us not be too selfish to exploit nature mindlessly when the very foundations of our civilisation rest on the harmonious co-existence with nature," he says.[3]

Managing climate change is not as easy as it may appear. It cannot be expected that overnight people would stop doing something they have been heedlessly practising over a long period of time. It needs a determined leadership and a committed bureaucracy to create awareness, plan mass action and implement the decisions taken without fear or favour. Gujarat is emerging as a shining example.

Gujarat Pollution Control Board (GPCB) and local authorities constructed five artificial ponds in Bharuch and Ankleshwar for immersion of Lord Ganesha idols after the Hindu festival Ganesh Chaturthi. These ponds are covered with high density poly-ethylene carpets and are filled with Narmada waters. Later, the polluted water would be taken for effluent treatment and discharged into the sea. People are catching up with this idea.[4] Most Gujarat cities have started looking positively at this practice.

Despite the steps being taken by the administration, Gujarat still has a long way to go. Industrial pollution is still one of the biggest obstacles before the state. Taming all of the thousands of industries at small and micro level is very difficult. At some places, due to irresponsibility of certain big industrial houses, environmental degradation is taking place. But the government must be analysed in terms of putting up a system that would tackle such issues and the awareness it is creating among people.

As a result of this consciousness, more and more people are likely to file an RTI with the government and PIL in courts, if there are any major issues of environment degradation. It is highly unlikely that the government that is preaching protection of environment will ignore these.

In 2013, the GPCB ordered closure of six industrial units of Jhaghadia, Panoli and Dahej. It ordered an immediate stop to production and directed disconnection of water and power supply. During checking, three industries were found to be discharging effluents in storm water drains, one was found to be discharging effluents in open trenches and another was found discharging effluents of higher value than prescribed. Another was found manufacturing a product without GPCB consent. The raids followed complaints by villagers.[5]

Another report said that the GPCB issued closure notices to 29 textile dyeing and printing mills in and around Surat for violating air and water pollution norms.[6]

Such news is not uncommon in the state showing that there are many more vigorous steps that need to be taken. But the good news is that the government is acting. It is not easy to bribe the officials and get away with such crimes.

Creating environment consciousness is a long-term strategy to check environment degradation. The Green (Golden Jubilee) Pledge was an innovative way to bring about climate change awareness. Gujarat completed 50 years of its foundation on 1 May 2010. But preparations to make this memorable had begun two years in advance. One of the components of the celebration was to encourage people to take a pledge to make Gujarat a better and prosperous state which meant a healthier, greener, cleaner, modern and inclusive Gujarat. The green pledge was a significant part of this pledge. The chief minister led the show in administering the pledges. All 5.5 crore people of the state (the population then) were asked to take a pledge to do that one little thing from the list of activities to enable the state to march forward.

The golden chariot moved into every village and town, encouraging people to take individual and collective pledges. Students from 9,133 schools and colleges participated in the pledge-taking events. More than one lakh trees were planted during the campaign.

Activities highlighted in the of pledges included: "I will plant and nurture ten trees; I will celebrate my kid's birthday by getting a tree planted; I will use water and electricity judiciously; I will judiciously use water for irrigation; I will use eco-friendly products; I will keep my classroom neat and clean."[7]

TERI (Tata Energy and Resources Institute) Director and international climate change expert Dr RK Pachauri was roped in and an orientation programme on climate change for ministers and bureaucrats was launched in 2008. This was the first time that any state government took up such an exercise. TERI and the state government signed a memorandum of understanding for capacity building of Gujarat and developing climate change adaptation and mitigation strategies.

The government established Management Education Centre on Climate Change at Ahmedabad-based Gujarat University to focus on short-term and long-term courses on climate change. It also looks after research and development and spreading and sharing knowledge through seminars, symposia, etc. Projects aimed at appropriate solutions are particularly encouraged.

One couldn't help but appreciate the grand vision when the chief minister set up a separate Department for Climate Change (DCC) under his own leadership in 2009. The state became the first government in Asia and fourth in the world to have such a department. Also, it became the fourth state/province in the world to have such a department.

The government's stated aim has been "to give a human face to environmental issues; empower people to become active agents of sustainable development; promote an understanding that communities are pivotal to changing attitudes towards environmental issues; and advocate partnership, which will ensure all citizens and people in Gujarat enjoy a safer and more prosperous future."[8]

The Green Priorities of DCC are "to promote Green Tech; earn more carbon credits; power saving; preserve ground water; promote CNG network; increase mangrove cover; fund research in Green Tech and preparation of comprehensive multi-dimensional Climate Change Policy of Gujarat state – Conservation of Land, Water and Air."

The DCC's mandate is to coordinate with all departments of the state on issues of environment, prepare curriculum for educational institutions and to spread public awareness. Achieving coordination with national and international agencies also falls under this department.

A study on the impact of global warming along the 1600-km long coastline of the state is being carried out. Gujarat currently has 29 per cent share of carbon credit of the entire country. A state-wide 'Green Credit Movement' is being contemplated on the lines of carbon credit. Under the Green Credit Movement, if someone cuts trees to set up an industry, he would have to replace them with the same number of full grown trees.[9]

Environmental Clearance for Industries

Although public hearing was made mandatory as a part of giving Environment Clearance in 1997, Environment Impact Assessment (EIA) was merely on paper. Ordinary citizens had no way to stop a polluting factory from coming up in their neighbourhood due to different reasons. The people of Gujarat had to wait till 2002.

There in an interesting anecdote on how an Environment Public Hearing (EPH) got institutionalised for giving environmental clearance.

Arvindbhai Padhiyar of Mujpur village in Padra *taluka* spoke about this incident. The area faced a serious issue of chemical pollution since there were about 300 chemical and dye factories in the *taluka*. The crops got destroyed and it even affected the health of the local population. When nothing worked, he got in touch with Mahesh Pandya in 2002. Pandya was working in *Paryavaran Mitra*—one of the three NGOs that work with the Government of Gujarat on environmental issues.

Pandya used to be a part of a litigating NGO earlier. He would file PILs in court and lose the cases since he had no institutionalised mechanism to embolden the cases. For one, the locals had no comparative data to demonstrate the soil, water and air qualities before and after the setting up of a factory. As a result, the factory owners used to get away with the excuse that they did not pollute the place; it was already polluted![10]

The job of these NGOs is to become an interface between the people or the industrialists who wished to set up a project in the area and the government.

Paryavaran Mitra wrote a letter to Chief Minister Modi after he assumed office. Modi took note of the grim situation and immediately asked the NGO, along with *Janpath* and *Janvikas* to be intermediaries in environment-related talks with the people.[11]

Now, a new project cannot be cleared until all concerns of the locals are addressed satisfactorily by the project proponent in an EPH held in the presence of government representatives. Once the draft EIA report is completed by the project proponent, the state government holds the EPH that enables the local population, immediately affected by the project, to publicly raise their objections and concerns. The businessman who wants to set up the project, in the presence of regulatory bodies, must answer their concerns. It is his job to satisfy the people and take their concurrence. It is only after clearance by the EPH that the government makes its own assessment and recommends measures and issues the environment clearance certificates.[12]

Water

We have already seen how the state's aquifers have got recharged due to the massive water conservation drive undertaken. These have helped in preventing water from becoming saline, checked desertification, improved soil quality, increased availability of drinking water and checked fluorine contamination. All these have had a direct impact on environmental and human health.

Steps taken to minimise the impact of deforestation as a result of the Sardar Sarovar Dam on river Narmada is a study in itself. The catchments' treatment in 27,204 ha in forest and 1,952 ha in non-forest area has been done besides compensatory forestation in 4,650 ha of non-forest area and 9,300 ha in forest area. Efforts at greening also include 550 ha dam vicinity area plantation; 4,120 ha canal side area plantation and 110 ha of mangrove plantation in the area of the dam's downstream. Satellite imageries of 2006 showed increase of 21.6 per cent in dense forest, 4 per cent increase in open forest and reduction of degraded forests by 26.57 per cent when compared to the figures of 1986.[13]

The state government has come out with incentives to promote drip irrigation and other environment friendly usages. It gives heavy subsidy for setting up drip irrigation structure. Modi has been at the forefront to popularise its use. Farmers have attested to getting benefits from drip and sprinkler irrigation.

Urban Issues

Gujarat is an urbanised state with problems facing most urban cities—vehicular pollution, discharge of waste and suspended particulate matter due to industrial activities. A lot of things can be controlled by planting trees, using CNG, putting systems in place to monitor pollution from industries and using effective mass transport system to decrease dependence on private vehicles.

In 2001, Ahmedabad figured among the list of India's sixteen most polluted cities. The Supreme Court intervention led to the formation of a special agency to make the cities better. The GPCB prepared an action plan in 2004 which is being constantly monitored to ascertain the progress. The state government also constituted a Task Force under the chief secretary to coordinate implementation of the action plan.

More than 80 cities in India are monitored in terms of presence of Respirable Suspended Particulate Matter (RSPM). As per the report of

Central Pollution Control Board (CPCB), Ahmedabad improved its position from the fourth most polluted in 2001 to 13th in 2005, 43rd in 2006 and 66th in 2009. The city has shown this remarkable result despite being one of the fastest growing cities in the world.[14]

Introduction of CNG and LPG in private vehicles, introduction of CNG in public transport, BRT corridors and check on industrial pollution in and around the city has made it better than many Indian cities. There are plans to construct new flyovers on the pattern of diamond city Surat to curb the problem of vehicular congestion during peak hours.

The success of a waste management system introduced in 50 cities on pilot basis to generate energy and produce fertilisers is likely to make the cities of Gujarat much better in coming days.

Non-Conventional Energy

The most environment friendly step by the government has been to encourage generation and use of wind and solar energy. The government has come out with a Wind Power Policy to increase the wind energy capacity from 1300 MW to 8000 MW.

While developing full-potential wind energy may take some time, the entire state appears to be excited about the prospects of generating commercial solar energy and popularising the use of this clean energy alternative. Gandhinagar is already being developed as the first solar city of India through the innovative rooftop policy.

Paryavaran Bhavan, the new building of GPCB, has been modelled on the concept of a green building. Modi inaugurated this fully solar-backed building in April 2012. The solar equipments installed generate 80 kW of electricity to run all 40 air conditioners in the complex, 600 fans and 1,000 CFL tube lights together.

Solar panels are spread over the top of the building in an area of over 2,000 square metres to generate this much energy. The GPCB said that it would recover the investment of one crore rupees in the next five years through less power consumption bills.[15] The building has also made provision for rainwater harvesting. Around 750 cubic metric tonne of rainwater per season/year is expected to be recharged into the underground aquifers through two separate recharge wells.[16]

Forestry

Between 1969 and 2002, social forestry was largely undertaken with the assistance of the World Bank. In 2002, these plantations were undertaken under the state scheme. Now it is self-dependent. Private organisations have also come up to support this effort. The CII in Vadodara took special initiative along with others to plant more than 15,000 saplings in 2012 on World Environment Day, said Stuti Ahluwlia, who handled a youth training programme to inspire young people to become more confident.

The Indira Priyadarshini Vrikshamitra Awards were instituted by the Union Ministry of Environment and Forests in 1986. A Forest department employee of Gujarat, BB Limbasiya, received this award in 2007. The Range Forests Office, Taluka Sewa Sadan, Khambat, received it the next year.

The Union Ministry instituted another award, Indira Gandhi Paryavaran Puraskar in 1987 to give recognition to those having made or having the potential to make measurable and major impact in the protection of environment. Dr Amrita Patel, Chairperson of the National Dairy Development Board, Anand, Gujarat, received the award for her wide ranging and incisive contributions to environmental conservation and awareness in 2005.[17]

India's leading news magazine *India Today* called Gujarat's agriculture "Green Revolution Lite". There is a boom in the production of *kesar* mangoes, Israeli dates, succulent sweet lemons and organically grown vegetables in the state. In this diversified choice of crops, *kesar* leads the output. Locally grown dates have been developed both in quality and quantity to turn them into export material. Indigenously devised techniques have turned sweet lime into a small industry. Taiwanese papaya and watermelon have been imported and are now grown on Kutch soil by local farmers using modern cultivation techniques like mulching—the use of plastic covers for underground fruits and vegetables to regulate humidity. To the Taiwanese papaya, Kutchi farmers are now adding vegetables like capsicum, which had never been grown in this region. And none of these crops deplete the soil of its essential elements, minerals and too much of ground water.[18]

The introduction of IT has helped the GPCB to better monitor the industries in terms of environment clearance and compliance after start of operation. The National Informatics Centre had developed a software application called Xtended Green Node (XGN) which is in use in the GPCB since June 2008. It has made the functioning of the GPCB 'transparent and accountable' and of course faster. GCP's head office and all its regional offices are connected with more than 17,000 industries spread across Gujarat, hospitals (private and government), and waste treatment facilities.

Before the advent of XGN, tracking of the activity by GPCB was difficult. For instance, it was difficult to keep track of when the consent of a particular industry would expire, when the last inspection was conducted, for how long an industrial unit had not paid water cess, or how many times it had violated the statutory norms. Now 15 issues including waste water generation, treatment and disposal, electricity consumption, inspection reports and monitoring results can be tracked on the click of a mouse.

Industries have been given an ID and a password to know their status whenever they want. For the first timer, all the information will have to be fed at the time of filling an application. The industry can then apply for consent to operate or establish the project.

The moment an application is made an SMS alert goes to the regional officer concerned to look into the application and send his or her queries. The applications have to be cleared within a specific time which is 120 days from the date of the application. The industrialist is informed about the clearance status through SMS.[19]

***

Khushboo Gujarat Ki
India's New Tourism Destination

Travel makes one modest. You see what a tiny
place you occupy in the world.

— **Gustave Flaubert, French author**

Narendra Modi and Amitabh Bachchan met in Mumbai. The chief minister discussed with him how to showcase Gujarat tourism. Modi passionately explained to him the beauty of the white Rann of Kutch. "You just need to be there to believe it. It is an out of the world experience," Modi told the Bollywood superstar. Then he proposed that the celebrity do the promotional advertisements. Amitabh Bachchan agreed.

When Modi asked for his conditions, he said "absolutely free". The living legend of the Indian film industry then requested for a longer cot to sleep and a treadmill wherever he would stay so that he could keep fit. And Bachchan has done advertisements of all important tourist places.

Amitabh Bachchan's mother had died in 2007. Sometime in 2011, Modi suggested to him that he should visit Sidhpur and perform the *matru shraddh* (a Hindu ritual that follows the death of one's mother). This place is considered the most auspicious in Hindu religion and mythology for performing the *shraddh* of one's mother, the same way Gaya in Bihar is considered holy for *pitru shraddh* (the corresponding ritual performed after the death of one's father). On 31 January 2012, Bachchan visited the place for *matru shraddh* and spent about five hours there. The short advertisement film about Sidhpur was also shot the same day.[1]

And Amitabh Bachchan produced one of the most powerful advertisements telling people why they should perform *shraddh* in Sidhpur. "People come here from across the world to perform the most difficult task *shraddh* for the departed soul of their mothers... They say that river Saraswati once flowed to Sidhpur. Saraswati, another name for

Maa… Sidhpur—the only pious destination that breathes the sanctity and sentiments of our mother's *shraddh!*"[2]

In the *Vedas*, Sidhpur is mentioned as Shristhal or a 'pious place'. It has the Bindu Sarovar, one of the five most holy lakes in India. Lord Parashurama performed his *matru shraddh* here. Sidhpur is also famous for its livestock camel fair during the month of Kartik, the first month of the Hindu calendar. The place is also known for buildings of European style architecture which the Bohra Muslim community had built.[3]

In September 2005, a grand function witnessed the waters of the Narmada flow into river Saraswati. It soon converted into a great tourist and religious attraction. So much so that former Prime Minister HD Deve Gowda visited Sidhpur to perform the *matru shraddh* for his mother.

'*Khushboo Gujarat Ki*' is one of the best advertisement series ever and has worked wonders for the state. Ask anyone and he would say that Amitabh Bachchan has brought hordes of tourists everywhere in Gujarat. The state bagged three national tourism awards— the best tourism film, innovative use of information technology and for being the best state for comprehensive development of tourism.[4]

Inbound tourists to Gujarat at the end of March 2013 numbered 2.54 crore as against a mere 60 lakh, 10 years ago.[5] No wonder tourism contributes 13.5 per cent to the state's economy. The number of foreigners and NRIs who visited Gujarat increased from 65,000 to 4,51,212 between 2002-03 and 2011-12.[6] "For the last 10 years during Narendra Modi's regime, tourism has been emerging as a sector contributing substantially to Gujarat's SDP," Kamlesh Patel said.[7]

A triumphant Modi is happy that efforts at promoting tourism have borne fruits: "I can proudly say that in such a small period of time, no other country or state can attract so much tourism like Gujarat has." He pointed out that the state witnessed 16 per cent growth in tourism compared to India's tourism growth of seven per cent.[8]

Gujaratis are known for their love for tourism. They travel a lot. But the state, despite having everything, was unable to showcase itself. At the best, people knew about the Gir forests and its Asiatic lions. For religiously-oriented Hindus, there was the Somnath temple. But things have changed today. In the last 12 years, the state has emerged as a major tourist destination.

The turnaround did not happen overnight. A visionary leader built the necessary infrastructure and repackaged the whole state. The "*Khushboo Gujarat Ki*" (fragrance of Gujarat) advertisements brilliantly present the Somnath temple as the power of belief; the Gir forest in the Girnam mountain range as the domain of the royal Asiatic lion; the importance of Kutch festivals and the beauty of white sands that light up immediately on the full moon night and "the earth becomes moon"; Dwarka as the city of *Moksha*, Lord Krishna and love; Porbandar, the birthplace of Mahatma Gandhi, and the memory of India's struggle for independence; the ancient city of Lothal and Dholavira, and the reasons our ancestors chose to settle there.

The Rann of Kutch festival (Rann Utsav) is held at Dhordo village, 85 km from Bhuj. Gujarat tourism department has been organising this event since 2005. Any such festival needs an elaborate law and order arrangement. There are no complaints that the safety and security of a tourist has ever been compromised. The month-long festival is visited by lakhs of tourists every year now. Hot air balloons, visit to the Mandvi beech and provision for spending the night in tents are some of the major attractions of the Kutch festival. There are also folk dances, music and trekking arrangements.

Mahatma Gandhi's grandson Tushar Gandhi was immensely impressed with the way Kutch has been rebuilt after the earthquake in 2001 and locals have been involved in development of tourism. "The entrepreneurial model that I saw being implemented in Dhordo is the closest to one envisaged by Bapu; one based on trusteeship, one where there is local participation and the benefit of the enterprise passes directly to the local community and benefits it. For this, Gujarat Tourism deserves hearty praise."[9]

He justified his praise thus: "Gujarat Tourism builds resorts and hands them over to the local village panchayat, which forms a Tourism Trust that takes over and manages the resort. This trust is headed by the collector, *sarpanch* and locals as well, while the revenue is shared by the government and local governing units. The locals run and supervise the day-to-day working of the resort, which is based on the trusteeship model."[10]

Gujarat's coastline provides a huge potential for beach tourism. The state is investing Rs 120 crore on developing infrastructure along the beaches. This will be carried out on a public-private partnership basis, where the investment by the state government itself will be negligible.[11]

In 2011, the state decided to open 16 beaches for private resorts. It set aside prime land overlooking these beaches after completing surveys with ownership details. Ten of these beaches are in the Saurashtra region. The government was keen to have at least 100 resorts in these beaches. Proposals worth Rs 18,000 crore were signed for building beach resorts at the Vibrant Gujarat summit the same year. The Atlantis group was keen to develop several resorts along Suvali beach near Surat with an investment of Rs 9,000 crore.[12]

Then, there is the 1954-vintage boat race in coastal Surat between Aaliya-bet in Dumas and Magdalla (20 miles). The Tourism Corporation of Gujarat Limited (TCGL) is now promoting the state's oldest race at different levels after including it in the list of prominent cultural events of the state. This is surely going to get it a prominent place on the tourism map.

The government intervened at a time when the number of contestants was dwindling and the race was getting limited to a few villages only.[13]

Water sports and adventure sports facilities may help to attract more international tourists, besides exposing domestic tourists to various forms of recreation. Financial assistance is being given by the state government to encourage these activities. However, water sports will not be permitted in the Narmada dam and the main canal. Adventure sports are being encouraged in forest and hilly areas.

Boat and water scooter, parasailing, water skiing and fun riding, jet skiing, wind surfing & sailing, kayaking, canoeing and scuba diving are some of the water sports being encouraged.

Gir Forest has been the main tourist attraction because of the majestic Asiatic lions. As per the last Lion census in 2010, the count was 411, which was 52 more than the last count in 2005. Now, since lions are in plenty, tourists find it easy to spot them and return home with the satisfaction of having seen the king of the jungle.

The increase in the number shows the cordial relation that exists between animals and humans. No incident of poaching has been reported. The walls around the wells have been raised to prevent cubs from falling into them. Earlier, more than 10 cubs used to die annually by falling into these wells.[14]

Appointment of women foresters helped achieve a greater balance with nature. Their presence has brought better forest discipline since they have been able to rope in tribal women for participation in forest conservation. These women assistants (*van sahayaks*) have been responsible for rescuing more than 250 leopards.[15]

The 60 seconds advertisement on Gir Forest was aired in October 2010. The first fortnight of November 2010 saw a record earnings for the Gir Sanctuary of over Rs 45 lakh from more than 35,000 visitors. Earlier, only 90 vehicles were permitted to be taken inside the sanctuary. Heavy rush forced the government to increase the number to 150. Monthly average of the last eight months between October 2009 and May 2010 was Rs 26 lakh.[16]

A record 4.16 lakh tourists visited Gir during the 2012-13 season.[17] Looking at the rush, the forest department was forced to introduce 12 additional 20-seater buses in 2012; earlier there were only two buses. On 16 November 2013, the Gir Sanctuary hosted a record 9,384 visitors in just one day. In 2012, it had seen 7,356 visitors a day during the same period. In all, close to 23,000 visitors came to see the Lions on Diwali and the three subsequent days after that.[18]

The Navratri festival happens in the month of October or November closer to Dussehra and the Kite Festival on 14 January. The Modi government has taken the celebrations to greater heights and now Gujarat is also being remembered for these festivals. The vibrant Navratri festival that goes on for nine days is promoted by the Gujarat government and is very popular with young boys and girls, who perform *garba* dance to the tune of traditional music.

The Kite flying festival is an old phenomenon but repackaged as a great event. "We showed how a kite can draw the world to Gujarat," Modi said while inaugurating the International Kite Festival in 2013.[19] The 20th International Kite Festival in 2010 became a major celebration when the government started hosting it on the newly constructed Sabarmati river front. More than 105 kite fliers from 34 countries and 120 kite fliers from nine Indian states participated in the event.

In 2013, the state decided to take the festival to different parts of the State—Vadodara, Surat and Modhera—to mark the silver jubilee of the international kite festival. The state also organised the festival in

Mumbai and Delhi.

The kite festival has given a big boost to the economic activities associated with making kites. The chief minister said in 2011 that revenue from the kite industry, which was estimated at Rs 30-35 crore, had jumped to Rs 400 crore. He also predicted that it would further go up to Rs 700 crore in the next few years.[20]

Modi tried to push spiritual tourism by developing the Rama trail in Dang district where Lord Rama had spent some time during his 14 years of exile. It is believed that Lord Rama, his wife Sita and brother Lakshmana spent the majority period of their exile in the forests of southern Gujarat. Sita Van, Ram Sarovar, Unai and Shabri Dham are taken as parts of the Rama Trail.

He also tried to develop the Buddhist remains in Vadnagar. Chinese traveller Hieun Tsang had visited Vadnagar in 640 AD. He spoke about the existence of 10 Buddhist monasteries and about 1000 monks.[21]

The idea of archaeological excavation in Vadnagar was first mooted by Modi.[22] He took keen interest in the activity and visited the excavation site.[23] A monastery, 1900-years old, was discovered there in 2009. Coins, seals, silver beads, clay utensils, ornaments, etc., were discovered in 2007.[24]

The government has decided to make a Buddhist tourism circuit in central Gujarat. The plan is to develop Devni Mori (Sabarkantha), Taranga in Junagarh, and Vadnagar in Mehsana as an integrated Buddhist circuit.[25] Developing Khambalida caves (Rajkot) and other Buddhist caves is a part of that circuit.

In 2010, the government organised the first ever tourist conclave attended by stakeholders in travel and hospitality sectors. In January 2010, both Modi and Buddhist spiritual leader Dalai Lama attended a seminar on Buddhist Heritage in Vadodara. Modi declared that the country's biggest Buddha temple would be built in Gujarat with the help of Dalai Lama.[26] More than 1,000 experts, scholars and lamas from 15 countries attended the seminar organised jointly by the state government and the Archaeological Survey of India.

The government has already initiated work on Rameshwar Dham and Shabri Dham at the cost of Rs 6.93 crore and Rs 12.21 crore respectively.[27] Rameshwar Dham in Mandavi in Surat district is situated on the bank of river Tapi. Lord Rama is believed to have performed his *pitru shradhh* here. Shabri Dham in Dang district is the place where Lord Rama had eaten the sweet *ber* (Chinese Apple/Jujube/Indian plum/Masau) offered by Shabari. She had tasted the fruit first to find out if they were sweet enough to be offered to Lord Rama.

During the peak tourist months of November-February, doctors in major Gujarat cities need to work overtime to cater to the huge demand for surgical treatment coming from Non-Resident Gujaratis (NRGs). Most NRGs club their visit with the need for medical treatment, mostly surgery and this is the time they prefer to visit the state.

A comparison between different rates in India and abroad would tell us why medical tourism is picking up. A knee replacement surgery could cost Rs 90,000 in Gujarat in place of USD 80,000 in the United States. A simple Lasik treatment would cost Rs 25,000, whereas one would need to shell out USD 3000 for the same in the US. A cervical disc surgery would cost Rs 1.5 lakh instead of USD 10,000. The highest demand is for ophthalmology, knee and joint replacements and spine surgeries.[28]

World class medical facilities in Gujarat are available at one-tenth of the cost abroad. There is no waiting, which means that a month-long advance planning is not needed. The super speciality hospitals set up with private sector participation have the best equipment in the fields of ophthalmology, urology, embryology, orthodontics, oncology and orthopaedics.

Indian medical tourism is expected to grow by 30 per cent and, by 2015, it would be worth USD 2 billion. The advantages are cost effectiveness, availability of the latest technology, global standards of medical care, and familiarity of English language. Of all the Indian cities, Ahmedabad has become one of the most preferred destinations for medical tourism.

The spurt in the growth of tourism sector attracting more and more international visitors is likely to boost this sector in coming days. There is international competition from Singapore and Thailand, and national competition from hospitals in the metros. But NRGs are the biggest asset for Gujarat, which no other state can match. Gujarat offers a hard-to-resist package of eco-tourism, religious tourism and medical tourism.

***

Healthcare to Every Citizen

*To keep the body in good health is a duty... Otherwise, we shall
not be able to keep our mind strong and clear.*
— **Gautama Buddha**

Anything against Gujarat makes headlines and rightly so, since
the state government constantly claims to lead the country in
matters of development, and has consciously or unconsciously exposed
itself to scrutiny. And if a state is developed, it cannot have bad social
indicators. This contradiction is apparent when one studies the initial
figures of Gujarat. However, a closer analysis would reveal a different
picture. The state has started witnessing change and the contradictions
are getting resolved.

The Comptroller and Auditor General of India (CAG) report in
October 2013 said that despite the government's claim of "providing
supplementary nutrition to the targeted children between the year
2007 and 2012, every third child in Gujarat was underweight
(malnourished)."[1]

This produced a sharp reaction from the state government that said
there was a steep decline in the rate of malnourishment in the state. "As
a result of various nutrition interventions undertaken by government
of Gujarat, the percentage of underweight children decreased from
73.04 per cent in March 2007 to 25.09 per cent in March 2013." This
showed a sharp decline of about 10.98 per cent since the number of
underweight children stood at 36.07 per cent in March 2012.

A careful analysis of the same CAG report had also highlighted the
decline in malnourishment. The report that studied implementation
of the Integrated Child Development Scheme (ICDS) from 2007-
12 said, "The percentage of moderately malnourished children in

Gujarat was 69.83 per cent in 2006-07, 60.74 per cent in 2007-08, 57.97 per cent in 2008-09, 53.88 per cent in 2009-10 and 34.21 per cent in 2010-11..." The CAG data was a proof of the improvement in the performance of the state, but these figures were drowned in the headlines that depicted Gujarat in bad light.

A comparison of the figures of malnutrition (overall) in other states from 31 March 2007 to 1 March 2011 would show that Gujarat has performed better than many. While significant reduction was witnessed in Gujarat from about 70.69 per cent to 38.77 per cent between the two dates, other states witnessed improvements of smaller degrees, such as Maharashtra which registered a decrease from 45.47 to 23.31, Karnataka from 53.39 to 39.50, Uttar Pradesh from 53.36 to 40.90, Uttarakhand from 45.71 to 24.93 and West Bengal from 52.75 to 36.92 per cent.[2]

The malnutrition percentage figures for other states that are in the 40-plus category are Bihar (82.12), Odisha (50.43), Delhi (49.91), Andhra Pradesh (48.72), Rajasthan (43.13), Haryana (42.95) and Uttar Pradesh (40.93). The national average stood at 41.16 per cent.

If this declining trend can be seen in the context of measures initiated to tackle the issue, the next survey would present a much improved figure. Gujarat is showing better health indicators such as higher life expectancy at birth for women, and lower infant mortality when compared to the time Modi came to power. The challenges he had faced also included the count of maternal mortality ratio, lack of the managerial capacity, shortage of skilled human resources, non-availability of blood in rural areas, and infrastructural and supply bottlenecks.

To get quicker results from government efforts, Modi launched Mission Balam Sukham in 2012. This was conceptualised as an integrated nutrition mission programme to tackle malnutrition on a war footing. Malnutrition among women, adolescent girls and children is the main reason for death from common ailments. In absence of proper nutrition, the body does not have the immunity to fight diseases. The departments of health and family welfare, and women and child development were made the nodal agencies to implement the mission.

It worked on both preventive and curative interventions at various stages such as adolescence, nine months of pregnancy to first two years of age (critical 1000 days) and for children up to six years. It recommended breast feeding within the first hour from birth, exclusive breast feeding up to six months and initiation of complementary feeding after six months. It also launched communication strategies to improve dietary practices and stressed de-worming of children, adolescent girls and pregnant women to improve absorption of nutrients.

The mission stressed community mobilisation at the level of panchayats, self help groups, *sakhi mandals* and *doodh mandalis* (milk cooperatives) to focus on deprived sections of the society. The mission adopted comprehensive monitoring through adequate sample surveys and launched mass awareness on infant and young child feeding practices.

Micronutrient supplementation was strengthened by making effective use of programmes such as village health and nutrition days, Mamta Divas (Day of Affection) and Annaprashan Divas (*Annaprashan* or *Upanayana* is a Hindu ritual performed on a male child in his eighth year). It sought to tackle malnutrition at the Bal Shakti Kendras in the Anganwadis, Bal Sewa Kendras at Primary Health Centres and Bal Sanjivani Kendras at district hospital and medical colleges.

To implement the mission, a separate structure under the Society Registration Act was created with the chief minister as its head. Three-tier operational structures were institutionalised at the state, district and *taluka* levels.

With an effort to bring down Infant Mortality Rate (IMR) and Maternal Mortality Ratio (MMR), innovative programmes such as Chiranjivi Yojana, Bal Sakha Yojana, Janani Suraksha Yojana and Janani Shishu Suraksha Karyakram were introduced.

Among others things, higher MMR is a factor of institutionalised delivery which depends on the availability of obstetricians at the time of delivery. Realising that the state has very few obstetricians working in rural areas, the government concluded that there was no way other than to outsource maternity services for poor people to private practitioners.

Under the Chiranjivi Yojana, aimed at safe motherhood and infant and child survival, the state entered into innovative partnership with private players including hospitals and private practitioners. Maternity services from these identified practitioners were made available to people living below poverty line and above poverty line tribal families absolutely free.

At present, the government gives Rs 2,80,000 for 100 deliveries, irrespective of whether the deliveries have been ordinary, complicated or caesarian section. If the enrolled private gynaecologist offers his/her services in the government hospital, he is paid Rs 86,500 for 100 deliveries.[3]

The beneficiaries do not have to pay charges related to delivery, medicine, anaesthesia and laboratory investigations or operations. During the year 2011-12, 1,50,187 deliveries were registered under the scheme.[4] Institutional delivery by December 2012 had reached 95 per cent. This was a great achievement compared to the figure of about 58 per cent a decade ago.

The scheme was given the prime minister's award for excellence in public administration for the year 2007-08. It has already received the Asia Innovation Award (Singapore) in 2006.

The Janani Surakhsha Yojana conceptualised to provide safe motherhood is a programme implemented under the National Rural Health Mission (NRHM). It also aims at promoting institutional deliveries. This is a 100 per cent centrally sponsored scheme and provides cash assistance of Rs 500 for nutrition support and Rs 200 for transport support to each pregnant woman from the marginalised sections (Scheduled Castes, Scheduled Tribes, and BPL families). This was implemented vigorously to add to the efforts of the Chiranjivi Yojana.

The Janani Shishu Suraksha Karyakram entitled all pregnant women access to public health institutions with absolutely no expenses to be borne by them or their families for 42 days, and the newborns are assured free treatment for the first 30 days after their birth, including to and fro transport.

Slow decrease in child mortality was primarily due to less number of paediatricians in the government system. Neonatal mortality accounted for majority of child deaths and many of these happened within the first seven days of birth. Bal Sakha Yojana intervention in 2009 brought private paediatricians to all children of BPL and tribal children born under the Chiranjivi Yojana or in government health care institutions.

The paediatrician attends to all eligible newborns at the place of birth, ensures their survival by proper early neonatal care including immunisations at birth, feeding advice, etc. The gynaecologist ensures a two-day long stay of mother and baby after delivery to cover the dangers of the immediate postpartum period. If a baby is found to have conditions that require further neonatal care, it is transferred and treated in his/her NICU. If the baby requires a very high level of care such as a ventilator, it is transferred to Level 3 NICU in medical college hospitals and given the facility or money for ambulance charges.

The much talked about and visible success story in Gujarat has been the Emergency Medical Service provided through the number 108. By dialling this number, a person can access police, medical and fire services on an emergency basis. This can be dialled for saving a life, reporting a crime or reporting a fire. The 108 service is mandated to reach in 18 minutes and its record is monitored on a regular basis.

The Emergency Medical Care service was launched on 29 August 2007. This has revolutionised response to quick medical needs and has become immensely popular. This service is available in the entire state. On an average, there are between 2000-2200 calls per day. This service is a hit, more particularly in tribal areas.

Shivajibhai, a cab driver, was gung ho about the 108 helpline: "Sir you call anytime, it comes within 20 minutes. Earlier, a person meeting with accident on road would certainly die due to lack of medical help. Also, we would look the other way fearing police harassment. Now, after seeing an accident, we just dial 108 without bothering about the police. This has helped save a lot of lives."

GVK Emergency Management and Research Institute (EMRI) is the nodal agency for implementation of this service which has now been linked to Chiranjivi Yojana for maternity services. Till June 2012, this was used for 10.19 lakh delivery cases, of which 29,126 women delivered in ambulance vans.[5]

The state-of-art medical van that ensures pre-hospitalisation care of patients till they are taken to the nearest health care facility has impressed one and all. The team of about 2,600 people and a fleet of 506 ambulances are working round the clock. Ninety nine per cent of the calls are picked up by the attendant within three seconds, which is at par with world standards. About 35 per cent of the cases handled are emergency delivery cases.[6]

All these efforts are bound to give results. Infant mortality rate, defined as death of an infant per one thousand births within one year, has declined substantially in the state. It has fallen from 57 in 2003 to 38 in 2012, as per Sample Registration System (SRS) adopted by the Union Government. The State's annual IMR decline for the last three years (2009-12) at 7.5 per cent is among the highest in the country. The central government's target under the Millennium Development Goal is pegged at seven per cent. The number will improve further as results of developmental initiatives and welfare measures start trickling in.

The Maternal Mortality Rate, defined as the number of deaths of mothers during childbirth out of one lakh live births, from 202 in 2001 got reduced to 148 in 2011.[7]

Independent studies have proved that the schemes have started yielding results.

A study by the Indian Institute of Management Ahmedbad analysed the Chiranjivi Yojana in 2007 and testified that the targeted beneficiaries were actually making the best use of the schemes.

Most of the Chiranjivi beneficiaries at that time had income levels less than Rs 12,000 per annum, indicating that the scheme was able to target the poor families. Also the cash incentives were being used even when some people had to shell out some cash.[8]

The average distance travelled by a Chiranjivi client to reach the health care facility was 13.79 km and the average time taken was 44 minutes. This was impressive for a state where health facilities were inaccessible a decade ago.[9]

Another credible report carried in the *Indian Journal of Community Medicine* said that the number of institutional deliveries increased even in absence of a conditional cash transfer programme linking cash transfer to institutional deliveries. It found that women, even from poor families, were more likely to deliver at an institution if there was availability of free emergency transportation, free and quality obstetric care at either public or private health facility for normal and complicated deliveries, and community-based mobilisation efforts to ensure that maximum number of women take advantage of government benefits.[10]

Most women who delivered in hospitals after initiation of maternity schemes chose hospitals for subsequent deliveries. Women who had previous home deliveries started having institutional deliveries. This indicates user satisfaction with the Chiranjivi Yojana and free emergency transportation along with effectiveness of grass-root mobilisation and quality in-patient obstetric services.

Sickle Cell Anaemia was a major problem particularly in tribal Gujarat. The government launched an unprecedented Sickle Cell Anaemia (SCA) control programme in tribal districts in 2006. The aim was to control this hereditary disease in four districts of south Gujarat dominated by tribal populations. This was extended in 2010 to all the 12 tribal districts with SCA disease.

The population is being screened and three kinds of cards are issued depending on the nature of the disease in a person. 'Yellow Card' is issued if they have sickle cell disease, 'Half White-Half Yellow Card' in case of sickle cell trait, and 'White Card' if they are sickle cell negative. The programme has been launched at the school level to screen the children. Asking two yellow card holders not to marry is the only way to prevent the disease from spreading since it is a genetic disease.

If either of the parents is having sickle gene, the child may be normal or may have the sickle gene. However, if both the parents have sickle gene, the child can either be normal or have sickle gene or sickle diseases. The state was awarded the Prime Minister's award for excellence in public administration in 2009-10.

About 20 million children are born with SCA in India every year. If it is not controlled now, then in another 25-40 years, over 15 million children will die from SCA disease. Of the total tribal population in Gujarat, about 10 per cent suffer from the disease.[11]

Health insurance or cashless medical treatment for people falling below poverty line is essential to protect the poor from going bankrupt in case of emergency. While the rich can afford costly healthcare treatment, one critical disease is enough to destroy any poor family. Modi has been talking about this every now and then because he is aware of the hardship disease brings to any average family. He launched a special health insurance scheme for 1.8 crore people living below poverty line. Called the Mukhyamantri Amrutam (MA) Yojana, the scheme was launched in September 2012 to cover hospitalisation expenses of up to Rs 2 lakh per family absolutely free of cost.

The MA Scheme would cover surgeries for cardiovascular diseases, neurosurgery, burns, poly-trauma, cancer (malignancies), renal and neo-natal diseases. The State government empanels public, private and trust hospitals for conducting surgeries. Each member is issued a quick response coded plastic card and he can get himself or his family treated without making any payment to the listed hospitals.[12]

E-Mamta can track pregnant mothers and children born to them, and to keep tabs on the general health of people. Information and Communication Technology (ICT) based software was introduced in 2010. This is now being used to monitor the health of the state's population. It uses various electronic systems and IT network to track the patient's location, keep record of their health history, monitor immediate health needs and provide medical help at the doorsteps.

Currently, e-Mamta contains records of 103 lakh families covering 4.9 crore individuals, that is, 82 per cent of the state's total population. During the year 2012-13 (up to December 2012), out of 11 lakh expected pregnant women, 8.77 lakh were tracked through ICT.[13] The central government has appreciated the ICT system and has decided to replicate it nationally.

E-Mamta was conferred the prestigious South Asia Manthan Award in 2010. This award was given jointly by the Digital Empowerment Foundation in partnership with World Summit Award, Department of Information Technology, Government of India.

Besides taking care of its citizens through these efforts, the state is promoting creation of world class medical facilities. It is developing into a hub of super health services. Ahmedabad, Surat, Vadodara and other fast growing cities are also getting known for high class hospitals with state-of-art technology. This has further helped to promote medical tourism.

***

Making Women Count

There is no chance of welfare of the world unless the condition of women is improved. It is not possible for a bird to fly on one wing.

— Swami Vivekananda

Gujarat has an adverse sex ratio. The good news is that women in the state are getting increasingly empowered and are taking democratic decisions in all walks of life. Though both appear mutually contradictory, they are both true. Based on indications of improving social indicators, we can safely say that the contradiction will get resolved as we approach closer to the 2021 Census.

While India's sex ratio is 940 women per 1000 men (according to the 2011 census), in Gujarat it was 918, a drop from 921 per 1000 in 2001. Along with Uttarakhand, Bihar and Jammu & Kashmir, Gujarat was the only state to have witnessed a negative trend. This was the biggest challenge before the Modi government and, if we look at the steps taken, there is no reason to believe that the situation will not improve.

The 2011 census also indicated towards positive development that proves that things have started brightening up as argued by Bibek Debroy.[1] The all India child sex ratio (female-male birth 0-6 years) was 945 in 1991, 927 in 2001 and 919 in 2011. This means that there has been a consistent decline. In Gujarat, the child sex ratio was 928 in 1991, 883 in 2001 and 890 in 2011. It can be said that while the child sex ratio declined over 10 years (2001-2011) at an all India level, it witnessed improvement over the same period in Gujarat. On the other hand, the adverse sex ratio in Gujarat today is also due to the adverse child sex ratio during 1991-2001 that saw a massive decline from 928 to 883.

Child sex ratio and sex ratio at birth are important indicators of the impact of the government's policies. At the all India level, the sex ratio at birth was 894 in 2001 and 906 in 2011. In Gujarat, it was 837 in 2001 and 909 in 2011. These figures are a clear indication that the state is catching up but may not be fast enough to undo the damage of the previous years. The impact of various schemes for women and child development must have started impacting people a couple of years after Modi came to power. The state government claimed the same when the census figures came. Then Principal Secretary (Planning) VN Maira said, "These efforts will bear fruits in the next few years." He pointed out that the state had reversed the trend of declining child ratio population.[2] The increase in the sex ratio may also be due to the various campaigns launched to save the girl child.

What must have added to the worsening situation could be labour migration to the state in search of better jobs. Sociologists have tried to explain this skewed sex ratio as a factor of urbanisation and industrialisation since these create dependence on nuclear families. Studies say that most young couples stop after one child, and therefore long for a male child.[3] Also, this means that there is sex determination that encourages female foeticide demanding stern governmental measures.

We must try to understand the status of women looking at government policies and the sincerity and determination of the government to implement them. Modi has been on the forefront of championing women's rights. In every meeting he has attended, where the practice is prevalent, he has made it a point to condemn it and has urged the people to take a vow not to continue it. At one such meeting in north Gujarat, he said, "It would be contradictory to worship female power on the one hand and to kill female foetus on the other... With such a cultural backdrop, it is necessary that our society take a vow to refrain from the sin of female foeticide."[4]

The practice is widely prevalent in the Kadva Patel community. In one such meeting of the community, he did not mince words and criticised the community openly: "I want to tell a bitter truth to the Kadva Patels. Unjha, which is the seat of their deity Ma Umiya, ranks the lowest in sex ratio in Gujarat. This isn't any natural phenomenon, but result of the evil practice of female foeticide." He asked people to take a pledge to end this practise. The community immediately responded by taking a vow to abolish the practice.[5]

The adverse sex ratio based on 2001 Census was a bitter reality when Modi became the chief minister. The situation became alarming when the state survey of 2004 showed the number of girl born as 824 against 1000 boys. In 2001 Census, it was 837.[6] The state government identified 43 *talukas* with child sex ratio of less than 850 for immediate intervention. It was after the state survey that the Beti Bachao Andolan was launched on 8 March 2005 (International Women's Day). Effective enforcement of the Pre-Natal Diagnostic Technique Act (PNDT Act) was launched simultaneously.

The PNDT act prohibits sex determination after conception, unless it is a medical emergency. Also, it mandates registration of all clinics with ultrasound machines since detection is possible only by using these machines. The very existence of widespread foeticide explains that the law was not being strictly implemented. The same administration became more vigilant when this part of law enforcement became a priority.

All elected representatives, including parliamentarians, were asked to go to their respective constituencies and spread awareness against the practice.

The government launched a crackdown on clinics offering sonography services. In 2006, hundreds of gynaecologists and radiologists came out on the streets to protest the government's move. About 150 clinics were closed, ultrasound machines were confiscated and legal proceedings were initiated against 30 such clinics.[7]

Gujarat registered all the clinics with ultrasound machines and appointed District Appropriate Authorities in all the districts to strictly oversee implementation of the PNDT Act. Further, State Inspection and Monitoring Committees were set up to undertake field visits and monitor implementation with powers to initiate action against unregistered institutions.

Advocacy groups and NGOs were roped in to spread awareness against the pre-natal sex determination test and support the Beti Bachao Andolan. An NGO used the *Garba* festival to highlight the plight of girls. One of the banners displayed prominently in some of the *Garba* venues was *"Arre Kyan Gayi Mari Saahelion"* (Where have all my girl friends gone?) It also distributed leaflets titled, *"Tamari Ladli No Pukar! Beti Bachao"* (Your daughters' voice! Save the girl). The NGO wanted to convey that if the practice of female foeticide was not stopped, there would be no girls to play *Garba*.[8]

The NCC girl cadets had decided to spread awareness in 17 districts that were considered the worst affected and an oath was taken by all cadets to make efforts to save the girl child. Girl cadets then took out a rally in the Ahmedabad city.[9] Mass swearing-in ceremonies were organised by the health department to encourage people to take a pledge against the evil practice.

Modi's vision on women empowerment was evident on the International Women's Day in 2013.

Modi said: "On this day, let us resolve to make women equal stakeholders in the decision-making processes and economic growth of the state as well as the nation... Let us affirm our commitment to eradicate any form of injustice against women and ensure that what the nation saw in the last few months does not happen ever again. A civilised society, etched in liberal democratic values, has no place for those who disrespect women."[10]

Modi has criticised the West that describes Indian women as housewives. He sees a woman as an entrepreneur such as the owner of *Jassu Ben's* pizza that produced more popular pizzas than the international brands, or as those leading democratic political institutions. "It's our role as a part of this society to promote and give power to women.[11] Every woman has entrepreneurial qualities and values. Women will become stakeholders in decision-making if they are financially independent," he added.

About 30 per cent reservation for women in government jobs ensures their larger participation in administration. Also, they get five years relaxation in upper age limit so that they can compete and join various administrative jobs. Women play a significant role in *pani samitis* spread all over the state. More than 72,582 women are members of 17,790 *pani samitis*. There are 2,119 women milk cooperatives. Also, 4,93,149 women are members of 3,205 participatory forest management committees. There are 17,675 village health and sanitation committees with about 70 per cent participation from women.

To give better social status to women, the government waived off registration fee of Rs 414.47 crore for about 11.72 lakh documents that were registered in the name of women by June 2012.[12] The state has reduced the stamp duty on property registered in the name of women. It has also made it mandatory for schools to mention the name of the mother, whereas mentioning the name of the father is not mandatory.

A direct impact of the government move was visible when GIDC made payment in 2013 for the land it bought from farmers in Khoraj village near Sanand. Over 400 villagers became *crorepatis*. Of these, 117 were women. This meant that more and more women were becoming owners of property.[13]

Women's representation in democratic institutions has been a factor of governmental efforts. There are 362 women *samras* gram panchayats—these are all women panchayats where the members have been elected through a consensus. The state has already provided 33 per cent reservation of seats to women in the civic bodies. The state Vidhan Sabha has passed a bill to sanction 50 per cent reservation for women in the assembly.

At the lowest level, the efforts of the government are seen through Anganwadi Workers (AWWs) and Anganwadi Helpers (AWHs) since they implement most of the welfare schemes for the weaker sections.

To keep them motivated, the state government has been giving more money to these workers than what has been prescribed by the Union government. In Gujarat, an Anganwadi worker is paid an honorarium of Rs 2,500 whereas the helper receives Rs 1,250. The state government spends Rs 95 crore over and above Rs 169.45 crore allocated by the Centre.

Every year since 2007, the state has also been giving the women workers a sari and blouse each along with stitching charges. A great way to make these women feel important and work with full enthusiasm!

To enable AWWs go into the interiors and access the socially excluded population, the state had started mobile Anganwadi vans equipped with facilities such as weighing scale, growth chart, pre-school educational kits, medicine kits, registers, etc.

Mata Yashoda Gaurav Nidhi Scheme (a group savings insurance scheme) for AWWs and AWHs has been implemented. A provision is made to pay Rs 50,000 as insured amount in case of death of an AWW or AWH with an interest of eight per cent on the last balance in the amount. In case of retirement, an eight per cent interest on the last balance is given. For this, each of them has to pay Rs 50 as their contribution with matching contribution from the state government.

Gujarat is the first state to set-up *Nari Adalats*. These are block level autonomous courts run by women for women. They seek to provide an alternative justice system for poor and illiterate women. These courts settle disputes mostly dealing with marital affairs.

According to the state government data of 2013, 37 *Nari Adalats* are already functioning and 50 more are in the process of being added These *adalats* are supported by *Mahila Samakhyas* (resource person). The five core members of the *adalats* are trained to think legally and resolve problems socially as per the policy of the government. The police are supportive and ensure compliance. If some cases merit punishment, these are referred to courts.[14]

Financial independence is key to women empowerment. *Sakhi Mandals* or women Self Help Groups (SHGs) have been created to provide training, infrastructure and credit support facility to rural women. This is intended to encourage self-employment. The women are provided skills and financial support to take on bigger activities.

The scheme was launched as an integrated poverty alleviation programme in 2010 by adding the *Sakhi Mandals* to the value chain making women entrepreneurs. A single platform was being created for stakeholders such as banks, industry partners, micro finance institutes and skill imparting institutions to get the desired results. It targeted at least one member from each BPL (below poverty line) family.

At present, there are about 2.39 lakh SHGs/*Sakhi Mandals* and they have an overall capital support of Rs 1,500 crore of which Rs 1,100 crore is the credit support from banks and Rs 400 crore is from savings of these *sakhi mandals*. The membership of these SHGs has crossed 29 lakhs.[15]

The plan is to use the skills of these women for mass production whereby these SHGs would act as linkages to private companies which will brand the products and sell them. Gradually, this would lead to standardisation as per demand. This would generate demands for rural products by urban people. The private companies would come to these SHGs rather than these women workers migrating to cities to get jobs in these companies. The women would own the assets jointly.

For example, these *Sakhi Mandals* could be used for mass scale production of honey, salt or manufacture of garments etc. These companies would get the products at a competitive rate since these SHGs receive both revolving fund and capital subsidy for undertaking economic activities. They have huge credit mobilisation potential and can avail low interest loans of range Rs 5-10 lakh per SHG for viable income generation activities.

Such a large trained workforce evenly spread across the state can take up any production challenge after initial training and guarantee of a market.

The concept had generated a lot of interest at the Vibrant Gujarat summit of 2011. Corporate houses had shown immense interest to involve themselves with Mission Mangalam.

The government took the bold step of involving more women in conservation of forest and wild life by appointing them as *van raksha sahayaks* in 2007. Tribal women from Junagadh, Amreli and Bhavnagar were deployed in the Gir forests. They not only protected lions and leopards but also the forest since they could easily interact with tribal women in the forest and educate them about the need to conserve forests. Modi provided them with cameras so that they could click pictures and make wildlife photography a hobby. Some have excelled in the art.[16] Gir forest is replete with stories of the valour of these women forest protectors.

Some credit for increase in the Lion population, as showed by the Lion Census of 2010, must be given to these women who save the animals, fight the poachers and teach the inhabitants of the villages how to deal with human-animal conflict situation. These *raksha sahayaks* conduct medical camps for villagers and nature education sessions for young girls.

Under the women's empowerment programme, the Gujarat State Road Transport Corporation (GSRTC) appointed 181 women as conductors in April 2013. Other than night shift duty, these women are provided with all facilities at par with men. However, No woman responded to the vacancy for drivers.[17]

The first wave of village empowerment in Gujarat came by way of dairy development unleashed by V Kurien through the White Revolution. It struck off the middlemen from the chain and strengthened dairy farmers. But men dominated the activities even when women played a significant role in milk collection. The farmers' cooperatives, which were the main drivers of the White Revolution, controlled procurement, processing and marketing.

Gradually, as the buzz of facilities for women—in terms of better access to loans and participation in local bodies—made news, more and more women moved to decision-making levels in the family and small groups of larger cooperatives. Now, one would hear success stories of women running dairies and animal husbandry in every corner of the state. In most cases, the cattle in the family are owned by the woman.

The Modi government's decision to make payment for the dairy business to the women of the family has made a lot of difference in social perceptions. It may look like a small step but, considering the village ambience, it has far-reaching consequences.

Some of the NGOs have also taken up women empowerment programmes through dairy cooperatives. Ahmedabad-based Self-Employed Women's Association (SEWA) was the first to start all-women dairy cooperatives in the Banaskantha district.[18]

When the state tries to implement something as a mission, it gets translated into a similar effort by other memebrs of the society. It is a chain reaction. There are many stories showing the private sector encouraging women. In 2012, Vodafone India announced the setting up of all-women retail outlets by the name 'Angel Stores'. The company claimed this was in line with their policy of encouraging diversity and inclusion at the workplace. Women will run services like security, pantry, customer service and management. Beginning with Ahmedabad and Vadodara, the chain will spread to Rajkot and Surat.[19]

***

Harnessing Human Resource: Education and Skill Development

We want that education by which character is formed, strength of mind is increased, the intellect is expanded, and by which one can stand on one's own feet.

—Swami Vivekanand

Six days in the month of scorching heat, everyone in the government takes a walk to different villages and towns to hold the hands of little toddlers and admit them to the nearest primary schools. Three days are spent in rural areas and three in urban. This is done under the motto: Education is *dharma* (duty).

About 3,000 class I and II officers, the entire council of ministers, all elected representatives and all secretaries descend on various villages in groups of five. Each group visits five schools daily during the six-day campaign. This is a unique initiative by the state to ensure 100 per cent enrolment in schools.

This programme has been named Shala Praveshotsav (enrolment drive). Along with this, the government simultaneously organises Kanya Kelavani (girl child education) campaign. The latter aims to ensure that girls don't drop out and enough financial incentives are given to them to continue their studies.

Since both the programmes complement each other, they were launched together in 2003.

A fund called Kanya Kelavani Nidhi has been created under the chief minister. Modi donates whatever gifts he gets from people to this fund. Other private institutions and individuals have come forward to contribute generously to this fund which is used to promote education of the girl child.

Under the Kanya Kelavani scheme, every girl child in areas where female literacy is less than 35 per cent or those who come from below poverty line families in urban areas, is issued a Rs 1,000 Vidya Laxmi Bond at the time of enrolment. This can be redeemed with interest at the time of completion of class VII when she would get Rs 2,200. Another bond of Rs 1,000 is issued when the girl child gets admitted to class VIII. This is redeemed with interest when she passes out from class XII.[1]

As a result of the Kanya Kelavani programme, female literacy increased from 57.8 per cent in 2001 to 70.73 per cent in 2011 in Gujarat. This upward trend is a good sign and will soon bring the state closer to the country's goal of providing free and compulsory education to all children between 6-14 years under the Sarva Sikhsha Abhiyan (universalisation of elementary education).

Bipin Chandra, a teacher in Rampur village of Bhanapur *taluka* in tribal Dahod district, said that the attendance of girls in the schools was more than that of boys due to government schemes. Parents were now more keen to ensure education of their girl child. Children of BPL families were also being given a bicycle when they reached class VIII, he said.

In many places in India, more so in rural areas, a child dropping out from school after the fifth grade is a common trend. The reason behind this is that they have to either change their school or village when there is no provision for secondary education or upper primary education (class VI-VIII) in the same school or village. There are nearly 2,600 government primary schools till Class V, where the students have to change their village to attend higher classes. There are around 8,000 primary schools where students are not required to change the village but the existing school. To take care of this issue, teachers have been assigned the job to get these students enrolled in other classes.[2]

At some places, as for example the Kutch, children moved to coastal areas for fishing and could not pursue schooling. Bipin Chandra pointed out that the dropout in Dahod happened mostly when the poor tribal people took their children out for employment. But if there were similar schools at the places of job, education would not suffer.

The other reason for the high dropout rate was absenteeism of teachers, particularly in tribal areas and remote villages. The chief minister tried to tackle teachers' shortage by recruiting more teachers. Since 2001, more than 1,41,000 vidya sahayaks (teaching assistants), including 8,000 in August 2013, have been appointed.

To ensure attendance of teachers, a biometric system is being introduced. For children with special needs, the government is making special provisions such as remedial classes, hostels, etc. The government would, however, need to have better rooms for computers and well-trained staff for maintenance since HCL staff, responsible for maintenance, visit the school either weekly or fortnightly.

But why girl students drop out? The main reason was absence of proper sanitation facilities in existing schools. The government, through a special drive, built around 71,000 sanitation blocks. It also added 1,04,000 classrooms for continuous education. The government was also constructing hostels for students who would have to leave their village for admission to other schools for higher education.

These, along with other incentives for girls, have ensured that the dropout rate in female enrolment has come down. The trend is positive. Under the Vidhyadeep Insurance Scheme, every student from primary to secondary government schools is provided insurance cover of Rs 50,000 for which premium is paid by the government. The guardian is paid this amount if the student dies from insurance claimable reasons.

As a result of the cumulative effort, the dropout rate (of standard I-V) reduced from 22.30 per cent in 1999-2000 to 2.07 per cent in 2011-12. During the same period, the dropout rate (for standard I-VIII) has decreased from 41.48 per cent to 7.56 per cent.

The hallmark of rudimentary primary education has been the introduction of computers. While computer-aided learning is being promoted, children are also being encouraged to develop English language skills.

The Gunotsav Programme (programme for celebrating virtues) ensures that a minimum quality and uniform standard is maintained in these government schools. On the same pattern as Shala Praveshotsav and Kanya Kelavani, the chief minister, ministers, officers of All India Services and over 3,000 officers of the state government from various departments move out for three days to assess the quality of education in government primary schools. This happens at a different time than Shala Praveshotsav.

About 25 per cent of the schools are assessed. The schools are picked randomly for assessment by the visiting officials. This keeps all schools and staff on tenterhooks. Among other things, the team reviews the infrastructure, quality of basic reading, writing and numerical skills, awareness among teachers and public for quality education, quality of classroom teaching and learning process. These can be classified as academic standards, co-curricular activities and utilisation of school infrastructure. The team makes data entry and suggests remedial action.

The role of a leader is to fire the imagination of the people and lead by example, if necessary. Modi excels in doing this with aplomb. The 'Vanche Gujarat campaign' to make the state read had an imprint of his personal life. He was a voracious reader. When others would gossip, he would pick up a book and read. During his stay at the RSS headquarters in the 1970s, his personal library comprised 1,000 books on different subjects; most of these books were gifted to him by people he met.[3]

The stated objective of Vanche Gujarat was to make Gujarat 'the knowledge capital and reading capital of India' and cultivate reading habit among children. The campaign began on 30 October 2010 with mass reading by school and college students in various libraries of the state from 9-10 am.

More than 60 lakh students participated in this mass reading campaign.[4] Modi kicked off the campaign by participating in the one hour reading session. He read the book *Hind Swaraj* by Mahatma Gandhi at the central library in Gandhinagar. Ministers and bureaucrats too joined in the reading session with students in various libraries.

The awareness campaign for the programme was launched much in advance through mobile reading vans, neighbourhood libraries, reading intervention in local schools, street theatres and donation of books. A special committee was formed with Modi as the chairman to make the programme a success.

During the campaign, different activities were organised such as best reading competition, favourite book, floating books programme, reading-thinking camps, promote reading diary and goal setting diary. Organising book fairs was also a part of the campaign.

School children participated in book reading competitions at their respective levels. They had to pick up at least four books of their choice, other than text books, and be prepared to talk about and answer questions related to them. The period in which the books were to be read was from

1 July to end of Diwali vacation. Teachers were appointed as guides. The best readers were awarded prizes.

Earlier, most schools were being given grants from the state government but there were few schools run by the government. Modi strengthened government intervention and the number of schools rose from 140 in 2001 to 744 in 2011.[5] Also, there are 5,500 schools under grants-in-aid at this level. The state has not abolished board examination for class 10 and uses this to test students' understanding of the subjects.

Another key initiative is to allow students undergoing diploma in Industrial Training Institutes (ITI), who dropped out of secondary school, to seek admissions for any graduation degree course. All in all, 28 technical institutes have been started for higher education.

For development of education in tribal areas, five agriculture polytechnic colleges, three engineering colleges and one physiotherapy college have been set up. If someone from the Scheduled Tribes has completed MBBS, the government provides him interest assistance of six per cent up to Rs 50 lakh. The objective is to facilitate them to open private clinics in tribal areas. It also provides liberal loans to tribal students for pursuing higher education abroad.

Eklavya Model Residential Schools (EMRS) have been implemented at 17 places mostly focussed in tribal areas and another seven were being planned. These schools gave result of 93 per cent in class 10 SSC examination as against the state average of 61 per cent (2009).

This project was launched in Gujarat by the name EMRS. The government spends an average of Rs 42,000 per student per year. All hostels have a mini library to provide access to books for the students after school hours. The school also provides state-of-art computer labs. All hostels have 24×7 computer accessibility.

EMRS have become very popular among the tribal folks. These are seen as the route to immediate advancement and empowerment. The rush for admission is so great that the government now conducts an EMRS entrance test to prepare a common merit list. Of the 3,570 students who enrolled in 2012, 48 per cent were girls.

There are also 35 Eklavya Girls Residential schools from Standard VIII to X. These schools aim to bridge the gap in the literacy level between general candidates and tribal women. They take care of all requirements of the students including medical facilities. The government also runs model non-residential schools and Surya Eklavya Sainik schools. It also provides transportation facilitates in such non-residential schools, to take and drop students at their homes.

The state has started SATCOM-based tutorials for English language teaching. This is to give exposure to students to learn the language in a natural environment outside the classroom.

Higher education in Gujarat has also seen a sea change. The state has 44 universities, 10 research institutes and 8 institutes of national importance. Of these, nine universities are run by the state, two by central university, one each is deemed and open respectively, 11 are special, four agricultural and 16 are run by private players. There are 1,032 colleges of which 71 are under the government, 357 under grant-in-aid and 604 under self-financing scheme. They together employ 12,000 people and cater to 13.5 lakh students.

Some of the novel universities in the special category are Yoga University, Children's University, Swarnim Gujarat Sports University and Raksha Shakti (Defence University).[6] Gujarat Forensic Sciences University is the first of its kind dedicated to forensic and investigative science.

More than nine lakh students are enrolled in these universities. The government has initiated Society for Creation of Opportunity through Proficiency in English (SCOPE) for imparting proficiency in English language. The state has started focussing on English education as a road to empowerment.

To raise awareness about internationalisation of higher education, the government organised an international conference for academic institutions in January 2013. Close to 145 international institutes from 56 countries and 14 Indian states participated in the knowledge pavilion which was visited by 45,000 students and professors and lakhs of general public.

The number of seats in degree and diploma engineering in government engineering colleges has been increased. Total seats in professional colleges have increased from 22,475 to 1,38,740, while those in colleges of grants-in-aid has increased from 13,470 to 33,955 in the last decade. The fee in these colleges is nominal and there is reservation of five per cent for economically weaker sections. Fee of students is waived off if the family income is less than Rs 2.5 lakh but he or she has secured a seat through the merit list. Similarly, students in the physically challenged category who have got a seat through the merit list are not required to pay any fee. About 25,000 students are provided free education under these schemes.

There is a huge shortage of skilled manpower in India and the country will need to move in a planned manner to achieve the target of 500 million skilled workers by 2022. Only about 10 per cent of its workforce has received some kind of skill training, of which only about two per cent received formal training. About 80 per cent of fresh entrants into the workforce did not have any training opportunity.[7]

Compared to this data, Korea has 96 per cent of its workforce in the trained category. The corresponding figures are 80 per cent for Japan, 75 per cent for Germany and 68 per cent for the United Kingdom.[8] If young Indian population has to compete with the world, this difference needs to be bridged. Due to salary expectations and mismatch with skill, about 48 per cent employers in India find it difficult to fill the vacancies.

As Gujarat embarked on the road to rapid industrialisation, the government started thinking of having its own skilled manpower to meet the demands. It realised that dependence on skilled manpower from other states was not the right option since it would dry up as more states catch up with development.

During a seminar at Vibrant Gujarat summit of 2011, the point was raised by industrialists that while Gujarat will have a demand of about 2.5 lakh skilled jobs per year, the availability will be only 1.5 lakh which meant there would be a shortage of about one lakh jobs.[9]

Modi spoke about his vision of skill development at a youth convention in Gandhinagar on the 150th birth anniversary of Swami Vivekanand in 2012. He gave the success mantra as "Skill plus Will plus Zeal is equal to WIN."[10] Skill leads to confidence and strengthens the will to do better. Zeal is the desire to do things in a positive way to better the future. "Many times we face a situation where a person has the degree but not the skill. *Jeevan mein hunar chahiye* (skill is needed in life)".

'Train them young' so that they become employable fast, get added to the productive population and contribute to the economy. With this motto, the State government has delinked skills from educational qualification and even a pass out of class five can avail training and become a part of the earning population. He pointed out the huge scope that had opened up because of 'even illiterate women adopting modern technology such as using electric oven'.

Modi learnt from his experience that vocational training decreases dependence on formal education and increases innovation. He spoke of a person who had started using biogas for running water pumps in the field. The local lad filled tubes with biogas and took them to the field. "The country is full of people who innovate on a day to day basis." He said that the need was to encourage them and integrate them with day to day life.[11]

In government schools too, vocational training has been introduced. The State Budget for 2013-2014 set aside Rs 800 crore for skill development. This figure needs to be contrasted with the figure of Rs 1000 crore allocated by the central government nationally.

Some of the initiatives for skill training include Skill Development Centers (SDCs) for short-term bridge courses under PPP mode; skills upgradation centres at GIDC estates/industrial clusters/industrial parks/ SEZs; and, specialised skill development centres for focus sectors.

A remarkable innovation has been the unique pre-paid Skill Voucher Scheme for better and credible interface between the private players and training institutes under governmental guidance. Gujarat became the first state to come out with this scheme launched in 2011 by the Gujarat Skill Development Mission (GSDM) under the department of Technical Vocational Education & Training (TVET).

The GSDM works as the nodal agency for monitoring various skill development programmes and issues pre-paid vouchers to private or government players in the name of candidates who have to be trained. The employers can plan the skill requirement and identify the people who are needed to fill the gap. The candidate can, thereafter, get training from any of the listed institute of his choice by producing the voucher at that institute. The training is given by any of the institutes listed by a department of the Union or state government.

Once the training is over, National Council for Vocational Training (NCVT), another autonomous institution, conducts an examination to test the candidate/s on the skills learnt and issues certification to successful candidates. In case the candidate fails to clear the examination, the money gets returned to the agency that originally paid.

After successful completion of the training, the institute that provided the training gets the vouchers redeemed. This ensures that the state acts as a guarantor of the money and this in turn helps the state to keep tabs on the standards of the institute and to keep their ratings up. The GSDM keeps a record of the trained candidates and looks after their employability as per the industry demands.

The auto industries in Sanand, including the Nano factory, employ such trained people from the local villages. Company buses ply to and fro to provide pick up and drop facilities to these workers. Such a symbiotic link has also helped to generate a lot of goodwill. GIDC, that develops the industrial areas, makes specific provision for such institutes so that the industries can have locally trained manpower.

The huge manpower shortage would be difficult to meet if one keeps women out of the workforce. One needs locally available skills to run industries and these skills can be best provided by women. Even otherwise, to make the best use of local resources in areas such as animal husbandry, agriculture and allied activities, a minimum level of skills training is required. Setting up Kaushalya Vardhan Kendras (KVKs) all across the state aims to achieve this.

The concept was a product of the *chintan shibir* that was organised in Kutch in 2009 and launched in 2010. Its mandate has been to impart desired skills to rural people and one KVK has been catering to a cluster of 7-10 villages for a population of 7,000 for the general category and 4,900 for the tribal areas. Instead of people going to distant towns for training, the government has come to provide them training at their doorsteps at a very nominal fee of Rs 50. More than 1,000 skills have been added to make the coverage comprehensive. All KVKs have DTH connection which helps in periodic lectures.

All those trained are awarded certificates by the Gujarat Council of Vocational Training (GCVT) that increases their employability by the private industries. KVKs also provide guidance for picking up a skill and then training the candidates.

KVK's training has received unprecedented response and demand for such training centres has increased. Women in particular are benefitting greatly. From August 2010, when the programme was launched, till March 2013, more than eight lakh people were trained. Of these over 4,80,000 were women.[12] This means that about 60 per cent of those trained were women. Popular courses at KVKs include computer fundamental, tally software, basic welding, electric wireman, beauty-parlour, make-up artist, hair dresser, other beautician related courses, garment stitching, hand embroidery, domestic appliance repairing, mobile repairing, plumbing, motor driving among others.

Superior Technology Centres have been started to meet the demand of emerging or potential sectors. The aim is to provide readymade manpower to emerging industries. Areas identified are chemicals, automobiles, solar photo voltaic electrician and environment technology. Modern laboratories have been established in 20 ITIs with the annual capacity of about 11,000.

E-MPower programme has been started to train at least 1,000 people in every *taluka* per year in computer and information technology. The certification is being referred to as Electronic Manpower or eMPower. The 40-hour duration course is to run in every *taluka*. Any person who has studied till fifth standard can get admission by paying a nominal fee of Rs 50 only. The certificate is awarded jointly by the GCVT and Microsoft.

All the *talukas* have an ITI (Industrial Training Institutes). That these institutes are serving their purpose is testified by the fact that their number has steadily increased from 275 in 2001 to 1054 in 2012. The decision to give weight to ITI training in admission to graduation course even without passing class XII has made the training more attractive. More than 50 per cent of the ITIs are running on PPP model.

The government has allowed industries or their associations to start ITI extension training centres with full or partial support from the government. This has encouraged industries to train manpower of their choice. Even otherwise, many private companies have involved themselves in training at these ITIs to get the desired manpower.

***

Statue of Unity

*Manpower without Unity is not a strength unless it
is harmonised and united properly, then it becomes
a spiritual power.*

—Sardar Vallabhbhai Patel

India will soon make its mark on the world map with the tallest statue in the world—a feat that is likely to make every Indian proud. The site for this statue would be Gujarat, thanks to the innovative thinking of Chief Minister Narendra Modi. Modi always dreams big and catches the public imagination with his vision. This time, the vision is to construct the tallest statue called the 'Statue of Unity' in memory of the Iron Man of India, Sardar Vallabhbhai Patel. The best part is that all Indians will get a chance to participate in the creation of this world record. The foundation stone for this huge structure was laid on 31 October 2013.

The statue will be 182 m tall standing over a base of 58 m, making it total of 240 m. The statue is to be built at Kevadia about 200 km from Ahmedabad and only 3.5 km away from Sardar Sarovar Dam. This will stand in the Sadhu-Bet Island which has a small hillock on the course of river Narmada between the Satpura and the Vindhyachal Ranges.

The statue will be placed on this hillock and a complete water body will be created around the statue. One would be able to move up inside the statue using a lift and look at the Sardar Sarovar Dam through the eyes of Sardar Patel. Hasmukhbhai, the guide at Kevadia, was extremely excited about this project as it would ensure manyfold increase in tourist inflows and his income. He was certain that the work would be over in a year because "Narendrabhai works to a target."[1]

Over 700 tonnes of agricultural iron implements are to be collected from over 6.5 lakh odd villages across the country. The project is being spearheaded by Sardar Vallabhbhai Patel Rashtriya Ekta Trust headed by Modi.[2] These iron implements will be melted and used to make the statue. Nearly 5,000 tonnes of steel will be needed for the Rs 2,000-crore project titled *"Ek Bharat, Shresth Bharat".*[3]

The Statue of Unity will remind generations about the life and times of the great man. It will be taller than the statue of Buddha at the Spring Temple, Lushan Country, Henan, China (153 m); Ushiku Daibutsu, Ibaraki prefecture, Japan (120 m); Statue of Liberty, New York City, US (93 m), the Motherland Calls, Volgograd, Russia (85 m) and Christ the Redeemer, Rio de Janeiro, Brazil (39.6 m).

On 28 December 2013, Modi flagged off 1,000 trucks with three lakh empty kit boxes to collect used iron implements and soil from all villages for the gigantic statue. These boxes were fitted with micro chips that would help the centralised headquarters to track the movement of these boxes.

About two crore citizens are supposed to sign a petition when the trucks move from one village to another. This will make the world's longest banner with the message of good governance. Also, school students will participate in essay writing competition to be held at 1.75 lakh schools during this period.[4]

The State government has already prepared the ground for the success of this programme. The latest was the 'Run for Unity' marathon organised all across the country on 15 December 2013, the death anniversary of Sardar Patel. The BJP organised such marathons at 565 places across the country to highlight the number of princely states Sardar Patel integrated into the Union of India. About 4,000 people participated in Mysore[5] whereas the number in Rajasthan was about 20,000.[6] The response was overwhelming and about five million participated across the county.[7]

Since this is a state government project, officials from the state go to various places to monitor collection of old iron pieces from various villages. They are noted to take the help of NGOs and village committees to mobilise farmers to donate the iron pieces. Farmers are being encouraged to donate a piece of used sickle or plough.

The Statue of Unity will be a symbol of India's unity. It was Sardar Vallabhbhai Patel who brought the country together. This not much sung architect of independent India made 565 princely states merge with the Union of India and thus united the country. Patel's grit, determination and strategic thinking amazed even his critics.

There is a genuine feeling in the country, where symbols play an important role, that Patel has not been given his due. His contribution and ideals have been consigned to ceremonial observance, largely because the political leadership dominated by the Congress never thought of resurrecting the glorious past of leaders other than those from the Gandhi-Nehru family. This is the theme Modi has been articulating everywhere. The idea to construct this statue to honour that great leader of the masses came to him in 2010.

Modi has also outlined the steps to translate this vision into reality through a step by step movement on the project that includes concept design, site development, collection of iron, etc. The project spread over 19,500 square metre will be completed in 168 weeks. The statue will be constructed in 48 weeks.

***

BJP's Trump Card: PM Candidate Modi

Na dainyam, na palayanam (Will neither plead nor flee)
—Atal Bihari Vajpayee

Goa has proved lucky for Narendra Modi. When everyone thought that his days were over, since Prime Minister Atal Bihari Vajpayee and others were mulling over Modi's resignation to save the NDA government's image, the Goa national executive gave a new lease of life to him. This was in 2002 when the entire national executive almost shouted in one voice that Modi could not be sacrificed at the altar of secularism.

When the national executive met in Goa in June 2013, everyone, from the media to the party leaders and millions of Modi's fans, waited eagerly for the outcome. Riding successfully on three election victories, Modi was inching closer to play a larger role at the national level. He had outgrown Gujarat and the cadre, in particular, wanted to see him lead the BJP's charge at the national level.

The excitement at the Goa meeting was palpable since everyone wanted to know if the BJP would play the Modi trump card in 2014 Lok Sabha polls. State health minister and national executive member Laxmikant Parsekar raised the expectation in the BJP saying "a signal may go out at executive meet that Modi may be BJP's prime ministerial candidate". He also admitted that there was some truth in the impression that Goa has been lucky for Modi. The party's national spokesperson Syed Shahnawaz Hussain made it clear that the party leadership was under tremendous pressure from its workers to ask Modi to lead from the front. "We cannot ignore the party workers' expectations", he said on the final day of the executive meeting.

Within hours of that the news was already out since Rajnath Singh announced the decision to the national executive on 9 June 2013. The meeting ended at 2 pm and the party president came out along with Arun Jaitley, Sushma Swaraj, Venkaiah Naidu and others, and declared that Modi would be heading the party's campaign committee for the Lok Sabha polls 2014.

"I have an important (piece of) information to share. All political parties take elections as their biggest challenge and so do we. We will move ahead with the resolve of victory. Today, I have appointed Gujarat Chief Minister Narendra Modi as chairman of the national election committee. This decision has been on the basis of unanimity."[2]

The architect of the BJP's rise to power at the centre in 1990s, LK Advani, was conspicuous by his absence. The official position stated that he was unwell. Party insiders knew that he was unhappy since he considered that everything was being done in haste.

RSS Chief Mohan Bhagwat had clearly instructed that Modi must be made chairman of the campaign committee. RSS joint general secretary in-charge for the BJP, Suresh Soni, was present at the executive meeting. He prevailed over other BJP leaders and Rajnath Singh saw merit in the proposal.[3] Based on its feedback, the RSS had already concluded that only Modi could revive the sagging fortunes of the BJP.

***

The first meeting Modi addressed after his elevation was that of party workers in Goa. He thanked Rajnath Singh for not only giving him responsibility of the new work but also for giving him a big honour in the eyes of party workers and the people in general. Rajnath Singh spoke before Modi and asked him to sit so that he would speak last.

Modi understood the significance: "Rajnathji stood to speak and asked me to sit. People from outside cannot understand this value. People don't do this when they have such a post. They do it when they have a big heart. He has shown large-heartedness. And this is what gives us the strength to work day and night." He reminded everyone that Goa gave him its blessing and he went on to work in Gujarat which "is competing with China". This time the blessings of Goa would make him work harder and make the party reach new heights of success.[4]

Advani apparently calculated that the move would alienate the BJP's allies. From his experience, he could say that while the euphoria was good, it would take a lot of effort to transform support into votes. The allies would be crucial, he thought. For the first time since formation of the BJP, he had missed the executive meeting. The party officially cited bad health as the reason for his absence.

But Advani has always been a man of conscience. He thought he must make his position clear. A day after the national executive meeting concluded, he wrote a one-page letter to Rajnath Singh. The letter said:

"All my life I have found working for the Jana Sangh and the Bharatiya Janata Party a matter of great pride and endless satisfaction for myself. For some time, I have been finding it difficult to reconcile either with the current functioning of the party, or the direction in which it is going. I no longer have the feeling that this is the same idealistic party created by Dr Mookerji, Pandit Deendayalji, Nanaji and Vajpayeeji, whose sole concern was the country and its people. Most leaders of ours are now concerned just with their personal agendas. I have decided, therefore, to resign from the three main forums of the party, namely, the National Executive, Parliamentary Board and the Election Committee. This may be regarded as my resignation letter."[5]

Rajnath Singh rejected the resignation instantly. Sushma Swaraj expressed confidence that Advani would be persuaded to withdraw the resignation. Sharad Yadav said he could not imagine the BJP without Vajpayee and Advani. Shiv Sena's Udhav Thackeray said that without Advani the NDA would break.

Advani clarified to those leaders who met him that he would not withdraw his resignation. He told Rajnath Singh that he had no problems with Modi but the manner in which events had unfolded. Advani repeatedly suggested that while Modi could head the central election committee for the Lok Sabha, Nitin Gadkari could lead another election management committee to supervise assembly elections in states.[6]

The BJP parliamentary board that met the same day rejected Advani's resignation. "We have rejected Advani's resignation unanimously. As the party president, I would not accept the resignation letter at any cost... All parliamentary board members were consulted on phone and personally. All members have requested Advani to take back his resignation. He is our guide, this role belongs to him."[7]

Narendra Modi spoke to Advani over the phone and requested him to withdraw his resignation. Modi's tweet said, "Had a detailed conversation with Advaniji on phone. Urged him to change his decision. I hope he will not disappoint lakhs of *karyakartas*."

The party succeeded and the next day Advani withdrew his resignation. The RSS intervened and Advani relented. "Mohan Bhagwat (RSS chief) has asked him to accept the parliamentary board decision and continue to guide the party. Advaniji has accepted his advice," Rajnath Singh said.[8] Bhagwat had spoken to Advani on the phone.

Modi heaved a sigh of relief and tweeted: "I had said yesterday that Advaniji will not disappoint lakhs of *karyakartas*. Today, I wholeheartedly welcome his decision." Modi came to Delhi on 18 June and met Advani at the latter's residence and spent about an hour with him.

During the Gujarat Gaurav Yatra in 2002, when the author had asked Modi if he needed Advani and Vajpayee for the campaign, Modi had come out of his motorised *rath* and said "Look at these photographs (while pointing to the images of Advani and Vajpayee). They are our most respected leaders. I cannot imagine doing anything without their blessings."

The move to make Modi the campaign committee chief was a clever ploy of the RSS to elevate the Gujarat chief minister without hurting the NDA coalition. The JDU had already raised its concerns with Advani. The Shiv Sena had also expressed some reservations.[9]

Modi's elevation had not happened overnight. Even before results of the 2012 assembly polls, people had started speaking about the need for Modi to lead the party's Lok Sabha election campaign in 2014.

Noted criminal lawyer and senior BJP leader Ram Jethmalani had sounded the bugle to make Modi the PM candidate as early as October 2012. In a letter to then party president Nitin Gadkari, Jethmalani stressed that the party must declare its prime ministerial candidate and he named Modi as the best candidate:

"I do not think that the choice is difficult... I would want Narendra Modi whose integrity and administrative ability are not in doubt," he said in the two-page letter.[10] During an election visit to Vadodara, Sushma Swaraj had declared that "Modi is a competent and proper leader to be the prime minister of India".[11] It was, therefore, natural that after the victory the issue would be debated intensely.

Modi's third successive victory in Gujarat raised his stature manyfold. Then Karnataka Chief Minister Jagdish Shettar said that the outcome showed "a new leader who can guide the nation is emerging". He described this as a victory for "exceptional development politics" pursued by Modi.[12] When Modi was addressing a rally of his supporters on the victory day, voices from the crowd could be heard saying that he should go to Delhi and play a bigger role.

The observations of these leaders were not mere statements but were reflections of the groundswell of support that Modi was gaining. A survey in January 2013 said that Gujarat chief minister was the country's most favourite prime ministerial candidate with 48 per cent votes, trailed by Rahul Gandhi at 18 per cent and Dr Manmohan Singh at 7 per cent. Rahul Gandhi had not become the number two in the Congress at the time of the survey.[13]

A few days after the survey, Jethmalani declared Modi to be the best man for the prime minister's job. He also declared Modi to be "100 per cent secular".[14]

Earlier, senior leader Yashwant Sinha had said, "I have no doubt in my mind that if we project Narendra Modi, there will be immense impact on the voters and the BJP will win....[15] Common people and party activists are strongly demanding that the BJP name Narendra Modi as its prime ministerial candidate... The party has to decide on this but such is the people's opinion."[16] Later, he said he was confident that Modi would be the country's next Prime Minister.

To set speculation to rest since this was embarrassing the party and forcing the chain of events, Rajnath Singh appealed to all party leaders not to speak on the issue. "I want to humbly appeal to BJP workers and leaders that there should be no statement from them on who will be the candidate for the prime minister's post. As I have said earlier, the BJP convention is that any decision on the chief ministerial or prime ministerial candidate is taken by the central parliamentary board."[17]

However, Rajnath's gag order could not quell the pitch. Three leaders—Maneka Gandhi, CP Thakur and Shatrughan Sinha, voiced their support for Modi the same day. Maneka said, "I think Modiji will become a good prime minister. He is good. He will run the government nicely." Senior BJP leader from Bihar CP Thakur said, "We have been taking name of only one person for the prime minister's post. There is no confusion in our mind." Shatrughan Sinha said, "Rajnath Singh has himself said that he (Modi) is a very popular leader of the country... If the decision about right leader is taken at the right time, then you will win the bet anyway."[18]

Modi was gradually being made part of Rajnath Singh's new team to recognise his growing importance. When the new party president constituted his team on 31 March 2013, he had inducted Modi as a member of the top decision making body of the party—the central parliamentary board. Also, he was made a member of the party's central election committee headed by Rajnath Singh.

However, speculation about Modi's final ascendancy was still not put to rest. And as BJP leaders continued to discuss and debate the possibility of his elevation to the top job, the nation got an opportunity to rate both Congress vice president Rahul Gandi and Narendra Modi, when they addressed meetings in Delhi within a gap of four days. Rahul addressed a meeting of the CII on 4 April 2013 and Modi addressed a meeting organised by FICCI's Women's chapter on 8 April.

It was clear to everyone that Modi demonstrated maturity backed by years of experience. The entire media went the whole hog comparing the two speeches and discussed the possibility of the Lok Sabha election being a contest between the leadership of Rahul Gandhi and Narendra Modi. The media had already projected Modi to be the BJP's face.

Rahul's speech became famous for giving the "beehive" analogy while comparing India with China. He said his advisors had told him not to get into the clichéd comparison between India and China: "I don't listen to them. Reason why I don't listen to them is because of my experience. Think about it. China applies power by hand; they are a manufacturing behemoth. India, on the other hand, applies people's power—the power of the mind. Forget the elephant and dragon analogy. India is the power of the beehive."[19]

Four days later when Modi made his speech at the FICCI, he tried to turn the tables on Rahul. He took strong objection to India being compared to a "beehive" and said that while India may be a beehive for Rahul Gandhi "but for us the country is our mother". Modi said he was shocked to hear Rahul Gandhi think of India in such a manner. Back in Ahmedabad, two days after Rahul's speech, Modi had ripped apart Rahul's comment on the 33rd foundation day of the BJP: "I happened to listen to a speech by a Congress leader two days back, whose words are considered to be very important for that party. I was deeply shocked and pained when he compared India to a beehive.... For you, this might be a beehive but for us this country is our mother. Hundred crore people of this country are our brothers and sisters. This is a sacred land of saints and seers. Atal Bihari Vajpayee used to say every particle of this land is Lord Shankar for us. Friends from Congress, please do not insult our country. If you do not understand the language of people of India, go and learn from somewhere. But due to your ignorance, do not try to destroy the culture and tradition of this country."[20]

Celebration of the BJP's foundation day in Ahmedabad on 6 April was another landmark. The BJP follows the practice of celebrating the foundation day at the national headquarters in Delhi and also at state headquarters. This time, Modi made a big show. Sardar Patel Stadium in Ahmedabad was packed to its capacity of 55,000 people. Party President Rajnath Singh was the special guest. Modi had organised a BJP *karyakarta sammelan* (conference of workers).

The highlight of the meeting, besides attack on Rahul Gandhi, was the vow he asked party workers to take while holding candles in their hands. The vow was to resolve to work hard to relieve people of their hardships. "On the banks of river Sabarmati, in presence of this pure light, we resolve to make India the greatest... In the leadership of BJP, we will establish a government that will work for continuous development of the country."

The bonhomie between Modi and Rajnath Singh was clear when the party president jumped the protocol and spoke before the chief minister. He justified this saying that he was doing so in the honour of "India's most popular Chief Minister Narendra Modi, who hails from the state of India's Iron Man Sardar Patel, the man who united the country."[21]

While praising Modi's leadership, the BJP president said, "I am not praising him because I am president of the BJP. The entire world accepts this reality that it is a model state of development... He is incorruptible. I am not alone in saying this and my remarks should not be taken wrongly, everybody says this."[22]

Three opinion polls conducted independently by three different groups gave one clear message that if the BJP wanted to come within striking distance of power in 2014, it must project Modi as its prime ministerial candidate. AC Nielsen did it for *ABP News*, C-Voter for *Headlines Today*, and GFK for *CNN-IBN*. These surveys helped assess the nation's mood.

CNN-IBN poll showed that urban voters favoured Modi as the PM candidate. He scored 38 per cent support as against 13 per cent for Dr Manmohan Singh and 14 per cent for Rahul Gandhi. *ABP News* put the figure as 36 per cent for Modi, 13 per cent for Rahul and 12 per cent for Dr Manmohan Singh. The *Headlines Today* tried to calculate the difference in the impact Modi could bring. With him, the NDA would get a five percentage additional vote share and 41 more Lok Sabha seats. It showed the BJP winning 29 Lok Sabha seats in Uttar Pradesh and 18 in Bihar even if the JDU under Chief Minister Nitish Kumar left (Nitish was a part of the NDA at the time of the survey).

These polls depicted the mood of the nation. And the party backed by the RSS decided to do what was needed to end the uncertainty at the Goa meeting.

Modi's elevation to chairman of the campaign committee empowered him to formally plan the party's campaign and decide its strategy for 2014 Lok Sabha polls.

The Goa decision also meant that Modi would not be projected as the PM candidate for quite some time. This is the way Rajnath had put the RSS case before Advani. The RSS had also said that this would leave the PM race open, at least within the NDA.[23]

Within a week, the situation changed. Bihar Chief Minister Nitish Kumar snapped ties with the BJP over Modi, and the 17-year-old alliance came crumbling down amidst charges and counter charges. There were reports that the JDU had given time to the NDA till December 2013 to declare its candidate for the Prime Minister. What happened then to justify the withdrawal?

Even before Modi's elevation, Nitish had expressed his discomfiture with the BJP. At its national executive meeting in Delhi on 14 April,

2013. Nitish launched a scathing attack on the BJP and Modi: "The NDA's prime ministerial candidate should be someone who can keep the country together… The PM should be secular, believe in inclusive growth and take backward states along," he declared. A resolution passed at the meeting said that the person should have a secular image. Nitish took a dig at Modi's development model as well.[24]

He attacked Modi without naming him. He said a leader aspiring to be the PM should be such *"Jise topi bhi pahanna padega aur tika bhi lagana hoga"* (A leader can only be one who is comfortable with Islamic skull cap and Hindu *tika*). This remark from Nitish came amidst reports that Modi had refused to wear skull cap during his Sadbhavna mission fast sometime back.

The BJP which had been guarded on giving a response decided to act tough. Within hours, the party came out with a written statement that was read out by its spokesperson Nirmala Sitharaman: "The need of the hour is to defeat the non-performing and corrupt UPA… The BJP expects allies to keep their main focus on that. It is unfortunate if they concentrate their energies on our chief ministers and dilute the focus of removing the UPA… We reject all unfounded references against Shri Narendra Modi."

Next day, the BJP came out with a stronger criticism against Nitish Kumar. Party spokesperson Meenakshi Lekhi said that Kumar was nobody to give a certificate of secularism to Modi.[25] BJP leaders from Bihar met Rajnath Singh and said that it was difficult to keep the alliance going.

Thus, when Nitish withdrew from the NDA, the BJP was not very surprised, although the reason was not enough provocation. The JDU's carefully drafted statement while withdrawing from the NDA gave more provocation:

"The Goa announcement of the chairmanship of the electoral campaign committee of the BJP has filled all of us with deep apprehensions about the future. It has left not a shadow of doubt that this is a mere ceremonial prelude to his [Mr Modi's] nomination as prime ministerial candidate. All efforts within the BJP to suggest care and moderation in the process were smothered with the authoritarian cult and imperious disdain. Needless to say that these developments do not augur well for the health of our secular and democratic polity…"[26] It further said, "The BJP's total disregard and the ominous recent development therefore compels the JDU to forthwith terminate and sever its present alliance with the BJP."[27]

The BJP countered this by releasing the speech of Nitish Kumar in 2003 in which he had praised Modi. In that speech Nitish had said, "I am certain that Narendrabhai will not be confined to Gujarat for long and the country will get the benefits of his services."[28] The BJP questioned the reason for the about turn.

Nitish gave his feeble defence: "When I used to visit other states as a railway minister, those speeches were never political. It's part of the protocol to praise the host state and not to speak against them."[29]

But Nitish's was never critical of Modi, not even when the images of riots were fresh. "The people of Gujarat were aggrieved with the kind of image painted outside the state and hence reacted in this way," Railway Minister Nitish Kumar had said while reacting to the BJP's victory in Gujarat in December 2002.[30] When Union Minister Ramvilas Paswan resigned from the NDA citing Gujarat riots as the reason, Nitish lambasted him and termed him an 'opportunist' who was trying to join Lalu Prasad Yadav through the Congress. "…But Paswan's decision had nothing to do with Gujarat. The Gujarat violence has been taking place for the last two months," Kumar said.[31] When the UC Banerjee committee submitted its report, Nitish described the report as a "political stunt": "It is a political stunt but they (the Centre) should know that they cannot take advantage of the Gujarat riots again and again."[32] How could Modi get transformed into a villain with the progress of time? Only Nitish Kumar would be able to explain.

The BJP described Nitish's act as the biggest betrayal in political history. Two days after they parted ways, workers of both the BJP and the JDU clashed on the streets of Patna during the Bihar bandh organised by the former as a part of Vishwasghat Divas (betrayal day).

In July 2013, Modi addressed more than 1,500 select workers of Bihar, from panchayat to state level through tele-links. He used audio bridge communication technology to link to them from Gandhinagar. BJP secretary Rameshwar Chaurasia said that the purpose was to guide ordinary BJP workers of the state who may not get a chance to talk to Modi directly. Of these, 500 workers were from Patna and the rest were from different parts of Bihar.

Modi used this occasion to launch a scathing attack on Nitish Kumar saying that people would not forgive those who "betrayed" the BJP. "There is a 1974-like anti-Congress wave prevailing in the country. The mandate of the people of Bihar was for the NDA. Those who betrayed the people's mandate will be taught a lesson."[33]

Bihar BJP was very impressed with Modi's public interactions. His tele-link address to workers had enthused them for a new beginning. They felt even happier after his rally in Hyderabad on 11 August that showed that the Gujarat chief minister had massive appeal across the country. His Independence Day speech at Bhuj—where he challenged the prime minister to a debate on governance saying the "nation is restless for change"—created a new aura about Modi. He had challenged the prime minister (an economist) for a debate on development—something that had never happened before.[34]

There were some sceptics who doubted if Modi's appeal was a pan-Indian phenomenon. India cannot be won merely on support from some states of north India. The answer was available at the Hyderabad rally where Modi used US President Barack Obama's style to connect with the youth. This was the first rally where people bought entry tickets to listen to any political leader. The money collected was contributed to the Uttarakhand flood relief. When he concluded his speech, Modi made the crowd chant with him "Yes We Can…Yes We Will!" He had achieved that rare connect with the youth most leaders long for.

He spoke about issues connecting youth such as intense nationalism wedded to the constitution. While talking about what kind of government he wanted, he said, "Its only religion should be 'India first', its mantra should be the Constitution, its belief should be '*Bharat Bhakti*', its power should be people's power and its worship should be the welfare of 125 crore people." He received thunderous applause from the crowd that was mostly young. The rally was termed 'Youth Conclave'.[35]

On the eve of Independence Day, Modi gave a big challenge to the UPA government by saying that on the Independence day, the nation would compare his speeches with those of the prime minister. "On one hand, there will be a series of promises, whereas on the other, there will be the account of the work done. On one side, there will be *nirasha* (despair) and on the other side *asha* (hope)."[36]

This prompted author Chetan Bhagat to tweet: "All the best to respected PM tomo (tomorrow) for his speech. As they say, before entrance exams: sleep early, be confident, and take extra pencils."

Modi articulated the frustration of a common man when he said people were desperate for a new ray of hope. They wanted a corruption-free government and a visionary government. "The country got independence but have we achieved true independence? We need to change our thought to gain true independence."

Criticising Dr Manmohan Singh for remembering only one family in his speech he said, "PM in his speech has unfortunately remembered only one family... Would it not have been befitting to remember Sardar Patel or Lal Bahadur Shastri? There should have been no politics in your speech... Lal Bahadur Shastri and Sardar Patel are people from your own party."

Talking further on development, Modi challenged the Prime Minister's team to have a competition of development between Gujarat and Delhi.

The nation watched Modi live. Even before he was pronounced the BJP's prime ministerial candidate, he had taken the UPA by the horns. He made fun of Dr Singh for saying "*aur faasla tay karna hai*" (we have to travel more distance). Modi asked "*Kaunsa faasla ab?*" (What more distance)? He pointed out that this was Dr Singh's last Independence Day speech.[37]

"When we are celebrating the Independence Day, let us promise that we will free the nation from the clutches of corruption. Just the way we attained the freedom from the British, we will free the nation from inflation, from old narrow-minded thinking and from the state of this trust deficit. We will build the bridge of trust and not allow the trust deficit to be part of India for long. Each one has lost faith, but we will work towards building the trust again."[38]

Both the Independence Day speech and the Hyderabad rally further testified to Modi's popularity. The Bihar unit of the party got so emboldened that the state executive meeting in Gaya passed a resolution requesting the central parliamentary board to announce Modi as the BJP's PM candidate (17 August). In doing so, the Bihar unit became the first state to make such a demand. They were bubbling with excitement at the prospect of an independent existence in Bihar. Alliance politics had not allowed the party to flex its muscles. Sushil Kumar Modi, who was deputy chief minister of Bihar till two months back, tweeted: "BJP state executive unanimously passed a resolution urging BJP parliamentary board to declare urgently NAMO as PM candidate." His second tweet was: "Bihar BJP is the fst (first) state to pass such resolution in favour of NAMO. Other states should follow."

Before other state units could catch up and emulate the example of Bihar, Rajnath Singh passed a gag order to state units saying that they should not pass any such resolution and that a decision on the issue would be taken after consulting all top leaders. Singh's writ came at a meeting of the Central Election Committee, state unit presidents and organisation general secretaries.[39]

Meanwhile, national BJP leaders debated the ifs and buts of projecting Modi as the PM candidate. The RSS was keen that an announcement be made as soon as possible to gain the advantage of being the first to declare the PM candidate. There was no coalition pressure since the JDU had already walked out. The Shiv Sena had clarified that they would support Modi.[40] The Shiromani Akali Dal president Sukhbir Singh Badal clarified that he had no objections to Modi's projection.[41] The Indian National Lok Dal (INLD) chief Om Prakash Chautala also declared that he would support Modi as prime Minister even if there was no alliance with the BJP.[42] When Modi gave a call to TDP Chief N Chandrababu Naidu at the Hyderabad rally to join hands with the BJP in order to throw out the Congress, Naidu did not react adversely even as he did not accept the bait. This opened the possibility for talks.[43]

Most allies or likely friends had, therefore, come around to supporting Modi. Everyone knew that with Modi getting more and more public support, more allies would join in due course. On 5 September, Modi surprised everyone by saying that serving the people of his state until 2017 was his priority. "I never see such dreams (of becoming PM), nor am I going to see such dreams. People of Gujarat have given me the mandate to serve them till 2017 and I have to do this with full strength," he said at a Teacher's Day function in Gandhinagar.

"Those who dream of becoming something end up destroying themselves. One should not dream of becoming something, but one should dream of doing something," he said in response to a query from a student. The student had asked him if he would continue to meet them if he became the prime minister after the 2014 elections.[44]

This clearly demonstrated that Modi was unhappy with the controversy in the party over whether or not he should be declared the BJP's prime ministerial candidate. He had never asked for being projected. The demand had come from the rank and file, but an impression was gaining that Modi was pushing himself. The RSS was putting pressure on the party to do so as early as September.

Swami Ramdev, the yoga guru, who has a network of his organisation almost everywhere in the country, announced on 6 September that he would not support the BJP if it did not make Narendra Modi its prime ministerial candidate.[45]

The RSS and its mass-based affiliates met in Delhi on 8-9 September to discuss their feedback about public mood. Members of BJP's parliamentary board were also invited. Narendra Modi attended the meeting only briefly because of his prior commitment.[46] The task was to enable the BJP's leadership to understand the mood of the people and prepare all organisations for Lok Sabha elections with far greater clarity.

On 7 September, a day before the meeting, the RSS said that it had apprised BJP of its opinion on projecting the prime ministerial face. RSS spokesperson M G Vaidya said, "It is for the BJP to decide who should it project and when." Two days later, while briefing on deliberations at the RSS meeting, he said, "There was no dilemma visible (inside the meeting), it may be outside." He was replying to a question whether the BJP would face a dilemma on Modi.[47]

Even before the RSS meeting, senior RSS leaders tried to blunt opposition to Modi. Suresh Bhaiyaji Joshi met Advani and Sushma Swaraj on 1 September at Advani's residence. Rajnath Singh was also present.[48] He reportedly told them that the party should not delay the appointment of Modi. On 5 September, Advani hosted a dinner for

RSS chief Mohan Bhagwat. Bhagwat wanted to apprise them about the need to respond to the call of most RSS workers who wanted Modi named as PM candidate.[49]

After the meeting, the only point of contention was when to declare Modi's name. While Advani and Sushma wanted that the party should wait till the results of the assembly elections were over, Bhagwat was keen that it be announced earlier. It is after these preliminary meetings of top BJP and RSS leaders that the two-day meeting began on 8 September.

It was after completing the necessary groundwork that the RSS asked Rajnath Singh to complete the formality of naming Modi as the PM candidate without further delay. However, the RSS was wary of adverse fallout if a miffed Advani was not mollified. On 10 September, the RSS sent former BJP president Nitin Gadkari to Advani's residence to persuade him to relent.[50] Gadkari argued with Advani that he should propose Modi's name. Advani told him that he had no problem in proposing Modi's name but he wanted to do the same after the assembly elections.[51]

RSS spokesperson Ram Madhav said on 10 September: "The country wants a change and we also realise it. During the two-day meeting between RSS and the BJP, this issue came up and it has been conveyed to the leadership in the party. Now, the decision has to be taken by them but from our side the message is clear."[52]

The month of *Pitri Paksha* (the fortnight to remember one's ancestors, considered inauspicious according to Hindu calendar) was to start from 20 September and was to last till 4 October. And after that would start *Navratra*. This clearly meant that they would then have to wait till the end of October. Clearly, the RSS was in no mood to wait for so long.[53]

Rajnath Singh met Advani on 11 September but there was no positive result. Advani was surprised by the haste with which the party was working. He wanted them to wait for some more time. Later, Rajnath Singh consulted other members of the parliamentary board in an attempt to build a consensus. His was a very difficult task. He could not have defied the RSS but he could not have gone against Advani, his mentor. And deep within, he was also convinced that the RSS was correct in its assessment.

Advani's reluctance was not going down well with other BJP leader.

His most trusted person from Bihar, Sushil Kumar Modi, who owed his rise to Advani and former BJP ideologue Govindacharya, questioned the patriarch. Advani had always encouraged others to speak their minds and Sushil Modi exercised this option against his mentor. One could understand the conflict in the party over the issue. His tweet criticised Advani for failing to understand public sentiment. "Advaniji has failed to gauge the public mood. Advaniji himself declared Atalji as PM candidate; now also he could have done the same for Namo." He appealed to Advani to respect the public sentiment.[54]

Rajnath Singh had to hurry. A delay in announcement could create a difficult situation. He also wanted to ensure that the respect Advani commanded should not be undermined at any cost. He announced that he would hold the much-awaited meeting of the central parliamentary board the next day, that is, on 13 September.

Even on the last day, BJP leaders tried to placate Advani. Among those who met him, either individually or in a group, included Nitin Gadkari, general secretary Murlidhar Rao and Sushma Swaraj. Rajnath Singh also met him on the day of the meeting. Advani told him that he would think about attending the meeting to explain his point.

At the last moment, Advani decided to skip the parliamentary board meeting that took place late in the evening. Instead, he sent a letter explaining the reason for his absence. The two-paragraph-letter said:

"This afternoon when you had come to my residence to inform me about the Parliamentary Board meeting, I had said something about my anguish as also my disappointment over your style of functioning. I had told you that I will think whether I should share my thoughts with the other board members or not. Now I have decided that it is better that I do not attend today's meeting."[55]

The meeting started at 6:05 pm. Except Advani and an ailing Vajpayee, all other members of the parliamentary board—Murli Manohar Joshi, Venkaiah Naidu, Nitin Gadkari, Sushma Swaraj, Arun Jaitley, Narendra Modi, Ananth Kumar, Thawarchand Gehlot and Ram Lal—were present. Within half an hour, the Board took the decision to anoint Modi as the prime ministerial candidate for 2014 Lok Sabha polls. Modi had joined the meeting towards the fag end so that others could discuss the issue freely.

Flanked by Sushma Swaraj on his right and Rajnath Singh on his left, Modi addressed the media and thanked the party and senior leaders for reposing faith in him. On Rajnath's left was Arun Jaitley and on Sushma's right were Nitin Gadkari and Venkaiah Naidu. Modi embraced Rajnath and touched Sushma Swaraj's feet.

A humbled and overwhelmed Modi said, "For several years as a *karyakarta*, I have undertaken several tasks and all the strength that I have got has gone in service of the nation. The party has given a big task to me, someone who came from a small family. The party has been built by the hard work of Atalji and Advaniji and the blessings of the *karyakartas* will give us success...In 2014, we hope the country will vote against corruption, price rise and will support the BJP for suraj (good governance) and development... I thank NDA allies for their blessings."

BJP President Rajnath Singh justified the decision: "The BJP has a tradition to declare the PM candidate before Lok Sabha elections and I called for a parliamentary board meeting to discuss this. The board has decided to project Narendra Modi as the prime ministerial candidate. We have taken this decision seeing the mood of the nation and the views of the *karyakartas*." He clarified that he had contacted presidents of alliance parties of the NDA and they had all agreed with the decision.

Arun Jaitley later explained the decision in realistic political terms: "First, elections are really contested to be won. Therefore, you put your best foot in front. And all surveys and opinion polls have shown that he has a very large popularity in this country. There was a criticism whether the BJP was not able to decide on the leader. I think this is the right time. We have a six-month run-up to the general elections... It was a winning decision which the party has consciously taken..."

Jaitley conceded the presence of an alternative view in the party but held that the rank and file of supporting constituencies could not be defied. "The groundswell was that we take the decision now... We had the choice between postponing the decision and taking the winning decision and we have taken the winning decision... The BJP's assessment is that the stronger the BJP emerges the stronger will be the NDA... The chemistry on the ground is changing and the analyst will have to ultimately analyse that the arithmetic will depend on the changed chemistry..."

This has also been a fact privately argued by almost everyone in the BJP that the party has been consistently losing its support base in successive Lok Sabha elections. And the Congress has been gaining. Till 1991, the Congress vote share of the valid votes hovered in the range of 35 per cent plus. In 1991 Lok Sabha elections, the BJP for the first time crossed the three figure mark and won 120 seats and polled 20.11 per cent valid votes. In 1996, the party polled 20.29 per cent votes and won 161 seats and emerged as the single largest party in the Lok Sabha. The Congress with 28.80 per cent won only 140 seats.

In 1998, the BJP polled 25.59 per cent votes and won from 182 seats. The Congress polled 25.82 per cent and won 141 seats. The next year, the BJP won the same number of seats 182 but polled 23.75 per cent votes, slightly less than 1998. The Congress polled 28.30 per cent and won 114 seats. In 2004, the BJP's vote declined to 22.16 per cent and it won 138 seats. The Congress polled 26.53 per cent votes and won 145. In 2009 Lok Sabha elections, the BJP deteriorated further to 18.80 per cent winning just 116 seats whereas the Congress improved to 28.55 and won 206 Lok Sabha seats.

Thus, the BJP has been consistently losing and the Congress has been consistently gaining. Something was needed to be done to at least take this vote percentage to the level of say 26-27 per cent. This can make the BJP win between 190 and 210 Lok Sabha seats. In the calculations of the entire Sangh Parivar, Modi is the only leader to make this happen by recharging the cadre, achieving that rare youth connectivity and attracting the middle class by his development vision. So, they have played their best card—'the winning decision'.

This was a rare moment in the BJP when Advani held an opinion different from his key second generation leaders. A correction was needed. And this came as a birthday gift to the PM candidate.

Advani hailed Gujarat government's feat of bringing 24-hour power supply to all villages in the state. "If the faith reposed in Mr Modi 'fructifies', good governance provided by BJP governments could be replicated across the country," he said at a rally in the Korba district of Chhattisgarh on 16 September 2013.

While dedicating the 500MW Hasdeo Thermal Power Expansion Project he said, "… If anyone has done this work (electrification in rural areas) first, it is my friend Narendra Modi."[56] There was no bitterness.

Modi's birthday on 17 September 2013 was a very simple affair. He began his day by visiting his 95-year-old mother, Hiraba, to seek her blessings. "I came for my mother's blessings. There is no bigger privilege than that." Later, he met Keshubhai and touched his feet. The BJP's Gujarat unit decided to launch a special drive to recruit about one lakh Muslim youth in the party. A large number of Muslim leaders met him to offer their good wishes.

Within a month, a more composed Advani endorsed Modi's candidature in an unqualified way. He said he would be happy if Narendra Modi became the prime minister of the country. He praised the unique quality of Modi in the following way: "I have seen this quality in Narendrabhai for a very long time; even before he came to power. He thinks about how to do things in a manner not done anywhere." Advani was in Modi's constituency Maninagar to inaugurate two river front parks launched in collaboration with the Institute of Infrastructure Research and Management.[57]

***

Modi and the Muslim Community

I learned that very often the most intolerant and narrow-minded people are the ones who congratulate themselves on their tolerance and open-mindedness.

—Christopher Hitchens, American author

"Mumbai 1993 was no less violent than Gujarat 2002. Can you tell which party's Chief Minister was ruling Maharashtra then?"

— Salim Khan

"Compared to the other states, Muslims in Gujarat are much happier."

— Maulana Mahmood Madani,
Jamiat Ulema-e-Hind

"I have travelled across states. In Gujarat, there are rich Muslims and poor Muslims. The economic status of poor Muslims in Gujarat has improved the most (during BJP rule). How can I deny that?"

— VV Augustine,
National Minority Commission

"It was childish to demand an apology. He should display in his character and through his actions that he cares for Muslims. If I see that Modi is making changes then I will back him."

— Maulana Kalbe Sadiq,
Shia cleric and renowned Islamic scholar

"We as civil society must acknowledge, applaud and reciprocate the gesture of Gujarat chief minister."

— Filmmaker Mahesh Bhatt

Why is Modi vilified so much? Is it merely because of Gujarat riots? Who gains by painting him as anti-Muslim? And the point to ponder over is whether a leader—who is spoken of as India's

PM-in-waiting—can afford to be non-inclusive by conviction? Who are these people who are hell bent on painting Modi a villain and why? Or, are these people trapped in their own self-orchestrated campaigns and can do nothing about it now?

While it is not ethical to compare riots since the loss of lives and the pain associated with them cannot be used to substantiate an argument, a comp.., 'son cannot be avoided. Those people who criticised Modi and his administration during the Gujarat riots of 2002 chose to stay mum when something similar happened in Muzaffarnagar (Uttar Pradesh) in 2013 right under the nose of Chief Minister Akhilesh Yadav. Some of these people had gone on to blame Modi as being an instigator of the riots but had nothing to say about the sheer inhuman behaviour of the UP government.

The Muzaffarnagar riots are considered the worst riots in India after the 1969 Gujarat riots since these spread to rural areas with untold brutality.[1] Congress leader Rashid Alvi described these riots as worse than the 2002 riots of Gujarat. The riots were limited to some pockets of Muzaffarnagar district but produced a devastating human tragedy, forcing innocent people to take shelter in relief camps.[2]

The Muzaffarnagar riots were confined to some villages. Imagine the situation if the same had happened across the entire state. Unlike in Gujarat, a chastened media this time knew how to report riots. In 2002, the electronic media was just beginning to learn to report and there was competition among a few journalists to become heroes while reporting on the riots rather than reporting them responsibly.

Chief of People's Democratic Party (PDP) Mehbooba Mufti spoke of the image this has produced: "The images of Gujarat riots shown on television are so strong that one cannot support him even when he is seen doing something good on the front of development."[3] She was appreciative of Modi's development initiative but held that his image, because of 24-hour television, had left "a permanent (negative) impression on the minds of Muslims".

Earlier, Mehbooba was in the news for praising Modi at a meeting of the National Integration Council (NIC) in 2011. Leader of Opposition Sushma Swaraj quoted Mehbooba's praise of Modi at the meeting. Mehbooba denied having praised Modi, but the transcript of the authentic tape did show that she was appreciative of the Gujarat chief minister for clearing the project of a Chennai-based Muslim businessman within 10 minutes of meeting him.[4]

This clearly shows that opposition to Modi is more political than substantive. In their heart of hearts the critics know that Modi cannot be faulted for what happened in Gujarat without blaming all other chief ministers who presided over riots in the country the same way.

The question arises, how does one deal with the image? Image is what the media paints. A verdict is delivered before trial and the subject's image gets irreparably damaged even without commission of the crime. Proprietors of two important newspapers from Gujarat came and met Modi and Arun Jaitley at the party's state office in Ahmedabad in 2002. They proposed that both newspapers must be given Rs 10 crore each if the party wanted positive coverage of the elections. Modi faced the Hobson's choice. If he disagreed, the media that commanded so much influence, would paint him in a negative light. If he agreed, he would be succumbing to the pressure tactics of the media and adopt unethical means. He discussed the issue with Jaitley, who was the in-charge for the state. "What should we do?" Modi asked Jaitley. The latter did not know what was to be done. Modi asked immediately whether the offer should be turned down.

Winning the elections was very important for the BJP and Modi. "I think we should tell them no," Modi persisted. Jaitley was upset at this blackmail by media. But wanted to test Modi's determination. He said, "But this would mean we will have to labour a lot." Modi's instant reply was: *"Mehnat se kaun darta hai? Aur hamare paas hai hi kya?"* (Who is scared of hard work? We do not have anything else to do). Modi went out, met the two proprietors and told them that the party would not pay as it would be compromising on its basic values. *"Aap apna kaam kijiye aur mujhe apna kaam karne dijiye"* (you do your work and let me do mine). The BJP rejected the request and attracted adverse publicity throughout the campaign.[5]

So, one creates an image of Modi as being anti-Muslim and a hard line Hindutva leader, and starts believing in this self-created image, which over a period of time becomes so strong that it does not allow facts to percolate down. Hitler's propaganda minister Joseph Goebbels—

who is credited with saying that "If you tell a lie big enough and keep repeating it, people will eventually come to believe it to be true"—also said that facts must be kept away because facts are antithetical to these lies. Facts have now come out destroying the lies one by one.

While his critics are caught in their own image trap, Modi has marched ahead. He had decided not to be cowed down by the propaganda against him and become the champion of India's development march in the footsteps of former Prime Minister Atal Bihari Vajpayee. Some feeble attempts are still being made to keep alive the ghost of Godhra; one such attempt was made by the editor of a leading English newspaper *The Hindu* who said that 2002 cannot go away easily.[6]

BJP spokesperson Prakash Javadekar presented some facts before the editor: "Of the total population in Gujarat, Muslims are less than 10 per cent. But 12 per cent of the police personnel in Gujarat are Muslims and 10 per cent of the government jobs are held by Muslims. The economic uplift of Muslims in Gujarat can be gauged from the fact that 18 per cent of the RTO registration of new two-wheelers is by Muslims. Their four-wheeler registration also is higher than their proportion in the overall population. On the contrary, West Bengal has the highest, 25 per cent, Muslim population, but even after 30 years of Left rule, only three per cent of Muslims are in government employment there."[7] The figures culled out from government records show that Muslims of Gujarat have decided to march forward.

It would not be wrong to say that there has been a Muslim turnaround for Modi's development agenda. The BJP won 12 out of 19 Muslim-dominated seats in 2012 assembly elections. Former Samajwadi Party leader and a journalist, Shahid Siddiqui, attributed this to the classical theory of division of Muslim votes among non-BJP parties allowing *The Hindu* candidate of the BJP to win. However, Asifa Khan, spokesperson of the Gujarat BJP, disagreed. She said that the vote was for development, education and health that were provided by Modi. These were more serious issues for Muslims than scoring brownie points.[8]

Siddiqui missed out that if Muslims had wanted they could have easily voted for the Congress since other parties in Gujarat are either marginal players or not strong enough to effect a division of vote. A large section of Muslims have started reaping the fruits of development and they do not want to risk the new found prosperity. Not all Hindus vote for the BJP and Siddiqui ignored this vital point as well. About 31 per cent Muslims voted for the BJP in the assembly elections of 2012.[9]

Asifa reeled out statistics to prove that six out of the eight constituencies with large Muslim population were won by the BJP despite the Congress fielding Muslim candidates. Nothing had prevented Muslims from voting against the BJP. As for example, Ahmedabad's Shahpur-Dariapur assembly with 60 per cent Muslim population was won by the Congress, but the Jamalpur-Kalupur assembly seat with 62 per cent Muslim population was won by the BJP. Muslim-dominated Juhapura-Sarkhej seat also went to the BJP. She also pointed out to the Vagra constituency (in her hometown Bharuch) which was a Congress bastion with a population of about 44 per cent Muslim voters. The Congress lost this seat to the BJP by a huge margin in spite of fielding a Muslim candidate. Similarly, Surat (West) and Surat Limbayat constituencies with large Muslim population were also won by the BJP. She was buoyant that the BJP's acceptability had increased "manyfold".

The success of 2012 assembly elections in terms of Muslim support would pale in comparison to the support the BJP got in 2013 municipal elections. Salaya, a small Muslim majority town in Jamnagar district (Saurashtra), threw out the Congress lock stock and barrel from a place that was considered its citadel for the last 25 years. The BJP won from all the 27 seats—24 of whom were Muslims. Women voted in large numbers. Salaya has 90 per cent Muslim population. Talking about other places, the BJP fielded 140 Muslim candidates in these elections, of whom 85 have won, said Gujarat minority morcha leader Sufi Mehbub Ali Bava.[10]

One of the prominent winners was Salem Mohammad Baghaad, who after meandering through the Samata Party (now called JD-U) and the Congress, finally embraced the BJP in 2010 and won the municipal seat on the BJP ticket. Till then, Salaya was notorious for smuggling and trafficking of contraband substances and had fallen off the development track.

"Honestly, joining the BJP was a tough decision for me... But I was confident about myself, about my decision. I knew if I joined hands with Modi, it will mean more benefits for the town and more development. *Mere ko khud ke oopar bahut confidence tha ki agar mere ko vikaas karna hai to bhajap mein ladoon to hi vikas karoon, baqi khali peeli mujhe ye nagarpalika lene ka koi matlab nahin tha* (I was confident that I could make the area prosper only by representing the BJP in the elections; otherwise, I had no fascination for becoming a councillor)."

After he won in 2010 from the BJP, Salaya began to pull in more funds for development. And this helped Baghaad and other Muslims who had come together to persuade others in the community to think about development.[11]

The BJP swept to power in six municipal corporations in the state in October 2010. Other than Jamnagar, where it won with a simple majority, the party won all the other five corporations with a two-third majority—Ahmedabad, Vadodara, Surat, Rajkot and Bhavnagar. The chief minister gave full credit to Muslims for supporting the BJP and asserted that the party had 'managed to win the hearts of Muslims'.

"More than 30 per cent of Muslims have voted for us. That is the reason we have been able to get over 80 per cent of votes... This (electoral support from Muslims) will dispel all the myths regarding Muslims of Gujarat," Modi said.[12] At most places, the party had won about 80 per cent of votes, he pointed out.

In these corporation elections, the BJP had fielded 12 Muslim candidates but only one Ms Babiben Habibbhai Sama (Rakjot) could win even as other candidates lost by a very slender margin. District panchayat, *taluka* panchayat and municipality elections that followed in the third week of October 2010 produced a completely different picture. The BJP fielded 21 candidates from the Christian community in Surat, Tapi, and Dang districts and most of them won. More than 100 Muslim candidates also won. "Over 100 Muslim candidates have won on the BJP ticket. Muslim candidates have crossed a century of winners. Christians and Muslims are voting for the BJP. They're disillusioned with vote-bank politics. Muslims have accepted the BJP's development politics. This is a turning point of India's political journey," a triumphant chief minister told the media.[13]

Modi's development effort had already started spreading its charm. Most people may have ignored the significance of the birthday gift Narendra Modi received on 17 September 2010. But it was not lost on the chief minister who knew Gujarat so well. The gift was the party's impressive win from Kathlal, a seat it had never won in the last 50 years. The seat was considered a Congress pocket borough.[14] The constituency has more than 65 per cent Muslim voters and the BJP victory surprised political pundits.[15] The BJP candidate Kanubhai Dabhi polled 62,120 votes and defeated Congress candidate Ghelabhai Zala by more than 21,000 votes.

One fact is very evident from all this—that Muslims in Gujarat have started coming out of the siege mentality much to the chagrin of those who would like to see them differently. They have started looking at Modi positively and want to take part in the state's development activities. In other words, they do not want to miss the bus.

Political aspirations would be one of the reasons for Muslims to look positively towards Modi in Gujarat. The real reason could be social empowerment. This is best described in the words of Justice Rajendra Sachar Committee that looked into the social, economic and educational condition of Muslims in India and submitted its report in 2006. The report discovered that the condition of Muslims in Gujarat was better than many Indian states.

The report came after Justice Rajendra's Sachar's meeting with Modi. Sachar asked Modi what the government had done for the minorities. Modi replied that his government "does not work for minorities". The members of the Sachar committee were stunned to hear his reply. But he continued, "My government does not work either for minorities or majority. It works for six crore Gujaratis".[16]

Muslim literacy in Gujarat stood at 73.5 per cent as compared to the national average of 59.1. While the figure for the urban males was 76, it was 81 for those living in rural areas as compared to the national average of 70 and 62 respectively in similar categories.[17]

The average literacy of Muslim women in urban Gujarat was five points higher than the national average, whereas their counterparts in rural areas of the state fared even better with a literacy rate of 57 per cent against the national average of 43.[18]

Also, a greater percentage of Muslims have attained primary, secondary and higher secondary education in Gujarat compared to the national average and compared to other states such as Uttar Pradesh. Against the national average of 60.9 per cent (and 42.2 per cent in Uttar Pradesh), Gujarat had 74.9 per cent Muslims at the primary level. The percentage at the secondary level in the state is 45.3 as compared to the national average of 40.5. In UP it was 29.2 per cent.[19]

In terms of employment, Gujarat had 5.4 per cent Muslims in government jobs. This compared favourably with states like West Bengal (2.1 per cent), then ruled by the Left Front led by the CPI(M), and Delhi (3.2 per cent).[20]

These points were quoted in LK Advani's blog as much as they were highlighted in all newspapers in 2006-07. And these were figures of 2006. If we see the current figures already there are signs of remarkable improvement. The latest government figures which are quoted about Muslim situation in Gujarat say that they occupy about 10 per cent jobs with 12 per cent representation in the state police force.[21]

But some critics either refuse to see the change that has taken place or are using outdated data to show the State in poor light. Christophe Jaffrelot's article in the *Indian Express* of November 2013 used Planning Commission's data to argue that the percentage of Gujarati Muslims living below the poverty line was 42.4 per cent. He said: "Not only is this higher than the national average—by 10 percentage points—but it is also higher than the comparable figures for West Bengal (34.9 per cent) and Rajasthan (29.5 per cent). The percentage of Muslims living below the poverty line in the rural areas in Gujarat is not very different from West Bengal: 31.4 per cent compared to 34.4 per cent. In the villages of Gujarat, the poverty of Muslims is largely due to the fact that they own little land—70 per cent of rural Muslims own less than 0.4 hectare, against 55.5 per cent of Hindus."[22]

A strong joint rejoinder came from Asifa Khan and Zafar Sareshwala. They said: "Jaffrelot has made sweeping one-sided comments on Muslims and Modi to the detriment of both—and his own credibility." They add, "Jaffrelot quotes old statistics to show that Muslims in Gujarat are worse off than Hindus—but what matters is how fast their lot is improving, not the historical disadvantage they have always had in almost all states outside the south."[23]

Choosing more recent data, leading economist Surjit Bhalla pointed out a large decline in the poverty levels of Muslims in Gujarat, about 26 points in the space of just two years. Using the figures of 2011-12 data he said, it appeared that Gujarat under Modi had delivered on both growth and governance. In a different article, Bhalla wrote: "The sharpest decline in poverty between 2009/10 and 2011/12 is observed for the Muslims, the very community against which a Gujarati-Modi bias is assumed and presumed. The poverty ratio for Muslims, which had not shown much change between 1999/00 and 2009/10, now collapses to 11.4 per cent level from the high 37.6 per cent level observed just two years earlier. At this level, the Muslim poverty rate is marginally below the 12.4 per cent poverty rate of the non-disadvantaged group consisting of OBCs and upper-caste Hindus."

In the case of Muslims, Gujarat was (in 2011-12) the second-best performing state, with West Bengal as the state where Muslims had the largest relative decline. However, the poverty level for Muslims in West Bengal in 2011/12 was more than twice the level observed in Gujarat and near identical to the national Muslim average of 25.5 per cent, Bhalla said.[24] Even the figure used by Bhalla is about a year old. In a faster developing pace, even one year is a long period. Modi's governance has started yielding results.

Modi has helped to take the kite festival in Gujarat to a new level of celebration where people want to spend. The Kite festival is now waited with bated breath and has emerged as an international event. It continues now for five days. The main beneficiaries of this festival are Muslims. In Jamalpur kite market, almost every Muslim house is involved in making kites. On an average, a woman makes 1,000 kites daily at home allowing her to earn Rs 100 as labour cost. Waheeda, a housewife, said: "We (Muslim women) feel empowered by this new kite fervour. I am uneducated but I want my children to get education at all cost." She earned enough by making kites to enable her to educate her two children even when her husband did not pay anything, she said. Kite festival used to be popular in Gujarat earlier too but it was not linked to the economy in such a big way.

Zafar Sareshwala pointed out that the largest contribution of

Muslims in the form of *zakat* (charity) came from Gujarat—more than 50 per cent. This indicated like nothing else that Muslims in the state were richer than their counterparts elsewhere in India. "More than 50,000 *safirs* (collectors of *zakat*) come to Gujarat to collect *zakat* during the month of Ramzan. If Modi is anti-Muslim, how will Muslims prosper? *Zakat* is a sign of prosperity. About 90 per cent *madrasas* of Uttar Pradesh, Bihar and West Bengal run on *zakat*."

He also gave the example of a large number of Gujarati Muslims going on Haj. Gujarat has a quota of 4,500 and the Haj committee on an average receives about 46,000 applications. "All the applications must be accompanied with money that is between Rs 2 and 2.5 lakh. This money is deposited through banks. So many applications prove that Muslims are prosperous. About 25,000 to 30,000 people from India go on Haj on private basis. Of these, about 70 per cent are from Gujarat. The cost of this private arrangement is between Rs 4 and 4.5 lakh. Besides this, about one lakh people go on mini haj called *Umra*." In Ahmedabad alone, more than 100 Haj tour operators have come up to meet the rush of people going on Haj.

Contrary to Muslims in other parts of India, Muslims of Gujarat have become as much a part of the aspirational class as their Hindu counterparts. The propaganda that Muslims were being discriminated against does not hold true for Modi, Sareshwala said.

Many Muslims have joined Modi and they have been trying their best to project the chief minster as the man who could be trusted with delivering justice. They have become Modi's supporters because of his plain speak. The earliest to become his supporter was Asma Khan Pathan based in Nadiad. During the 2002 riots, her *hing* (asafoetida) factories were burnt. She found that both BJP and Congress workers were participating in the riots including senior congressman. When she sought to know why, Congress leaders had no answer. Her father-in-law Abdul Rahim Khan Hingwala was a Congressman. Her husband's brother Navroz Khan was arrested and put behind bars. A senior Congress leader was responsible for that, she said. "I heard then Congree parliamentarian Dinsha Patel, who was at the police station, telling DSP Manoj Aggarwal to ensure that Navroz was not released."

Finally, she met Modi in Gandhinagar at a public function. She put vermillion on her head to hide her identity of being a muslim. "When people tried to stop me, he encouraged me to speak, and when I finished, he said he would see what could be done. This was in March 2002. Within three days, Navroj was a free man." Ever since then, she has become a big fan of Modi.[25]

Asifa Khan comes from Bharuch. She was a journalist for many years before she was picked up by senior Congress leader Ahmed Patel to be a part of the Congress in the state. Ever since 2009, when she joined the Congress, she did not find anything substantial to do. While people thought she had access to Patel, the latter did not have much time for the state. She said she felt stifled in the Congress and finally decided to join the BJP and support Modi on the eve of 2012 assembly elections.

What acted as a clincher for her decision was the experience of Chanchvel, a Muslim-dominated village near Bharuch. "In Chanchvel, Modiji's known annual girl enrolment campaign in schools had such an impact that many Muslim girls started going to schools. It impressed a local businessman so much that he donated Rs 20 lakh to him for the campaign," she said. After that she sought an appointment with the chief minister and got five minutes but the meeting stretched to 55 minutes. She realised that he was quite different from the image that was being projected of him by the critics. Ever since then, she has emerged as a key spokesperson to demolish anyone who says Modi is anti-Muslim.

While touring various parts of Bharuch and Kutch as a Congress leader, she had discovered that most Muslims had shifted to the BJP. They came to meet her but told her that nothing would happen and the Congress was merely interested in token gestures. She remembered the case of a Muslim widow demanding pension from the postal department. Despite her best attempts, Asifa could not make Delhi move in this case.

"I had come to politics from journalism to deliver goods to my people. When I couldn't do that, despite Ahmed Patel being my patron, I saw no point continuing in the party. I told him I would not continue as a rubber stamp and that I would rather work under a leader who was working for the community."[26]

Zafar Sareshwala was based in London and was planning to file a case against Modi in the international court of justice. A thought came to him: why not to talk to Modi and counter him and find out what he had to say. So when Modi visited London in August 2003 in connection with Vibrant Gujarat summit, Sareshwala and few others met him in London. This meeting changed the course of Sareshwala's thinking on Gujarat.

Sareshwala asked Modi tough questions about 2002 riots including why he did not visit Juhapura. Maulana Masuri who was also present at the meeting was unsparing. Sareshwala argued before Modi that he was the chief minister and the buck must stop with him. Modi listened to the delegation patiently and after they waited for an answer, he said in a low voice, "*Haan ye mere kaal ka kalank hai, aur mujhe usko dhona hai.*" (Yes, this is a blot on my past, and I alone will have to clean it). He then promised that justice would be done and everyone could come to him with whatever problems they had, Sareshwala said.

After a frank talk with Modi, Sareshwala became his admirer. As he started working closely with Modi on minority issues, he realised that Modi would be instrumental in improving the plight of the minority community. He has now emerged as the most trusted spokesperson of Modi, outside the BJP. "The welfare of my community is supreme for me," said Sareshwala, who is a devout Muslim and has a flourishing business to take care of his needs.[27]

Strong support to Modi has come from Salim Khan, who is a veteran film script writer of the Salim-Javed duo era and father of film actor Salman Khan. He had written an article on Gujarat and Modi liked that. When Modi visited Mumbai, he expressed a desire to meet Salim Khan. Ever since then, Salim Khan is an admirer of Modi. "These Congress ministers do not have time for anyone. When the home minister wants to talk to me, he sends his police officer who makes me talk. They can't even make a call. And here is a chief minister who always gives a return call."[28] Salim Khan turning positive for Modi is a big development since Congress leaders always took his home to be their first port of call in Mumbai.

Salim Khan held that Muslims of India cannot afford to keep living in the past. They must move ahead. "No one can deny that the development that has taken place in Gujarat has helped all sections of society. Muslims outside Gujarat must visit the state to verify the claim. Seeing is believing."

He wanted his "fellow religionists" to know that Modi has been a different politician. "Whenever a problem is brought to his notice, he tries to address it immediately. No other politician I know listens to people with so much of intent and tries to solve their problems to the extent possible. I believe he is the right contender to be the country's prime minister. He is a very efficient man, and has a lot of time in his life to work for the country. He should be given a chance."

Recently, a group of Muslim clerics went to Modi with a list of 14 complaints and the chief minister accepted all the demands except "treating Muslims as a separate entity within India," Salim Khan said, "Modi is right when he asks why treat Muslims separately. They also are citizens like anyone else."

"Muslims of the country must remember what Prophet Mohammed had told one of his followers. When asked what the greatest worship was, the Prophet said, 'Love'. When asked what the greatest charity was, he said, 'Forgiveness'. The only way that the two large communities of India can progress is by living in peace and mutual harmony."

There has been a softening in the attitude of Mahesh Bhatt, who was one of Modi's most vocal critics. After listening to Bhatt spitting venom against him, Modi called him on the phone and told him that he was ready to listen to everything that he (Bhatt) had to say. "I believe you are very angry and you have a lot of complaints," Modi told him. Bhatt then told him about the desperate situation of the riot victims and that there was no relief or rehabilitation. Nothing seemed to be moving. "He told me, 'Maheshbhai I am interested in solving the problems. You come in group of 5, 25, 50, 500 or 5000 and wherever you want to come. I want to address the issues. I want harmony to return as quickly as possible.'"

I told him you have taken a very big step by calling me directly and giving me this offer. But because I was speaking from the forum of Jamiat Ulema-e-Hind I will ask them to take their complaints to you."[29]

Bhatt then called general secretary of the organisation Maulana Mahmood Madani and told him to respond to the call: "*Mahmood bhai… bhai* (referring to Modi) *ka phone aaya tha.* I said *ki lagta hai*

*ki Prophet Mohammad ki Hadis ne jaa ker… apna jaadu dikha diya hai.
Kyunki unhone phone kiya tha aur unhone ye kaha hai ki main aapko
ye* convey *karun ki ab aap kya karna chahte hai aap foran unhe itila
karen. To unhone meri baat suni aur kaha ki haan main ab ye jo offer
hai usko le jaa ker hamari* general body meeting *mein rakhunga aur
unki* consultation *se baad mein kya karna chahiye wo agla kadam hum
wahan se uthayengey.*" (Modi had called. It seems the Prophet (PBUH)
has influenced his mind. Modi has asked me to convey to you that he
is keen to listen to what you want to do next. Mahmood listened to me
and said that he would bring up the issue at the general body meeting
of Jamiat Ulema-e-Hind and decide the next step)

Mahesh Bhatt said that the offer was not taken by Madani: "*Meri
aaj bhi shikayat Mahmood Madani saheb se hoti hai ki sahib main kaise
is baat ko jhooth ker dun ki Narendra Modi ka 2003 mei phone aaya
tha. Sach to ye hai ki unhone offer kiya tha aapne offer swikara nahi. Ye
sacchayi hai. To kahin per chook aap se ho gayi hai*". I keep on telling
this to him. But they say *ki nahin Sir, agar hum us waqt jaate to shayad
hamari jo ek* following *hai, hamari ek* constituency *hai jo, wo usko galat
samajhti. Maine kahan bhaiya aap to Allah ke bande hai.* Politician *to
woh hai. Political constituency ko madde nazar rakhte hue to ye political
log kaam karte hain. Aapko kya darna hai? Aapki niyat pak hai, saaf hai.
Aap apne bandon ki raksha karna chahte hai, unki haalat mein sudhar
lana chahte hain. Aapki… jab aapki niyat saaf hai to aap kyun nahi karte
hai?*" (I still have complaints that the offer was not taken by Madani. I
cannot deny that the phone call came. The truth is that the offer was not
taken by the other side. 'Somewhere, you have committed a mistake,' I
keep telling him. But they told me that their core support base would
not have liked if they had gone to meet Modi. I told him, 'You are the
people of God; they are politicians. Politicians work keeping in mind
their constituencies. You people are honest and you want to safeguard
the interests of your people. Why don't you take the initiative?')

"I did not get an answer from Mahmoodbhai. Today he says
gracefully that his *waalid* (father), who was alive then, had told him
that they should talk to Modi. His father told Mahmood, "*Aapki Hadis
bolti hai ki baat karni chahiye. Aap Prophet (PBUH) ki baat manenge
ki political game ke takaze ke anusar chalengey? To aap to Allah ke bande*

hain to aap jaaiye baat kijiye. (*Hadith* says that we should talk. Will you accept what the Prophet said or will you go as per the need of politics?)"

They lost the chance in 2003 but the aggrieved side should now take the initiative to set aside the acrimony and create conditions to enable people to live in peace and harmony, he said. "I personally feel, whenever anybody, no matter how opposed I may be to his politics, makes a gesture of reconciliation, talks about harmony and talks about healing the wounds; it must be applauded, acknowledged and reciprocated. This is my response. If I keep talking about peace and I do not take the initiative to bring peace, then I do not want peace. And do not live off conflict, there are people who live off conflict," Bhatt said.

Mahmood was instrumental in the ouster of Maulana Vastanvi in 2011 as vice-chancellor of Darul Uloom Deoband when Vastanvi indirectly praised Modi and said that Muslims had benefitted from the development initiatives of the Gujarat chief minister.[30]

The same Mahmood Madani, however, demonstrated a softening of stand on Modi and Gujarat in October 2013. "More riots have taken place in Uttar Pradesh and Rajasthan than in Gujarat. The number of Muslim youths in the jails of Maharashtra and Rajasthan exceed those in Gujarat," he said.

"I don't say any such thing in private or in public to show that I support Modi. But if I compare Gujarat with Maharashtra and Rajasthan, then people will say I support Modi."[31] A few months back, Madani had articulated a similar view: "More innocent Muslims are wallowing in prisons of Maharashtra than in Gujarat. The human rights record of several states is deplorable. They don't have a Modi at the helm. This is a ground reality we can't ignore," Madani explained.[32]

Madani had admitted that there was a change in Muslim opinion of Modi. "In Gujarat, Jamiat workers have told me that in several assembly segments, Muslims voted for Modi," he said and pointed out that Muslims in Gujarat were better off than their counterparts in other States.

Mufti Aijaz Arshad Qasmi has studied from JNU and he was spokesperson of the Darul-Uloom, Deoband. He was dead against Modi and held him responsible for the 2002 riots. He had refused to attend a conclave of young leaders in Gandhinagar in June 2013 because Modi was going to preside over the function. He met Modi in July 2013 and he was a changed man. "Modi said he would not allow injustice to happen with Muslims and that he would work for equal opportunity for all communities. He is a rare politician who listens to people and listens to criticism too", the Mufti said.[33]

It is clear that certain vested interests have been working overtime to create an impression about Modi being anti-Muslim. Now cobwebs have begun to clear. Facts are beginning to prevail over lies and insinuations. Muslims in Gujarat have begun to realise that no other political leader has benefitted the minority community as much as Narendra Modi has.

A group of Muslims in Bhachau, Mohammad Sharif, Ghulam Ali and Maulana Zia-ur Rehman agreed that Modi had delivered on the front of development. Earlier ladies used to walk long distance to get water, Ghulam Ali of Lakadiya village said. "We used to take bath once in a week, now we are able to take bath daily. There is no problem of water. The wells that had dried up have got water now. We will have to give credit to Modi for this."[34] Sharif, also from Lakadiya, added that since productivity of agriculture had increased, nobody wanted to sell his land. Muslims constitute about 50 per cent of Lakadiya population.

Poor Muslims who depend on daily earning for living are the worst sufferers of any riot or imposition of curfew. Earlier, riot-like situation was a norm. The poor would suffer and often depend on credit. A riot-free and tension-free state has helped them a lot. Not even one hour of curfew has been imposed in the last 10 years, said Sheru Khan Pathan, who owns a garment business in Ahmedabad. Asma Khan Pathan said that the youths of Gujarat did not know curfew or police *lathi*-charge because the state had not witnessed any conflict for more than a decade. This was the biggest contribution of Modi to the welfare of the minorities, she stressed.

Ashfaqbhai runs a food stall at Ahmedabad's Lal Darwaja. He is thankful that there has been peace and communal harmony. "Earlier people were not sure if one would return home safe. Muslims had stopped growing beard and those Hindus, who had to pass through minority populated areas, had stopped putting *tilak*. Now the situation has changed completely. You can see people moving freely without the fear of getting stabbed," he said.

He disagreed with Modi's critics who painted him as an anti-Muslim. He recalled the incident of 2002 to prove his point: "Towards the beginning of March 2002, when some Muslims were returning from Haj, Modi made special arrangements for their security from airport to their respective homes. Ashfaqbhai recalled how these Hajis were escorted in a bus under full police protection. One DSP and one SP were deputed to take care of the Hajis who kept coming continuously for eight days," he said.

Hasan Ali from Vadnagar was not willing to blame Modi for the riots and gave pearls of wisdom to those who want to pick them up. It was not the job of one person. "*Kisi ek aadmi ne thodi hi kiya sahib. Vo hamara padosi hai. Humlog usko jante hain. Yahan pe koi hamara bahiskar nahi karta.*" (He is our neighbour. We know him. Nobody does our social boycott here).

Muslims have started supporting Modi also because he is seen as the one who has helped control organisations such as the Vishwa Hindu Parishad and the Bajrang Dal. When Modi became the CM, he was a novice and people like Pravin Togadia must have prevailed. Now, Modi is in complete command of the situation and does not allow any nonsense, said Wakf Board Chairman, AI Saiyad.[35] Asifa Khan said that it was good to see people such as Pravin Togadia lose their clout. "Now when he comes to the airport there are not even four people to receive him," she added.

Mufti Aijaz Arshad Qasmi held the same: "When I was in Deoband, statements of some hardliners in the VHP such as Pravin Togadia used to create lot of problems. These people are silent now. Modi has tackled these people well." He held that with his governance agenda Modi would keep such people in check.

Those who say Modi is anti-Muslim often rake up the skull cap controversy. Bihar Chief Minister Nitish Kumar said that those who want to lead the country will at times have to wear skull caps and at times put tilak on the forehead.[36] Although people have short memories, Nitish himself should remember that he had refused to wear a skull cap and take a shawl at Patna airport given by some Muslim leaders.[37]

While isolated incidents should not be used to pass judgement, one also has to learn to separate such tokenism from defining secularism. It would be sufficient to know that Modi wrapped a shroud that had *kalma* written all over. (*Kalma* refers to this Islamic mantra in Arabic: *la Ilaha il-Allah, Mohammed ul-Rasool Allah* which means there is no god but Allah, and Mohammed is His prophet). This fact was pointed out by Asifa Khan when she was asked to react on the skull cap controversy.[38]

The reason why Modi did not wear such public symbolism was obvious. A person who has been critical of people resorting to such symbolism in the name of secularism did not wish to become a part of the same. He has always tried to avoid such symbolism. And the Sadbhavna fast in 2011, when he refused to wear the skull cap, was a message of peace for all and he did not wish to convert this into an occasion for obvious symbolism. But, he did not disappoint the clerics and accepted the shawl (*chaddar*) instead.[39]

His interview to Reuters wherein he gave the 'puppy remark' became controversial. When Reuters' reporter asked him whether he regretted what happened in Gujarat in 2002, Modi replied: "I'll tell you. India's Supreme Court is considered a good court today in the world. The Supreme Court created a special investigative team (SIT) and top-most, very bright officers who oversee the SIT. That report came. In that report, I was given a thoroughly clean chit, a thoroughly clean chit. Another thing, any person if we are driving a car, we are a driver, and someone else is driving a car and we're sitting behind, even then if a puppy comes under the wheel, will it be painful or not? Of course it is. If I'm a chief minister or not, I'm a human being. If something bad happens anywhere, it is natural to be sad."[40]

This interview created a storm since his critics went to town saying that Modi was comparing Muslims with 'a puppy'. The remark was innocuous without any malice and just came by way of comparison. It was not intended at any community and the expression is used by an ordinary Indian in the day-to-day life. It meant to denote compassion rather than contempt. The chief minister's office clarified that there had been a "gross distortion" of the chief minister's remark.[41] Sruthi Gottipati, who had interviewed him, clarified that the remark was not put in the right context by Indian media.[42]

Mufti Aijaz Arshad Qasmi of the All India Muslim Personal Law Board said Modi had clarified in private talks that he did not mean Muslims in the puppy statement and I find him truthful. The Mufti said he was confident that Muslims would get justice under Modi. Former IAS officer KJ Alphons said Modi had told him that as a chief minister he should have been more careful about giving such a comparison, more so since media is waiting for one such slip to rip him apart.

But the question which many Muslims like Asifa Khan and Zafar Sareshwala have started asking are: Are these real issues for Muslims? "Muslims in India are no longer interested in tokenism and symbolism. Whether Modi wears a skullcap or not is of little interest to Muslims; it does not matter if Modi throws *iftar* parties or not, for Muslims can see through this hypocrisy. In the aspirational politics of today, these are empty gestures."[43]

Khan and Sareshwala added that Muslims need empowerment and the only way to empower them is to give them 'Education, Education and Education'. In Ahmedabad, there were only three schools for Muslims. Today, there are 25 run by Muslims—a 10-fold increase in 10 years—and this is the case in many other parts of Gujarat.[44]

Some people are charged up and have been demanding an apology from Modi about what happened in Gujarat in 2002, like the one Congress leaders offered for the 1984 anti-Sikh riots. After having failed to paint him as guilty, they now want him to apologise. The issue was raised in Modi's interview with Shahid Siddiqui. This was a rare occasion when Modi had agreed to speak about 2002 riots since he did not wish to be seen as one who was not keen to reach out to the minority community. It was because of some really sincere people such as Salim Khan, who wanted to bridge the divide, that the interview had taken place.[45]

The interview was given for Urdu weekly *Nayi Duniya*. Modi gave his reason for not apologising: "… In my interview to Prabhu Chawla for *Seedhi Baat* in 2005 or 2006, he asked if I was willing to apologise, to that I responded that why should I be forgiven? If any head of state has committed such a crime then he should be hanged in public so that for the coming hundred years, no other head of state should ever think of committing such a heinous crime. If anyone pleads for their forgiveness, then they are encouraging such crimes.

"If Narendra Modi has committed such a crime, then he should be hanged, this is my upfront demand, but if people are attacking me with criticism for political purposes without considering my effort of saving people's lives, then I don't have an answer for them."

When Siddiqui asked him the same question again, he asserted: "No, I was able to stop it. I don't agree that I have not been able to stop it."[46] Modi has maintained this consistent line ever since.

The tallest Shia cleric and Islamic scholar, Maulana Kalbe Sadiq, held a different viewpoint. He said that it was childish to demand an apology. "He should display in his character and through his actions that he cares for Muslims. If I see that Modi is making changes then I will back him. I can't say this for all Muslims, but I will personally back him."[47] Kalbe Sadiq is vice president of the All India Muslim Personal Law Board. "Modi is not a political untouchable for Muslims, and can win their votes if he 'changes himself' and shows that he cares for them."

Mahesh Bhatt believed that expressing remorse through apology was not needed as these were empty words. "He must make an attempt to take India to that zone which Nelson Mandela had taken post his release from Northern Island after 27 years of imprisonment. He fought against White domination and against Black domination with vigour, and refused to become a Prophet. He said, 'Don't make me a Prophet. I am one of you. But I will fight both White and Black domination with my might.' Then he went about creating situations where there was reconciliation between the communities which had moved far away."

Muslim leaders have been meeting Modi to know his view on controversial issues as well. Modi has told them in numerous conversations that there need not be any apprehension about any of the issues facing them. One such issue is uniform civil code. He told them that any step taken would always be in consultation with the affected people. It would never be thrust upon them, Asifa said quoting Modi. The same was the case on opposition to the communal violence bill. Did Modi need this bill to control riots in Gujarat, she asked. "It is a sensitive issue and needs to be debated fully," Modi told her.

It is only after talking to the chief minister heart to heart that many Muslim leaders have decided to come out and rebut the negative campaign against him. Now there are plans to apprise Muslims outside Gujarat of the realities in the state. The state BJP unit has documented the success stories of Gujarati Muslims. It has prepared a booklet *Naaz Hai Gujarat Pe* (Proud of Gujarat). The 32-page booklet states that Muslims in Gujarat are better off than their counterparts elsewhere in the country. The claims are backed by facts and statements of other leaders. It focusses on education, healthcare and employment.

Modi has refused to see Muslims as a separate identity and this has alienated a number of leaders who thrive on identity politics. But this should be welcomed since he is treating everyone as a citizen of the state he has been ruling. "If I have built a road, it's for everyone, welfare is for everyone. I have come out with a scheme called Mukhyamantri Amrutum Yojna where we have spent Rs 200 crore for the treatment of poor people who are suffering from serious health issues and everyone has benefited from this scheme."[48]

At his massive rally in Patna, Modi had asked: "Do Hindus need to fight Muslims or poverty? Do Muslims need to fight Hindus or poverty?" He added, "Poor Hindus and poor Muslims will have to fight together against their condition. Let's unite to fight poverty."[49] This was a brilliant attempt to take politics away from identity to aspiration. Hindus and Muslims are not different in that way.

Empowerment automatically brings prosperity and fulfils aspirations. Ask any Muslim and one may hear him or her expressing the desire to go on Haj. But they can go to Haj only if they can afford it. At his Patna rally Modi gave a new yardstick to calculate the prosperity of Muslims.[50]

Gujarat had a Haj quota of 4813 (as per data of 2013). But it got applications from more than nine times of this quota. There were 36,171 excess applicants. Bihar had the quota of 11,817 but it received only 6,533 applications. West Bengal received only 10,111 applications against a quota of 17,430. Uttar Pradesh had 35,082 applicants against a quota of 32,214.[51]

And to make a new beginning on Modi's 63rd birthday on 17 September 2013, the Gujarat BJP announced a special drive to recruit about one lakh Muslims into the party. The drive had actually started in the month of June 2013 but was announced on 17 September. And by 15 November, the party had already recruited about one lakh Muslims, state minority morcha chief Sufi Sant Mehbub Ali said. Similar steps are likely to be taken at the national level too.

***

The Fuss Over Visa

The world is indeed a mixture of truth and make-believe.
Discard the make-believe and take the truth.

— **Ramakrishna**

The United States finally decided to end the boycott of Narendra Modi. US Ambassador to India Nancy Powell met the Gujarat chief minister on 13 February 2014. This was the first such high profile meeting after the US revoked Modi's US visa in 2005. The move is reflective of the US rethink influenced by the general mood across the globe.

The UK had already made course correction after diplomatically preventing him from visiting the country since 2003. Although the UK did not formally deny a Visa to Modi, it boycotted the State government from 2002-2012 and used the issue of security threat to prevent Modi's visit in 2005. UK High Commissioner James Bevan ended the boycott by calling on the Gujarat chief minister in October 2012.

We need to understand why this happened. The most controversial riots of Gujarat happened in 2002. Modi visited the United Kingdom in August 2003. Although there was opposition to him from various NGOs and other social groups, the UK government did not think it fit to cancel his visa then. Suddenly, in March 2005, Modi had to cancel his visit to the UK after reports of security threats. The UK then reiterated its stand of not having any relation with the Gujarat state government. Technically, the UK did not deny a Visa to Modi yet it kept him away from the UK. Any person could question the reason for the shift in the stand.

Defending his meeting with Modi in 2012, Bevan said, "This is about engagement. This is not about endorsement. If you want to engage effectively with an Indian state, you need to engage with the government of that state, you need to engage with the chief minister of that state and Mr Modi is the democratically elected leader of Gujarat."[1]

This visit was to prepare the ground for the visit of British minister of state for the foreign office, Hugo Swire, in March 2013. Swire's visit came after Modi's third successive victory in the state. Those he spoke to after the meeting said that he was immensely impressed with the personality of the Gujarat chief minister.

"I am confident that active engagement is the best way to pursue British interests in Gujarat. This includes support for the British nationals in Gujarat, for the large Gujarati community in the UK, for human rights, and good governance," he said after the meeting.[2]

The UK, however, moved a step closer when the BJP projected Modi as its Prime Ministerial candidate in September 2013. UK Prime Minister David Cameron announced within 10 days of the projection that Britain favoured closer engagements with Gujarat and its chief minister.[3] On a short visit to Delhi in November 2013, Cameron said: "We have started a proper engagement with Gujarat and the chief minister there. Our foreign office minister has met with him... The connection is there, the engagement is there. I think the engagement should continue." When asked if he would like to meet Modi in the near future, he said: "In time, yes. It's good to meet. We have an approach of meeting all politicians and leaders. In the end, it will be for the people of India whom to elect. But I'm open to meeting elected leaders."[4]

Modi held the US visa since 1998. He was supposed to visit the US in 2003 on invitation of private US citizens but he did not go. The US denied him visa in March 2005, when he was making plans to visit the country on an invitation from some Indian American groups. It invoked the Section 212(a)(2)(G) that makes any foreign government official "who was responsible for or directly carried out, at any time, particularly severe violations of religious freedom" ineligible for the visa. The Indian government under United Progressive Alliance (UPA) protested but the US did not relent.

Also, why did the US not revoke the visa in 2002? Why did it wait till 2005? Modi had rightly raised this issue in the context of the US move.[5]

President George Bush had secured a second term as US President in 2005. His first term of presidency was known for terrorists' attack on the World Trade Center and his statement that he would "smoke them out from their holes and make them pay".[6]

After having angered the entire Islamic world, the US was looking for reconciliation in Bush's second term. Was denying a visa to Modi a clever ploy to please Pakistan whom the US desperately needed in its war against terrorism, and to demonstrate that it was not anti-Muslim per se? The BJP did say that the US decision was taken to please Pakistan.[7]

It must be questioned whether the US would have taken this step if the NDA was still in power. The NDA had lost the Lok Sabha elections in 2004 and the UPA led by the Congress had come to power at the Centre.

Leader of the Opposition LK Advani questioned US administration's concept of religious freedom. "While it denied visa to the Gujarat chief minister for the alleged violation of religious freedom, it welcomed with open arms, the leaders of those countries where religious freedom never existed and minority rights were trampled down under the feet."[8] Advani pointed to Saudi Arabia and Egypt where even religious books like the Bhagvad Gita and the Holy Bible were banned.

The US, however, has kept the same stance as before and has stressed that there was no change in its visa policy vis-à-vis Narendra Modi. "There is no change in our longstanding visa policy with regard to the chief minister (Gujarat)," US State department spokesperson Marie Harf said.[9]

The clause of religious freedom is very dicey and gives a lot of scope to foreign governments to use it at whim. It also talks about perception and does not confine to an indictment by the law. Perception is based on reports that appear in newspapers. The embassy denying the visa does not need to justify its decision.

In the case of Modi, if perception is taken as the reason then the fact that he won elections successively should also count while assessing the perception. That Muslims voted for him in Gujarat should also go towards shaping the perception. And for the US to keep saying that its policy remains unchanged, despite various evidences that disprove the perception about Modi, is nothing but prejudice.

Arun Jaitley summed it up well by accusing the US administration of buckling under pressure from vested interests as it happens in a kangaroo court. "The American stance on the issue has clearly been one determined by their 'kangaroo court'. To proclaim Modi guilty even when there was no evidence against him despite investigations and reinvestigation amounts to immature diplomacy. It constitutes interference in India's internal affairs," Jaitley said.[10]

In December 2012, about two dozen US parliamentarians wrote a letter to then US Secretary of State Hillary Clinton asking for a 'no change' in the US policy.[11] Why were these Congressmen so agitated? Who was provoking them and putting constant pressure on them?

In November 2012, more than five dozen Indian parliamentarians wrote to US President Barack Obama urging him not to change the 2005 US stand on no visa to Modi. This letter was supposedly signed by 25 members from Lok Sabha and 39 from Rajya Sabha. The same letter was sent to British Prime Minister David Cameron.

The letter was released to the media in July 2013. Apparently, this was a clever way to derail BJP President Rajnath Singh's visit to the United States where he was likely to raise the issue of visa to Modi. The letter was released to the media on 23 July, a day after Singh told the media in New York that he would take up the visa issue with US lawmakers.[12]

The letter exposed those MPs who had signed it since it was akin to appealing to an external government to resolve an internal issue of India. Also, it went against the government of India's stated policy of opposition to the US stand on Modi.

Nine Indian parliamentarians including CPI(M) Leader Sitaram Yechuri denied having signed the letter and claimed that their signatures were forged.[13] This further raised questions about the motive of people who were behind the campaign.

The blame should not lie only with these NGOs or individual citizens but the US administration that persuades itself into believing their versions. Even the officials of the embassies of the US and the UK in India meet only those kind of people who help shape the perception they want to strengthen. Rightist NGOs or intellectuals do not figure in their list. These officials pick up these hearsays and lies and send their dispatches as truth. One such dispatch quoted a senior journalist to say that a big industrial house must have paid a bribe. The dispatch also added that they could not verify the claim.[14]

Former US Ambassador to India Robert Blackwill believes that the US should grant visa to the Gujarat chief minister. "He is a prominent political thinker in India. And, I don't believe the United States is in a position, thousands of miles away, to have a magisterial opinion about what happens here in India... That's up to the Indians...," he said after meeting Modi in Gandhinagar on 30 August 2013.[15] In that context, Nancy Powell's visit is a welcome move. The US has realized that the official boycott made no sense when most US firms were keen to be there in Gujarat.

There is support for Modi internationally which these governments will find difficult to ignore. British MP Barry Gardiner said, "This is a man who has been re-elected three times as the chief minister of the state in India with which Britain does the most business. In fact, we do more business with Gujarat than with the rest of India put together. He is now the leader of India's official opposition party. He is obviously a key player in Indian politics, and as such he is somebody British politicians need to hear from."[16]

Other countries of Europe have softened towards Modi. German Ambassador to India Michael Steiner said in November 2013 that by ending the boycott of Modi and his government, Germany was not endorsing anybody but giving respect to India's democracy. "This has nothing to do with an endorsement. I am a representative of a foreign country, like my European colleagues. We have to respect that India is a democracy with functioning institutions and we have to stay neutral, that is what we are doing," Steiner said when asked if his three-day visit to Gujarat was an endorsement of Modi.[17]

The European Union (EU) made it official that it had ended its decade-long boycott of the Gujarat chief minister after Modi-led BJP's third consecutive electoral victory in the state. EU officials in Delhi said that they recognised that Modi was "already unofficially playing a national role" in India. Part of the decision to renew relations with Mr Modi was based on the court verdict which sentenced a former Gujarat minister Maya Kodnani to 28 years in jail for playing a leading role in the riots. The conviction signalled that those responsible for the deadly riots would be punished, and gave the EU a solid argument to renew ties. "This is a new phase," Steiner summed up the EU's upbeat mood about Modi.[18]

China has proved itself to be Modi's friend. Modi has publicly endorsed China's progress and has been trying to emulate it. While going on his China tour in 2011, he had said that Gujarat was not competing with any Indian state but with China. His talk about economies of scale and largescale planning and operations reminds one of China.

During his visit, Modi said that "Gujarat is the Guangdong of India", the province that had kicked off economic reform in China. When Modi was listing out the achievements of Gujarat, one Chinese leader whispered into the ear of another leader loud enough to be heard, 'Narendra Modi may be the Deng Xiaoping of India'. But Modi also spoke about the sensitivity of India towards the perception that Chinese were using Islamabad against India. The Chinese leaders listened to him in rapt attention.[19]

The Chinese investment in Gujarat has been growing. Many Gujarati businessmen are looking towards China to strengthen their technology and scale. The red carpet welcome to Modi has helped a lot in changing Guajrat's perception about China.

Modi spoke glowingly about the warmth in Sino-India relations, invited China to invest in Gujarat and declared that "the two great countries will make Asia the centre-stage of the global economy."[20]

He also developed a close relation with Japan. He had visited Tokyo along with other chief ministers in 2007 and showed his keenness to understand Japan's growth. This was followed by a visit of a Japanese delegation to Gujarat. Modi revisited Japan in July 2012. He was given the protocol befitting a Union Minister of India.

The Japanese newspaper noted that "in contrast to many other states, Gujarat was a haven for international investors: its government, headed by Modi, was responsive to investor's needs and, just as important, could deliver. It is this that reinforced the perception among international leaders that Modi is someone they could do business with. He is a strikingly different leader who had earned their respect."[21]

***

The GameChanger

Once you make a decision, the universe conspires to make it happen.

—Ralph Waldo Emerson

Not all chief ministers are biography material. There are few who are able to impress the entire nation with their vision. Narendra Modi's dedication, vision and pan-India appeal have put him in a different league. While still working for six crore Gujaratis as the chief minister, he has impressed the country with his national vision. He has charged up the BJP's rank and file and the party's decision to declare him as its prime ministerial candidate for 2014 Lok Sabha elections was a natural call.

It is not merely because of development and for translating Gujarat into a growth powerhouse that Modi is being talked about. It is growth with equity. And, above all, it is a growth story that has failed to sully his image of being honest even when he rubs shoulders with the who's who of Indian industries. He fits into the mould of those who become popular with the middle class with their undiluted patriotism and unquestionable integrity.

Even his worst critics concede that he is "incorruptible". Senior Congress leader Digvijaya Singh told US consul general Michael S Owen that even BJP leaders were worried about Modi. They feared that he would take action against corrupt politicians and cadre in the BJP.[1] He has brought fear among the Delhi elite who acquire strength due to their proximity to those in power. Those who thought that ministerial positions were rewards for struggle in politics are uncertain if the same trend would continue since Modi's main criteria are performance and integrity.

When Atal Bihari Vajpayee became the prime minister in 1998 his regime expedited the dismantling of the license-quota *raj* that had stifled the nation's entrepreneurial energy. He impressed people with his development vision that included converting national highways into four lane highways, inter-linking of river waters (that did not take off) and freeing space for private sector participation in major government monopolies including telephony.

Most BJP leaders learnt from Vajpayee that development could be a winning electoral plank.

In that sense, Modi has been a true follower of Vajpayee. When he was sent to Gujarat as chief minister, his immediate task was to rebuild the State from the debris of a devastating earthquake. And despite the backing of the central leadership of the BJP, there were repeated pin pricks from his detractors within the State unit since he was considered an imposition from outside.

This was, therefore, not an easy task in a party where various pulls and pressures worked at the same time, creating unimaginable hurdles. On the one hand, he had to tackle factional opposition from within the BJP and on the other, he had to tackle the bureaucracy that was known as inefficient and slow moving.

In cricketing terms, we can say he was given a bat he did not know how to wield. He was sent to bat on a pitch which was not his own. And he was sent as the last batsman with a mandate to win the match at any cost. He had only one thing — the vast experience of working in the RSS and the BJP as their organisational man. He had an acute sixth sense that told him who was the right man for the job. And above all, he had the right intent. He was guided by only one goal: how to provide relief to the common man.

Very soon the bureaucracy was eating out of his hand and waiting for his nod like dutiful school children awaiting the teacher's approving eyes. His dedication, punctuality, full time devotion and determination did the trick. He chose honest bureaucrats and gave them positions of power and responsibility. Things began to fall in place. Most people recall the way he used to come to office at 9 am sharp and go back home late in the night.

From day one, Modi's focus was development. He tackled sick

public sector undertakings (PSUs) by making them profit making enterprises. Political patronage that contributed to internal bleeding was stopped — something that did not go down well with traditional politicians who held these as parking places for their key supporters. He converted loss making Gujarat Electricity Board (GEB) into a profit making entity and forced the power producers to renegotiate the power purchase agreements that were considered too high. He clearly sent a strong message that he meant business and would not accept the old order as it was.

At a time when people thought of winning elections through populist promises such as free electricity and water, Modi brought discipline and more accountability. Power for agriculture is subsidised but farmers in Gujarat are paying for the power they consume domestically. There is a separate line and meter for non-agriculture use by farmers. Power theft and transmission and distribution losses have been brought down to an all time low. This involved taking tough steps but the chief minister was ready to take the risks. The RSS affiliated Bharatiya Kisan Sangh stood up in opposition but he refused to budge. His question was, 'do you want regular and dependable power to irrigate the fields or you want free but irregular power.' People accepted the new credo.

Bringing governance to the doorsteps of people is another landmark which Modi can pride in. Farmers do not have to go to the government offices to get their compensation. Officials go to them to make the payments and receive their signatures. This is something unheard of in any other state. There are more than 100 government services for which a citizen can apply online and get them within 24 hours. One does not have to go through the humiliation of paying bribes to get things done.

Instead of trying to earn a few brownie points in the media by holding *Janata Darbar* (people's court) to resolve problems of those who could come, he developed a system of institutionalised delivery of government services. For those who do not get their problems resolved, there is a SWAGAT system of grievance resolution at the Chief Minister's Office. The Chief Minister sits with his officials and the complainant to directly interact with concerned local officials to discuss why the issue could not be resolved. Anybody has the right to approach the CMO directly without going through any bureaucratic channel.

Take any sector of Gujarat's development story: One cannot help but get impressed by the scale and the vision. If one drives along the State's coastline one would be surprised to see thousands of windmills that rotate with the power of wind to produce energy. It appears there is a windmill revolution. And the State has well laid roads that run along the coast and at some stretches one runs through windmills on both sides. Incentivising wind energy has done the trick.

If one visits any of the GIDC sites, one can't remain unimpressed by the scale of operation. The same is the case with agriculture experiments such as growing cotton or adopting drip irrigation.

Once, a group of young interns from an NGO met Narendra Modi to discuss village empowerment. The NGO wanted to adopt a few villages for implementing education schemes under corporate social responsibility (CSR). When Modi asked how many villages they needed, they said five. While Modi did not discourage them, he told them that the scale has to be really big to make an impact in a vast country like India.

Modi believes in doing everything in a big way. He not only dreams big but translates them into reality through a step by step process that includes launching a pilot project to see whether it would be successful. Once it succeeds with or without amendments, the scheme is replicated all across the state. This was seen in encouraging dairy farming through animal hostels, agriculture through soil testing and waste disposal through better waste management.

This energy to do everything big seems to have been transplanted into every Gujarati. They talk of everything being vibrant—Vibrant Navaratri festival, Vibrant Mall, Vibrant Park. "Even when one is going to set up a school in Gujarat now, the promoters want to make it globally competitive. Earlier an average Gujarati wanted to be happy with whatever earnings he made. Now he wants to compete, not nationally but globally," Hiren Diwan said.

When the iron collection programme for the Statue of Unity in honour of Sardar Vallabhbhai Patel was launched on 28 December 2013, the sheer size of the exercise left one in awe. About three lakh boxes were kept in 1000 trucks to collect soil and iron implements from about 6.5 lakh villages across country. All these boxes were fitted with microchips to track their movement. One had not heard about such a massive exercise organised this way before. The same was the case when the 'Run for Unity' march was held across the country on 15 December 2013. About 50 lakh people participated.

Every political party or politician grapples with the problem of mass mobilisation. It is easier said than done. Even the ones considered most popular fail to draw crowds. One often comes across reports that people were paid to come for the rallies.

Modi has breathed fresh life into political mobilisation, at least for the BJP. It is after this, that the party decided he would address about 100 rallies before the Lok Sabha elections in 2014. None of Modi's rallies get less than a lakh people. The BJP cadre is happy since they are getting a huge response everywhere without much effort. They are experiencing a new wave of mass power that is, in turn, making them more active.

Among the recent crowd pulling leaders, Anna Hazare deserves special praise since people flocked to his *dharna/*protest venue spontaneously. The middle class saw hope in the anti-corruption crusader. Swami Ramdev also demonstrated his mass mobilisation power when he came to Delhi at the Ramlila Maidan in February 2011 and addressed a rally of more than one lakh. Those who had not seen such a big rally in Delhi for a long time were mesmerised by the yoga guru who promised change. These two — Anna Hazare and Swami Ramdev — captured the imagination of the nation in different ways. They both promised change and people were ready to listen to them.

Modi is drawing crowds bigger than either of them and at every place, whether it is Kochi, Hyderabad, Bangalore, Delhi or Patna.

Only a party that is confident of the leader would dare to test if people would pay to come to listen to him. The BJP experimented with this at the Hyderabad rally that was branded as a rally of youths. Those who wanted to attend the meeting were asked to purchase Rs 5 tickets as contribution for relief fund of Uttarakhand flood victims. The Lal Bahadur Shastri Stadium in the capital city of Andhra Pradesh was full of people.

The crowd comprised those who would normally not go to listen

368 Narendra Modi: The GameChanger

to political leaders. They were mostly college students and young IT professionals. Many people who could not go inside the stadium watched him on the giant screens displayed outside — there were six such screens that demonstrated the organisers had expected such a response.[2]

Modi has started a new trend in India where people are paying to listen to their leader. At the Bangalore rally on 17 November 2013, the fee was hiked to Rs 10 and the money was to be donated for construction of Sardar Patel's statue. The rally had an unprecedented response greater than —any BJP leader had received till then. More than three lakh people had registered online.

At the Kolkata rally on 5 February 2014, the BJP had put a voluntary entry fee of a minimum of Rs 100. There were reports that some people paid as high as Rs 2 lakh. The seats were booked online.

That he was equally popular in South India was proved much earlier when he addressed people in Tiruchirapally (Trichy) in Tamil Nadu on 27 September 2013. Modi enthralled the large crowd that had gathered at the G-corner of the city by his no -holds barred attack on the UPA and Prime Minister Dr Manmohan Singh. In a bid to establish connect with the crowd, mostly youth, he spoke about Tamil Nadu, some of it in Tamil.

Modi the communicator had an instant connect with the masses. His speech in Hindi did not deter his audience from appreciating the punch of his attack on UPA. A senior journalist KV Lakshmanan while describing the Trichy rally wrote: "He had the masses eating out of his hands — despite his speech in Hindi, a language that most in this part of the country do not understand. Luckily, the Tamil translation that followed retained his punch and style. Modi struck the chord with the masses from the moment he began — in Tamil. His pronunciation of Tamil words may have annoyed language purists, but the masses lapped it up."[3]

If Modi could get such a massive response in Tami Nadu and Andhra Pradesh, where the BJP has a marginal presence, the situation in other States where the party is fighting fit was bound to be much better. At the rally in Jaipur (10 September 2013), Modi told the crowd of more than two lakh that the country was on the verge of destruction.[4]

This was dubbed the largest rally ever in the Pink city's history.

The Jaipur rally was marked for a large attendance by the minority community as well.[6]

Straight talk and patriotism pull ex-servicemen to Modi. The Rewari meeting was the first rally he addressed (though not planned that way) after being declared the BJP's prime ministerial candidate. He addressed their concerns and spoke about the need for a strong leadership at the Centre. He touched an emotional chord by saying that he had wanted to join the army but could not do so due to lack of money. But he compensated by serving tea to soldiers during the 1962 war with China.

Even the organisers had not anticipated such a huge response. The venue was packed with people.[7] Commenting on the rally, BJP-affiliated website 272+ noted, "Far more than the rhetorical flourish of Narendra Modi, it was the electric connect that Narendra Modi had established with the audience that should worry the Congress-led UPA the most."

The Bhopal rally on 25 September 2013 was a Shivraj show. Senior leader LK Advani was also present and this generated considerable interest since Modi and Advani were sharing the dais for the first time after Modi was made the PM candidate. There were more than five lakh party workers (the rally was dubbed '*Karyakarta Mahamumbh*') and it was not a public meeting.

The *karyakartas* had their clear favourite. They started shouting "Modi, Modi, Modi" when other BJP leaders came to speak. The shouts became louder when Murli Manohar Joshi came to speak. Joshi could not ignore it and told the crowd that "Modiji will also come. All these arrangements are for him alone." And the frenzy of workers would not have gone unnoticed on master craftsman Advani. The sound of the animated crowd was not lost on anyone.[8]

You may organise big rallies in smaller towns and cities but unless you do a grand show in Delhi, your popularity is not accepted by critics. This is because Delhi is a difficult territory for crowd response. The Delhi unit had made elaborate arrangements for Modi's rally on 30 September. About 100 LED big screens were placed at strategic points all across the city to enable people to watch, in case they would not be able to reach the venue on Delhi's outskirts at Rohini.

Even conservative estimates put the figure at more than a lakh. And it was a young and enthusiastic crowd comprising mostly of the middle class that cheered every time Modi spoke. Modi bristled at reports that Pakistani Prime Minister Nawaz Sharif had referred to the Indian Prime Minister Dr Manmohan Singh as a *"dehati aurat"* (illiterate woman). To the delight of the audience, Modi thundered that the "the nation of 1.2 billion will not tolerate its prime minister's insult".[9]

Bihar has always been a politically sensitive state. In every nook and corner, people talk and breathe politics. They talk about rights, social empowerment and development. However, the caste conscious society seldom rises in one voice and when it does it becomes the harbinger of change. It empowered a frail Jayaprakash Narayan to dethrone a mighty Indira Gandhi.[10] and it strengthened an unsure VP Singh to vanquish the powerful Rajiv Gandhi.[11] Mahatma Gandhi realised the strength of people power when he launched the Champaran *satyagraha* from Bihar — his first ever agitation in India.[12]

Will Modi succeed was the main issue in Bihar when the BJP planned the *"hunkar rally"* (rally of clarion call for change) in Patna on 27 October 2013. Former Chief Minister of Bihar, Lalu Prasad Yadav, claimed complete sway over the dominant Yadava community and present Chief Minister Nitish Kumar claimed the same over Kurmis and other backward castes. After exiting from the government, the BJP was unsure if people would come. It was their first real test at mass mobilisation.

As the time for the rally drew closer, the cadre got enthused with new confidence. Everyone wanted to come and listen to Modi. Professor RN Sharma who teaches Sociology in Patna University said, "We wanted to see if Modi's rally would be bigger than that of Jayaprakash Narayan in June 1974 at the same venue. Had the bomb blast not taken place, the city would have witnessed a never before kind of crowd presence."[13]

A commentator said: "Make no mistake, Modi sent a strong message from Gandhi *maidan*. No other leader in Bihar today is capable of attracting such a big crowd to a rally. Most, in fact, avoid the *maidan* to hide their inability to fill up the ground."[14]

An attempt to thwart the rally was made by miscreants who

triggered bomb blasts at the venue. In any other situation, people would have panicked. Although the BJP tried to downplay the incident as 'fire-crackers or tyre blasts', people in the crowd must have come to know the news about casualties and injuries. No one was ready to move out. Everyone appreciated Modi for the way he handled the crowd. MJ Akbar said one can plan for a speech but one can't plan for a crisis.

People thronged to the venue in large numbers. There was a sea of humanity all around. Modi was moved by such a huge crowd presence — the largest rally the BJP had organised till then. A visibly moved Modi said: "This is not a mere historic rally but an event to write a new history. The love which Bihar has shown...other political leaders may not be fortunate to see such a scene (crowd).. I will repay your love with interest. And our mantra is '*vikas*'" (development).

Overwhelmed by the energy of the crowd, he said while concluding: "*Main aap sab ko naman karta hun; bhaiya main aap sab ko naman karta hun. Aaj aapne pure Hindustan ka dil jeet liya hai doston, pure Hindustan ka dil jeet liya hai.*" (I salute you brother, I salute you. You have today won the heart of India, friends, you have won the heart of India). The crowd was animated, responsive and people waved and jumped.[15]

Uttar Pradesh has been the BJP's political battleground on the road to power at the Centre. It won 52 of the 85 Lok Sabha seats in the State in 1996.[16] Subsequently, the party's tally dipped since regional parties — the Samajwadi Party (SP) and the Bahujan Samaj Party (BSP) — performed better. After formation of a separate state of Uttarakhand, Uttar Pradesh now has 80 Lok Sabha seats.

The first few rallies of the nine Modi addressed in the state rattled other parties so much that their leaders could not restrain themselves from attacking him. In November 2013, chief minister of the state Akhilesh Yadav said, "You know an outsider is moving around the state and misleading people. He is telling lies. He is created by media and the hype created by TV channels is false and misleading."[17]

BSP chief and former Uttar Pradesh chief minister, Ms Mayawati, who is known to have complete sway over her core support base could also not restrain herself. A day after Modi's rally in Agra, the area which has sizeable presence of Dalits, she said: "wherever Modi goes, he is raising local issues but... his knowledge about Uttar Pradesh is poor and is misleading people through his lies… Media is giving him too much space, which he does not deserve." Mayawati's fort appeared to have been breached.

The Agra rally (21 November 2013) was the fourth Modi addressed in Uttar Pradesh after Kanpur, Jhansi and Bahraich. A huge crowd awaited Modi's arrival despite his getting late by three hours. A similar rally of the SP was taking place almost simultaneously about 200 Km away in Bareilly. In that rally, speaker after speaker referred to Modi's rally as the one not getting a good response. Modi did not mention the Bareilly rally even once but pointed out that every rally in UP was surprising him with a large crowd presence.

He clearly focused on development and sought to know why the city of Taj Mahal did not have an airport despite housing one of the Wonders of the World. He sought to know why the city did not get adequate drinking water despite having river Yamuna.

Modi's first rally in Uttar Pradesh was in Kanpur (19 October 2013) and BJP leaders were overwhelmed by the crowd response. "It is almost after more than a decade that such a huge crowd assembled at a BJP rally in UP. Earlier such a crowd used to come for Atal Bihari Vajpayee… Today's crowd was because of Modi…" said state BJP spokesperson Chandramohan.[18]

The Congress could not digest the massive response Modi got in Kanpur. Its spokesperson Renuka Chowdhary said in Delhi, "do not measure one's strength from one's obesity. The famous film star Rajkumar once said that a large crowd gathers even when some circus comes to town."[19]

The Mumbai rally on 22 December 2013 was also remarkable for the large crowd presence. About 10,000 *chaiwalas* (tea vendors) were invited to attend the rally as VIPs. This was an answer to senior Samajwadi Party leader Naresh Agarwal's comment that "a *chaiwala* cannot become the prime minister of the country."

Corruption must stop and the youth must get jobs, he said at the *Maha Garjana* Rally and stressed that the BJP would get back the black money of corrupt Indians stashed in Swiss banks.

Modi's biggest advantage is his connect with youth. He speaks the language of their aspirations and he has young people manning his campaign. He has emerged as a symbol to fight corruption and a source of youth empowerment. Gone are the days when the youth would be lured with populist slogans or promises of the moon. They can debate issues and are logical.

India's population in the 15-34 age group increased from 353 million in 2001 to 430 million in 2011. The country is set to become the world's "youngest" country by 2020 with 64 percent of its population in the working age group.[20] Modi is targeting these voters with his India first campaign.

What do these millions of youngsters want? They aspire for conditions that would enable them to shape their own destinies away from clutches of region, religion or other narrow considerations. This explains why a Nirmal Kumar from Bihar decides not to go for a job after IIM Ahmedabad and sets up his G-Auto in Gujarat. First he tried to do the same in Bihar but did not get any encouragement from the establishment. Also, a Harshad Patel in Himmatnagar after B. Tech decides to set up his own switching system rather than apply for a job.

The youths are fiercely competitive and oppose regressive or populist economic measures although they would support government help for the poor irrespective of their origin. It is this class that Modi is addressing. This also explains why they don't mind paying to listen to their leader — from Rs 5 a ticket in Hyderabad to Rs 10 a ticket in Bengaluru. Their response is coming at a time when people are disinterested in politics and disillusioned with politicians!

Look at the way they wait for his rallies and the way they go home satisfied after hearing his speech. After Modi delivered his speech before students of the Sri Ram College of Commerce of Delhi University in 2013, this is how they reacted to it: "I don't know much about politics and wouldn't know if he would make for a strong prime minister but I really liked his speech where the emphasis was on development," said Priyanka Sharma, a first-year student. "This is a commerce college and his speech was expectedly more on growth and business than politics," said Sanjita Gupta, another first-year student. "He is a good orator and might be a good prime ministerial candidate," said Gaurav Verma, a second-year student.

He has a phenomenal craze among the youth. One needs to recall the incident of the Wankhede Stadium in Mumbai where Sachin Tendulkar played his last test match on 15 November 2013. When people in the crowd came to know that Congress vice president Rahul Gandhi had come to watch the match, they started shouting 'Modi', 'Modi'. Such hysteria for any one leader has not been seen before.

Of definite advantage to Modi is his massive youth following on the social media. The young crowd get their information from various blogs, Status Updates, quite a few *Facebook* pages, including one that is authenticated, Modi's website, *Twitter* handle, Mission 272+ Application etc. The impression that they get about Gujarat creates hope in them about an India that will be strong, prosperous and corruption free. They come to hear him whenever he is in their town or city.

The craze among the youth for Narendra Modi is apparent on the social media. When last checked (20 November 2013), these were the number of followers the most popular political leaders had on *Facebook* and *Twitter*.

	Narendra Modi	Arvind Kejriwal	Rahul Gandhi
Facebook page	6.2 million	850,000	185,000
Twitter handle	2,832,125	734,469	43,744 (run by fans)

But the youth are not from the urban middle class alone. Modi is getting tremendous response even in the small towns from where people come to rally venues in large numbers to hear him speak.

A veteran journalist, Rajdeep Sardesai noted this Modi phenomenon on his blog: "In the last five years, while Rahul has stayed mostly closeted behind the forbidding walls of Lutyens Delhi — barring the occasional foray into a UP — Modi has made a conscious and sustained attempt at engaging with young India. Be it a Google Hangout, a *Twitter* account with regular updates and addressing students, Modi has almost been like a Shah Rukh Khan on a 24×7 Chennai Express promotional overdrive in seeking young audiences. [21]

Like a young man, Modi has kept himself abreast with technology. His smart phone is as fast as the new generation phone and he tweets at will. He was IT savvy even when he was in Delhi and when IT had just begun to penetrate every office. He used to tell BJP workers to keep pace with technology.

This is also the reason for the youth to identify with him. You write to him something and he responds. Ask any question or raise any doubt, you get an answer. He caught the imagination of the tech-savvy generation through his 3D campaign during 2012 assembly elections — something that India had not witnessed before.

The new mobile application "India 272+" is an extension of Modi's IT vision. Anyone downloading this application will get all the information about who said what and can also get ideas about what should be done.

Modi's undiluted patriotism has made him popular with the youth. They see him as a leader who can give a befitting reply to China, stand up to Pakistan and laugh at the US intransigence. A nation struggling with its basic problems needs a strong leader to suit the aspirations of the youth — someone who can redefine India's personality. This will mark India's transition to an assertive nation in the international community.

Even those who oppose him do not fail to realize this feeling he evokes in a common Indian. Time magazine commented: "…But when others think of someone who can bring Indian out of the mire of chronic corruption and inefficiency- of a firm, no-nonsense leader who will set the nation on the course of development that might finally put it on part with China- they think of Modi."[22] And they are not wrong to think so. During his visit to China in 2011, Modi actually gave a test of how things may take shape. China had arrested about two dozen diamond merchants in 2010 on charges of smuggling and most were Gujaratis. Indian side tried their best but nothing could influence the Chinese decision. Before leaving for China, Modi promised families of the diamond merchants and others concerned that he would bring them back.

He was given a grand reception by the Chinese and was received at the Great Hall of People reserved for national leaders, Jagan Shah, the chairman of the India China Economic and Cultural Council, said. Shah was a member of the delegation. At the first official engagement with Chinese leaders, Modi raised the issue of the diamond merchants but the Chinese brushed it aside saying such small issues should not figure in high level discussions and that the Chinese law would take care of this. At the second meeting, which was with another leader, Modi did not raise the issue at all. Instead he presented a policy framework for India-China cooperation. He spoke of the Buddhist circle in Gujarat and cultural exchanges and also of immense business potential. At the third meeting, which was also the concluding one, with Chinese leaders, the Chinese side was relaxed since the issue of the diamond merchants was not raised at the previous meeting. At the end of the meeting, Modi said: "My diamond merchants are in jail for two years. I don't want to discuss that. But I want to understand as a student how much time it takes in Chinese law for the start of proceedings after arrest and for punishment to be awarded after trial. Also suggest to me what I should do now that I have promised my diamond merchants in Gujarat that I will get the diamond merchants released?" The trial for the merchants was over but the judgement had not come for the last three months, Shah said while narrating the incident.

The Chinese leader was forthright and said the legal system was there and he could not do anything about it. At this Modi said, "Oh yes! There are certain small mistakes people commit but relations of national leaders should go beyond this. For example, we have liquor prohibition but the Chinese engineers working in Gujarat ports drink liquor daily. But we do not put them behind bars because they support nation building as well." His body language suggested that their engineers could be put behind bars. This changed the facial expressions of the Chinese leaders. When Modi was leaving the meeting, a Chinese leader stopped him and said: "We promise the judgement will come in 15 days and two things will be kept in mind—the Chinese law and the relation with Gujarat," Shah said.

After 10-12 days, the Gujarati diamond merchants were given two years of punishment which they had already served and therefore released. The non-Gujarati diamond merchants were given six years' imprisonment. When a jubilant Shah informed Modi about this, Modi was upset that other Indians were not released. "What about other Indians? Make sure we create legal assistance to other Indian diamond merchants even at the cost of Gujarat's relation with China", he told

Shah. Also, Modi did not go to town to claim credit for the release of the Gujarati merchants. After six months, others were also released.

The change in the stand of the United States demonstrates that even the most powerful fall in line if there is dogged determination to succeed on one's part. Modi never complained when the US denied visa to him in 2005, but pointed at the inconsistency in the American stand. He used satellite links to address his supporters in the US whenever they wanted and stuck to his agenda of outlining his vision for India. The US could not explain what made the difference in 2005 and why it waited for three years after 2002 riots to boycott Gujarat and Modi. Even in private talks with US officials, Modi was not apologetic or supplicative. When US consul general Michael S Owen met him in Gandhinagar in 2006 to discuss trade issues, Modi told him that the US stand vis-à-vis Gujarat was not correct since it relied far too much on fringe NGOs that did not know the real pictures and had an axe to grind. Modi had clarified to Owen, "The events of 2002 were an internal Gujarati matter and the US had no right to interfere."[23]

Rather than wooing the US administration, he created a climate very friendly for business and investment. This persuaded hordes of US-based companies to come and invest in Gujarat. He cultivated China as a natural ally without compromising on his basic principles. The West and Europe realised that it was fruitless to be staying out of Gujarat that promised better returns and transparency of operations compared to other Indian states with their uncertainties. Foreign governments value political stability and predictability as crucial factors in bilateral ties. The vast Gujarati Diaspora in the US, other persons of Indian origin and business interests exerted a lot of pressure on the US administration to change its policy.

The fact that he is fast emerging as India's most powerful contender for the prime minister's post did the trick. Earlier, the US and others were persuaded to believe that the Indians would not accept a person as their leader who was not treated honourably by the US and other major foreign powers. On the contrary, most Indians took this as an affront. The strategy boomeranged on the US and Modi marched ahead. Americans were forced to do a rethink and change its stand. The US cannot be seen as hostile to a person who is being projected as a strong contender for India's top job. Nancy Powell's visit to Gujarat to meet Narendra Modi on 13 February 2014 should be seen in this context. A course correction, yes, but also a way to accept that they were wrong!

Modi had not appealed against the Visa revocation and the Indian government should have protested loudly since this was being done against an elected head of a State. Modi had said that there was a need for the country to become so strong that the US would not dare to take India lightly. Powell's visit was his moment of triumph.

"Powell has shared and listened to views on the US-India relationship" and she "continues to emphasize that the partnership is important and strategic, and that the United States looks forward to working closely with the government that the Indian people choose in the upcoming elections," a statement released by the US embassy said after the meeting.

Like young people don't want to talk about their caste, Modi has never brought up his backward caste origin to increase his acceptability. When some BJP leaders tried to do that in Bihar, he told them it should not be done. The only concession he has given to himself is that he has spoken about his humble background. However, he had to forego the restriction when senior Congress leader Mani Shankar Aiyar ridiculed his background saying that he would never become the prime minister but could sell tea at the Congress headquarters, if he so desired.[24] At the BJP's national council meeting on 19 January 2013, a day after Aiyar's remark, came Modi's reply. Modi spoke about his backward caste origin and said that the Congress was perhaps refusing to name its prime ministerial candidate since it was governed by "forward caste family with higher status" and they would find it demeaning for a person from the dynasty to contest against "a backward caste *chaiwala*".[25]

Modi is driven by a great sense of purpose resulting sometimes in self-imposed isolation. This is because he does not wish to deviate from the chosen path. He rarely lets down his guard but if you are lucky enough to see his inner self, he is like anyone of us—deeply emotional and driven by passion. Senior journalist and former editor of *The Times of India*, MD Nalapat said that his ability to keep his personal life out of public gaze, such as his family members, has ensured that his personal relationships do not influence policies.

When a TV journalist wanted to do one full day's shoot in the life of Modi, the chief minister's advisors laughed since Modi's life veers around work, office, meetings, rallies etc. This devotion to work and the desire to do something for the country has endeared him to the RSS — an organisation known for domination of Brahmins. But Modi never felt sidelined or isolated because of his backward caste origin. The organisation always trusted him with more and more responsibilities.

Projecting Modi as the prime ministerial candidate is nothing short of a revolution in India. The United States created history by making Barack Obama the first Black president. The BJP has already created history by projecting Modi, a person from a backward caste, as the party's prime ministerial choice.

We will have to wait and see whether India will vote for Modi and create history. HD Devegowda was the only Prime Minister who came from the agriculture (Vokkaliga) community. He was never identified as a backward caste leader and belonged to a politically dominant caste group as well.

It may not have been by design but most of India's Prime Ministers have been *Brahmins* or upper caste people — Jawahar Lal Nehru, Indira Gandhi, Morarji Desai, Rajiv Gandhi, PV Narasimha Rao and Atal Bihari Vajpayee were all *Brahamins*. IK Gujral was a Punjabi Khatri (upper caste), whereas Lal Bahadur Shashtri was a forward caste Kayastha. VP Singh and Chandrashekhar belonged to the powerful Thakur caste.

In that sense, a new era has begun in the saffron party. Modi is a product of social engineering done by Modi's guru Vakil Saheb when the former had barely reached his teen years. The RSS is aware of the importance and is leaving no stone unturned to ensure Modi reaches the top.

Very few chief ministers of an Indian State can dare to challenge an Oxford educated economist Prime Minister on the concept of development. Modi has done this without mincing words. This has been a characteristic of Modi ever since his childhood. If he feels very strongly he says it loudly. He is speaking the language of Vajpayee. He is talking of basic things, those little things that affect the common man.

The story of Modi surmounting difficulties despite all odds and marching ahead despite opposition is inspiring for an average Indian who struggles on a daily basis. He may see a reflection of his struggle in him. No chief minister has been vilified so much. "In fact, I have never seen any leader who can climb up in public opinion by defeating media negativity. Nobody in the history of modern Indian has got as much negative press. The same media — I won't mention names — which is raising the same questions like 'What right do you have to rule?' and so on, or finding artificial dummy props to challenge him, never raised these questions with Narasimha Rao." veteran journalist MJ Akbar said.

Modi's success is also because he comes from the ground and is not a part of the elite who have been trying to dominate politics since a long time. Like when you struggle too hard, you become a fighter with a never die attitude. Akbar says, "if you want to analyse any leader, you must do a graph, a basic chart of where he is over a one-way period. The interesting thing about Modi is that he is not a flash in the pan; he is not another Kejriwal puffed up by media."

While comparing him with Rahul Gandhi, Akbar gave an interesting take: "You are basically.. This is chalk and cheese. One side there is experience, deliverables and the other side there is a constantly reinvented persona. Problem with Rahul Gandhi is that there is total absence of any consistency. He seems to reinvent himself according to the needs of his latest set of advices....He was promising 17 per cent reservations for the minorities. Today he is two steps ahead of the AAP (Aam Aadmi Party)...But what is he protesting against? He is protesting against Congress corruption not opposition corruption. And he has been taken for a ride by the Congress party. Because Congress party does Adarsh and says yes we will listen to you and then does nothing."

But, the Gamechanger's task is not going to be easy. A bruised and wounded media, animosities across the political spectrum and antagonism of NGOs and other Left of the Centre opinion makers are likely to combine to oppose his march. Internationally, vested interests would never accept a strong nationalist government at the Centre. Modi is for market economy but he is smart enough to see international design in their India operations. An officer of the British intelligence had once told the author that the US or any country in the West would not like to see a nationalist government in India.[26] The problems that the prospect of Modi becoming the prime minister will entail for the United States have already started being debated.[27]

MD Nalapat concurred that no foreign country will accept a strong man as the leader of India today. "Modi doesnot have a foreign account and hence you can't blackmail him. The West is facing problems from China and Korea. They are scared of Indian brains. They do not want India to stand up and start competing. India is seen as a threat. Modi has the potential to empower people and create a new India," he said.

Members of Delhi circle who thrive on their connection with power are scared because they are apprehensive of an outsider. Modi may take steps to tackle corruption and destabilise the system of patronage that has been going on. Akbar put it differently: "I think media also...those sections which are part of the Delhi establishment are also worried because Modi represents huge uncertainty. He actually interferes with the comfort level of the system."

Ram Jethmalani believes Modi would bring freshness in politics and better the delivery system that has been rotting and taking the common people away from government. "He is young, energetic and honest. And he has been running Gujarat successfully for the last many years. He has not looted anything. Narendra Modi is an avatar who will kill the demons, the thugs and the dacoits in politics who have looted the poor people's wealth," he said.

"There is anarchy in India everywhere. Only Modi can set it right", said former DDA commissioner KJ Alphons, while talking about the reason for youths' attraction towards Modi. Nalapat, held that there was an increasing realization that Modi was the country's only hope. India must not lose this opportunity. "This is the last chance for the country. If he fails this time, the next time, the country will be a failed state," he added.

Many people from outside Delhi get a sense of affiliation with Modi because they see him as someone who has come up through the struggle of politics with an unblemished record. "Actually we have, in Modi's case, gone through something equivalent to American primaries. Every step you have to fight not one election, (but) challenge after challenge after challenge in a series of concentric circles before you are eligible to a claim there. And quite a few of the challenges are within the party itself," Akbar said.

Modi's biggest challenge will be to increase his acceptability in the minority community. Things have begun to look up. A group of Muslims offered chadar at Ajmer Sharif shrine when Modi won the assembly elections in 2012. They announced that they would offer chadar again if Modi would become the Prime Minister.[28]

Many leaders from the community have come out and spoken openly in his favour. Mufti Aijaz Arshad Qasmi, the youngest member of the All India Muslim Personal Law Board, was one of his bitterest critics, but has now turned into his supporter. "If Modiji becomes the Prime Minister, I think, there will be no discrimination in the country," the Mufti who has also studied at Delhi's Jawaharlal Nehru University said. "We must make a fresh assessment of the BJP's prime ministerial candidate."

Before turning into a Modi supporter, the Mufti was known for his extremist views. "I was an extremist Muslim for a long time and now I have no shame in accepting this." He was dead against the United States and a US delegation came to India to read his mind. "They stayed here for a week but could not change my thinking. But one meeting with Modi and I was a completely transformed man," the Mufti said. He used to hold Modi solely responsible for 2002 riots till he met him in July 2012.

What is that which makes Modi win over his enemies in one meeting? Whether it was meeting Zafar Sareshwala in 2003, speaking to Mahesh Bhatt the same year or meeting Qasmi in 2012, the results have been the same. One reason is he is simple and straight and speaks out his mind without fear. All three of them say that you can trust him. Salim Khan went to the extent of saying that here is one leader you can openly speak with. He always calls back and is ready to listen.

Salim Khan told Modi not to bother about anything but lead people with honesty. People may not come for the party but they may come for you, he told Modi: *"Modi Sahib ek baat mai bataun? Duniya mein jab bhi koi revolution aaya hai to kisi party se ya kisi committee se nahi aaya hai…Hamesha jab bhi revolution aaya hai, ek aadmi le ke aaya hai. Jesus Christ, Gautam Buddha, Mohammad ek hi aadmi le ke aata hai.*

Ek hi aadmi ko log follow karte hai. Ek aadmi pe trust hota hai ek aadmi pe bharosa hota hai, aur ek hi aadmi ke liye samajhta hai ki ye sahi jaa rha hai. Jahan humko le ke jaa rha hai sahi hai isko hum follow kare.

I told Modi "whenever revolution has come in the world it has not come due to any party or committee. …Always, when revolution has come it has been brought by one man. Jesus Christ, Gautam Buddha, Mohammad. Only one man bring revolution and people follow only one man. People trust only one man and understand that he is right."

Both Qasmi and Sareshwala said that they were surprised the way Modi listened to them for hours. Modi clarified to them that he is not against Muslims and that he could be trusted for delivering justice. It is no wonder that cine star Salman Khan after meeting Modi turned out to be his biggest defender. "Narendra Modi should not apologise for Gujarat riots as he has been given a clean chit by the judiciary" he said.[29]

The Gamechanger's final salvo came at the party's national council in Delhi on 19 January 2013. This was as much in what he said as to how he said. Like a pied piper, he made the entire national council chant nationalistic slogans along with him. The entire party leadership appeared charged up with the energy that Modi generated. Among others who were shouting the slogans included party patriarch LK Advani and president Rajnath Singh. The slogans centred around "My idea of India". There were close to 3 dozen slogans that included *Satyamev Jayate* (truth alone triumphs), *Vasudev Kutumbhakam* (the world is one family), *Sarva Panta Sambhav* (equal treatment to all the religions), freedom from corruption, freedom from dynasty, for employment, women uplift and India's unity.

Minutes before that, he unrolled his national vision for the country calling it a 'rainbow vision'. These could be described as strengthening the family values that have stood the test of time for thousands of years; the village life that includes agriculture and livestock; women empowerment and their transformation from home makers to nation builders; safeguarding environment through proper care of *Jal* (water), *Jangal* (forests), *Zameen* (land) and *Jalvayu* (eco-system); channelising youth power through proper manpower planning and skill development; strengthening and respecting institutions of democracy including federalism; and, respecting the power of knowledge to elevate the existence of the common man.

At the recent assembly elections in December 2013 in Madhya Pradesh, Chattisgarh, Rajasthan, Delhi and Mizoram, the topic of discussion was not how the Congress failed to retain Rajasthan and Delhi, but how Modi failed to capture Delhi. The Congress which lost Delhi and ranked a distant third with only eight seats, 35 seats less than its tally of 2008, was not attacked as much as the BJP that emerged the single largest party with 32 seats (31 won by the BJP and one won by its alliance partner the Shiromani Akali Dal), 9 more than its tally of 2008 and 4 more than the tally of the Aaam Aadmi Party (AAP) that won 28. This was the first election campaign in which Modi campaigned as a national leader. And the BJP's performance was spectacular. Many analysts felt that had Modi been not there, the Aam Aadmi Party would have registered a clean sweep in Delhi.

Senior journalist Abhilash Khandekar who reported on Madhya Pradesh elections said that everyone including chief minister Shivraj Singh Chauhan knew that the party was walking on a razor's edge in Madhya Pradesh. Modi's elevation and his campaign changed the complexion, he said. The party won 165 seats out of 230, which was 22 seats more than its tally of 143 in 2008.

BJP Rajya Sabha member and the party's state election management chief Anil Madhav Dave said that Modi had an electrifying connect with the youth and this helped the party achieve spectacular results in Madhya Pradesh. What was true of Madhya Pradesh was also true of Rajasthan where the party managed a decisive victory and Chattisgarh, where it won narrowly. The BJP won 162 of the 199 seats* in Rajasthan.

British documentary film maker Antonia Filmer found Modi's personality to be very powerful and impressive. She drew a comparison with former British Prime Minister Margaret Thatcher, the Iron Lady of Britain. Like her, Modi is also a nationalist and a champion of free market economy and he is equally capable of empowering the poor and the deprived, she said.

---

* The state has 200 seats out of which 199 went for polling. In one constituency, elections were postponed due to death of a BSP candidate.

Also, there is another comparison. Thatcher was a workaholic and daughter of a grocer, Modi is her male equivalent. Modi is getting the same kind of response which Thatcher got.

The situation of India today and that of the UK in 1980s seems to be almost similar. When Thatcher became the Prime Minister in 1979, the United Kingdom was faced with major economic crisis due to recession and unemployment. But, she successfully steered the country away from the crisis taking tough decisions that made her unpopular.

This is rare that an Indian election is being talked about in the foreign media so much in advance and with so much of interest. And almost everywhere the topic of discussion is Narendra Modi. They are discussing every aspect of Modi and the impact it may have on international relations. This speaks as much about the leader as about the Indian Diaspora that sees hope in Modi. Antonia said that "there have been positive comparisons and good things about Modi in British press too."

Modi has an emotional connect as well. Undeterred by criticisms Modi gave his final election *mantra* to the national council in Delhi. Go to the people and tell them that a *chaiwala* (tea vendor) was contesting the polls and he had nothing of his own. At least 10 crore families will donate funds to contest elections and the BJP would contest elections on donations from people, he said. The issue is, will the nation rally behind the person whose mother used to fill waters and clean utensils at the houses of others? (*ek aisa vyakti jiski maa ados pados ke ghar mein panni bharti thi bartan saaf karti thi.*).[30] Will this emotional connect translate into support.

***

Bibliography

1. Advani, LK, *My Country My Life*, Rupa & Co, 2008.
2. Ahmed, Akbar S, Islam Under Siege: Living Dangerously in a Post-Honor World, Polity Press, 2003.
3. Bunsha, Dionne, Scarred: *Experiment's With Violence In Gujarat*, Penguin, 2005.
4. Campbell, John, Chris Seiple, Dennis Hoover, Dennis R. Hoover, Pauletta Otis (ed), *The Routledge Handbook of Religion and Security*, Routledge, 2012.
5. Debroy, Bibek, *Gujarat—Governance for Growth and Development*, Academic Foundation, 2012.
6. Desai, Akshayakumar Ramanlal, D'Costa, Wilfred, *State and Repressive Culture: A Case Study of Gujarat*, Popular Prakashan, 1994.
7. Gangoli, Geetanjali, Nicole Westmarland, Geetanjali Gangoli, ed. *International Approaches to Rape*, Policy Press, 2012.
8. Ghassem-Fachandi, Parvis, *Pogrom in Gujarat — Hindu Nationalism and Anti-Muslim Violence in India*, Princeton University Press, 2012.
9. Gopal , Krishna, *Gujarat Pogrom – 2002*, Jaunpuri Shiksha Mission, 2006
10. Goradia, Prafull, *The Saffron Book*, Contemporary Targett Ltd, 2001.
11. Hansen, Thomas Blom and Jaffrelot, Christophe (ed), *The BJP and the Compulsions of Politics in India*, Oxford University Press, 1998.
12. Hansen, Thomas Blom, *The Saffron Wave — Democracy and Hindu Nationalism in Modern India*, Oxford University Press, 1999.
13. Horvitz, Leslie A, Christopher Catherwood, *Encyclopedia of War Crimes and Genocide* (Revised ed.), Chelsea House Publishers, 2011.
14. Hibbard, Scott W, *Religious Politics and Secular States: Egypt, India, and the United States*, Johns Hopkins University Press, 2010.
15. Jaffrelot, Christophe, *The Hindu Nationalist Movement*, Penguin Books, 1996.

16. Jaffrelot, Christophe, *Religion, Caste, and Politics in India*, C Hurst & Co, 2011.
17. Kabir, Ananya Jahanara, Sorcha Gunne, Brigley Zoe and Brigley Thompson, ed., *Feminism, Literature and Rape Narratives: Violence and Violation* (Reprint ed.), Routledge, 2011.
18. Kamath, MV and Randeri, Kalindi, *The Man of the Moment*, Wide Canvas (Vikas Publishing House Pvt Ltd), 2013.
19. Kannabiran, Kalpana, *Tools of Justice: Non-discrimination and the Indian Constitution*, Routledge, 2012.
20. Khan, Yasmin. Andrew R Murphy, ed., *The Blackwell Companion to Religion and Violence*, Wiley-Blackwell, 2011.
21. Khanna, Renu, "Communal Violence in Gujarat, India: Impact of Sexual Violence and Responsibilities of the Health Care System", *Reproductive Health Matters*, 2008.
22. Kishwar, Madhu, *Modinama, Manushi*, 2013.
23. Kulkarni, Atmaram, *Portrayal of a Charismatic Leader*, Mumbai: Leelavati Publications, 1998.
24. Lal, RB, Padmanabham, PBSV, Krishnan, G and Azeez, M (ed), *People of India — Gujarat*, Volume XXII Part One.
25. Mohideen Margatt, Ruth. Cynthia E Cohen, Roberto Gutierrez Varea, Polly O, Walker, ed., *Acting Together: Resistance and reconciliation in regions of violence*, 2011.
26. Martin-Lucas, Belen, Sorcha Gunne, Zoë Brigley, ed. *Feminism, Literature and Rape Narratives: Violence and Violation* (1st ed). Routledge, 2010.
27. Modi, SK, *Godhra: The Missing Rage*, New Delhi: Ocean Books Pvt Ltd., 2004.
28. Modi, Narendra, *Apatkal men Gujarat* (Hindi), Prabhat Prakashan, 2007.
29. Modi, Narendra, *Jyotipunj*, Praveen Prakashan Pvt Ltd, 2008.
30. Modi, Narendra, *Samajik Samrasta* (Gujarati), Makwana, Kishore (ed), Image Publications Pvt Ltd, 2010.
31. Modi, Narendra, *Convenient Action — Gujarat's Response to Challenges of Climate Change*, Macmillan Publishers India Ltd, 2011.
32. Mukhopadhyay, Nilanjan, *Narendra Modi: The Man, The Times*, Westland Ltd, 2013.

33. Nag, Kingshuk, *The NaMo Story — A Political Life*, Roli Books, 2013.
34. Nene, Rajabhai and Modi, Narendra (ed), *Setubandh*, Praveen Prakashan Pvt Ltd, 2012.
35. Oommen, TK, *Crisis and Contention in Indian Society*, SAGE, 2005.
36. Oommen, TK, *Reconciliation in Post-Godhra Gujarat: The Role of Civil Society*, Pearson Education India, 2008.
37. Oza, Dr Ramesh, Makwana, Kishor and Desai, Dinesh (compiled by), *Apana Narendrabhai* (Gujarati), Sri Modh Modi Samaj Hitvardhak Trust, 2012.
38. Rosser, Yvette Claire, *Curriculum as Destiny: Forging National Identity in India, Pakistan, and Bangla*, University of Texas at Austin, 2003.
39. Rubin, Olivier, *Democracy and Famine*, Routledge, 2010.
40. Sanghvi, Nagindas, *Gujarat: A Political Analysis*. Surat: Centre for Social Studies, 1995.
41. Shani, Ornit, *Communalism, Caste and Hindu Nationalism: The Violence in Gujarat*, Cambridge University Press, 2007.
42. Shiva, Vandana, *India Divided: Diversity and Democracy Under Attack*, Seven Stories Press, 2003.
43. Simpson, Edward, *Muslim Society and the Western Indian Ocean: The Seafarers of Kachchh*. Routledge, 2009.
44. Singh, DP, *Narendra Modi — Yes, He Can*, Self-published, 2012.
45. Smith, Paul J, *The Terrorism Ahead: Confronting Transnational Violence in the Twenty-First Century*, ME Sharpe, 2007.
46. Vaidik, Ved Pratap, *Bhajpa, Hindutva aur Musalman* (Hindi), Rajkamal Prakashan, 2010.
47. Varadarajan, Siddharth, *Gujarat: The Making of a Tragedy*. Penguin (India), 2002.
48. Varshney, Ashutosh, *Ethnic Conflict and Civic Life: Hindus and Muslims in India*, New Haven, Yale University Press, 2002.
49. Vidyaranya, MK, *Gujarat Elections 2012*, Press Club of Bangalore, 2013.
50. Vijay, Tarun, *Saffron Surge — India's Re-emergence on the Global Scene and Hindu Ethos*, Har-Anand Publications Pvt Ltd, 2008.
51. Wilkinson, Steven, *Religious politics and communal violence,* Oxford University Press, 2005.

52. Zavos, John, *The Emergence of Hindu Nationalism in India,* Oxford University Press, 2000.

Reports, expositions and theses

1. "Agriculture Performance in Gujarat since 2000," by Gulati, Ashok, Shah, Tushaar, Sridhar, Ganga, International Water Management Institute, May 2009.
2. "Compounding Injustice: The Government's Failure to Redress Massacres in Gujarat". Fédération Internationale des Droits de l'Homme, 2003.
3. "Communal Riots in Gujarat: The State at Risk?" by Jaffrelot, Christophe, Heidelberg Papers in South Asian and Comparative Politics, South Asia Institute, Department of Political Science, South Asia Institute, July 2003, University of Heidelberg.
4. "Communal Riots in India — A Chronology (1947-2003)", by Rajeshwari, B, Institute of Peace and Conflict Studies.
5. Report by the Commission of Inquiry Consisting of Justice GT Nanavati and Justice Akshay H Mehta.
6. Report by the Supreme Court-appointed Special Investigation Team, headed by former CBI director RK Raghavan.
7. "The Gujarat pogrom — Compilation of Various Reports", Indian Social Institute, 2002.
8. "We Have No Orders To Save You". Human Rights Watch, April 2002.

Documents

1. "Compendium of Good Governance — Exploring Innovative Approaches, Recent Best Practices in Gujarat", Administrative Reforms & Training Division, General Administration Department, Government of Gujarat, 2013.
2. Election Commission of India documents.
3. "Encyclopaedia of Backward Castes, Vol II" by Mathur, ML, Kalpaz Publications, Delhi, 2004.
4. "Gujarat Earthquake Rehabilitation and Reconstruction Programme (GERRP), a Report", indiagovernance.gov.in.
5. "Gujarat Electricity Board's Turnaround: Complete Rural

Electrification in Gujarat," by Joshi, Rakesh Mohan, London Business School, October 2008.

6. "Government of Gujarat: Jyotirgram Yojana", Marico Innovation Foundation and Erehwon Innovative Consulting, 2010.

7. "Impact of Restructuring on the Financial Performance of Organisation: A Case Study of Reforms in Gujarat Power Sector" by Panchal, Nilam, Singh, Wahengbam Chandbabu, International Journal of Applied Research and Studies (iJARS), Volume 2, Issue 8, August 2013.

8. "Judgment of Special Judge for GR Mumbai at Mumbai in Bilkis Bano's case", Sessions Case No. 634 of 2004.

9. Power Tariff, Socio-Economic Survey Gujarat 2012-13.

10. "State of Indian Agriculture, 2012-13", Ministry of Agriculture, Government of India.

11. "Swantah Sukhaya Initiative", Sardar Patel Institute of Public Administration.

12. Social-economic Review 2010-11, Gujarat State", Budget Publication no. 34, Directorate of Economics and Statistics, Government of Gujarat.

13. Socio-economic Review 2012-13 Gujarat State Budget Publication No. 34, Directorate of Economics and Statistics, Government of Gujarat, February 2013.

14. "The Investment Destination: Vibrant Gujarat Summit 2009", Government of Gujarat.

15. "The Politics of Preference: Democratic Institutions and Affirmative Action in the United States and India" by Parikh, Sunita, The University of Michigan Press, 1997.

Newspapers, magazines, journals and websites

1. *Frontline*
2. *Gujarat Samachar*
3. *Hindustan Times*
4. *India Today*
5. *Indian Journal of Applied Research*
6. *Indian Journal of Community Medicine*
7. *Journal of Indian Social and Political Economy*

8. *narendramodi.in*
9. *Niti Central*
10. *Outlook*
11. *PTI*
12. *Rediff.com*
13. *Reuters*
14. *Sandesh*
15. *The Business Standard*
16. *The Hindu*
17. *The Indian Express*
18. *The Statesman*
19. *The Sunday Guardian*
20. *The Telegraph*
21. *The Times of India*
22. *The Tribune*
23. *The Week*
24. *Time*
25. *Wall Street Journal*
26. *Zeenews.india.com*

Endnotes

Chapter - 1

1. Sikander Khan Qureshi a property dealer, told the author in an interview at Vadnagar.
2. Editors R B Lal, PBSV Padmanabham, G Krishnan and M Azeez Mohideen, *People of India—Gujarat*, Volume XXII, Part One, Pages 397 to 401.
3. Gopal Narain Singh, former BJP Bihar State President, in an interview to author.
4. "Nothing bigger than mother's blessings, says Modi on his birthday", *timesofindia. indiatimes.com*, 17 September 2013.
5. "My son has worked hard, he should now become PM: Modi's mother", *zeenews.india. com*, 20 December 2012.
6. "Modi meditates in Swami space—Room opens for CM who couldn't be monk", *telegraphindia.com*, 10 April 2013.
7. Nilanjan Mukhopadhyay, *Narendra Modi: The Man the Times*, page 30-32, Westland Ltd, New Delhi, 2012.
8. Ambalal Koshti, an old RSS worker, in an interview to author
9. MV Kamath and Kalindi Randheri, *The Man of the Moment—Narenda Modi*, page 10, Vikas Publishing, New Delhi, 2013.
10. Rajabhai Nene and Narendra Modi, *Setubandh*, page 41, Pravin Prakashan, Rajkot, 1986.
11. Ibid, page 31
12. MV Kamath and Kalindi Randheri, *The Man of the Moment—Narenda Modi*, page 12, Vikas Publishing, New Delhi, 2013.

Chapter - 2

1. Narendra Modi, *Apatkal mein Gujarat*, page 13-14, Prabhat Prakashan, New Delhi, edition 2007. The original book *Sangharsh ma Gujarat* in Gujarati language was published in 1978.
2. Praful Raval in an interview to author.
3. Narendra Modi, *Apatkal Mein Gujarat*, page 19.
4. Ibid, page 120.
5. Ibid, page 31-33.
6. Ibid, page 52.
7. S Gurumurthy, "Will They Follow Kalam", *newindianexpress.com*, 23 November 2011.
8. Thomas Blom Hansen, *The Saffron Wave*, page 130, Oxford University Press, New Delhi, 1999.
9. Narendra Modi, *Apatkal Mein Gujarat*, page 77.
10. Ibid, page 78.
11. Ibid, page 161.
12. Praful Raval in an interview to author.

13. Narendra Modi, *Apatkal Mein Gujarat*, page 147.
14. Ibid,162.
15. Christophe Jaffrelot, *The Hindu Nationalist Movement and Indian Politics*, Page 285-286, Penguin Books, New Delhi, 1999.
16. Rajabhai Nene and Narendra Modi, *Setubandh*, p 135-136, Pravin Prakashan, Rajkot, in Gujarati.

Chapter - 3

1. Data from Election Commission India, *eci.nic.in.*
2. Sunita Parikh, *The Politics of Preference: Democratic Institutions and Affirmative Action in the United States and India*, The University of Michigan Press, 1997
3. Rajabhai Nene and Narendra Modi, *Setubandh*, page 145, Pravin Prakashan, Rajkot, in Gujarati.
4. Nilanjan Mukhopadhyay, *Narendra Modi: The Man the Times*, page 148, Westland, 2013.
5. ML Mathur, *Encyclopaedia of Backward Castes*, Vol II, page 35-37, Kalpaz Publications, Delhi, 2004.
6. "Journey of Awareness", *indiatoday.intoday.in*, 15 January 1988
7. Blog by LK Advani, Serial no.432/285, *lkadvani.in*
8. Kingshuk Nag, *The Namo Story*, page 55, Roli Books, New Delhi, 2013.
9. Christophe Jaffrelot, *The Hindu Nationalist Movement and Indian Politics*: 1925 to the 1990s, page 417, Penguin Books, New Delhi, 1999.
10. LK Advani, *My Country My Life*, page 375, Rupa Publications, New Delhi, 2008.
11. *narendramodi.in/ektayatra*, 27 September 2013.
12. Version of J & K administration and Version of the BJP.
13. Ajay Umant and Harit Mehta, "3-day fast rocks 30-year bond", *timesofindia.indiatimes.com*, 25 Sep 2011
14. Uday Mahurkar, "Tottering bastion", *indiatoday.intoday.in*, 15 October 1995.
15. Priyavadan Patel, "Gujarat: Hindutva mobilisation and electoral dominance of the BJP", *Journal of Indian School of Political Economy*, Vol. 15, page 129, Nos. 1 and 2, January-June 2003.
16. Uday Mahurkar, "Tottering bastion", *indiatoday.intoday.in*, 15 October 1995.
17. MV Kamath and Kalindi Randheri, *The Man of the Moment; Narendra Modi*, page 42, Vikas Publishing, New Delhi.
18. Ibid, page 44
19. Arun Verma, "Crisis because of Khajurias", *rediff.com*, 18 November 2009
20. Priyavadan Patel, "Gujarat: Hindutva mobilisation and electoral dominance of the BJP", *Journal of Indian School of Political Economy*, Vol. 15, page 129, Nos. 1 and 2, January-June 2003.
21. "Fragile Victory," *indiatoday.intoday.in*, 15 November 1996.
22. V Gangadhar, "Muslims can be divided into two. Those with the BJP and those who are indifferent", Narendra Modi Interview, *rediff.com*, 25 February 1998.

Chapter - 4

1. "Civic polls keenly watched, past results mirrored in Assembly", *indianexpress.com*, 14 November 2011

2.   Sanjay Sharma, "Modi played a big role in BJP success in HP, Haryana", *The Sunday Guardian*, 15 June 2013
3.   Data from Election Commission of India, *eci.nic.in*.
4.   Ibid
5.   Manohar Lal Khattar, a senior BJP leader from Haryana, in an interview to author.
6.   The author had visited Himachal Pradesh to report on the elections and had found that Modi had created an army of youngsters who were ready to do his bidding.
7.   "A rough ride for the BJP", *frontline.in*, Vol 20, Issue 3, 1-14 February, 2003
8.   Roop Upadhyay, "One time rival joins hands to win elections", *hindustantimes.com*, 27 October 2012.
9.   "A government on tenterhooks", *frontline.in*, Vol. 15, No. 10, 9-22 May 1998.
10.   NK Singh, "Broadening his Base", *India Today*, 15 April 1996
11.   Praveen Swami, "A BJP wipe-out", *frontline.in*, Vol. 19, Issue 5, 2-15 March 2002
12.   Raj Bhatia in an interview to author.
13.   Manoj Singh Chauhan in an interview to author.
14.   LK Advani, *My Country My Life*, p 490-491, Rupa Publications, New Delhi, 2008
15.   A state office bearer of the then Gujarat unit told author.
16.   Onkar Singh, "Atalji was on the Offensive", Narendra Modi's interview, *rediff.com*, 19 July 2001
17.   V Venkatesan, "Who is In, Who is Out", *Frontline*, Vol 17, Issue 19, 16-29 September 2000.
18.   Priyavadan Patel "Gujarat: Hindutwa Mobilisation and Electoral Dominance of the BJP", *Journal of Indian School of Political Economy*, Page 130, Pune, Jan-June 2013.
19.   Nilanjan Mukhopadhyay, *Narendra Modi: The Man the Times*, page 205 Westland, New Delhi, 2013.
20.   Priyavadan Patel "Gujarat: Hindutwa Mobilisation and Electoral Dominance of the BJP", *Journal of Indian School of Political Economy*, Page 130, Pune, Jan-June 2013.
21.   V Gangadhar, "Muslims can be divided into two. Those with the BJP and those who are indifferent", Narendra Modi Interview, *rediff.com*, 25 February 1998.
22.   "Hello, I am home again", *indiatoday.intoday.in*, 2 March 1998.
23.   V Gangadhar, "Muslims can be divided into two. Those with the BJP and those who are indifferent", Narendra Modi Interview, *rediff.com*, 25 February 1998.
24.   Ibid
25.   Aditi Phadnis, "Political Profiles of Cabals and Kings", page 116 *Business Standard*, 2009, New Delhi.
26.   Mihir R Bhatt, "Corporate Social Responsibility and Natural Disaster Reduction: Local overview of Gujarat—a report", page 3, All India Disaster Mitigation Institute, August 2002.
27.   National Disaster Management, Government of India, *ndmindia.nic.in*.
28.   Dionne Bunsha, "New Oarsman", *Frontline*, Vol. 18, Issue 21, 13-26 October 2001
29.   Jana Krishnamurthy to the author on the eve of Thakre's visit to Gandhinagar in 2001.

Chapter - 5

1.   "Bureaucrats excited over likely postings," *timesofindia.indiatimes.com*, 5 October 2001.
2.   Ross Colvin and Satarupa Bhattacharjya, *Special Report: The Remaking of Narendra Modi*, Gandhinagar, 12 July 2013.

3   Amitabh Sinha, a senior BJP leader in an interaction with author at Bhuj.

4.   Bharat Desai, "Modi's CMO usurps quake relief from GSDMA," *The Times of India*, Ahmedabad, *timesofindia.indiatimes.com*, 20 October 2001.

5.   "CM spends Diwali with quake-affected families", *timesofindia.indiatimes.com*, 18 November 2001.

6.   "The Rise and Shine", *indiatoday.intoday.in*, 15 October 2001.

7.   Ashok Malik, "Know Narendra Modi, learn why Gujarat needs him", *hindustantimes. com*, 19 October 2012.

8.   "Relief in Sales Tax for Kutch Industries," *timesofindia.indiatimes.com*, 5 November 2001.

9.   "Gujarat Earthquake Rehabilitation and Reconstruction Programme GERRP, a Report", *indiagovernance.gov.in*.

10.   Sharamana Ganguly Mehta and Parag Dave, *The Economic Times*, 27 January 2011.

11.   Udai Mahurkar, "The high road to recovery," *indiatoday.in*, 27 September 2004.

12.   "Gujarat bags UN award for disaster management," *The Times of India*, 22 October 2003.

13.   Modi's inaugural speech at the International Conference on "Post Earthquake Reconstruction—Lessons Learnt and Way Forward", *narendramodi.in*, 14 April 2011.

14.   Chirag Bhatt has been working in BHDA for the last 12 years and has seen the hard work done by the organisation. He was proud to brief us on the work done in Bhuj.

15.   The author and his team toured extensively to figure out the extent of development in the Kutch region. Shakeel was employed at one of the hotels where the team stayed.

16.   Ghulam Ali, a farmer, told this to author at Bhachau, 2013.

17.   Gujarat Earthquake Rehabilitation and Reconstruction Programme GERRP, a Report, *indiagovernance.gov.in*.

18.   "Gujarat to give Rs 10 crore," *tribuneindia.com*, 27 December 2004.

19.   "Modi in Rambo act saves 15,000", *epaper.timesofindia.com*, 23 June 2013.

20.   "More on Modi's 'Rambo act', *deshgujarat.com*, 23 June 2013.

Chapter - 6

1.   Pingle Jaganmohan Reddy, *The Judiciary I Served*, pages 191-193, Orient Blackswan, 1999.

2.   Ghanshyam Shah in an interview to *rediff.com* on 1 May 2002.

3.   "Chronology of communal violence in India", *hindustantimes.com*, 9 November 2011.

4.   "History of Communal Violence in Gujarat", by Concerned Citizens Tribunal, *outlookindia.com*, 22 November 2002.

5.   Akshayakumar Ramanlal Desai; Wilfred D'Costa, *State and Repressive Culture: A Case Study of Gujarat*, page 99, Popular Prakashan, 1994.

6.   Ornit Shani, *Communalism, Caste and Hindu Nationalism: The Violence in Gujarat*, pages 161–164, Cambridge University Press, 2007.

7.   B Rajeshwari, "Communal Riots in India — A Chronology 1947-2003", Institute of Peace and Conflict Studies.

8.   "History of Communal Violence in Gujarat", Concerned Citizens Tribunal, *outlookindia. com*, 22 November 2002.

9.   B Rajeshwari, "Communal Riots in India: A Chronology 1947-2003" for March 2004 IPCS Research Papers.

10. Justice PB Sawant, Justice Suresh Hosbet, KG Kannabiran, Dr KS Subramanian, "Concerned Citizens Tribunal Report, 2002".
11. Christophe Jaffrelot, "Communal Riots in Gujarat: The State at Risk?" Heidelberg Papers in South Asian and Comparative Politics, South Asia Institute, Department of Political Science, South Asia Institute, July 2003, University of Heidelberg.
12. *The Indian Express*, 17 December 2009.
13. Official figure given by Union Minister of State Sriprakash Jaiswal in the Rajya Sabha on 11 May 2005.
14. "A Beast Asleep", *Outlook*, 5 March 2012.

Chapter - 7

1. "It was not a random attack on S-6 but kar sevaks were targeted, says judge," *The Hindu*, 6 March 2011
2. "Gujarat Govt challenges acquittals in Godhra verdict before HC," *deccanherald.com*, 25 June 2011.
3. "Amicus curiae erred by relying on Bhatt: SIT report", *ibnlive.in.com*, 8 May 2012.
4. "Amicus curiae: Prosecute Narendra Modi for Gulbarga massacre", *timesofindia. indiatimes.com*, 8 May 2012.
5. "'We will not remain silent spectators: VHP", PTI report published in *rediff.com*, 27 February 2002.
6. "Sabarmati Express set ablaze, 57 dead 'Ramsevaks' among victims, shoot-at-sight orders in Godhra", *tribuneindia.com*, 27 February 2002.
7. TK Oommen, *Crisis and Contention in Indian Society*, page 12, SAGE, New Delhi, 2005.
8. The chief minister's movements and actions on 27 February 2002 have been presented here based on his deposition before the SIT, pages 468-472
9. Newspaper clippings attached to the Nanavati-Shah Commission report.
10. Sheela Bhatt, "Mob sets fire to Wakf Board Office in Gujarat Secretariat", *rediff.com*, 28 February 2002
11. SIT report page 429
12. The chief minister's movements and actions on 28 February 2002 have been presented here based on his deposition before the SIT, page 474
13. "Curfew in Ahmedabad, Rajkot", PTI report, *rediff.com*, 28 February 2002.
14. SIT report pages 430-432
15. "Fernandes tours Ahmedabad, two Army brigades for Gujarat", *rediff.com*, 1 March 2002.
16. "Hindu Rioters Kill 60 Muslims in India", The New York Times, *nytimes.com*, 1 March, 2002
17. "Mobs rule Ahmedabad streets", *economictimes.indiatimes.com*, 1 March 2002.
18. "Ethnic cleansing in Ahmedabad", *outlook.com*, 10-11 March 2002
19. Fédération internationale des droits de l'homme 1999. India. Human Rights Watch, Retrieved 1 September 2012, pages 15–21.
20. The Gulbarg Society riot has been narrated based on SIT closure report, pages 201-203.
21. "Ahmedabad court rejects Zakia Jafri's petition, clean chit to Modi stands", *indiatvnews. com*, 26 December 2013
22. SIT Report, page 430

23. "Fernandes tours Ahmedabad, two Army brigades for Gujarat", *rediff.com*, 1 March 2002
24. "Shoot orders in many Gujarat towns, toll over 200", *hindu.com*, 2 March 2002.
25. "Shoot-at-sight order issued in Ahmedabad", *rediff.com*, 1 March 2002
26. "136 dead in two days of violence in Gujarat: CM", *rediff.com*, 1 March 2002
27. "33 People burnt alive near Godhra", *rediff.com*, 1 March 2002
28. Compilation of reports in *The Times of India* and *The Indian Express* on onlinevolunteers. org, 8 April 2002
29. "How has the Gujarat massacre affected minority women?" *Hindustan Times*, 27 March 2002.
30. "Sardarpura riot case: 31 convicted, 42 acquitted", *timesofindia.indiatimes.com*, 9 November 2011 and "First whiff of justice for Gujarat riot victims", *thehindu.com*, 17 November 2011.
31. "British national visiting Gujarat killed", *timesofindia.indiatimes.com*, 2 March 2002
32. "Modi denies making provocative statements", *rediff.com*, 3 March 2002.
33. "Gujarat violence toll mounts to 427", *rediff.com*, 3 March 2002
34. "Judgement of Special Judge for GR Mumbai at Mumbai in Bilkis Bano's case", Sessions Case No. 634 of 2004.
35. "Landmark case: How Bilkis Bano got justice", *hindustantimes.com*, 11 February 2012
36. "Silent march in Ahmedabad to protest violence", *timesofindia.indiatimes.com*, 5 March 2002
37. "Govt acted quickly to control communal flare up: Modi", *rediff.com*, 10 March 2002
38. Sheela Bhatt, "Politicians, gamblers keep Gujarat's cycle of violence going", *rediff.com*, 2 April 2002.
39. "Muslims not alone in times of crisis: Vajpayee", *rediff.com*, 4 April 2002.
40. Video of Atal Bihari Vajpayee's press conference on *youtube.com*
41. "Record 65 per cent turnout in Gujarat panchayat polls", *rediff.com*, 7 April 2002.
42. "Modi turns peace broker", *timesofindia.indiatimes.com*, 2 May 2002
43. "Gujarat violence flares", *news.bbc.co.uk*, 8 May 2002
44. "5 dead, widespread arson in Ahmedabad", *timesofindia.indiatimes.com*, 11 May 2002

Chapter - 8

1. Narendra Modi's blog on 2002 Gujarat riots", ibnlive.in.com, 27 December 2013
2. "Narendra Modi's riots baggage will remain: Kapil Sibal", *dnaindia.com*, 29 December 2013.
3. Mahesh Bhatt in an interview to author.
4. MJ Akbar in an interview with author on 10 January 2014
5. Barry Gardiner's interview on *NDTV*, 13 August 2013, *ndtv.com/video*.
6. Various comments of the SIT put together. For details on the SIT please see the chapter, "Godhra and post-Godhra Riots"
7. "My men have done a commendable job: PC Pande", *rediff.com*, 4 March 2002.
8. "Sins Of Modi", *indiatoday.com*, 18 March 2002.
9. "Police to people ratio: 3 cops for every VIP but just 1 for 761 commoners", *dnaindia. com*, 25 August 2013.
10. SIT report quoted in the earlier chapter.

11. "Centre delayed deployment of paramilitary forces", *timesofindia.indiatimes.com*, 2 March 2002.
12. Nirmala Sitharaman, "Face the facts on riots", *thehindubusinessline.com*, 6 October2011.
13. Steven I Willkinson, *Votes and Violence: Electoral completion and ethnic riots in India*, page 95, Cambridge University press, 2004.
14. "Assam violence: Was the Army deployed too late? Home ministry to take up the issue with the Prime Minister", *ndtv.com*, 30 July,2012.
15. "Assam on edge: six dead, PM phones chief minister", *ndtv.com*, 15 November 2012.
16. "What led to Muzaffarnagar communal riots", *tehelka.com*, 8 September 2013.
17. "UP government announces Rs 5 lakh each to 1,800 families displaced in Muzaffarnagar riot", *timesofindia.indiatimes.com*, 26 October.
18. SIT Report, page 448.
19. "Curfew imposed in 26 cities", *The Hindu*, 1 March 2002.
20. Ram Jethmalani in an interview to author.
21. "Amicus curiae erred by relying on Bhatt: SIT report", *ibnlive.in.com*, 8 May 2012
22. SIT report, page 43.
23. SIT report, page 49.
24. Modi's reply, SIT Report, page 484.
25. "When Select Phrases are Lifted and Distorted out of Context", *Modinama8, manushi. in*
26. "SIT endorses Modi's 'action-reaction' theory", *hindustantimes.com*, 11 May 2012.
27. "SIT says Ehsan Jafri 'provoked' murderious mob", *thehindu.com*, 12 May 2012
28. "I don't look at the religion of the dead", *indiatoday.intoday.in*, 8 April 2002
29. Modi's deposition, SIT report page 474
30. SIT Report page 204.
31. Modi's deposition, SIT Report, page 475
32. "Committee to oversee relief work in Gujarat", *rediff.com*, 25 March 2002.
33. "BJP cites govt statistics to defend Modi", *expressindia.indianexpress.com*, 12 May 2005.
34. "2002 Gujarat riots: No evidence that Narendra Modi incited rioters or pressured police, says SIT," *indiatoday.intoday.in*, 26 April 2013.
35. "*Swadeshi* vs *videshi*", *hindu.com*, 16 July 2000.
36. "Interview with BJP leader Narendra Modi", *reuters.com*, 12 July 2013.
37. Mufti Aijaz Arshad Qasmi in an interview to author.
38. Mahesh Bhatt in an interview to author.
39. Ibid
40. Salim Khan in an interview to the author on 19 December 2013.
41. LK Advani, *My Country My Life*, pages 759-760, Rupa Publications, New Delhi, 2008.

Chapter - 9

1. "I wanted to visit Gujarat earlier: PM", *rediff.com*, 4 April 2002
2. "Muslims not alone in this time of crisis: Vajpayee", *rediff.com*, 4 April 2002
3. "PM asks Modi to follow raj dharma", *rediff.com,* 4 April 2002
4. Interview given by Arun Shourie to Shekhar Gupta for NDTV, published by *rediff.com*, 5 August 2009.
5. Jaswant Singh told Shekhar Gupta in programme Walk The Talk for *NDTV 24 x 7*, published on 22 August 2009.

6. LK Advani, *My Country My Life*, page 758-759, Rupa Publications, 2008.
7. Sheela Bhatt and Sandesh Prabhudesai, "Modi gives in, submits his resignation", *rediff. com*, 12 April, 2002
8. Radhika Ramaseshan, "When tormentor was saviour", *The Telegraph*, Calcutta, 11 June 2013
9. The chain of events about what happened inside the executive meeting has been reconstructed on the basis of recollections of the meeting by some senior BJP leaders who were members of that national executive.
10. Onkar Singh, "Shanta Kumar calls for Modi's resignation", *rediff.com*, 11 April, 2002
11. "I had decided to seek fresh mandate five days ago: Modi", *rediff.com*, 13 April 2002.
12. Sheela Bhatt and Sandesh Prabhudesai, "Modi gives in, submits his resignation", *rediff. com*, 12 April 2002
13. Text of this speech taken from Annexure-18 of a report titled "An enquiry into the carnage in Gujarat".
14. "Gujarat House dissolved, Modi to be interim CM", *timesofindia.indiatimes.com*, 19 July 2002.
15. A report of the Press Trust of India as reported in *rediff.com*, 4 May 2002
16. J Venkatesan, EC rules out early polls in Gujarat", *The Hindu*, 17 August 2002
17. Prime Minister Atal Bihari Vajpayee's statement in the Lok Sabha on 6 May 2002 as reported by PTI and carried by *rediff.com*.

Chapter - 10

1. Tara Shankar Sahay, "EC's Gujarat order against the Constitution: BJP," *rediff.com*, 17 August 2002
2. "EC suggestion on President's rule made Govt challenge order: Advani" *rediff.com* 19 August 2002
3. Supreme Court Judgement "Under Article 1431 of the conssitution of India vs Unknown," *indiankanoon.com*, 28 October 2002.
4. NHRC statement of 1 July 2002.
5. Editorial "Gaurav Yatra is Off", *tribuneindia.com*, 4 July 2002.
6. "Sonia Writes to PM on Yatra", *The Hindu*, online edition, 30 June 2002
7. Manasdas Gupta, Narendra Modi postpones Gaurav Yatra to Sept.7, *hindu,com*, 2 September 2002.
8. Ibid
9. "Cong's move to launch yatra confirms Guj is normal: BJP", *economictimes.indiatimes. com*, 3 September, 2002
10. MV Kamath and Kalindi Randheri, *Narendra Modi:The Man of the Moment*, page 108, Vikas Publishing, New Delhi, 2013.
11. Christophe Jaffrelot, *Communal Riots in Gujarat: The State at Risk?* Working paper no. 17, Page 10, South Asian Institute, Department of Political Science, University of Heidelberg, July 2003.
12. Ibid
13. "Modi Kicks off Gujarat Gaurav Yatra", *timesofindia.indiatimes.com*, 8 September 2002.
14. 'Should we run relief camps? Open child producing centres?', *indianexpress.com*, 19 September 2002.

15. "Vikas Yatra: Narendra Modi's juggernaut rolls out today", *indianexpress.com*, 22October 2012

16. Milind Ghatwai, 'Modi's speech' *Navsari dateline,* 22 September 2002. *The Indian Express* carried the story on the front page with title "25 top 625: Look Modi's Counting". This article was found in *www.gujaratfiles.net,* 14 October 2013.

17. "Modi Begins Second Phase of Gujarat Gaurav Yatra", *rediff.com*, 14 September 2002.

18. "'5 crore Gujaratis will chop off Miyan Musharraf's hands'- Modi", *outlookindia.com,* 15 September 2002.

19. "Musharraf speaking Cong language: Modi", *timesofindia.indiatimes.com,* 15 September 2002

20. "Modi Slams Musharraf's UN speech", *timesofindia.indiatimes.com,* 14 September 2002.

21. "If I die, thousands of Modis will rise: CM", *timesofindia.indiatimes.com,* 5 October 2002

22. "That Missing Healing Touch", *outlookindia.com,* 14 October 2002

23. "BJP will not hesitate to raise Godhra issue during Gujarat election: Advani", *rediff.com,* 28 November 2002

24. "Gujarat polls: Parties launch full-scale offensive", *Asia News Agency, teleradproviders. com,* 2 December 2002

25. "Sonia Kicks Off Poll Campaign: Flays Modi's Gaurav Yatra", *tribuneindia.com,* 3 December 2002.

26. "Modi hits back at Congress", *hindu.com,* 4 December 2002

27. "I see an emotional frenzy in the BJP's favour", *rediff.com,* 12 December 2002

28. The author had covered Gujarat elections including Modi's Gaurav Yatra for *The Statesman.*

29. "My son loves everyone: Modi's mother", *rediff.com,* 7 December 2002

30. Election Commission of India *eci.nic.in*

31. "Rebels rally behind Keshubhai Patel", *hindu.com,* 17 August 2005

32. "BJP rebels flay Modi at Koli meet", *timesofindia.indiatimes,* 18 June 2007

33. Manas Dasgupta, "BJP rebels campaign for Congress", *thehindu.com,* 15 Sep 2007.

34. Rathin Das, "Modi Shifts 41 IPS Officers", *hindustantimes.com,* 1 October 2007

35. RK Mishra, "Hanging Modi Fire", *outlookindia.com,* 5 November 2007.

36. Ibid.

37. "If possible, set me on fire: Modi to opponents", *rediff.com,* 22 October 2007.

38. RK Mishra, "Hanging Modi Fire", *outlookindia.com,* 5 November 2007.

39. "Send Taslima to Gujarat, says Modi in first election speech", *rediff.com,* 27 November 2007.

40. "Congress releases charge sheet against Narendra Modi", *timesofindia.indiatimes.com,* 30 November 2007

41. Quoted in the complaint the BJP filed before the Election Commission along with the CD of her speech as reported in *The Hindu, thehindu.com,* 10 December 2007.

42. This happened on 3 December 2007. The BJP sought an apology from him on the same day. The Commission's notice was reported in *The Hindu, thehindu.com,* 10 December 2007

43. "Modi owns up Sohrabuddin killing", *economictimes.indiatimes.com,* 5 December 2007

44. Point no. 2 and 6 of his reply to the Election Commission, sent on 8 December 2007

45. *news.oneindia.in,* 7 October 2007

46. Saroj Nagi, "Cong Confident, Rejects Exit Poll Predictions", *hindustantimes.com*, 18 December 2007
47. M V Kamath & Kalindi Randeri, *The Man of the Moment: Narendra Modi*, Page 205, Vikas Publishing, New Delhi, 2012.
48. Transcription of Modi's Bardoli speech, video published in *deshgujarat.com*, 6 February 2012.
49. "Vote for Congress's Rabari candidate, but not for BJP's Kshatriya candidate: Shankersinh asks Kshatriyas in Patan rally", *deshgujarat.com*, 7 May 2012
50. Manish Macwan, "After Keshubhai, now Cong woos Patidars", *thesundayindian.com*, 4 June 2012
51. "Gujarat Congress woos tribals ahead of Assembly polls", *indianexpress.com*, 5 June 2012.
52. "SC ruling has vindicated our stand: BJP", *thehindu.com*, 13 September 2011
53. Ahead of his fast, Narendra Modi condemns 'communal frenzy and casteism', *timesofindia. indiatimes.com*, 16 September 2011
54. Narendra Modi's speech after Sadbhavna Mission, *narendramodi.in*, 16 February 2012.
55. Narendra Modi's speech after Sadbhavna Mission, *youtube.com*, 19 September.
56. "Message clear as Narendra Modi begins poll yatra: it's Gujarat vs Centre", *indianexpress. com*, 11 September 2012
57. "Gujarat Congress compares Narendra Modi to a monkey, BJP files complaint", *ndtv. com*, 8 November 2012
58. "Narendra Modi uses 3D telecast to address audiences in four cities", *timesofindia. indiatimes.com*, 19 November 2012
59. "Liberate Gujarat from divisive politics: Manmohan", *thehindu.com*, 10 December 2010
60. "Gujarat polls 2012: Modi targets Sonia, Congress' 'vote-bank politics'", *zeenews.india. com*, 11 December 2012.
61. "Rahul Gandhi sharpens attack on Modi, calls him a 'marketeer'", Report by Agencies, *hindustantimes.com*, 11 December 2012
62. At his public rally on 14 December that was beamed at 53 places simultaneously, *indianexpress.com*, 15 December 2012
63. "Narendra Modi reacts to Rahul Gandhi's speech" Video, deshgujarat.com, 11 December 2012
64. "We won 2 seats but hit BJP's chances in 15 seats', *timesofindia.indiatimes.com*, 23 December 2012
65. "Narendra Modi's 3D show enters Guinness Book of World Records", The Indian Express, *indianexpress.com*, 15 March 2013
66. *narendramodi.in*, 19 October 2013
67. Gujarat CM Narendra Modi's victory speech, *economictimes.indiatimes.com*, 20 Dec 2012.

Chapter - 11

1. Bibek Debroy, "Gujarat: Governance for growth and development", pages 40-41 Academic Foundation, New Delhi, 2012.
2. Narayan B Bhatt, "Gujarat PSU's worth Rs 1,000 crore", *timesofindia.indiatimes.com*, 18 September 2003
3. "Gujarat: The Issue of Debt Management", Dr Sangita Agrawal, Faculty Member, Department of Business Economics Faculty of Commerce, M.S. University of Baroda,

Indian Journal of *Applied Research*, page 1, Vol. 2, Issue 1, October 2012.

4. "State Update: Government of Gujarat", CARE ratings, Professional Risk Opinion, 24 March 2013.

5. "It's Stupid if you are not in Gujarat: Ratan Tata", *Rediff*, 13 January 2007

6. Directorate of Economics & Statistics of respective state governments; for All-India Central Statistics Office, *mospi.nic.in*.

7. R Jagannath quoted in "The Gujarat Growth Story... Victim of Lies", *ibtl.in/news*, 11 Mar 2013

8. "Gurgaon and Faridabad—An Exercise in Contrasts", a study paper of the Centre on Democracy, Development, and The Rule of Law, Freeman Spogli Institute for International Studies, Stanford University, *Bibek Debroy and Laveesh Bhandari*, September 2009.

9. Bibek Debroy, "Gujarat: Governance for growth and development," page 27, Academic Foundation, New Delhi, 2012.

10. Ibid, page 161.

11. Social-economic review 2010-11, Gujarat State, Directorate of Economics and Statistics, Government of Gujarat, Budget Publication no. 34.

12. The author had travelled along with his team to Bhachau and other areas of Kutch in December 2013 to understand development.

13. An overview of Economy, Socio-Economic Review, Gujarat State, 2010-11 XI

14. Bibek Debroy, "Gujarat: Governance for growth and development," Page 159, Academic Foundation, New Delhi, 2012.

15. Gujarat Economic Profile — July 2011, *gidb.org*

16. Gujarat drought sparks protests, *news.bbc.co.uk*, 19 April 2000.

17. Weekly Drought Report: No.10, as on 3 July 2001, *ndmindia.nic.in*

18. Lyla Bavadam, "Gujarat's thirst", *frontline.in*, Volume 17, Issue 10, 13-26 May 2000

19. Ibid.

20. "No water means no bride for suitors in this Gujarat village", *ndtv.com*, 6 May 2013

21. "Advani gets heckled", *rediff.com*, 2 September 1999.

22. "Water Sector in Gujarat: Challenges and Opportunities", A report prepared by Tata Strategic Management Group, *tsmg.com*, 2010.

23. Ibid

24. 2001 figures as quoted by Kapil Dave, "Gujarat faces grim water scenario", *timesofindia. indiatimes.com*, 13 April 2013.

25. Bibek Debroy, "Gujarat: Governance for growth and development", Academic Foundation, page 50, New Delhi, 2012.

26. Rakesh Mohan Joshi, "Gujarat Electricity Board's Turnaround — Complete Rural Electrification in Gujarat", A report by Indian Institute of Foreign Trade, New Delhi, supported by Aditya Birla India Centre at London Business School, 2008, page 8.

27. Gopal Krishna, "Gujarat Electricity Board Ranks First Among Losing State Electricity Boards", Independent Media Centre, *india.indymedia.org*, 17 February 2003

28. GEB losses mount to Rs 2,312.35 cr", *thehindubusinessline.in*, 30 January 2002

29. In an interview with author.

30. "Is Keshubhai up to it? Gujarat earthquake: Gujarat CM Keshubhai Patel hardpressed to explain sluggish response", *indiatoday.intoday.in*, 12 February 2001

31. "Corruption in buildings dept: Gujarat govt", *timesofindia.indiatimes.com*, 7 September 2001.

32. Report by Harnath Jagawat, "Drought in our Project Area", NM Sadguru Water Development Foundation, 2001.

33. Bipinchandra J Divan & Other V State of Gujarat And Ors., AIR 2002 Guj 99.

34. Uday Mahurkar, "And greed hits home," *indiatoday.intoday.in*, 19 February 2001.

35. A city builder who had already built buildings in Ahmedabad told this to the author in an interview.

Chapter 12

1. The journalist, who is associate editor with a major TV channel, narrated this incident to the author but refused to be named

2. "Narendra Modi the man behind the mask", *asianage.com*, 23 September 2013

3. Ibid

4. A source close to Modi narrated this incidence to author

5. Akshat Khandelwal, "De-coding Narendra Modi's Governance and Gujarat's Development Model" *albrightstonebridge.com*, 22 April 2013

6. "Narendra Modi the man behind the mask", *asianage.com*, 23 September 2013

7. "Don't take oral orders from netas: SC", *The Times of India*, New Delhi, 1 November 2013

8. During an interactive session on the Pravasi Divas 2003

9. "Babus Modified: Narendra Modi trains his bureaucrats to become better at work", *indiatoday.intoday.in*, 21 October 2011

10. Ibid

11. MV Kamath and Kalindi Randeri, *The Man of the Moment: Narendra Modi*, page 164, Vikas Publications, New Delhi, 2012,

12. "Babus Modified: Narendra Modi trains his bureaucrats to become better at work", *indiatoday.intoday.in*, 21 October 2011

13. "Narendra Modi the man behind the mask", *asianage.com*, 23 September 2013

14. "Politicians should learn to say 'no', bureaucrats to say 'yes': Modi", India Dialogue Programme of Network 18, *ibnlive.in.com*, 8 April 2013

15. Modi's valedictory, speech at the chintan shibir 2011, Mehsana.

16. "Develop Gujarat as a knowledge-based society", *dnaindia.com*, 6 December 2009

17. "Gujarat: Beyond the obvious—a report on initiatives for inclusive growth", a compilation by Ernst and Young, *gujaratcmfellowship.org*, 25 September 2007

18. Prof TKG Namboodhiri, "The Meaning of Karma Yoga in Bhagvad Gita", *speakingtree.in*, 26 Jun 2012.

19. If I have committed any mistake, I apologise: Narendra Modi", *timesofindia.indiatimies.com*, 20 December 2012

20. "Swantah Sukhaya Initiatives", page 6, A Report by Sardar Patel Institute of Public Administration, Ahmedabad, *spipa.gujarat.gov.in*.

21. "Is Lalu's feudalism rubbing off on Nitish?" NR Mohanty wrote this on 26 October 2007. He mentions a statement of Lalu published by the *Indian Express* where he is taking credit for getting *khaini* made by the chief secretary when he was the chief minister of Bihar, *sangharshindia.wordpress.com*.

22. Ex-Additional DG AI Saiyed in an interview to author in Ahmedabad

23. "Gandhinagar water to be metered soon", *timesofindia.indiatimes.com*, 4 March 2012.
24. Waste puts Gujarat in hot water", *timesofindia.indiatimes.com*, 18 July 2011
25. Narendra Modi, *Convenient Action, Gujarat's Response To Challenge Of Climate Change*, page 71, Macmillan Publishers India Ltd., Delhi, 2011.
26. Data as per government figures
27. "Socio-Economic Survey–Gujarat", Directorate of Economics and Statistics, Government of Gujarat, 2012-13
28. "Water harvesting a social movement in Gujarat", *financialexpress.com*, 26 Dec 2005
29. Statistics taken from *guj-nwrws.gujarat.gov.in*
30. "CAPAM recognises Gujarat's innovative khet-talavadi scheme", *news.oneindia.in*, 31October2006
31. "State Economy and Socio-Economic Profile" by India Brand Equity Foundation and Ernst & Young, 2008
32. "Secret of Gujarat's Agrarian Miracle after 2000", Tushar Shah and others, *Economic and Political Weekly*, Vol. XLIV, No.52, 26 December 2009
33. "Gujarat water surplus state, claims GWSSB official", *indianexpress.com*, 27 September 2013.
34. "Gujarat water surplus state, claims GWSSB official", *indianexpress.com*, 27 September 2013
35. Narendra Modi, *Convenient Action, Gujarat's Response To Challenge Of Climate Change*, page 86, Macmillan Publishers India Ltd., Delhi, 2011,
36. "Manjula sets out priorities for GEB", *timesofindia.indiatimes.com*, 15 December 2001
37. N Madhavan, "The transformer", *businesstoday.intoday.in*, 5 February 2012
38. Ibid
39. Rakesh Mohan Joshi, "Gujarat Electricity Board's Turnaround: Complete Rural Electrification in Gujarat" Indian Institute of Foreign Trade, London Business School, 2008.
40. Ibid, page 9
41. "Reforms in offing; Subsidy to GEB slashed", *timesofindia.indiatimes.com*, 4 April 2003
42. Transcript of Modi's speech at Rewari Rally quoted in *firstpost.com*, 15 September 2013
43. Rakesh Mohan Joshi, "Gujarat Electricity Board's Turnaround: Complete Rural Electrification in Gujarat" page 10, Indian Institute of Foreign Trade, London Business School, 2008.
44. Ibid, page 14.
45. "The Transformer" by N Madhavan, *businesstoday.intoday.in*, 5 February 2012
46. "Gujarat discoms get high ratings", *financialexpress.com*, 21 March 2013
47. Bibek Debroy, "Gujarat: Governance for Growth and Development" page 50, Academic Foundation, New Delhi, 2002,
48. Statement of Ministry of Power on per capital consumption, Press Information Bureau, Government of India, *pib.nic.in*, 12 August 2011
49. Kavita Kanan Chandra, "A grass root innovation of windmill to operate tube well has caught on", *theweekendleader.com*, Vol 4, Issue 51, 20-26 December 2013
50. Darshan Desai, "The Sunshine State" *thehindu.com*, 5 May 2013
51. "NAMO Way To Clean Energy Security", *dailypioneer.com*, 3 May 2012
52. "Damodar Valley to replicate Gujarat's canal-top solar plant", *business-standard.com*, 22 May 2012

53. "Ajay Devgan invests in Gujarat solar power plant", *zeenews.india.com,* 20 April 2012
54. "Gujarat's canal-top solar power plant: 10 must-know facts", *economictimes.indiatimes.com,* 10 April 2013
55. Ibid
56. Narendra Modi, *Convenient Action, Gujarat's Response To Challenge Of Climate Change,* page 167, Macmillan Publishers India Ltd., Delhi, 2011.
57. Bandish Patel in an interview to author
58. Rakesh Mohan Joshi, "Gujarat Electricity Board's Turnaround: Complete Rural Electrification in Gujarat" page 16, Indian Institute of Foreign Trade, London Business School, 2008
59. "Gujarat Empowers the Power Sector", *narendramodi.in,* 29 May 2013
60. N Madhavan, "The Transformer" *businesstoday.intoday.in,* 5 February 2012.
61. "Gujarat has better roads, observes Bombay High Court", *zeenews.india.com,* 2 December 2009
62. "Follow Gujarat Path to Road Reform: World Bank", *timesofindia.indiatimes.com,* 24 August 2010
63. "Gujarat roads closer to international standards: WB" by Rajiv Shah, *timesofindia.indiatimes.com,* 11 August 2011
64. Figures of Government of Gujarat
65. "Creating dynamic, people oriented cities of the future: The Gujarat Experience", *narendramodi.in,* 21 August 2013
66. Figures of Government of Gujarat
67. Clell Harral, Graham Smith & William Paterson, "Maintaining Road Assets" page 15, DFID — World Bank, 2011
68. Port-led development in Gujarat: a short film by Gujarat Maritime Board, *firstpost.com*

Chapter - 13

1. Clell Harral, Graham Smith & William Paterson, "Maintaining Road Assets", DFID-World Bank, p16, 2011
2. *twitter.com from @thekiranbedi,* 5 January 2014
3. Rohinee Singh, "After S Jaganmohan Reddy, N Chandrababu Naidu warms up to Modi, praises Gujarat model", *dnaindia.com,* 3 October 2013
4. "State-Wide Attention on Grievances by the Application of Technology—SWAGAT", *indiagovernance.gov.in,* Governance Knowledge Centre, Government of India
5. "Gujarat—where bureaucracy delivers the goods happily", *newsbharati.com,* 11 November 2012
6. "Bhilad check post earns Rs 23.5 cr more than Acchad", *timesofindia.indiatimes.com,* 3 April 2012
7. Niral Patel in an interview to the author at Vadodara
8. Ravindrabhai Vepari in an interview to author at Surat
9. Sandesh, an article carried in the government compendium on Good Governance, 29 August 2004
10. Niral Patel in an interview to the author at Vadodara
11. Clell Harral, Graham Smith & William Paterson, "Maintaining Road Assets", DFID-World Bank, p 16, 2011
12. 23 new talukas "created in Gujarat" *zeenews.india.com,* 9 september 2013

13. Despatch of Michaels Owen, US Consul General, Mumbai, on his Meeting with Gujarat Chief Minister Narendra Modi published by WikiLeaks, *wikileaks.org*, Despatch of 27 November 2006

14. The Congressional Research Service CRS on India, 2011

15. Ex- CVC N Vittal praises Narendra Modi for 'unpopular decisions', *indianexpress.com*, 2 October 2012

16. "Gujarat Police release three sketches", *thehindu.com*, 6 August 2008

17. Kishore Trivedi, "Gujarat's 10-year tryst with peace, unity & brotherhood" *news.oneindia. in*, 26 February 2012

Chapter - 14

1. "How Saurashtra is driving Gujarat's agricultural growth", *rediff.com*, 27 February 2013

2. Swaminathan S Anklesaria Aiyar "Agriculture: Secret of Modi's success", *economictimes. indiatimes.com*, 22 July 2009

3. Bibek Debroy, Gujarat: Governance for Growth and Development, Academic Foundation, page 138, New Delhi, 2012.

4. State government data

5. Figures of latest state government data in 2013

6. "Gujarat's decade of agricultural success", *thehindubusinessline.com*, 24 May 2013

7. Ibid

8. Ibid

9. "Gujarat's decade of agricultural success", *thehindubusinessline.com*, 24 May 2013

10. "Agriculture, industry thriving side by side: Modi", *zeenews.india.com*, 20 May 2012

11. Socio-economic Review 2012-13 Gujarat State Budget Publication No. 34, Directorate of Economics and Statistics, Government of Gujarat, February 2013.

12. "Agriculture, industry thriving side by side: Modi", *zeenews.india.com*, 20 May 2012

13. "NCF to submit final report on October 2", *thehindu.com*, 25 June 2006

14. RN Bhaskar, "How did Gujarat become a farming paradise", Forbes India, *forbesindia. com*, 18 March 2010

15. Abhishek Kapoor, "Gujarat set to give mandis a corporate look", *indianexpress.com*, 23 April 2008

16. Ravindrabhai Vepari in an interview to the author at Surat

17. Japan K Pathak, "Columbia University's eye-opening report on north Gujarat", *deshgujarat.com*, 4 April 2011

18. "Gujarat woman milking millions in dairy den", *timesofindia.indiatimes.com*, 6 July 2012

19. "On Janmashtami, Narendra Modi attacks UPA on cow slaughter 'promotion'", *economictimes.indiatimes.com*, 10 August 2012

20. The author and his team visited the animal hostel in Akodara village and interacted with the villagers there.

21. Uday Mahurkar, "Gujarat reaps a rich harvest", *indiatoday.intoday.in*, 28 April 2012

22. Ibid

23. "10 villages in Gujarat practice 100% drip-sprinkler irrigation", *deshgujarat.com*, 8 June 2009

24. Mahendrabhai in an interview to the author and his team at his farmland in Khoraj village.

25. "600 Gujarat farmers fly to Israel to learn agriculture technology", Himans Dhomse,

dnaindia.com, 15 May 2012

26. "Krishi Mahotsav: a mix of fun and learning for Gujarat farmers", *indianexpress.com*, 22 May 2008

27. "Krishi Mahotsav boosting farm sector in Gujarat: Modi", *business-standard.com*, 1 June 2012

28. "Narendra Modi courts farmers, says think big on agriculture", *articles.timesofindia. indiatimes.com*, 9 September 2013

29. *gujaratinformatics.com*

30. Figures of the Planning Commission

31. Rasheeda Bhagat, "Vibrant Gujarat agri-meet: Modi wows farmers", *thehindubusinessline. com*, 10 September 2013.

32. Avinash Nair and Hiral Dave wrote about these farmers in their report "In Modi's global agro summit, farmers treated as state guests", *financialexpress.com*, 12 September 2013

33. "Togadia slams Modi for 'toilets first temples later' comment", *thehindu.com*, 3 October 2013

34. "Govt starts drive for use of toilets in rural Gujarat", *indianexpress.com*, 6 February 2013.

35. Reported in the official blog of the Department of Information, Government of Gujarat, *thegujaratblog.net*, 15 April 2013

Chapter - 15

1. "Raise Nano like Yashoda's Krishna: Narendra Modi", *timesofindia.indiatimes.com*, 11 October 2008

2. "Modi's Gujarat bags Tata's Nano: There is a good 'M' and a bad 'M' and we have made the transition: Ratan Tata", *business-standard.com*, 8 October 2008

3. "Raise Nano like Yashoda's Krishna: Narendra Modi", *timesofindia.indiatimes.com*, 11 October 2008

4. "Modi's Gujarat bags Tata's Nano: There is a good 'M' and a bad 'M' and we have made the transition: Ratan Tata", *business-standard.com*, 8 October 2008

5. Raise Nano like Yashoda's Krishna: Narendra Modi", *timesofindia.indiatimes.com*, 11 October 2008

6. "The Auto Wars—Tamil Nadu vs Gujarat", *thehindubusinessline.com*, 18 March 2013

7. N Madhavan, "Why Ford chose Sanand in Gujarat to set up its 2nd plant over Chennai", *businesstoday.intoday.in*, 30 July 2011

8. Murali Gopalan and N Ramakrishnan, "The Auto Wars—Tamil Nadu vs Gujarat", *thehindubusinessline.com*, 18 March 2013

9. "Maruti Suzuki India to invest Rs 4,000 crore to set up new plant in Gujarat", *economictimes.indiatimes.com*, 2 July 2012

10. "Will Tatas pay more for Singur?" *rediff.com*, 24 September 2008

11. Nirmal Kumar in an interview to author in Ahmedabad

12. Unless otherwise mentioned the data used is from the latest data of the government of Gujarat

13. "Gujarat government green lights single-window clearance for filmmakers", *bollywoodtrade.com*, 30 April 2013

14. Hiteshbhai Sanghi in an interview to the author in Ahmedabad

15. Gujarat State profile, *nabard.org*

16. "Gujarat—pharmacy to the nation", *thehindubusinessline.com*, 29 September 2013
17. Modi's inaugural speech at 'Sparkle International 2013', Surat
18. "Panel Probing Congress charges against Gujarat government seeks Info", *dnaindia.com*, 10 April 2012

Chapter - 16

1. "Liquor permits to be made easy: Minister", *timesofindia.indiatimes.com*, 27 August 2003.
2. Ibid
3. "Modi rallies faithful in London", *rediff.com*, 18 August 2003.
4. Ibid
5. Sheela Bhatt, "I want Gujarat to compete with China: Modi", *rediff.com*, 1 November 2006.
6. "India's tallest building to tower over Gujarat?", *timesofindia.indiatimes.com*, 13 January 2005.
7. Ramakant Jha told this in an interview to author at Gandhinagar
8. "Modi, his team visit Three Gorges Dam in China", a UNI report published in news. *oneindia.in,* 4 November 2004
9. Subha Ranjan Tampi, who had accompanied the delegation on behalf of the CII, told the author in an exclusive interview.
10. "Land acquisition not an issue in Gujarat: Narendra Modi", *thehindu.com*, 29 January 2007.
11. Newsletter of Vibrant Gujarat, *vibrantgujarat.com*, Issue 16, December 2012-January 2013
12. Ibid
13. Ibid
14. "Gartex Mart garners Rs 10,600 crore offers", *rediff.com*, 2 October 2003.
15. Figures from the Government of Gujarat
16. Uday Mahurkar, "State Modi-Fied: Narendra Modi lures India Inc, investors with Vibrant Gujarat summit", *indiatoday.intoday.in*, 29 January 2007
17. "Vibrant Gujarat Global Investors' Summit -2009 Touches Golden Heights", *narendramodi.in,* 16 January 2009
18. "Rs 20.83-lakh-cr MoUs at Vibrant Gujarat", *business-standard.com*, 14 January 2011

Chapter - 17

1. "Spend on urban development to be Rs 75,000 crore in 5 yrs: Modi", *business-standard. com,* 27 July 2013
2. "NaMo's Gujarat is way ahead of other states", *niticentral.com*, 29 October 2013
3. Modi addressed a panel discussion on "'Rurbanisation': a transformative process to foster sustainable, equitable and inclusive growth," 8 January 2013. This programme was held during 2013 Vibrant Gujarat Summit.
4. "Jairam Ramesh criticises APJ Abdul Kalam's PURA, launches his own version", *dnaindia. com,* 24 February 2012
5. "Gujarat water surplus state claims GWSSB official", *indianexpress.com*, 27 September 2013.

6. "Gujarat: A glorious decade of development", *news.oneindia.in*, 22 January 2013

7. Ibid

8. "Gujarat to generate energy from waste in 50 cities: Narendra Modi", *economictimes. indiatimes.com*, 17 October 2013

9. "No end to abuse of Sabarmati, waste still dumped in river", *timesofindia.indiatimes. com*, 21 June 2013

10. "BRTS adds another jewel in its crown", *timesofindia.indiatimes.com*, 28 May 2013

11. "Ahmedabad BRTS wins silver rating from globally renowned experts", *nitientral.com*, 16 May 2013

12. "Rajkot BRTS rolls out today, free ride for three months", *indianepress.com*, 1 October 2012

13. "Gujarat to extend BRTS to Surat, Rajkot", *livermint.com*, 14 September 2012.

14. "Wonder what Delhi CM does, Narendra Modi says", *timesofindia.indiatimes.com*, 24 November 2013

15. "Sabarmati river front body gets PM's award", *thehindubusinessline.in*, 11 April 2003

16. All figures from 2011 census

17. "Free flats for Gujarat slum-dwellers", *thehindubusinessline.com*, 8 October 2011

18. "Modi promises 30 lakh new jobs for youth, 50 lakh houses for poor", *thehindubusinessline. com*, 3 December 2012

19. "Gujarat govt gives nod to four housing schemes", *business-standard.com*, 18 July 2013.

20. "90,000 houses allotted to slum dwellers in 2 years in Modi's Gujarat", *ibnlive.in.com*, 21 October 2013

21. Ramakant Jha in an interview to author at GIFT City

22. Jay Patel, an NRI businessman in an interview to author at GIFT city

23. Original orders of the High Court of Gujarat, PIL No. 97 of 2013 order 8 October 23013, and The Supreme Court of India in SLP C No. 32507 of 2013, order 22 November 2013

24. M Ramesh, "Sun Edison, Azure win rooftop contracts", *hindubusinessline.com*, 12 February 2012

25. "Rays of hope: Rooftop solar panel, a new hit in states", *indiatoday.in*, 31 May 2013.

Chapter - 18

1. "With 30.14 crore trees, Gujarat gets greener by 20% in 10 years!" *dnaindia.com*, 1 August 2013

2. Narendra Modi, *Convenient Action: Gujarat's Response to Challenges of Climate Change*, page 11, Macmillan Publishers, New Delhi, 2011.

3. Ibid, page 228

4. "Artificial ponds in Bharuch, Ankleshwar for Ganesha idols", *timesofindia.indiatimes. com*, 15 September 2013

5. "Six industrial units get closure notice for pollution", *timesofindia.indiatimes.com*, 4 September 2013

6. "Gujarat Pollution Control Board issues closure notice to dyeing mills", *timesofindia. indiatimes.com*, 7 September 2013

7. Narendra Modi, *Convenient Action: Gujarat's Response to Challenges of Climate Change*, page 216, Macmillan Publishers, New Delhi, 2011.

8. "Global Warming: Climate Change Initiatives", Gujarat State Portal, *gujaratindia.com*
9. Ibid
10. Maulik Pathak, "Balancing public and private interests", *livemint.com*, 1 November 2013
11. "Climate Change: Clean Development Mechanism", *paryavaranmitra.org.in*
12. "Paryavaran Mitra: Balancing public and private interests", *livemint.com*, 1 November 2013
13. Narendra Modi, *Convenient Action: Gujarat's Response to Challenges of Climate Change*, page 73, Macmillan Publishers, New Delhi, 2011
14. "Environmental Protection Sustains Development: Some initiatives in Gujarat", Gujarat Pollution Control Board, *gpcb.gov.in*, 2011
15. "Gujarat Pollution Control Board's solar-powered building inaugurated", *timesofindia. indiatimes.com*, 7 April 2012
16. "Environmental Protection Sustains Development: Some initiatives in Gujarat", Gujarat Pollution Control Board, *gpcb.gov.in*, 2011
17. "Dr Amrita Patel, Gujarat, won the Indira Gandhi Paryavaran Puraskar", *The India Post*, 8 June 2008
18. Uday Mahurkar, "The Good Earth", *India Today*, 26 June 2010
19. Nivit Kumar Yadav, "Gujarat pollution board gets a makeover in efficiency", *downtoearth. org.in*, 1 October 2012

Chapter 19

1. "Amitabh Bachchan performs 'shraddh' for his mother", *timesofindia.indiatimes.com*, Ahmedabad, 31 January 2012
2. Transcript of the advertisement featuring Amitabh Bachchan.
3. Sidhpur, *gujarattourism.com*
4. "Gujarat bags three national tourism awards", Gujarat tourism newsletter, Issue 10 April 2013, *gujarattourism.com*
5. Kamlesh Patel, Tourism Corporation of Gujarat, "Tourism flourished under Modi's rule, contributing largely to SDP: TCG", *post.jagran.com*, 26 October 2013
6. Tourist arrival data from official website of Gujarat tourism, Government of Gujarat
7. "Tourism contributing substantially to Gujarat's SDP", *business-standard.com*, 25 October 2013
8. "Efforts to promote tourism sector in Gujarat have been fruitful: Modi", *sify.com*, 13 January 2013
9. "Trusteeship model in Rann of Kutch" by Tushar Gandhi in Financial Chronicle, *mydigitalfc.com*, 10 November 2013
10. Ibid
11. "Gujarat to spend Rs 120 crore to develop 10 beaches" by IANS for *newindianexpress. com*, 31 October 2013
12. Rajiv Shah, "Gujarat opens 16 beaches for private resorts", *timesofindia.indiatimes.com*, 17 February 2011
13. "Tourism dept to support Surat boat race", *dnaindia.com*, 27 October 2013
14. "Lion census: Gujarat's pride crosses 400", *indianexpress.com*, 3 May 2010
15. "Gujarat women script unique chapter in conservation", *firstpost.com*, 31 August 2013
16. "Narendra Modi's strategy works, Big B pulls in tourists", *ndtv.com*, 15 December 2010

17. "Record tourists flock Sasan Gir to watch lions as new season begins", *indianexpress.com*, 17 October 2013
18. "With 9,000 tourists a day, Gir roars a record", *dnaindia.com*, 17 November 2013
19. "Even a kite can draw the world to Gujarat: Modi", *indianexpress.com*, 14 January 2013
20. "When Gujarat Chief Minister Narendra Modi took to kite flying", *ndtv.com*, 11 January 2011
21. "1900-Year-Old Buddhist Monastery discovered in Gujarat's Vadnagar", *deshgujarat.com*, 11 October 2008
22. M V Kamath and Kalindi Randeri, *Narendra Modi: The Man of the Moment*, page 266, Vikas publications, New Delhi 2012
23. "Buddhist circuit: Gujarat government speeds up work", *indianexpress.com*, 5 April 2011
24. "1900-Year-Old Buddhist Monastery discovered in Gujarat's Vadnagar", *deshgujarat.com*, 11 October 2008
25. "Buddhist circuit: Gujarat government speeds up work", *indianexpress.com*, 5 April 2011
26. "India's largest Buddhist temple to come up in Gujarat", *ndtv.com*, 15 January 2010
27. "First phase of Rama trail project kicked off", *deshgujarat.com*, 29 September 2012
28. "Medical tourism picking up in S Gujarat", *timesofindia.indiatimes.com*, 13 September 2013

Chapter 20

1. "Every third child in Gujarat is underweight, says CAG", *thehindu.com*, 5 October 2013
2. "Guess which State improved most in malnutrition? Gujarat", *firstpost.com*, 6 March 2013
3. Socio Economic Review, Budget Publication No. 34, Directorate of Economics and Statistics, Government of Gujarat, February 2013
4. Ibid
5. Ibid
6. "The Miracle Called 108", *ehealth.eletsonline.com*
7. "Vibrant Gujarat 2013", by PK Taneja, Principal Secretary, Public Health and Family Welfare, Industrial Extension Bureau, Government of Gujarat, *vibrantgujarat.com*, 22 March 2013
8. Ramesh Bhat, Dileep Mavalankar, Prabal V Singh and Neelu Singh, "Maternal Health Financing in Gujarat: Preliminary Results from a Household Survey of Beneficiaries under Chiranjivi Scheme", Indian Institute of Management, Ahmedabad, 2007
9. Ibid
10. Pankaj P Shah, Dhiren K Modi, Shobha P Shah and Shrey A Desai, "Effect of maternity schemes on place of delivery in a tribal block of Gujarat", Department of Community Health, SEWA Rural, Jhagadia, Bharuch, Gujarat, India, Indian Journal of Community Medicine
11. "10 per cent tribal population in State has sickle cell gene: Study", *timesofindia.indiatimes.com*, 15 January 2013
12. "Gujarat government rolls out healthcare scheme for poor" by *Himanshu Darji, articles.economictimes.indiatimes.com*, 4 September 2012
13. Socio Economic Review, Budget Publication no 34. Directorate of Economics and Statistics, Government of Gujarat, February 2013.

Chapter - 21

1. Bibek Debroy, "Why Raghuram Rajan Ranked Gujarat Low…", *businesstoday.intoday. in*, 27 October 2013
2. "Gujarat puts brakes on declining child sex ratio", *news.oneindia.in*, 18 April 2011
3. "Gujarat's sex ratio was once enviable", *timesofindia.indiatimes.com*, 20 December 2012
4. "Modi calls on Gujarat to stop female foeticide", *firstpost.com*, 3 June 2013
5. "Root out menace of female foeticide: Modi to Kadvas", *indianexpress.com*, 10 February 2012
6. "Girls gasp for breath in garvi Gujarat", *timesofindia.indiatimes.com*, 13 June 2006
7. Ibid
8. "In 2020, a Navratri sans women?", *timesofindia.indiatimes.com*, 25 September 2006
9. "NCC launches 'Save the Girl Child' campaign in Gujarat", *news.oneindia.in*, 24 July 2008
10. "Narendra Modi pays tribute to Naari Shakti on International Women's Day", *niticentral. com*, 15 November 2013
11. "Empower women to strengthen India, says Narendra Modi", *zeenews.india.com*, 9 April 2013
12. Socio Economic Review, Budget Publication No 34, page 68, Directorate of Economics and Statistics, Government of Gujarat, February 2013.
13. "This Gujarat village has 117 women crorepatis", *timesofindia.indiatimes.com*, 24 December 2013
14. Madhurima Mallik, "Nari Adalats—Redefining social justice", *narendramodi.in*, 5 October 2012
15. "Mission Mangalam: Empowering Gujarat's women", *narendramodi.in*, 14 May 2012
16. "Gujarat women script unique chapter in conservation", Business Standard, 16 November 2013
17. "Gujarat road transport authority appoints 181 women conductors", *ndtv.com*, 23 April 2013
18. "Gender Revolution, after White Revolution", *indiatogether.org*, 20 September 2005
19. "Vodafone launches women-run 'Angel Stores' in Gujarat", *thehindubusinessline.com*, 6 November 2012

Chapter - 22

1. Education Department, Government of Gujarat
2. "This time, Praveshotsav to focus on school dropouts", *indianexpress.com*, 9 May 2013 The number of primary school was 40,943 in 2011-12 Socio Economic Survey, 2012-13, Budget Publication No. 31, Government of Gujarat, February 2013
3. One of the persons whom Modi inspired to join RSS told this in an interview with author
4. As per government figure though some newspapers reported this to be 50 lakh, "Vanche Gujarat campaign launched", *timesofindia.indiatimes.com*, 30 October 2010
5. "A sea change in education sector", *thehindubusinessline.com*, 2 May 2013
6. All data as per Government of Gujarat, 2012-2013
7. Quoted in Ernst and Young report for FICCI—"Knowledge paper on skill development in India Learner first", September 2012, page 4.

8. Figures of the Planning Commission, 2008, quoted in the Ernst and Young Report, Ibid, page 3.

9. "Industry Responsive Skill Development—Emerging Trends in Gujarat", Vibrant Gujarat Seminar and Panel Discussion, 2011, prepared by iNDEXTb, Government of Gujarat, page 8

10. Modi's speech on 12 January 2012

11. "Industry Responsive Skill Development—Emerging Trends in Gujarat", page 8, Vibrant Gujarat Seminar and Panel Discussion, 2011, prepared by iNDEXTb, Government of Gujarat

12. State government figures carried in "Gujarat's KVKs win PM's Award for Excellence in Public Administration", 21 April 2013, posted in *narendramodi.in*

Chapter - 23

1. Hasmukhbhai told author when the latter visited Kevadia in 2013 to understand the Statue of Unity development plan.

2. "NE metal for Iron Man's Statue", *timesofindia.indiatimes.com,* 29 November 2013

3. "For iron to build Sardar Patel statue, Modi goes to farmers", *indianexpress.com,* 8 July 2013

4. "Modi flags off 1,000 trucks for iron collection for Sardar Patel's statue", *timesofindia. indiatimes.com,* 28 December 2013

5. "Over 4000 people take part in Run for Unity in Mysore", *newindianexpress.com,* 16 December 2013

6. "Unprecedented turnout at run for unity", *timesofindia.indiatimes.com,* 16 December 2013

7. "Nation Runs for Unity", *dailypioneer.com,* 16 December 2013

Chapter - 24

1. "BJP leaders view Goa as 'lucky venue' for Narendra Modi," *timesofindia.indiatimes. com,* 4 June 2013

2. Mohua Chatterjee, "Narendra Modi anointed chairman of BJP 2014 Lok Sabha election campaign committee", *timesofindia.indiatimes.com,* 9 June 2013

3. A BJP leader who was privy to the constant interaction Advani had with BJP leaders including Rajnath Singh, told the author

4. His first address after becoming the chairman of the central election committee was before a convention of BJP workers. Extract from video tape of this speech, *youtube. com,* published 26 July 2013

5. "LK Advani resigns from all positions in BJP", *timesofindia.indiatimes.com,* 10 June 2013

6. "BJP Board rejects LK Advani's resignation, says party chief Rajnath", *ibnlive.in.com,* 11 June 2013

7. "BJP Board rejects LK Advani's resignation, says party chief Rajnath", *ibnlive.in.com,* 11 June 2013

8. "LK Advani relents, agrees to withdraw resignation", *jagran.com,* 12 June 2013

9. "Narendra Modi unlikely to get Shiv Sena support as BJP PM candidate", *indianexpress. com,* 19 July 2013

10. "Make Narendra Modi BJP's PM candidate, Ram Jethmalani writes to Nitin Gadkari", *economictimes.indiatimes.com,* 17 October 2012

11. "Modi competent and fit to be a PM: Sushma Swaraj", *hindustantimes.com*, 1 December 2012

12. "Clamour for Narendra Modi to play bigger role grows", *hindustantimes.com*, 21 December 2012

13. "Narendra Modi best bet for PM's post: Survey", *hindustantimes.com*, 25 January 2013

14. Modi 100% secular, best man for PM: Jethmalani bats for Modi after Yashwant Sinha", *currentnews.in*, 29 January 2013

15. In an interview to Headlines Today news channel, *indiatoday.intoday.in*, 28 January 2013

16. "Yashwant Sinha Bats for Modi as Prime Minister", *paper.hindustantimes.com*, 29 January 2013

17. "Rajnath Singh gag order on PM issue", *timesofindia.indiatimes.com*, 5 February 2013

18. "BJP leaders defy Rajnath's gag order, back Modi as party's PM candidate", *indiatoday.intoday.in*, 5 February 2013

19. Rahul Gandhi's speech at CII Delhi on 4 April 2013, *indianexpress.com*

20. "For you, India may be a beehive but for us this country is our mother, Narendra Modi takes a dig at Rahul Gandhi", *indiatoday.intoday.in*, 6 April 2013

21. "Rajnath skips protocol in honour of Modi", *thehindu.com*, 7 April 2013

22. Ibid

23. A senior RSS leader who refused to be named told this in an interview to the author.

24. "JDU gives 8-month deadline to BJP to declare its PM nominee", *zeenews.india.com*, 14 April 2013

25. "Nitish Nobody To Give Certificate On Secularism To Modi: BJP", *tehelka.com*, 15 April 2013

26. "JDU ends ties with BJP, Nitish drops all BJP ministers," *timesofindia.indiatimes*.com, 16 June 2013

27. "JDU snaps ties with BJP on Modi issue," *thehindu.com*, 17 June 2013

28. "BJP Releases Nitish Kumar's 2003 speech praising Narendra Modi", *timesofindiatimes.com*, 17 June 2013

29. "BJP takes a potshot at Nitish Kumar, says will soon expose his real face", *ibnlive.in.com*, 17 June 2013

30. "Gujarat victory - a verdict against Cong: BJP's allies", *timesofindia.indiatimes.com*, 15 December 2002.

31. "Paswan is an opportunist, says Nitish", *timesofindia.indiatimes.com*, 6 May 2002

32. "Nitish terms Godhra report as a political stunt", *expressindia.indianexpress.com*, 17 January 2005

33. "Nitish will be taught a lesson: Modi", *timesofindia.indiatimes.com*, 7 July 2013

34. "Narendra Modi challenges Manmohan Singh to a debate on development", *dnaindia.com*, 15 August 2013

35. "Narendra Modi chants Obama's 'Yes, we can!' at Hyderabad rally", *ibnlive.in.com*, 11 August 2013

36. "Narendra Modi dares PM Manmohan Singh, says India will compare Independence Day speeches from Bhuj and Lal Qila", *indiatoday.intoday.in*, 14 August 2013

37. "Let's have competition of development between Gujarat, Delhi: Narendra Modi to PM: Highlights", *ndtv.com*, 15 August 2013

38. "Shri Narendra Modi's speech on 67th Independence Day Celebrations at Bhuj", *narendramodi.in*, 15 August 2013

39. "Don't pass resolutions on Modi-for-PM: Rajnath to State units", *economictimes. indiatimes.com*, 18 August 2013

40. "Shiv Sena backs Narendra Modi: Uprooting Congress main priority, says Uddhav Thackeray", *ndtv.com*, 21 July 2013

41. "NDA must declare PM candidate: Sukhbir Badal", *timesofindia.indiatimes.com*, 31 July 2013

42. "INLD to support Narendra Modi for PM if need arises", *zeenews.india.com*, 10 August 2013

43. "Chandrababu Naidu parries questions on Narendra Modi's overture", *economictimes. indiatimes.com*, 13 August 2013

44. "I have to serve Gujarat, have no PM dreams: Modi", *hindustantimes.com*, 5 September 2013

45. "Will support BJP only if Modi made PM candidate, says Ramdev", *indiatoday.intoday. in*, 6 September 2013

46. "On Day 1 of meet, Parivar keeps off PM nominee issue", *indianexpress.com*, 9 September 2013

47. "It's for BJP to decide on Narendra Modi: RSS", *indianexpress.com*, 7 September 2013

48. "Modi's projection- RSS leaders meet Advani, Sushma, Rajnath", *deccanherald.com*, 2 September 2013

49. "Advani, Swaraj, RSS chief meet over dinner", *business-standard.com*, 6 September 2013

50. "RSS sends Gadkari to convince Advani on Modi", *timesofindia.indiatimes.com*, 10 September 2013

51. "Advani sticks to his guns—'Let us wait till Assembly polls'", *thehindu.com*, 12 September 2013

52. "Advani refuses to relent on Modi", *enewspaperofindia.com*, 11 September 2013

53. "Modi's rise likely before Pitra Paksh", *sundayguardian.com*, 7 September 2013

54. "Advani should gauge public mood on Narendra Modi: Sushil Modi", *thehindu.com*, 12 September 2013

55. "Narendra Modi anointed BJP PM candidate, Advani disappointed", *timesofindia. indiatimes.com*, 13 September 2013

56. B Muralidhar Reddy, "Advani gives in, endorses Modi's candidacy", *thehindu.com*, 17 September 2013

57. Darshan Desai, "I will be happy if Modi becomes PM, says Advani", *thehindu.com*, 17 October 2013

Chapter - 25

1. "The danger signal from the Muzaffarnagar riots", *rediff.com*, 19 September 2013

2. "Muzaffarnagar riots worse than in Gujarat: Rashid Alvi", *dnaindia.com*, 19 September 2013

3. Mehbooba Mufti in an interview to Priya Sehgal, *NewsX* Television, 14 April 2013

4. "Mehbooba Mufti did praise Modi reveals NIC transcript", *business-standard.com*, 2 January 2012

5. Amitabh Sinha, a senior BJP leader told this in an interview to author. He had handled the BJP's media in Gujarat during 2002 assembly elections.

6. "Narendra Modi and why 2002 cannot go away", *thehindu.com*, 8 November 2013

7. "People want to move on, want good governance", *thehindu.com*, 11 November 2013

8. Asifa Khan in an interview to the author

9. Modi is a de-polarising figure in Gujarat", *ibnlive.com*, 13 September 2013

10. "BJP Muslim candidates sweep Gujarat town", *indianexpress.com,* 14 February 2013

11. NDTV video on *youtube.com*, 13 February 2013

12. "Huge win for BJP in Gujarat civic polls due to Muslim support: Modi", *timesofindia. indiatimes.com*, 12 October 2010

13. "Gujarat civic polls: Several minorities candidates win on BJP ticket", *economictimes. indiatimes.com*, 25 October 2010

14. "BJP wins Kathlal by-poll on Modi's birthday", *rediff.com*, 17 September 2010

15. "Gujarat civic polls: Several minorities candidates win on BJP ticket", *economictimes. indiatimes.com*, 25 October 2010

16. From Narendra Modi's speech after Sadbhavna Mission on 19 September, *youtube.com*

17. Sachar Committee report: Appendix table 4.1, Page 287

18. Sachar Committee report: Appendix table 4.1(b), Page 289

19. Sachar Committee report: Appendix table 4.6 & 4.7, Pages 295-296-297-298

20. Sachar Committee report: Appendix table 9.4, Page 370

21. "Muslims are safer, more prosperous in NaMo's Gujarat", *niticentral.com,* 18 June 2013

22. "Modi attempts a new tone towards Muslims. But facts from Gujarat tell another story", *indianexpress.com*, 7 November 2013

23. Asifa Khan & Zafar Sareshwala, "Debunking the 'facts' on Narendra Modi and Muslims", *firstpost.com*, 8 November 2013

24. "Lessons to be learnt from Narendra Modi's Gujarat", *indianexpress.com,* 26 October 2013

25. Asma Khan Pathan in an interview to author at Nadiad

26. Asifa Khan in an interview to author

27. Zafar Sareshwala told this in an interview to author

28. Salim Khan in an interview to author

29. Mahesh Bhatt told author

30 Yagnesh Mehta, "New Deoband chief praises Modis Gujarat: No Bias Against Muslims, Says Darul Uloom V-C", *timesofindia.indiatimes.com*, 19 January 2011

31. "More riots in UP than in Gujarat: Madani", *timesofindia.indiatimes.com,* 27 October 2013

32. "Madani admits hard-line Muslims in Gujarat are warming to Modi", *dailymail.co.uk,* 18 February 2013.

33. The Mufti said this in an interview to author

34 The author interacted with these farmers at Bhachau

35. AI Saiyad in an interview to author

36. "Sometimes one has to wear a cap, sometimes a tilak: Nitish's dig at Modi", *indiatoday. intoday.in,* 21 September 2013

37. "Nitish Kumar refuses shawl offered by Muslims", Newxlive, *youtube.com,* 18 April 2013

38. ABP News video on *youtube.com,* 20 December 2012

39. "Narendra Modi refuses to put on 'skull cap' offered by Muslim cleric", *timesofindia. indiatimes.com,* 19 September 2011

40. "Interview with BJP leader Narendra Modi", *blogs.reuters.com,* 12 July 2013

41. "Modi's 'puppy' remark triggers new controversy over 2002 riots", *in.reuters.com,* 12 July 2013

42. "Modi's 'puppy' comment poorly contextualised, tweets Reuters journalist", *firstpost. com*, 15 July 2013

43. Asifa Khan & Zafar Sareshwala, "Debunking the 'facts' on Narendra Modi and Muslims", *firstpost.com*, 8 November 2013

44. Ibid.

45. "Salman's father behind interview", *telegraphindia.com*, 27 July 2012

46. The Modi Interview: I won't apologise for 2002 riots" by Shahid Siddiqui published by *rediff.com*, 27 July 2012

47. Narendra Modi not a political untouchable for Muslims: Shia cleric", *ndtv.com*, 25 October 2013

48. In the interview to Shahid Siddiqui quoted above

49. "Modi slams Nitish in Patna, woos Yadavs, calls for Hindu-Muslim unity," *hindustantimes. com*, 27 October 2013

50. "In Patna battle cry, Modi lauds Gujarat Muslims' progress", *hundustantimes.com*, 27 October 2013.

51. "Haj applicants from Gujarat outnumber rest of India, *indianexpress.com*, 1 May 2012

Chapter - 26

1. "Narendra Modi: UK high commissioner meets Gujarat chief", *bbc.co.uk*, 23 October 2012

2. "Meeting with Narendra Modi 'logical next step' in ties: British Foreign Minister", *ndtv. com*, 20 March 2013

3. "UK favours closer engagement with Gujarat, Narendra Modi, David Cameron says", *timesofindia.indiatimes.com*, 18 September 2013.

4. "UK PM Cameron 'open to meeting' with Modi", *dailymail.co.uk*, 15 November 2013.

5. "No Entry for Modi", *frontline.in*, Vol 22, Issue 7, 12-25 March 2005

6. "We are going to smoke them out: President airs his anger", *The New York Times, nytimes. com*, 19 September 2001

7. "US decision to please Pak: BJP", *rediff.com*, 21 March 2005

8. "NDA rally thanks Manmohan for stand on Modi's visa", *hindu.com*, 21 March 2005

9. "No change in Visa policy for Modi: US", *thehindu.com*, 14 September 2013

10. "Arun Jaitley advises Narendra Modi not to apply for US visa" *economictimes.indiatimes. com*, 28 December 2013

11. "US Congressmen urges Clinton to continue denying visa to Narendra Modi" by PTI in *thehindubusinessline.com*, 4 December 2012

12. "64 MPs urged Obama to keep visa ban for Modi", *thehindu.com*, 24 July 2013

13. "Rights group suspected of forging anti-Modi letter", Millennium Post, *millenniumpost. in*, 25 July 2013.

14. Despatch of Michael Owen, US Consul General, Mumbai, On his Meeting with Gujarat Chief Minister Narendra Modi and interaction with others published by Wikileaks, *wikileaks.org*, Despatch of 27 November 2006

15. "US can't be judgemental, should give Narendra Modi visa: Robert Blackwill", *economictimes.indiatimes.com*, 31 August 2013

16. Barry Gardiner's interview on *NDTV*, 13 August 2013, *ndtv.com/video*

17. "Germany defends Gujarat visit,", *ibnlive.in.com*, 15 November 2013

18. "After 10 years of boycott, European Union envoys meet Narendra Modi, say this is a

'new phase''', *ndtv.com*, 8 February 2013

19. Madhav Nalapat, "Modi woos China in Mandarin", *sunday-guardian.com*, 13 November 2011

20. "Modi courts Chinese investment, showcasing the 'Gujarat model'", *thehindu.com*, 10 November 2011

21. "On Japan tour, Modi is seen as India's rising sun", *firstpost.com*, 23 July 2012

Chapter - 27

1. Despatch of Michael Owen, US Consul General, Mumbai, On his Meeting with Gujarat Chief Minister Naerndra Modi published by Wikileaks, *wikileaks.org*, Despatch of 27 November 2006.

2. "Huge crowd but mixed reactions to Modi's speech in Hyderabad", *timesofindia. indiatimes.com*, 12 August 2013.

3. KV Lakshmana, a senior journalist sent his description exclusively for this book after a request by author.

4. "Narendra Modi matinee show grips Jaipur, over 2 L attend rally", *timesofindia.indiatimes. com*, 11 September 2013.

5. "Narendra Modi takes 'ABCD' jibe at Cong in Jaipur," *hindustantimes.com*, 10 September 2013.

6. "In Jaipur, Modi's skull cap, burqa of secularism", *indianexpress.com*, 11 September 2013

7. "Narendra Modi addresses rally in Haryana, his first as BJP's PM candidate": Edited by Nadim Asrar on 15 September 2013

8. "Modi at mega show: CBI, not Congress, will fight elections", *hindustantiems.com*, 26 September 2013

9. "Modi storms Capital; launches blistering attack on Rahul, Manmohan, Sheila": *hindustantimes.com*, 29 September 2013.

10. The Emergency movement against Indira Gandhi during 1975-77 was led by Jayaprakash Narayan who was 75. Indira Gandhi was vanquished in the Lok Sabha elections in 1977

11. VP Singh who came to power in 1989 riding anticorruption wave against Rajiv Gandhi and the Congress had received unprecedented support in Bihar

12. Gandhiji's first Satyagraha in India was launched from Champaran in Bihar in 1917 in support of the indigo farmers.

13. Prof RN Sharma told this to author during a chat in Delhi.

14. "Narendra Modi rocks Patna, record crowd at Hunkar rally", report by Rahul Kanwal, *indiatoday.intoday.in*, 27 October 2013.

15. "Shri Narendra Modi Addresses BJP Hunkar Rally at Patna", posted through the official account of Narendra Modi on *Youtube*, Published on 27 October 2013

16. "Result of Uttar Pradesh in 1996", *ibnlive.in.com*, undated

17. "In Uttar Pradesh, Modi is talk of the town", *niticentral.com*, 24 November 2013

18. "A turnout like Atal's rallies", *indianexpress.com*, 20 October 2013.

19. "Congress unfazed ove rlarer turnout at Modi's Kanpur rally", *timseofindia.indiatimes. com*, 20 October 2013.

20. "State of the Urban Youth, India 2012", IRIS Knowledge Foundation, UN-HABITAT, *esocialsciences.org*, 21 March 2013.

21. "Why Modi strikes a chord with the youth and not Rahul" by Rajdeep Sardesai, *ibnlive. in.com*, 23 August 2013.

22. Jyoti Thottam, "Boy from the Backyard", *time.com,* 26 March 2012.

23. "2002 riots an 'internal Gujarati matter': Modi told American diplomat", *thehindu.com,* 22 March 2011.

24. "Modi will never be PM, but he can sell tea: Mani Shankar Aiyar", *firstpost.com,* 18 January 2014.

25. "Modi plays OBC caste to taunt Congress, ridicules Sonia for not naming PM candidate", *hindustantimes.com,* 19 January 2014. Also "Shri Narendra Modi addressing BJP's National Council Meeting in Delhi: Speech", *youtube.com,* posted by Narendra Modi's official youtube account, 19 January 2014.

26. British intelligence officer told this to the author when he was working with the British High Commission as a senior political analyst.

27. "Time magazine sees Narendra Modi as 'America's Other India Problem'", *ibnlive.in.com,* 18 January 2014

28. "Pro-Narendra Modi Muslims offered prayer at Ajmer Dargar to see Gujarat CM as PM", daily.bhaskar.com, 21 August 2013.

29. "Salman Khan defends Narendra Modi for Gujarat riots, says he shouldn't say sorry", *indiatoday.intoday.in,* 20 January 2014

30. "Shri Narendra Modi addressing BJP's National Council Meeting in Delhi: Speech", *youtube.com,* posted by Narendra Modi's official *youtube* account, 19 January 2014.

Index

3D campaign   173, 375
3D technology   16, 171, 174

A

Aapno Taluko Vibrant
   Taluko   194
Abhishek Singhvi   164
Agra summit   79, 155
Ahmed Patel   346
AI Saiyed   197
Akhilesh Yadav   128, 337
Akshardham   155
Al Gore   173, 271
Amarsinh Chaudhary   48, 148
Ambaji temple   156, 168
Ambalal Koshti   25
Amitabh Bachchan   281
Amitabh Sinha   87
Amul   233
Anand Agriculture
   University   237
Anandiben Patel   22
Ananth Kumar   144
Anil Ambani   259
Anil Sharma   73
Animal hostel   234, 372
Anna Hazare   215, 373
Anti-US   31
Arif Mohammad Khan   47

Arjun Modhwadia   170
Arjun Munda   61
Arun Jaitley   80, 111-167, 318,
   332, 359
Arun Shourie   142, 164, 257,
Asiatic Lions   282
Asifa Khan   138, 339-353
Asma Khan Pathan   345
Atal Bihari Vajpayee   34-177,
   339, 370, 383
Azam Khan   128

B

Babri Masjid   49, 99
Babu Bajrangi   116
Babubhai Patel   33, 38
Bachubhai Thakur   37
Bahujan Samaj Party   74, 377
Bajrang Dal   51, 116, 352
Bal Sakha Yojana   290
Balam Sukham   289
Balraj Madhok   96
Banas Dairy   233
Bangaru Laxman   80
Bangladesh war   28, 31
Bansi Lal   67, 69
Bapurao Moghe   41
Barack Obama   327, 360, 377
Barry Gardiner   127, 361

Becharji 154
Bengaluru 180, 373
Best Bakery case 120
Beti Bachao Andolan 298
Bhairon Singh Shekhwat 257
Bharatiya Kisan Sangh 42, 136, 371
Bhatiji Maharaj 152
Bhilad Check post 219
Bhogilal Gandhi 39
Bharatiya Janata Party 319
Bijlibhai Chowdhary 17
Bilkis Bano 121
BN High School 3-23
Bofors kickbacks 49
Boribands 200
Buddhist circuit 286
Bus Rapid Transit System 264

C

Central Parliamentary Board 321, 332
Chamanlal Gupta 76
Chandrashekhar 378
Chhote Sardar 254
Chimanbhai Patel 49, 55, 99
chintan shibir 193, 312
Chiranjivi Yojana 290, 294
Citizen Charter 191, 215, 294
Congress Seva Dal 24
CP Thakur 321

D

Dalai Lama 286
Dalit Yatra 155
Damodardas Modi 1

Dandi 40
Dasrathbhai Laxmandas Patel 10
Dattopant Thengdi 41
Dave Commission 99
David Cameron 359
Deendayal Upadhyaya 319
Deng Xiaoping 362
Deputy Mamlatdar 223
Digvijaya Singh 162, 224, 363
Dilip Sanghani 63, 80, 236
Doodh mandalis 290
Dhordo tent city 194
Dr APJ Abdul Kalam 194
Dr Manmohan Singh 143, 170, 321, 368
Dr Prahlad Patel 19, 23
Dr Rajendra Prasad 50
Drip irrigation 234, 277, 366

E

Earthquake 83-181, 283, 364
East African countries 255
e-City centres 218
e-Dhara 222
e-governance 216-224
e-Gram 223, 237
Ehsan Jafri 110-134
e-Kiran 237
e-Krishi Kiran 237
Election Commission 69, 148, 170
E-Mamta 295
Emergency 11, 253, 292, 294, 298
Emergency Medical Service 292,

Environment Impact Assessment   275
Environment Public Hearing   275
e-procurement   197, 221
e-urja   208
Ex-servicemen rally   208

G

Gamthi Shala   20
Ganesh Visarjan   99
Gaurav yatra   151, 156, 320
Gautam Adani   255
George Bush   357
George Fernandes   28, 35, 118
Ghanchi Caste   2
Ghanchi Muslims   98
Ghelabhai Zala   342
Gir forests   255, 282, 302
Global Agriculture Summit   238
Goa National Executive   142, 317
Godhra   56-170, 339
Gopal Narain   6
Gopinath Munde   161
Gordhan Zadaphia   112-166
Govindacharya   77, 80, 332
Green Credit Movement   275
Green pledge   274
Green revolution   188, 235, 279
Greenfield ports   214
Guangdong   362
Gujarat Agro Vision   229
Gujarat Electricity Board   185, 205, 365

Gujarat Industrial Development Corporation   247
Gujarat International Finance Tec-city   268
Gujarat Parivartan Party   166
Gujarat Pollution Control Board   209
Gulbarg   110-166
Gulf of Khambhat   205
Gunotsav   193, 306
Gyan Chand Gupta   64
Gyan Shakti   189

H

Haj   345-356
Harin Pathak   118
Haryana Vikas Party   67
HD Deve Gowda   59, 282
Hedgewar Bhavan   27, 28
Hillary Clinton   360
Himachal Kranti Morcha   71
Himachal Vikas Congress   71
Hind Swaraj   307
Hiraba   7-23, 157, 335
Hitendra Desai   97, 158
Hussain Dalvi   170

I

Incorruptible   324
India 272+   375
Indian National Lok Dal   67, 329
Indira Gandhi   28-97, 194, 279, 370, 378
Investment Regions   250, 261

J

Jagan Shah   375
Jagannath temple   96
Jagdish Shettar   321
Jal Shakti   189
Jama Masjid   39
Jamat-e-Islami   39
James Bevan   358
James Michael Lyngdoh   148,151
Jamiat Ulema-e-Hind   336, 348,
Jan Shakti   189
Jana Krishnamurthy   85, 87,
    143, 144
Jana Sangh   25, 37, 56, 71, 96,
    164, 319
Janata Morcha   33, 38
Jangbir Singh   67
Janmarg BRTS   265
Jaswant Singh   142
JP Mathur   87
JS Bandukwala   115
Judge Jyotsna Yagnik   116
Judge PR Patel   110
Justice PM Chauhan   99
Justice Rajendra Sachar   342
Justice Shamim   123
Justice TU Mehta   107
Justice UC Banerjee
    Committee   108
Jyotigram Yojana   211, 212

K

Kadva Patel   297
Kailash Mansarovar   12, 13,
Kalpasar Dam   205
Kalraj Mishra   161

Kamalam   64
Kangaroo court   359
Kanya Kelavani   304, 306
Kargil War   70, 79
Karmayogis   194
Karsanbhai Patel   255
Kashiram Rana   55, 57, 158,
    160, 166
KD Desai   37
Keshavrao Deshmukh   34, 42
Keshubhai Patel   45-172, 201
Khajuraho   57
khet talavadi   201
Khushboo Gujarat ki   282
Kiran Bedi   216
Kisan Cedit Cards   237
Kite festival   257, 285
KN Govindacharya   77
KPS Gill   124, 148
KR Narayanan   73
Krishi Mahotsav   235
Krishi raths   236
Kushabhau Thakre   78, 87

L

Lalu Prasad Yadav   51, 196,
    326, 370
Largest pumping station   200
Larry Pressler   257
Laxmanrao Inamdar   26
Laxmikant Parsekar   317
LD Engineering College   32
Lee Kuan Yew   255
Lion census   284, 302
LK Advani   34, 46, 47, 55, 78,
    99, 114, 130, 142, 167, 257,

259, 318
Lok Sangharsh Samiti   34

M

M Greene   89
M Venkaiah Naidu   77, 78, 156
Madan Lal Khurana   85
Madandas Devi   62
Madhavrao Scindia   60
Madhavsinh Solanki   45-55
Madhu Limaye   28
Maha Garjana Rally   372
Maha Gujarat Janata Parishad   24
Mahagujarat Janata Party   166
Mahatma Gandhi   95, 172, 283, 307, 370
Mahendra Darji   10
Mahesh Bhatt   126, 138, 348-382
Mahila Samakhyas   301
Mahila Samras Gram   239
Makrand Desai   38
Mandvi beech   283
Maneka Gandhi   321
Mani Shankar Aiyar   70, 378
Maniben Patel   40
Manohar Lal Khattar   69
Mass mobilisation   367, 370
Mata Yashoda Gaurav Nidhi Scheme   301
matru shraddh   281
Maulana Kalbe Sadiq   355
Maulana Mahmood Madani   348, 350
Maulana Masuri   347
Maulana Vastanvi   350

maut ka saudagar   162
Maya Kodnani   116, 361
Mayawati   371, 372
Meenakshi Lekhi   325
Mehbooba Mufti   337
M G Vaidya   330
Michael Clarke   257
Michael Steiner   361
Millennium Development Goal   293
Mission Mangalam   94, 302
MN College   20, 22
Mohan Bhagwat   318, 320, 331
Morarji Desai   33, 95, 97, 154, 379
Ms Babiben Habibbhai Sama   341
MS Swaminathan   230
Mukesh Ambani   257
Mukhya Mantri Aawas Samruddhi Yojna   268
Mukhyamantri Amrutam   295
Mukund Deovankar   160
Mukhyamantri Amrutum Yojna   356
Mulayam Singh Yadav   128
Murli Manohar Joshi   51, 64, 332, 369
Murlidhar Rao   332

N

N Chandrababu Naidu   216, 329
N Vittal   224
Nancy Powell   378, 360
Naaz Hai Gujarat Pe   355

Nanaji Deshmukh   35
Nanavati-Shah
    Commission   106, 127
Narendra Modi
    Organising secretary   47-55
    OTC training   29
    National election
    committee   318
    Nyay Yatra   47, 48
    Lok Shakti Rath Yatra   47,48
    Ram Rath Yatra   48-99
    Ekta Yatra   51-76
    Masterji   76
    vibhag pracharak   41
    vyavastha pramukh   41
    prant padadhikari   41
    sambhag pracharak   41
    Prakash   34
    Khabardar   40
Naresh Agarwal   372
Narhari Amin   165
Nari adalats   301
Narmada Main Canal   198, 204
Narmada Valley River
    Development Project   198
Naroda Patiya   115
Nathabhai Jhagda   34, 47
National council   78, 312, 378,
    385
National Democratic Alliance   73
National Human Rights
    Commission   123, 148,
    152
Navjyot Singh Sidhu   161
Navnirman Movement   32-64
Navratri festival   285

Nawaz Sharif   370
Nelson Mandela   138, 355
Nigel Shaw   257
Nirmal Gujarat   238, 239
Nirmal Kumar   245, 373
Nirmala Sitharaman   325
Nitin Gadkari   319, 333
Nitish Kumar   122, 245-370
Non-cooperation movement   95
non-one day governance   218
Noorani Mosque   115

O
Om Prakash Chautala   67,69,329

P
Panchamrut   189
Panchavati yojana   240
Pani samitis   198, 203, 299
Parashurama   282
Parivartan Yatra   165
Parliamentary Board   319-333
Parvez Musharraf   79
Paryavaran Bhavan   278
PC Pande   113, 128
People's Democratic Party   337
Pepper's Ghost Illusion   174
Piloo Mody   37
Prabhudas Patwari   35, 42
Praful Raval   33
Praful Sanjaliya   160
Prakash Javadekar   339
Pramod Mahajan   52, 77, 144,
    147
Praveen Togadia   137
Prem Kumar Dhumal   72

Punsari village   263
PV Narasimha Rao   52, 379

R

Radhakrishna   36
Rahul Gandhi   171, 321, 374
Raj Bhatia   76
Rajdharma   123,134,140,141, 149
Rajendra Prasad   50
Rajendrasinh Rana   152
Rajiv Gandhi   47, 52, 370, 379
Rajkumar   372
Rajnath Singh   153, 161, 318-383
Raju Ramachandran   110, 125, 131, 166
Raksha Shakti   189, 309
Ram Bilash   67
Ram Jethmalani   131, 320, 381
Ram Lal   332
Ram Madhav   331
Ram Naik   257
Ram Rajya   160, 219
Ram Rath Yatra   48-99
Ramakant Jha   255, 269
Ramakrishna Mission Ashram Almora   14
Ramesh Chand   73
Rameshwar Chaurasia   327
Ramjanmabhoomi movement   47
Ramlila Maidan   367
Ramvilas Paswan   326
Randhir Singh Bedi   65
Rann of Kutch   91,194,281,283

Rann Utsav   283
Ras Behar Maniar   21
Rashtriya Janata Party   82
Rasikbhai Dave   24, 31
Ratan Tata   179, 241, 256
Ravindra Varma   36, 43
Ravishankar Prasad   161
Record of Rights   223
Reddy Commission   97
Renuka Chowdhary   372
Riots
    Assam Riots 2012,   130, 185
    Anti-Sikh 1984   74,130,354
    Bhagalpur riot   119
    Bombay riots 1993   130
    Gujarat 1893   95
    Gujarat 1969   96
    Muzaffarnagar   128, 130, 139, 337
    Sardarpura riots   119
RK Raghavan   110, 117
Robert Blackwill   361
RS Jamur   135
Run for Unity   315, 367
Rurbanisation   262

S

Sabarmati Ashram   122
Sabarmati River Front Development Corporation 204
Sachar Committee   168, 342
Sadbhav yatra   46
Sadbhavana Mission   166
Sadhu-Bet Island   314
Sakhi Mandals   290, 301, 302

Salaya 340

Salem Mohammad Baghaad 340

Salim Khan 126, 139, 347, 352, 382

Salman Khan 139, 347, 383

Samajwadi Janata party 68

Samras Gram Yojana 239

Sangh Priya Gautam 78

Sangharsh ma Gujarat 33

Sanjiv Bhatt 111, 131, 132,

Sanskar Dham 53, 54, 58

Sardar Patel Utkarsh Samiti 159, 160

Sardar Sarovar Project 155, 209, 210

Sardar Vallabhbhai Patel 50, 154,165, 314, 315, 366

Sarva Sikhsha Abhiyan 305

Sarvodaya movement 35

Sasakawa Award 90

Satyapal Jain 65

Shah Alam Relief Camp 141

Shahid Siddiqui 339, 354

Shala Praveshotsav 304, 306

Shankersinh Vaghela 29, 53, 55, 58, 82, 99, 170

Shanta Kumar 72, 144

Sharad Pawar 236

Sharad Yadav 319

Sharmishtha Lake 11, 30

Shashi Ruia 254, 256, 257

Shiv Sena 319, 320, 329

Shivraj Singh Chauhan 369, 384

Shiromani Akali Dal 65, 74, 329, 384

Shyamji Krishna Varma 254

Sickle Cell Anaemia 294

Sitaram Yechuri 360

Smriti Irani 161

Sohrabuddin 163

Solar city 270, 278

Somnath temple 48, 95, 282, 283

Sonia Gandhi 121, 152, 153, 156, 162, 163, 164, 171

Special Economic Zones 213, 248, 268

Special Investigation Team 110, 117, 127

Special Investment Regions 250, 259, 261

Statue of Unity 314, 315, 316, 366,

Subramanian Swamy 37

Sudha Yadav 70

Sudheendra Kulkarni 77

Sudhir Joshi 17, 22

Sudhir Mankad 269

Sudhir Mehta 254

Sufi Mehbub Ali Bava 340

Sujalam Suphalam Yojana 198, 199

Sukh Ram 71, 72, 73

Sukhbir Singh Badal 329

Sumitra Mahajan 78

Sundar Singh Bhandari 85

Suraj Bhan 66, 67

Suresh 'Bhaiyaji' Joshi 330

Suresh Mehta 37, 58, 59, 63, 81, 85, 160

Suresh Soni 318

Surjit Bhalla   344
Sushil Kumar Modi   161, 329, 332
Sushma Swaraj   66, 77, 161, 167, 318, 319, 320, 330, 332, 333, 338
Suvali beach   284
SWAGAT   197, 220, 221, 224, 365
Swami Atmasthananda   15
Swami Madhavananda Maharaj   15
Swami Ramdev   330, 367
Swami Vivekananda   15, 16, 27, 169, 178
Swami Vivekananda Yuva Vikas Yatra   169
Swantah Sukhaya   193, 195, 196
Swarna Jayanti Rath Yatra   77
Syed Shahnawaz Hussain   317

T

Teerth gram   240
Telugu Desam Party   143, 329
TN Chaturvedi   144
Train them Young   311
Tree Census   271
Turkman Gate   39
Tushar Gandhi   283
Twin-city   263

U

Udhav Thackeray   319
United Kingdom   173, 310, 357, 385

United Progressive Alliance   161, 325, 328, 357, 358, 368, 369
US visa   357

V

Vaidya Vishnu Datt   76
Vakil Saheb   25, 26, 27, 28, 33, 34, 41, 45, 379
Van raksha sahayaks   302
Vanche Gujarat   307
Vasantbhai Gajendra Gadkar   36
Venkaiah Naidu   77, 78, 144, 147, 156, 161, 318, 332, 333, 347
Vibrant Gujarat   252, 256, 259, 260, 262, 264, 284, 302, 310, 347
Vidhyadeep insurance Scheme   306
Vidya Laxmi Bond   305
Vidya Sahayaks   305
Vinay Katiyar   161
Virbhadra Singh   72, 73
Vishnubhai Pandya   38, 43
Vishwanath Bhagat   5
Vishwasghat divas   326
Visnagar   2, 3, 7, 22
VP Singh   48, 49, 51, 370, 379

W

Water and Sanitation Management Organisation   202
Water riots   184
Wind Power Policy   278
World Environment Day   279
Worst drought   83, 183

Y

Yashwant Sinha   321

Z

Zafar Sareshwala   343, 345,
    346,382,
Zaheera Sheikh   120
Zakat   345
Zakia Jafri   110, 111, 117, 118,
    125, 166,
Zinabhai Darji   45